Punishing the Poor

A JOHN HOPE FRANKLIN CENTER BOOK

Politics, History, and Culture
A series from the International Institute at the University of Michigan

Sponsored by the International Institute at the University of Michigan and published by Duke University Press, this series is centered around cultural and historical studies of power, politics, and the state—a field that cuts across the disciplines of history, sociology, anthropology, political science, and cultural studies. The focus on the relationship between state and culture refers both to a methodological approach—the study of politics and the state using culturalist methods—and a substantive one that treats signifying practices as an essential dimension of politics. The dialectic of politics, culture, and history figures prominently in all the books selected for the series.

Punishing the Poor

THE NEOLIBERAL GOVERNMENT OF SOCIAL INSECURITY

Loïc Wacquant

Duke University Press
Durham and London
2009

Printed in the United States of
America on acid-free paper ♾
Designed by C.H. Westmoreland
Typeset in Warnock by Tseng
Information Systems, Inc.

Duke University Press gratefully
acknowledges the support of
the International Institute at the
University of Michigan, which
provided funds toward the publication
of this book.

Library of Congress Cataloging-
in-Publication Data
Wacquant, Loïc J. D.
[Punir les pauvres. English]
Punishing the poor : the neoliberal government
of social insecurity / Loïc Wacquant.
p. cm. — (Politics, history, and culture)
"A John Hope Franklin Center book."
Includes bibliographical references and index.
ISBN 978-0-8223-4404-9 (cloth : alk. paper)
ISBN 978-0-8223-4422-3 (pbk. : alk. paper)
1. Imprisonment—Social aspects—United
States. 2. Imprisonment—Social aspects—
European Union countries. I. Title. II. Series:
Politics, history, and culture.
HV9471.W3313 2009
365'.6086942—dc22 2009003275

A la mémoire de tata Odile et tonton André,
pour m'avoir donné mes palmes de vie

Contents

Tables and Figures

TABLES

FIGURES

Prologue

America as Living Laboratory of the Neoliberal Future

Present-day society, which breeds hostility between the individual man and everyone else, thus produces a social war of all against all which inevitably, in individual cases, notably among uneducated people, assumes a brutal, barbarous, violent form—that of crime. In order to protect itself against crime, against direct acts of violence, society requires an extensive, complicated system of administrative and judicial bodies which requires an immense labor force.—FRIEDRICH ENGELS, Speech at Elberfeld, 8 February 1845

To punish is to reprove, it is to blame. Thus, at all times, the main form of punishment has been to blacklist the guilty party, to hold him at a distance, to isolate him, to create a vacuum around him, to separate him from law-abiding folks. . . . But punishment is only a material sign through which an interior state is conveyed: it is a notation, a language through which the public conscience of society . . . expresses the sentiment that the reproved act inspires among its members.—ÉMILE DURKHEIM, "Academic Penality," 12th lecture, 1902

The public agitation over criminal "security" (*insécurité, Sicherheit, seguridad*) that has rippled across the political scene of the member countries of the European Union at century's close, twenty years after flooding the civic sphere in the United States, presents several characteristics that liken it closely to the pornographic genre, as described by its feminist analysts.[1] A rough sketch of its main figures and springs can help us discern the evolving contours of the transformation of the state in the age of economic deregulation and social insecurity that is the empirical topic of this book and set out the parameters of the analytic agenda the latter pursues.

Figures and Springs of Penal Pornography

First, the rampant gesticulation over law and order is conceived and carried out not so much for its own sake as *for the express purpose of being exhibited and seen*, scrutinized, ogled: the absolute priority is to put on a spectacle, in the literal sense of the term. For this, words and deeds proclaiming to fight crime and assorted urban disorders must be methodically orchestrated, exaggerated, dramatized, even *ritualized.* This explains why, much like the staged carnal entanglements that fill pornographic movies, they are extraordinarily repetitive, mechanical, uniform, and therefore eminently *predictable.*

Thus the authorities responsible for law enforcement in the different governments succeeding one another in a given country, or within different countries at a given time, all combine, in the same staccato rhythm and with only a few minor variations, the same mandatory figures with the same partners: they go down to patrol and extol anti-crime measures in the subway or on an inner-city train; they visit in procession the police station of an ill-reputed neighborhood; they slip into the team victory picture after an unusually large seizure of drugs; they hurl a few virile warnings to the outlaws who had better "keep a low profile" now or else; and they train the headlights of public attention on teenage scofflaws, repeat offenders, aggressive panhandlers, drifting refugees, immigrants waiting to be expelled, street prostitutes, and the assorted social detritus that litter the streets of the dualizing metropolis to the indignation of "law-abiding" citizens. Everywhere resound the same praise for the devotion and the competence of the forces of order, the same lament over the scandalous leniency of judges, the same avid affirmation of the sacrosanct "rights of crime victims," the same thundering announcements promising, here to "push the crime rate down by 10 percent every year" (a promise that no politician dares make about the ranks of the unemployed), there to restore the hold of the state in "no-go-areas," elsewhere to increase the capacity of the prison system at the cost of billions of euros.*

As a result, the law-and-order merry-go-round is to criminality what pornography is to amorous relations: a mirror deforming reality to the point of the grotesque that artificially extracts delinquent behaviors from the fabric of social relations in which they take root and make sense, deliberately ignores their causes and their meanings, and reduces their treatment to a series of conspicuous position-takings, often

*Brought into office by surfing on the surging law-and-order wave of the presidential campaign of winter 2002, prime minister Jean-Pierre Raffarin pushed anti-crime pornography to the point of nominating to his first cabinet a junior "minister in charge of justice real estate investments," in other words, entrusted with building prisons. This world première (which made France the triste laughingstock of penologists around the planet) was rather inconclusive, since the junior minister in question was later forced to resign after having been indicted for "passive corruption" and speedily replaced by a junior "minister for crime victims."

acrobatic, sometimes properly unreal, pertaining to the cult of ideal performance rather than to the pragmatic attention to the real. All in all, the new law-and-order *geste* transmutes the fight against crime into a *titillating bureaucratic-journalistic theater* that simultaneously appeases and feeds the fantasies of order of the electorate, reasserts the authority of the state through its virile language and mimics, and erects the prison as the ultimate rampart against the disorders which, erupting out of its underworld, are alleged to threaten the very foundations of society.

Whence comes this curious manner of thinking and acting about "security," that, among the "basic functions of the state" identified by Max Weber—the elaboration of legislation, the enforcement of public order, the armed defense against external aggression, and the administration of the "hygienic, educational, social and cultural needs" of its members[2]—grants unprecedented priority to its missions of police and justice, and exultantly heralds the capacity of the authorities to bend indocile categories and territories to the common norm? And why has this punitive approach, targeting street delinquency and declining urban districts, which purports to make criminal offenses recede inch by inch through the full-blown activation of the penal apparatus, recently been embraced not only by right-wing parties but also, and with surprising zeal, by politicians of the governmental Left from one end of the European continent to the other? This book seeks to answer these questions by mapping out one of the major political transformations of the past half-century—and yet one that has gone virtually unnoticed by political scientists and by sociologists specializing in what is conventionally called, due to intellectual hysteresis, the "crisis of the welfare state": namely, the *irruption of the penal state* in America, and its practical and ideological repercussions upon the other societies subjected to the "reforms" fostered by neoliberalism.

Over the past decade, the grand American experiment of the "War on crime" has indeed imposed itself as the inevitable reference for all the governments of the First world, the theoretical source and practical inspiration for the general hardening of penality that has translated in all advanced countries into a spectacular swelling of the population behind bars.* It is in the United States, this country "where imagination is

*I retraced in *Les Prisons de la misère* (Paris: Raisons d'agir Editions, 1999; expanded English trans. *Prisons of Poverty*, Minneapolis: University of Minnesota Press, 2009) the three stages of the planetary diffusion of the notions, technologies, and policies of public safety "made in USA": gestation and implementation (as well as exhibition) in New York City under the tutelage of the neoconservative think tanks that led the campaign against the welfare state; import-export through the agency of the media

at work," according to an official report by a French government expert in urban safety, that penal innovation has proven that "it is possible to make real delinquency and the feeling of subjective insecurity recede" by the deployment of zealous police, judicial, and correctional policies aimed at the marginal categories caught in the cracks and ditches of the new economic landscape.[3] It is in the United States that, forsaking all "sociological complacency," criminology is said to have demonstrated that the cause of crime is the personal irresponsibility and immorality of the criminal, and that the merciless sanctioning of "incivilities" and assorted low-level disorders is the surest means of damming up violent offenses. It is in the American metropolis that the police are said to have proven capable of "reversing the crime epidemic" (the title of the best-seller autobiography of New York City's chief of police is *Turnaround*), here by applying "zero tolerance" and there by the "coproduction" of safety with the residents of dispossessed neighborhoods. It is in America that the prison has turned out, in the end, to be a judicious tool for taming the "violent predators" and other "habitual offenders" who roam the streets in search of innocent prey. Better yet, according to a leading journalist at *Le Monde*, "to focus on the repressive policies of the United States," in relation to the urban policies implemented in that country, would enable us to "open our eyes to what is being invented there, day after day, and without connection with the sole punitive obsession: schemes to promote autonomy, buttressed by the instituting capacity of civil society."*

This book discloses and dismantles the springs of the international legend of an *American law-and-order El Dorado* by showing how the

---

and of the kindred policy centers that have mushroomed throughout Europe, and particularly in Great Britain, acclimation chamber of neoliberal penality with a view toward its dissemination on the continent; scholarly "dressing up" by local *passeurs* (smugglers) who bring the warrant of their academic authority to the adaptation to their countries of theories and techniques of order maintenance that come from the United States.

*Jean Birnbaum, "Insécurité: la tentation américaine," *Le Monde*, April 4, 2003 (an article that reviews and extols the books by Didier Peyrat, *Éloge de la sécurité*; Jacques Donzelot, Catherine Mével, and Anne Wyvekens, *Faire société*; and Hugues Lagrange, *Demandes de sécurité*, and whose introductory caption confirms: "The United States is becoming an ever-more important source of inspiration for French researchers interested in urban insecurity"). Birnbaum writes with the superb assurance that comes from the smug ignorance of US realities combined with the doxic belief in the new neoliberal security-think: "Here we find what is perhaps one of the strong constants of the present time: whatever their political sensibilities, from now on the renewal of a democratic doctrine of public safety seems to have to pass through this double resort to civil society and to the US reference."

penal categories, practices, and policies of the United States find their root and reason in the neoliberal revolution of which this country is the historical crucible and the planetary spearhead. Explosive growth of the incarcerated populations, which increased fivefold in twenty-five years to exceed two million and are stacked in conditions of overpopulation that defy understanding; continual extension of criminal justice supervision, which now covers some seven million Americans, corresponding to one adult man in twenty and one young black man in three, thanks to the development of computer and genetic technologies and to the frenzied proliferation of criminal databases freely accessible on the internet; runaway growth of the budgets and personnel of correctional administrations, promoted to the rank of third-largest employer in the country even as social expenditures undergo deep cuts and the right to public aid is transformed into the obligation to work at underpaid, unskilled jobs; frenetic development of a private incarceration industry, darling of Wall Street during the roaring 1990s, which has taken on a national and even international scope in order to satisfy the state's demand for expanded punishment; targeting of police surveillance and judicial repression onto the residents of the collapsing black ghetto and onto sex offenders, now aggressively repulsed to the infamous margins of society; finally, diffusion of a racialized culture of public vituperation of criminals endorsed by the highest authorities in the land and relayed by a cultural industry feeding (off) the fear of felons: the irresistible ascent of the penal state in the United States over the past three decades responds not to the rise in crime—which remained roughly constant overall before sagging at the end of the period—but to the dislocations provoked by the social and urban retrenchment of the state and by the imposition of precarious wage labor as a new norm of citizenship for those trapped at the bottom of the polarizing class structure.[4]

The Material and Symbolic Charges of Incarceration

To understand why and how the law-and-order upsurge that has swept most postindustrial countries around the close of the century constitutes a *reaction to, a diversion from, and a denegation of, the generalization of the social and mental insecurity* produced by the diffusion of desocialized wage labor against the backdrop of increased inequality, it is both necessary and sufficient to break with the ritual opposition of intellectual schools and to wed the virtues of a *materialist* analysis, inspired by Karl Marx and Friedrich Engels, and the strengths of a *symbolic* approach, initiated by Émile Durkheim and amplified by Pierre

Bourdieu. The materialist perspective, elaborated by various strands of radical criminology, is attuned to the changing relations that obtain in each epoch (and particularly during phases of socioeconomic upheaval) between the penal system and the system of production, while the symbolic outlook is attentive to the capacity that the state has to trace salient social demarcations and produce social reality through its work of inculcation of efficient categories and classifications.[5] The traditionally hostile separation of these two approaches, the one stressing the instrumental role of penality as a vector of power and the other its expressive mission and integrative capacity, is but an accident of academic history artificially sustained by stale intellectual politics. This separation must imperatively be overcome (as suggested by the epigrammatic joining of Engels and Durkheim), for in historical reality penal institutions and policies can and do shoulder both tasks at once: they simultaneously act to enforce hierarchy and control contentious categories, at one level, and to communicate norms and shape collective representations and subjectivities, at another. The prison symbolizes material divisions and materializes relations of symbolic power; its operation ties together inequality and identity, fuses domination and signification, and welds the passions and the interests that traverse and roil society.*

By paying attention to both the social-economic and discursive dynamics at work in the growing linkage between revamped welfare and penal policies, "workfare" and "prisonfare," one gains the means to discover that the explosive growth of the scope and intensity of punishment—in the United States over the past thirty years and in Western Europe on a smaller scale over the past dozen—fulfills three interrelated functions, each corresponding broadly to a "level" in the new class structure polarized by economic deregulation. At the lowest rung of the social ladder, incarceration serves to physically neutralize and warehouse the supernumerary fractions of the working class and in particular the dispossessed members of stigmatized groups who persist in entering into "open rebellion against their social environment"—to recall the provocative definition of crime proposed a century ago by W. E. B. Du Bois in *The Philadelphia Negro*.[6] One step higher, the rolling out of the police, judicial, and correctional net of the state fulfills the function, inseparably economic and moral, of imposing the disci-

*A forceful argument for recognizing the full "complexity of structure and density of meaning" of punishment as a multilayered social institution, that skillfully draws on Marx, Durkheim, Elias, and Foucault, is deployed by David Garland, *Punishment and Society: A Study in Social Theory* (Chicago: University of Chicago Press, 1990), esp. 280–92.

pline of desocialized wage work among the established fractions of the proletariat and the declining and insecure strata of the middle class, in particular by raising the cost of strategies of escape or resistance that drive young men from the lower class into the illegal sectors of the street economy.* Lastly and above all, for the upper class as well as the society as a whole, the endless and boundless activism of the penal institution serves the symbolic mission of reaffirming the authority of the state and the newfound will of political elites to emphasize and enforce the sacred border between commendable citizens and deviant categories, the "deserving" and the "undeserving" poor, those who merit being salvaged and "inserted" (through a mix of sanctions and incentives on both the welfare and crime fronts) into the circuit of unstable wage labor and those who must henceforth be durably blacklisted and banished.

So much to say that this book does not belong to the genre, which is coming back into fashion these days, of the "political economy of imprisonment," inaugurated by the classic work of Georg Rusche and Otto Kirschheimer, *Punishment and Social Structure*,[7] since my ambition is to hold together the material and symbolic dimensions of the contemporary restructuring of the economy of punishment that this tradition of research has precisely been unable to wed, owing to its congenital incapacity to recognize the specific efficacy and the materiality of symbolic power. Deploying Pierre Bourdieu's little-known but potent concept of *bureaucratic field* enables us at once to construe the perimeter and missions of the state as sites and stakes of sociopolitical struggles, to (re)link developments on the welfare provision and crime control fronts, and to fully attend to the constitutive capacity of the symbolic structures embedded in the public organization, implementation, and representation of punishment.** Just as Bourdieu broke with the Marxist conception of class to expound his multidimen-

*To get a raw experiential sense of the steep escalation of police intrusion and penal sanction at ground level, compare the autobiographical narratives of criminal life on the streets of the Big City given by Piri Thomas in *Down These Mean Streets* (New York: Vintage, 1967) for the 1950s, and by Reymundo Sanchez (a.k.a. "Lil Loco") in *My Bloody Life: The Making of a Latin King* (Chicago: Chicago Review Press, 2000) for the 1990s.

**"When it comes to the social world, the neo-Kantian theory that confers upon language, and upon representations more generally, a properly symbolic efficacy in the construction of reality is perfectly justified." This is why "social science must encompass a theory of the theory effect which, by contributing to impose a more or less authorized manner of seeing the world, contributes to making the reality of that world." Pierre Bourdieu, *Language and Symbolic Power* (Cambridge: Polity Press, 1990 [1982]), 105–6. My translation.

sional theory of social space and group-making through classification struggles,[8] we must escape from the narrowly materialist vision of the political economy of punishment to capture the reverberating roles of the criminal justice system as cultural engine and fount of social demarcations, public norms, and moral emotions (as dramatized by the feverish campaign to banish sex offenders analyzed in chapter 7, which would appear irrelevant and inexplicable from the standpoint of an economistic paradigm).

Punishing the Poor is intended as a contribution to the *historical anthropology of the state* and of the transnational *transformations of the field of power in the age of ascending neoliberalism*, in that it purports to link the modifications of social policies to those of penal policies so as to decipher the *double regulation* to which the postindustrial proletariat is now subjected through the joint agency of the assistantial and penitential sectors of the state. And because the police, the courts, and the prison are, upon close examination, the somber and stern face that the Leviathan turns everywhere toward the dispossessed and dishonored categories trapped in the hollows of the inferior regions of social and urban space by economic deregulation and the retrenchment of schemes of social protection. In sum, the present volume is a study, not of crime and punishment, but of the remaking of the state in the era of hegemonic market ideology: penal expansion in the United States, and in the Western European and Latin American countries that have more or less slavishly followed its lead, is at bottom a *political project*, a core component of the retooling of public authority suited to fostering the advance of neoliberalism. Tracking the Malthusian retraction of the social wing and gargantuan enlargement of the penal clutch of the state in America after the peaking of the Civil Rights movement thus paves the way for moving from a narrowly economic conception to the fully sociological characterization of neoliberalism essayed in the conclusion to this book. This characterization proposes, first, that we construe the prison as a core political institution, instead of a mere technical implement for enforcing the law and handling criminals, and, second, that we recognize that "workfare" and "prisonfare" are two integral components of the neoliberal Leviathan, and not passing contradictions or accidental sideshows to the grand narrative of the alleged advent of "small government." And it puts in the spotlight the distinctive *paradox of neoliberal penality*: the state stridently reasserts its responsibility, potency, and efficiency in the narrow register of crime management at the very moment when it proclaims and organizes its own impotence on the economic front, thereby revitalizing the twin historical-cum-scholarly myths of the efficient police and the free market.

The provisional account offered here of the rise of the penal state in the United States as an integral component of neoliberal restructuring is admittedly one-sided and overly monolithic. It does not probe policy misfirings, ambiguities, and contradictions, which abound in the penal field as in every realm of public action, and the manifold metamorphoses and devolutions that state activity undergoes as it percolates down from central conception to local implementation at ground level.[9] It does not survey efforts to resist, divest, or divert the imprint of the penal state from below, which have been variegated if remarkably ineffectual in the United States. Nor does it elucidate the contests that have raged at the top, inside policy-making circles, to steer public programs in divergent directions on both the welfare and the punishment tracks.* This choice of focus is deliberate and justified on three grounds.

First, this book is not an inquiry into penal policies (or their social-support cousins) in their full scope and complexity but, rather, a *selective excavation* of those changing activities of the police, courts, and especially the prison that are specifically *turned toward managing the "problem" categories* residing in the lower regions of social and urban space, and so it overlooks other forms of offending (such as white-collar, corporate, and regulatory crimes, for instance) and other missions of the law-enforcement machinery. Second, it seeks to highlight the discursive and practical arrangements that work to join penal sanction and welfare supervision into a single apparatus for the cultural capture and behavioral control of marginal populations. Accordingly, it stresses a selfsame logic cutting across policy domains at the expense of multiple logics competing within a single domain.[10] And, thirdly, the analysis offered here is necessarily provisional and schematic insofar as it tackles policy developments that are ongoing, unfinished, and diversified along regional as well as local lines. To paint patterns that are not fully congealed, whose elements crystallize at varying paces, and whose effects have yet to ramify fully across the social structure and play out over the long run (in the case of workfare), requires that one exaggerate the meshing of trends tying punishment and marginality, at the risk of giving the impression that penalization is an irresistible totalizing principle that crushes everything in its path. This (over)simplication is an unavoidable *moment* in the analysis of the surge of the penal state

*This book also concentrates on the nexus between penality and emerging forms of urban marginality at the expense of a full treatment of the powerful prismatic effects of ethnoracial division, as the latter are tackled frontally in another study. See Loïc Wacquant, *Deadly Symbiosis: Race and the Rise of the Penal State* (Cambridge: Polity Press, 2009).

in the neoliberal age and a *cost* well worth paying if it gets students and activists of criminal justice to pay attention to germane developments in poverty policies and, conversely, if it alerts scholars and militants of welfare—as traditionally defined—to the urgent need to bring the operations of the overgrown penal arm of the Leviathan into their purview.

It should be clear, then, that the high degree of internal coherence and external congruence displayed by the radiography of the nascent government of social insecurity after the collapse of the Fordist-Keynesian order drawn here is partly a function of the analytic lens deployed. It should not mislead the reader to think that the penalization of poverty is a deliberate "plan" pursued by malevolent and omnipotent rulers—as in the conspiratorial vision framing the activist myth of the "prison-industrial complex."[11] Nor does it imply that some systemic need (of capitalism, racism, or panopticism) mysteriously mandates the runaway activation and glorification of the penal sector of the bureaucratic field. The latter are not preordained necessities but the results of struggles involving myriad agents and institutions seeking to reshape this or that wing and prerogative of the state in accordance with their material and symbolic interests. Other historical paths were open, and remain open, however narrow and improbable they may appear to be. It goes without saying—but it is better said nonetheless—that, with Pierre Bourdieu, I forcefully reject the "functionalism of the worst case" which casts all historical developments as the work of an omniscient strategist or as automatically beneficial to some abstract machinery of domination and exploitation that would "reproduce" itself no matter what.* At the same time, it is the empirical claim of this book that neoliberal penality does coalesce around the shrill reassertion of penal fortitude, the pornographic exhibition of the taming of moral and criminal deviancy, and the punitive containment and disciplinary supervision of the problem populations dwelling at the margins of the class and cultural order. Bringing developments on the social welfare and crime control fronts into a single analytic frame reveals that, for the precarious fractions of the urban proletariat that are their privileged clientele, the programmatic convergence and practical interlock of restrictive "workfare" and expansive "prisonfare" gives the neoliberal state a dis-

*"One of the principles of sociology consists in recusing this negative functionalism: social mechanisms are not the product of some Machiavellian intention. They are much more intelligent than the most intelligent of the dominant." Pierre Bourdieu, *Questions de sociologie* (Paris: Minuit, 1980), 111, translated as *Sociology in Question* (London: Sage, 1990), 71. My translation.

tinctively paternalistic visage and translates into intensified intrusion and castigatory oversight.*

The undivided hegemony of neoliberal "security-think" on both sides of the Atlantic hides the fact that contemporary societies have at their disposal at least three main strategies to treat the conditions and conducts that they deem undesirable, offensive, or threatening.[12] The first consists in *socializing* them, that is, acting at the level of the collective structures and mechanisms that produce and reproduce them—for instance, as concerns the continual increase in the number of the visible homeless who "stain" the urban landscape, by building or subsidizing housing, or by guaranteeing them a job or an income that would enable them to acquire shelter on the rental market. This path entails (re)asserting the responsibility and (re)building the capacities of the social state to deal with continuing or emerging urban dislocations. The second strategy is *medicalization*: it is to consider that a person is living out on the street because she suffers from alcohol dependency, drug addiction, or mental deficiencies, and thus to search for a medical remedy to a problem that is defined from the outset as an individual pathology liable to be treated by health professionals.

The third state strategy is *penalization*: under this scenario, it is not a matter of either understanding a situation of individual distress or a question of thwarting social cogs; the urban nomad is labeled a delinquent (through a municipal ordinance outlawing panhandling or lying down on the sidewalk, for instance) and finds himself treated as such; and he ceases to pertain to homelessness as soon as he is put behind bars. The "legal construction of the homeless as bare life" abridges his

*This diagnosis contrasts with the influential views of Nikolas Rose, for whom advanced countries have witnessed "a bewildering variety of developments in regimes of control" displaying "little strategic coherence"; David Garland, who sees penal change over the past three decades as stamped by schizophrenic "bifurcation" betraying the limits of the sovereign state; Pat O'Malley, who also stresses dispersal, inconsistency, and volatility; Jonathan Simon and Malcolm Feeley, for whom postmodern disintegration deepens the disconnect between the actuarial logic of the "new penology" and popular understandings of crime and punishment; and Michael Tonry, who highlights the cyclical nature and absurdist tenor of recent trends in criminal policies. See respectively, Nikolas Rose, "Government and Control," *British Journal of Criminology* 40, no. 3 (Spring 2000): 321–39; David Garland, *The Culture of Control* (Chicago: University of Chicago Press, 2001); Pat O'Malley, "Volatile and Contradictory Punishment," *Theoretical Criminology* 40, no. 1 (January 1999): 175–96; Jonathan Simon and Malcolm Feeley, "The Forms and Limits of the New Penology," in *Punishment and Social Control*, eds. Stanley Cohen and Thomas Blomberg, 75–116 (New York: Aldine de Gruyter, 2003); and Michael Tonry, *Thinking about Crime: Sense and Sensibility in American Penal Culture* (New York: Oxford University Press, 2004).

or her rights, effectively reduces him to a noncitizen, and facilitates criminal processing.[13] Here penalization serves as a *technique for the invisibilization of the social "problems"* that the state, as the bureaucratic lever of collective will, no longer can or cares to treat at its roots, and the prison operates as a judicial garbage disposal into which the human refuse of the market society are thrown.

Inasmuch as they have developed the necessary organizational and ideological capacity, advanced countries can implement these three strategies in diverse combinations and for diverse conditions. There is, moreover, a dynamic interrelationship between these three modalities of state treatment of deplorable states of affairs, with medicalization often serving as a conduit to criminalization at the bottom of the class structure as it introduces a logic of individual treatment.* What matters here is that the weighing and targeting of these manners of governing indocile populations and territories is *doubly political*. First, they are political in that they result from ongoing power struggles between the agents and institutions which contend, in and around the bureaucratic field, to shape and eventually direct the management of "troubled persons" and troubling collective states. Second, the shifting dosage and aim of socialization, medicalization, and penalization are political in that they result from choices that engage the conception that we have of life in common.

It is crucial that these choices be made with full knowledge of the causes and consequences, in the middle and long run, of the options offered. The most portentous scientific and civic mistake here consists in believing and making people believe, as the hypersecuritarist discourse that saturates the political and journalistic fields today asserts, that police and carceral management is the optimal remedy, the royal road to the restoration of sociomoral order in the city, if not the only means of ensuring public "safety," and that we have no alternative to

*In American history, the adoption of the medical model to deal with a variety of disquieting activities (opiate use and addiction, homosexuality, abortion, child abuse and madness) has repeatedly led to their penalization. Peter Conrad and Joseph W. Schneider, *Deviance and Medicalization: From Badness to Sickness* (Philadelphia: Temple University Press, 1992). An instructive case study of how medicalization worked to divert attention from the socioeconomic roots of the rising presence of homeless people on the streets of New York City in the 1980s (namely, the steep decline in stable jobs and severe penury of affordable housing) and to justify a policy of physical removal of social discards from public space is Arline Mathieu, "The Medicalization of Homelessness and the Theater of Repression," *Medical Anthropology Quarterly*, n.s. 7, no. 2. (June 1993): 170–84. For a germane analysis in the French case, see Patrick Gaboriau and Daniel Terrolle, eds., *Ethnologie des sans-logis. Etude d'une forme de domination sociale* (Paris: L'Harmattan, 1998).

contain the social and mental turbulence induced by the fragmentation of wage work and the polarization of urban space. The sociological analysis of the stupendous ascent of the penal state in the United States after the peaking of the Civil Rights movement demonstrates that such is not the case. Entering into the living laboratory of the neoliberal revolution also has the virtue of revealing in quasi-experimental fashion the colossal social cost and the irreversible debasement of the ideals of freedom and equality implied by the criminalization of social insecurity.

New York, May 2004—Berkeley, December 2006

1

Social Insecurity and the Punitive Upsurge

Comparative analysis of the evolution of penality in the advanced countries over the past decade reveals a close link between the ascendancy of neoliberalism as ideological project and governmental practice mandating submission to the "free market" and the celebration of "individual responsibility" in all realms,* on the one hand, and the deployment of punitive and proactive law-enforcement policies targeting street delinquency and the categories trapped in the margins and cracks of the new economic and moral order coming into being under the conjoint empire of financialized capital and flexible wage labor, on the other hand.

Beyond their national inflections and institutional variations, these policies sport six common features.[1] First, they purport to put an end to the "era of leniency" and to attack head-on the problem of crime, as well as urban disorders and the public nuisances that border the confines of penal law, baptized "incivilities," while openly disregarding their causes. To do so, they claim to rely on the recovered or renewed capacity of the state to bend so-called problem populations and territories to the common norm. Whence, second, a proliferation of laws and an insatiable craving for bureaucratic innovations and technological gadgets: crime-watch groups and "guarantors of place"; partnerships between the police and other public services (schools, hospitals, social workers, the national tax office, etc.); video surveillance cameras and computerized mapping of offenses; compulsory drug testing, "Tazers" and "flash-ball" guns; fast-track judicial processing and the extension of the prerogatives of probation and parole officers; criminal profiling,

*One would need to deconstruct these two notions, which function in the manner of mutually supporting magical incantations. Such an exercise would remind us that, just as no durable system of commodity exchange can exist without a vast infrastructure of social relations and a recognized juridical framework, the autonomous individual and her free will are, as Durkheim showed long ago, not universal anthropological givens but creations of the modern society and state. Émile Durkheim, *Leçons de sociologie* (Paris: Presses Universitaires de France, 1950), esp. 93–99. Translated by Cornelia Brookfield as *Professional Ethics and Civic Morals* (London: Routledge and Kegan Paul, 1957), 57–64.

satellite-aided electronic monitoring, and generalized genetic fingerprinting; enlargement and technological modernization of carceral facilities; multiplication of specialized detention centers (for foreigners waiting to be expelled, recidivist minors, women and the sick, convicts serving community sentences, etc.).

Next, the need for these punitive policies is conveyed everywhere by an alarmist, even catastrophist discourse on "insecurity," animated with martial images and broadcast to saturation by the commercial media, the major political parties, and professionals in the enforcement of order—police officials, magistrates, legal scholars, experts and merchants in "urban safety" counseling and services—who vie to propose remedies as drastic as they are simplistic. Woven of amalgamation, approximation, and exaggeration, this discourse is amplified and ratified by the prefabricated productions of a certain magazine sociology that shamelessly lumps together schoolyard brawls, stairwell graffiti, and riots in derelict housing projects, in accordance with the demands of the new political common sense.*

Fourthly, out of a proclaimed concern for efficiency in the "war on crime" as much as for proof of solicitude toward this new figure of the deserving citizen that is the crime victim, this discourse overtly revalorizes repression and stigmatizes youths from declining working-class neighborhoods, the jobless, homeless, beggars, drug addicts and street prostitutes, and immigrants from the former colonies of the West and from the ruins of the Soviet empire, designated as the natural vectors of a pandemic of minor offenses that poison daily life and the progenitors of "urban violence" bordering on collective chaos.[2] Following which, on the carceral front, the therapeutic philosophy of "rehabilitation" has been more or less supplanted by a managerialist approach centered on the cost-driven administration of carceral stocks and flows, paving the

*From among the unstoppable flood of books, each catchier than the last, that has submerged French bookstores these past few years, the most representative (and thus the most grotesque) are those by judge Georges Fenech, *Tolérance zéro. En finir avec la criminalité et les violences urbaines* (Paris: Grasset, 2001); Socialist house representative Julien Dray, *État de violence. Quelles solutions à l'insécurité?* (Paris: J'ai lu, 2001); the merchants in "urban safety" consulting, Alain Bauer and Xavier Raufer, *Violences et insécurité urbaines. Les chiffres qui font réfléchir* (Paris: Presses Universitaires de France, 2002); and the former general director of the national police Olivier Foll, *L'Insécurité en France. Un grand flic accuse* (Paris: Flammarion, 2002), whose title ("Insecurity in France: A Top Cop Accuses") is revealing of the logic of indignant denunciation that is typical of the genre, and which opens with this fiery tirade: "I say it, I yell it: the state is responsible for failure to assist persons in jeopardy with regard to thousands of minors and citizens" ("failure to provide assistance to a person in jeopardy" is a criminal offense according to the French penal code).

way for the privatization of correctional services. Lastly, the implementation of these new punitive policies has invariably resulted in an extension and tightening of the police dragnet, a hardening and speeding-up of judicial procedures, and, at the end of the penal chain, an incongruous increase in the population under lock, even though their impact on the incidence of offenses has never been established other than by pure proclamation, and without anyone raising the question of their financial burden, social costs, and civic implications.

These punitive policies are the object of an unprecedented political consensus and enjoy broad public support cutting across class lines, boosted by the tenacious blurring of crime, poverty, and immigration in the media as well as by the constant confusion between insecurity and the "feeling of insecurity." This confusion is tailor-made to channel toward the (dark-skinned) figure of the street delinquent the diffuse anxiety caused by a string of interrelated social changes: the dislocations of wage work, the crisis of the patriarchal family and the erosion of traditional relations of authority among sex and age categories, the decomposition of established working-class territories and the intensification of school competition as requirement for access to employment.[3] And how would the rolling out of the penal arm of the state not be popular when the parties of the governmental Left in all of the postindustrial countries have converted to a narrowly behaviorist and moralistic Rightist vision that counterposes "individual responsibility" and "sociological excuses" in the name of the (electoral) "reality principle"? It follows that penal severity is now presented virtually everywhere and by everyone as a healthy necessity, a vital reflex of self-defense by a social body threatened by the gangrene of criminality, no matter how petty.[4] Caught in the vise of the biased alternative between catastrophic and angelic visions, anyone who dares to question the self-evident commonplaces of the *pensée unique* (one-way thinking) about "insecurity" that now rules uncontested is irrevocably (dis)qualified as a vain dreamer or an ideologue guilty of ignoring the harsh realities of contemporary urban life.

The Generalization of Social Insecurity and Its Effects

But reality, properly speaking, is not what we are made to think it is. The sudden proclamation of a "state of emergency" on the police and penal front in the United States starting in the mid-1970s, and then in Western Europe according to the same schemas a quarter-century later, does not correspond to a rupture in the evolution of crime and delinquency, which we shall see did not abruptly change in scale and physiognomy at the start of the two periods in question on either side of the Atlantic. Neither does it translate a forward leap in the efficiency of the repressive apparatus that would justify its reinforcement, as the zealots of "zero tolerance" now spread around the world would have us believe. And it is not the spawn of advances in criminological science authorizing a refining of deterrence and judicial pressure, as claimed by the myth of the "broken window." It is not criminality that has changed here so much as the *gaze that society trains on certain street illegalities,* that is, in the final analysis, *on the dispossessed and dishonored populations* (by status or origin) that are their presumed perpetrators, on the place they occupy in the City, and on the uses to which these populations can be subjected in the political and journalistic fields.

These castaway categories—unemployed youth left adrift, the beggars and the homeless, aimless nomads and drug addicts, postcolonial immigrants without documents or support—have become salient in public space, their presence undesirable and their doings intolerable, because they are the *living and threatening incarnation of the generalized social insecurity* produced by the erosion of stable and homogenous wage work (promoted to the rank of paradigm of employment during the decades of Fordist expansion in 1945–75) and by the decomposition of the solidarities of class and culture it underpinned within a clearly circumscribed national framework.[5] Just as national boundaries have been blurred by the hypermobility of capital, the settlement of migration flows, and European integration, the normalization of desocialized labor feeds a powerful current of anxiety in all the societies of the continent. This current mixes the fear of the future, the dread of social decline and degradation, and the anguish of not being able to transmit one's status to one's offspring in a competition for credentials and positions that is ever more intense and uncertain. It is this diffuse and multifaceted social and mental insecurity, which (objectively) strikes working-class families shorn of the cultural capital required to accede to the protected sectors of the labor market and (subjectively) haunts large sectors of the middle class, that the new martial discourse of politicians and the media on delinquency has captured, fixating it onto the sole issue of physical or criminal insecurity.

Indeed, the generalized hardening of police, judicial, and correctional policies that can be observed in most of the countries of the First World over the past two decades[6] partakes of a *triple transformation of the state,* which it helps simultaneously to accelerate and obfuscate, wedding the amputation of its economic arm, the retraction of its social bosom, and the massive expansion of its penal fist. This transformation is the bureaucratic response of political elites to the mutations of wage work (the shift to services and polarization of occupations, flexibilization and intensification of work, individualization of employment contracts, discontinuity and dispersion of occupational paths) and their ravaging effects on the lower tiers of the social and spatial structure. These mutations themselves are the product of a swing in the balance of power between the classes and groups that struggle at every moment for control over the worlds of employment and their proceeds. And in this struggle, it is the transnational business class and the "modernizing" fractions of the cultural bourgeoisie and high state nobility, allied under the banner of neoliberalism, that have gained the upper hand and embarked on a sweeping campaign to reconstruct public power in line with their material and symbolic interests.[7]

Three trends implicate and intricate with one another in a self-perpetuating causal chain that is redrawing the perimeter and redefining the modalities of government action: (1) the commodification of public goods and the rise of underpaid, precarious work against the backdrop of working poverty in the United States and enduring mass joblessness in the European Union; (2) the unraveling of social protection schemes, leading to the replacement of the collective right to recourse against unemployment and destitution by the individual obligation to take up gainful activity ("workfare" in the United States and the United Kingdom, ALE jobs in Belgium, PARE and RMA in France, the Hartz reform in Germany, etc.), in order to impose desocialized wage labor as the normal horizon of work for the new proletariat of the urban service sectors;[8] and (3) the reinforcement and extension of the punitive apparatus, recentered onto the dispossessed districts of the inner city and the urban periphery which concentrate the disorders and despair spawned by the twofold movement of retrenchment of the state from the economic and social front.

The Keynesian state, coupled with Fordist wage work operating as a spring of *solidarity*, whose mission was to counter the recessive cycles of the market economy, protect the most vulnerable populations, and reduce the most glaring inequalities, has been succeeded by a state that one might dub *neo-Darwinist*, in that it erects *competition* and celebrates unrestrained individual responsibility—whose counterpart is collective and thus political irresponsibility. The Leviathan then withdraws into its regalian functions of law enforcement, themselves hypertrophied and deliberately abstracted from their social environment, and its symbolic mission of reasserting common values through the public anathematization of deviant categories—chief among them the unemployed "street thug" and the "pedophile," viewed as the walking incarnations of the abject failure to live up to the abstemious ethic of wage work and sexual self-control. Unlike its *belle époque* predecessor, this new-style Darwinism, which praises the "winners" for their vigor and intelligence and vituperates the "losers" in the "struggle for [economic] life" by pointing to their character flaws and behavioral deficiencies, does not find its model in nature.[9] It is the market that supplies it with its master-metaphor and the mechanism of selection supposed to ensure the "survival of the fittest." But only after this market itself has been naturalized, that is to say, depicted under radically dehistoricized trappings which, paradoxically, turn it into a concrete historical realization of the pure and perfect abstractions of the orthodox economic science promoted to the rank of official theodicy of the social order *in statu nascendi*.

Thus the "invisible hand" of the unskilled labor market, strengthened by the shift from welfare to workfare, finds its ideological extension and institutional complement in the "iron fist" of the penal state, which grows and redeploys in order to *stem the disorders generated by the diffusion of social insecurity* and by the correlative destabilization of the status hierarchies that formed the traditional framework of the national society (such as the division between whites and blacks in the United States and between nationals and colonial immigrants in Western Europe). The regulation of the working classes through what Pierre Bourdieu calls "the Left hand" of the state,[10] that which protects and expands life chances, represented by labor law, education, health, social assistance, and public housing, is *supplanted* (in the United States) or *supplemented* (in the European Union) by regulation through its "Right hand," that of the police, justice, and correctional administrations, increasingly active and intrusive in the subaltern zones of social and urban space. And, logically, the prison returns to the forefront of the societal stage, when only thirty years ago the most eminent specialists of the penal question were unanimous in predicting its waning, if not its disappearance.*

*Recall that, in the mid-1970s, the three leading revisionist historians of the prison, David Rothman, Michel Foucault, and Michael Ignatieff, agreed with radical sociologists Stanley Cohen and Andrew Scull, as well as with mainstream penologists Hermann Manheim and Norval Morris, that it was an institution in inevitable decline, destined to be replaced in the medium run by more diffuse, discrete, and diversified instruments of social control. See Franklin E. Zimring and Gordon Hawkins, *The Scale of Imprisonment* (Chicago: University of Chicago Press, 1991), chap. 2. The penal debate then turned decisively toward the implications of "decarceration" and implementation of community sentences. Since this Malthusian prognosis, the evolution of punish-

The renewed utility of the penal apparatus in the post-Keynesian era of *insecure employment* is threefold: (1) it works to bend the fractions of the working class recalcitrant to the discipline of the new fragmented service wage-labor by increasing the cost of strategies of exit into the informal economy of the street; (2) it neutralizes and warehouses its most disruptive elements, or those rendered wholly superfluous by the recomposition of the demand for labor; and (3) it reaffirms the authority of the state in daily life within the restricted domain henceforth assigned to it. The canonization of the "right to security," correlative to the dereliction of the "right to employment" in its old form (that is, full-time and with full benefits, for an indefinite period, and for a living wage enabling one to reproduce oneself socially and to project oneself into the future), and the increased interest in, and resources granted to, the enforcement of order come at just the right time to *shore up the deficit of legitimacy* suffered by political decision-makers, owing to the very fact that they have abjured the established missions of the state on the social and economic front.

Under these conditions, one understands better why, throughout Europe, the parties of the governmental Left smitten with the neoliberal vision have proven so fond of the security thematics incarnated by "zero tolerance" that have come from the United States in the past decade, or its British cousins such as "community policing." For, in their case, the adoption of policies of economic deregulation and social retrenchment amounts to a political betrayal of the working-class electorate that brought them to power in the hope of receiving stronger state protection against the sanctions and failings of the market. Thus the punitive turn taken by Lionel Jospin in France in the fall of 1997, like those negotiated by Anthony Blair in Britain, Felipe González in Spain, Massimo d'Alema in Italy, and Gerhard Schröder in Germany around the same years, after William Jefferson Clinton had plainly adopted the ultra-repressive agenda of the Republican Party in the United States in 1994,[11] has little to do with the alleged "explosion" in youth delinquency or with the "urban violence" that have invaded public debate toward the end of the past decade. (The climax of this media crescendo in France was reached during the presidential campaign of 2002, which saw the Socialist Party mimicking the positions of the RPR, the main right-wing party, which had aligned itself with the more punitive stance

ment has made an about-face in almost all Western societies: the population behind bars has doubled in France, Belgium, and England; it has tripled in Holland, Spain, and Greece; and it has quintupled in the United States.

of the National Front, reducing the debate on "insecurity" to a frantic bidding up in severity.)* It has everything to do with the generalization of desocialized wage labor and the establishment of a political regime that will facilitate its imposition. It is a regime that one may call "liberal-paternalist," insofar as it is *liberal* and permissive at the top, with regard to corporations and the upper class, and *paternalist* and authoritarian at the bottom, toward those who find themselves caught between the restructuring of employment and the ebbing of social protection or its conversion into an instrument of surveillance and discipline.

"Sociological Excuses" and "Individual Responsibility"

Just as neoliberal ideology in economic matters rests on an impermeable separation between the economic (supposedly governed by the neutral, fluid, and efficient mechanism of the market) and the social (inhabited by the unpredictable arbitrariness of powers and passions), so the new penal *doxa* come from the United States postulates a clean and definitive caesura between (social) circumstances and (criminal) acts, causes and consequences, sociology (which explains) and the law (which regulates and sanctions). The same behavioristic mode of reasoning then serves to devalue the sociological point of view, implicitly denounced as demobilizing and "deresponsibilizing"—and thus as infantile, even feminizing—in order to substitute for it the virile rhetoric of personal uprightness and responsibility, tailor-made for deflecting attention away from the abdications of the state on the economic, urban, schooling, and public health fronts. This is indicated by this typical statement of prime minister Lionel Jospin in an interview of January 1999, curiously entitled "Against the International '*Pensée Unique*'" even though it would appear to have come straight out of the mouth of an expert from a "think tank" of the new American Right:

*According to the UBM index (*Unité de bruit médiatique*, Unit of Media Noise, elaborated by the firm TNS Media Intelligence, to measure the space occupied in eighty press outlets and television and radio news segments in France), "insecurity" weighed eight times more than unemployment in public debate during the election campaign of winter 2002 (even as official crime figures were declining and those for joblessness were rising). On the eve of the second round of the election, the mad race for audience ratings even led *Le Monde* to cover the magazine kiosks of Paris with a poster promoting a "Special Dossier" on "Insecurity" with this panicked interpellation: "Is France a Dangerous Country?" (which senior editor Thomas Ferenczi answered in the positive, thus illustrating the wry observation of sociologist Philippe Robert in the same supplement on "the poverty of the French debate"). The political mistake of candidate Jospin in that race was to believe that he could draw electoral profits from manipulating the thematics of crime in order to mask the rise of precariousness and poverty under an allegedly Left government.

> From the moment we took office, we have insisted on problems of security. To prevent and to punish are the two poles of the action we are conducting. These problems are linked to serious issues of badly managed urbanism, family breakdown, and social misery, but also to the deficit of integration of part of the youths living in the *cités* [public housing projects]. But these do not constitute, for all that, an *excuse* for delinquent *individual behaviors*. One must not confound sociology with law. *Each remains responsible for his acts*. So long as we allow *sociological excuses* and we do not implicate *individual responsibility*, we will not resolve these questions.[12]

Social and economic structures disappear to make room for reasoning of a marginalist kind that debases collective causes to the rank of "excuses" in order to better justify individual sanctions. Being assured of having little durable traction on the mechanisms generative of delinquent conduct, these sanctions can have no other function than to underline the authority of the state on the symbolic level (with a view toward electoral dividends) and to reinforce its penal sector on the material level, to the detriment of its social sector. It is therefore not surprising to find this same individualistic and repressive philosophy in countless speeches by leaders of the Right in the United States, such as in this "Address to Students on the 'War on Drugs'" delivered by President George H. W. Bush in 1989:

> We must raise our voices to correct an insidious tendency—the tendency to blame crime on society rather than on the criminal. . . . I, like most Americans, believe that we can start building a safer society by first agreeing that *society itself doesn't cause the crime—criminals cause the crime.**

In March 1999, in a speech delivered via video to the "National Meetings of Agencies for the Prevention of Delinquency," justice minister Elisabeth Guigou bid up on the imperative necessity to disassociate social causes from individual responsibility, in conformity with the root schema of the neoliberal vision of the world. And she even found Reaganite tones in which to excoriate a "culture of indulgence" allegedly fostered by "prevention" programs, bluntly dismissing the advocates of the social treatment of precariousness as utopians:

> The turn we undertake together must be a turn towards the *reality principle*. . . . Who does not see that certain methods of prevention support, sometimes inadvertently, a certain culture of indulgence that *relieves individuals of responsibility* [literally: "de-responsibilizes"]? Can one develop a young person's autonomy by ceaselessly conceding that his infractions have *sociological, even political, causes*—causes which, more

*George Bush, "Remarks at a Briefing on Law Enforcement for United States Attorneys," 16 June 1989. My emphases. This *forte pensée* can be found over and over again in the statements of French Socialist leaders ten years later, for example on the lips of Paris congressman Christophe Caresche, who asserted with remarkable aplomb in *Le Parisien* of 31 October 2001: "We know that delinquency has no social nature whatsoever and that it pertains to the individual responsibility of each person."

often than not, he would not have thought of on his own—even though a mass of his peers, placed in exactly the same social conditions, do not commit any offense?[13]

It is this same "reality principle" to which Ronald Reagan himself never missed a chance to summon us, as indicated in these "Remarks at a Conservative Action Committee Dinner" made in 1983:

> It is abundantly clear that much of our crime problem was provoked by a social philosophy that saw man as primarily a creature of his material environment. The same liberal philosophy that saw an era of prosperity and virtue ushered in by changing man's environment through massive federal spending programs also viewed criminals as the unfortunate products of poor socioeconomic conditions or an underprivileged upbringing. Society, not the individual, they said, was at fault for criminal wrongdoing. We were to blame. Well, today, a new political consensus utterly rejects this point of view.[14]

One can measure how much this "new consensus" on the individual foundations of social and penal justice, which reduces delinquency to the simple sum of the private acts of delinquents, each exercising their free will the better to invite repression, transcends the traditional political divide between the Right and the governmental Left in France by noting the frank and full agreement between congressman Julien Dray, the Socialist Party "expert" on security issues, and Nicolas Sarkozy, the human spearhead of the hyperactive law-and-order policy engaged by the Right after its return to power in the spring of 2002, during the parliamentary debate on the implementation of that policy. Under the approving exhortations of the Right deputies, the socialist Drey held forth:

> Following our Prime Minister, Jean-Pierre Raffarin . . . , for us, *a delinquent is a delinquent*. So there is not, on the benches of this Assembly, on the one side those who are undecided and, on the other, those who are determined—contrary to the Manicheans for whom life is so simple and whose views are often expressed the loudest. Yes, there exists a propitious soil for delinquency. But to recognize this neither excuses delinquency nor, for all that, justifies it. If you do not choose where you were born, you do choose your life and, at a given moment, *you choose to become a delinquent. Whence society has no other solution than to repress these acts*. . . . For the well-being of our country and fellow citizens, . . . I can only wish your success. Your project is an extension of the strategic plan prepared by the previous [Socialist] government and comes out of the discussion of November 2001.[15]

Taking much care to distance himself from any "sociological complacency," Julien Dray then struck up the anthem that serves as the slogan (and screen) for the repressive policy of Tony Blair's New Labour, which is responsible for an unprecedented increase in the incarceration rate in England. "It is necessary to be tough on crime, but also on the causes of crime." To which Nicolas Sarkozy was happy to respond:

> I would like to say to you, and through you to all the members of the Socialist Party, that I found your intervention courageous and useful. It rests on your competence as a grassroots representative and it expresses your refusal to make something ideological out of the issue [sic]. . . . Monsieur Dray, it gave me such *pleasure to hear you hail the American model*, and with such talent, such honesty, and such exactitude! Never would I have dared to go so far. Thank you for doing me this service! [Laughter and applause from the benches of the Union pour la Majorité Présidentielle and the Union pour la Démocratie Française, the two main right-wing parties.][16]

An American Invention with Planetary Implications

The resolutely punitive turn taken by penal policies in advanced societies at the close of the twentieth century thus does not pertain to the simple diptych of "crime and punishment." It heralds the establishment of a *new government of social insecurity*, "in the expansive sense of techniques and procedures aimed at directing the conduct of the men"[17] and women caught up in the turbulence of economic deregulation and the conversion of welfare into a springboard toward precarious employment, an organizational design within which the prison assumes a major role and which translates, for the groups residing in the nether regions of social space, in the imposition of severe and supercilious supervision. It is the United States that invented this new politics of poverty during the period from 1973 to 1996, in the wake of the social, racial, and antistatist reaction to the progressive movements of the preceding decade that was to be the crucible of the neoliberal revolution.[18] This is why this book takes the reader across the Atlantic to probe the entrails of this bulimic penal state that has surged out of the ruins of the charitable state and of the big black ghettos.

The argument unfolds in four steps. The first part ("Poverty of the Social State") shows how the rise of the carceral sector partakes of a broader restructuring of the US bureaucratic field tending to criminalize poverty and its consequences so as to anchor precarious wage work as a new norm of citizenship at the bottom of the class structure while remedying the derailing of the traditional mechanisms for maintaining the ethnoracial order (chapter 2). The planned atrophy of the social state, culminating with the 1996 law on "Personal Responsibility and Work Opportunity," which replaced the right to "welfare" with the obligation of "workfare," and the sudden hypertrophy of the penal state are two concurrent and complementary developments (chapter 3). Each in its own manner, they respond, on the one side, to the forsaking of the Fordist wage-work compact and the Keynesian compromise in the mid-1970s, and, on the other side, to the crisis of the ghetto as a device for the sociospatial confinement of blacks in the wake of the Civil Rights Revolution and the wave of urban riots of the 1960s. Together, they ensnare the marginal populations of the metropolis in a *carceral-assistantial net* that aims either to render them "useful" by steering them onto the track of deskilled employment through moral retraining and material suasion, or to warehouse them out of reach in the devastated core of the urban "Black Belt" or in the penitentiaries that have become the latter's distant yet direct satellites.[19]

The second part ("Grandeur of the Penal State") dissects the modalities and identifies the engines behind the ascent of the penal state in the United States. Chapter 4 retraces the onset of a regime of permanent and generalized carceral hyperinflation without precedent in a democratic society, while crime rates stagnated and then receded, and sketches the lateral expansion of the "penal dragnet" that now holds several tens of millions of Americans in its mesh by means of judicial supervision and criminal databanks. Chapter 5 documents the stupendous expansion of the means devoted to the punitive supervision of the poor and weighs the astronomical financial and social costs of the ascent of the correctional institution among public bureaucracies while the economic and social weight of the state diminishes. It also shows how the country's authorities have strived to enlarge their carceral capacity by resorting to private imprisonment, by hardening conditions of detention, and by shifting part of the cost of their confinement onto the inmates and their families.

The third part ("Privileged Targets") explains why the "great confinement" of fin-de-siècle America strikes first and foremost the subproletariat of the black ghettos undermined by deindustrialization, among the declining fractions of the working class (chapter 6), and the reviled figure of the "sex offender," among vectors of deviance in violation of the Puritan ethic of work and domestic order (chapter 7). It gives us an opportunity to stress the *properly symbolic effects of the unleashing of the penal system*, especially how the latter reinforces, by dramatizing it, the legal, social, and cultural demarcation between the community of "law-abiding citizens" and criminals, so as to turn the latter into a sacrificial category that concentrates within itself all of the negative properties (immorality, poverty, blackness) that this community wishes to expel outside itself. The penalization of poverty thus vividly reminds everyone that, by its sole existence, poverty constitutes an intolerable offense against this "strong and definite state of the collective conscience"* of the nation that conceives of America as a society of affluence and "opportunity for all."

The central thesis of the present book resides in its very architecture, that is, in the empirical and analytical rapprochement it effects between social policy and penal policy. These two domains of public action continue to be approached separately, in isolation from each other, by social scientists as well as by those, politicians, professionals, and activists, who wish to reform them, whereas in reality they already function in tandem at the bottom of the structure of classes and places. Just as the close of the nineteenth century witnessed the gradual disjunction of the social question from the penal question under the press of working-class mobilization and the reconfiguration of the state it stimulated, the close of the twentieth century has been the theater of a renewed fusion and confusion of these two issues, following the fragmentation of the world of the laboring classes**—its industrial dismantlement and the deepening of its internal divisions, its defensive retreat into the private sphere and crushing feeling of downward drift, its loss of a sense of collective dignity, and, lastly, its abandonment by Left parties more concerned with the games internal to their apparatus than with "changing life" (the motto of the French Socialist Party in the late 1970s), leading to its near disappearance from the public scene as a collective actor.[20] It follows that *the fight against street delinquency now serves as screen and counterpart to the new social question*, namely, the generalization of insecure wage work and its impact on the territories and life strategies of the urban proletariat.

In 1971, Frances Fox Piven and Richard Cloward published their classic book *Regulating the Poor*, in which they argue that "relief programs

*To borrow the language of Durkheim, who reminds us that "to gain an accurate idea of punishment, one must reconcile the two contrary theories that have been offered of it: that which sees in it an expiation and that which makes it a weapon for social defense." Émile Durkheim, *De la division du travail social* (Paris: Presses Universitaires de France, 1930 [1893]), 77. My translation. *The Division of Labor in Society* (New York: Free Press, 1984), 63.

**In the French case, this dissociation was accomplished between 1888 and 1914, as shown by Christian Guitton, "Le chômage entre question sociale et question pénale en France au tournant de siècle," in *Aux Sources du chômage, 1880–1914. Une comparaison interdisciplinaire entre la France et la Grande-Bretagne*, ed. Malcolm Mansfield, Robert Salais, and Noel Whiteside, 63–91 (Paris: Belin, 1994). Future historians will perhaps date their renewed conjunction to October 1997, the date of the famous Villepinte Symposium organized by the Jospin government on "Safe Cities for Free Citizens" ("*Des villes sûres pour des citoyens libres*"—note in passing the masculinist character of this designation, which partakes at the discursive level in the virilization of state action, and the priority it gives to security over freedom).

are initiated to deal with dislocations in the work system that lead to mass disorder, and are then retained (in an altered form) to enforce work."[21] Thirty years later, this cyclical dynamic of expansion and contraction of public aid has been superseded by a *new division of the labor of nomination and domination of deviant and dependent populations* that couples welfare services and criminal justice administration under the aegis of the same behaviorist and punitive philosophy. The activation of disciplinary programs applied to the unemployed, the indigent, single mothers, and others "on assistance" so as to push them onto the peripheral sectors of the employment market, on the one side, and the deployment of an extended police and penal net with a reinforced mesh in the dispossessed districts of the metropolis, on the other side, are the two components of a single apparatus for the management of poverty that aims at effecting the authoritarian rectification of the behaviors of populations recalcitrant to the emerging economic and symbolic order. Failing which, it aims to ensure the civic or physical expurgation of those who prove to be "incorrigible" or useless.* And much as the development of modern "welfare" in the United States from its origins in the New Deal to the contemporary period was decisively shaped by its entailment in a rigid and pervasive structure of ethnoracial domination that precluded the deployment of inclusive and universalist programs, we shall see (especially in chapters 2 and 6) that the expansion of the penal state after the mid-1970s was both dramatically accelerated and decisively twisted by the revolt and involutive collapse of the dark ghetto as well as by the subsequent ebbing of public support for black demands for civic equality.[22]

In the era of fragmented and discontinuous wage work, the regulation of working-class households is no longer handled solely by the maternal and nurturing social arm of the welfare state; it relies also on the virile and controlling arm of the penal state. The "dramaturgy of labor" is not played solely on the stages of the public aid office and job placement bureau as Piven and Cloward insist in the 1993 revision of their classic analysis.[23] At century's turn it also unfolds its stern scenarios in police stations, in the corridors of criminal court, and in the darkness of prison cells.[24] This dynamic coupling of the Left and Right hands of

*This coupling of the assistantial and penitential sectors of the state rises to the level of a deliberate strategy for remaking public authority among some apostles of the new government of poverty in America, such as Lawrence Mead, ed., *The New Paternalism: Supervisory Approaches to Poverty* (Washington, D.C.: Brookings Institution, 1997); for a discussion, see Wacquant, *Les Prisons de la misère* (Paris: Raisons d'agir Editions, 1999), 36–44.

the state operates through a familiar sharing of the roles between the sexes. The public aid bureaucracy, now reconverted into an administrative springboard into poverty-level employment, takes up the mission of inculcating the duty of working for work's sake among poor women (and indirectly their children): 90 percent of welfare recipients in the United States are mothers. The quartet formed by the police, the court, the prison, and the probation or parole officer assumes the task of taming their brothers, their boyfriends or husbands, and their sons: 93 percent of US inmates are male (men also make up 88 percent of parolees and 77 percent of probationers). This suggests, in line with a rich strand of feminist scholarship on public policy, gender, and citizenship,[25] that the invention of the *double regulation of the poor* in America in the closing decades of the twentieth century partakes of an overall (re)*masculinizing of the state* in the neoliberal age, which may be understood in part as an oblique reaction to (or against) the social changes wrought by the women's movement and their reverberations inside the bureaucratic field. Considering that feminist social scientists have conclusively demonstrated that one cannot explain the constitution and trajectory of welfare states without factoring gender into the core equation, there is reason to think that fully elucidating the rise of the penal state will likewise require bringing masculinity from the periphery toward the center of the analysis of penality.*

Within this sexual and institutional division in the regulation of the poor, the "clients" of both the assistantial and penitential sectors of the state fall under the same principled suspicion: they are considered morally deficient unless they periodically provide visible proof to the contrary. This is why their behaviors must be supervised and regulated by the imposition of rigid protocols whose violation will expose them to a redoubling of corrective discipline and, if necessary, to sanctions that can result in durable segregation, a manner of *social death for moral failing*—casting them outside the civic community of those entitled to

*So far, masculinity has entered into the analysis of punishment only indirectly and marginally, through the "backdoor" of crime. See, for instance, the pioneering books by James W. Messerschmidt, *Masculinities and Crime* (Lanham, Md.: Rowman & Littlefield, 1993); Tim Newburn and Elizabeth A. Stanko, eds., *Just Boys Doing Business? Men, Masculinities, and Crime* (London: Routledge, 1995); and the survey by Tony Jefferson, "Masculinities and Crime," in *The Oxford Handbook of Criminology*, ed. Mike Maguire, Rod Morgan, and Robert Reiner, 535–58 (Oxford: Oxford University Press, 1997). Moreover, what research exists remains confined to the narrow intellectual cell of crime-and-punishment, instead of looking more expansively at penality as a full-fledged institution in relation to broader structures of inequality, identity, and community.

social rights, in the case of public aid recipients, outside the society of "free men" for convicts. Welfare provision and criminal justice are thus animated by the same punitive and paternalist philosophy that stresses the "individual responsibility" of the "client," treated in the manner of a "subject," in contraposition to the universal rights and obligations of the citizen,[26] and they reach publics of roughly comparable size. In 2001, the number of households receiving Temporary Assistance to Needy Families, the main assistance program established by the 1996 "welfare reform," was 2.1 million, corresponding to some 6 million beneficiaries. That same year, the carceral population reached 2.1 million, but the total number of "beneficiaries" of criminal justice supervision (tallying up inmates, probationers, and parolees) was in the neighborhood of 6.5 million. In addition, as we shall demonstrate in chapter 3, welfare recipients and inmates have germane social profiles and extensive mutual ties that make them the two gendered sides of the same population coin.

It follows that if one wishes to decipher the fate of the precarious fractions of the working class in their relation to the state, it is no longer possible to limit oneself to studying welfare programs. One must extend and supplement the sociology of traditional policies of collective "well-being"—assistance to dispossessed individuals and households, but also education, housing, public health, family allowances, income redistribution, etc.—by that of penal policies. Thus the study of incarceration ceases to be the reserved province of criminologists and penologists to become an *essential chapter in the sociology of the state and social stratification, and, more specifically, of the (de)composition of the urban proletariat* in the era of ascendant neoliberalism. Indeed, the crystallization of a liberal-paternalist political regime, which practices "laissez faire et laissez passer" toward the top of the class structure, at the level of the mechanisms of production of inequality, and punitive paternalism toward the bottom, at the level of their social and spatial implications, demands that we *forsake the traditional definition of "social welfare"* as the product of a political and scholarly common sense overtaken by historical reality. It requires that we adopt an expansive approach, encompassing in a single grasp the totality of the actions whereby the state purports to mould, classify, and control the populations deemed deviant, dependent, and dangerous living on its territory. The study of welfare-turned-workfare must thus be closely coupled with the investigation of what I call *prisonfare*: the extended policy stream that responds to intensifying urban ills and assorted sociomoral turbulences by boosting and deploying the police, the courts, custodial institutions (juvenile detention halls, jails, prisons, retention centers), and their extensions (probation, parole, criminal data bases and assorted systems of surveillance, supervision and profiling such as "background checks" by public officials, employers, and realtors), as well as the commanding images, lay and specialized idioms, and bodies of expert knowledge elaborated to depict and justify this deployment (chief among them the tropes of moral indignation, civic urgency, and technical efficiency).

In the 1993 edition of their classic study *Regulating the Poor*, Piven and Cloward note that "the welfare state literature generally is plagued by theoretically significant definitional problems, such as the question of whether education is a welfare-state policy, or whether non-governmental services and income supports are appropriately part of the definition."[27] But at no point do they envisage the possibility of including in their perimeter of study the penal sector of the state. The prison and the jail appear fleetingly in their historical account of the invention of relief policies in Europe: carceral institutions are mentioned a total of five times, in Piven's and Cloward's discussion of their use in the sixteenth century to stem rising vagrancy and begging in France and England, in response to popular disorders in England in the early nineteenth century, and later as penal sanction for the wayward husbands of welfare clients in the twentieth century.[28] But they are never granted even a marginal role as a labor-clearing or labor-shaping device in the contemporary period. Indeed, in the chapter added to the 1993 edition to cover "Relief, Deindustrialization, and the War Against Labor, 1970–1990," the very period when the carceral boom took off in the United States, Piven and Cloward concentrate solely on work and welfare developments, on grounds that "the workhouse is no longer a politically feasible way to enforce market discipline." Alluringly, they remark in a passing *footnote*: "However, imprisoning the poor—the US has the highest incarceration rate among Western countries—could be construed as a partial equivalent of the poorhouse,"[29] not realizing that this footnote misses the advent of a new regime of poverty regulation combining restrictive workfare and expansive prisonfare.

Similarly, the canonical works of Theda Skocpol, Michael Katz, Linda Gordon, and Jill Quadagno are silent on the targeting of the poor by judicial policies, in spite of the pivotal role of punishment in the early history of state institutions in the country—as demonstrated, among others, by David Rothman's *The Discovery of the Asylum* and Thomas Dumm's *Democracy and Punishment*.[30] The thorough discussion of "current policies, efforts, and programs designed to deal with the poor" offered in *We the Poor People* by Joel Handler and Yeshekel Hasenfeld on the morrow of the 1996 "welfare reform" typically leaves penal institutions entirely out of the picture.[31] A comprehensive overview of recent scholarship on social policy in the United States by Edwin Amenta and his colleagues contains all of one line and a single cursory reference to the part played by criminal justice in the management of precarious populations. A similar survey of scholarship on urban poverty research and policy in America after "welfare reform" by Alice O'Connor published in 2000, the year the United States passed the two-million-inmate mark, is blissfully mum on how the penal state patrols that novel socio-racial landscape. The same conspicuous absence is found in a broad panorama of comparative studies of changing welfare regimes in political science by Paul Pierson, when comparison would seem to highlight America's distinctive move to mate workfare with prisonfare just as it captures the title of world leader in incarceration.[32] The penal state has surged suddenly, grown voraciously, and forced itself into the center of the institutional horizon faced by America's poor, directly and dramatically impacting their life chances and conditions, without students of poverty and welfare seeming to notice it.

On the penal front, scholars have likewise overlooked the roots and ignored the significance of the restrictive and punitive revamping of welfare into workfare for the established clientele of criminal justice. In spite of their growing and glaring disconnection, criminologists have continued to study the causes, shape, and consequences of carceral trends strictly in relation to crime and its suppression, without regard to the broader reconstruction of the American state of which these trends are but one fractional indicator. The typical textbook in correctional studies contains no analysis of social policies aimed at marginalized populations outside of prison walls.[33] Two notable yet only partial exceptions to this entrenched analytic myopia are legal scholars Michael Tonry and David Garland. In *Malign Neglect: Race, Crime, and Punishment in America*, Tonry discerns well that "crime control and social welfare policies are inextricably connected." He points to the concurrent debasement of both policy streams, based on the activation of the same racial enmity toward blacks ("Willie Horton is to crime control as the Welfare Queen is to welfare policy"), and he highlights the disastrous impact of the War on drugs on the African-American community. But he sees changes in social welfare and penal control as parallel and *conflicting* developments, which he attributes to the fact that both "have been converted by conservative politicians from subjects of policy to objects of politics."[34] In reality, we shall show that they are fully congruent and linked transformations *converging* into a novel disciplinary apparatus to supervise the poor in the post–civil-rights era of deregulated low-wage work, and an apparatus whose diligent erection has transcended partisan politics—we will see in chapter 3 that it is William Jefferson Clinton who orchestrated its completion on both the welfare and the prison front in the mid-1990s.

In *The Culture of Control*, Garland stresses similarly that "the institutional and cultural changes that have occurred in the crime control field are analogous to those that have occurred in the welfare state more generally."[35] But he sees these changes as parallel and independent responses to the advent of "late modernity" and "the cluster of risks, insecurities, and control problems" that come with it. Even as they become invested by the same "discursive tropes and administrative strategies," these two domains of state action toward the poor remain empirically separate and theoretically separable. For, according to Garland, "the changes that have occurred in the crime control field" as on the social welfare front "have been mainly a matter of redeploying and redirecting the practices of existing institutions. It has not been a process of inventing new institutions." In his eyes, they entail not the creation of novel structures of control—those that now effectively mate restrictive workfare with expansive prisonfare—but operate primarily "at the level of the *culture* that enlivens these structures, orders their use, and shapes their meanings."[36] Isolating penal policy from its social welfare counterpart leads Garland to conclude that "the problem of crime control in late modernity has vividly demonstrated the limits of the sovereign state."[37] Coupling the analysis of the changing roles of the Left and Right hands of the state reveals, on the contrary, that the "sovereign state strategy" pursued by advocates of the penalization of poverty has been enormously successful, not only in its historic cradle of the United States, but increasingly in other First-World countries that have imported the punitive government of social insecurity precisely because it enables them to stage the newly reasserted potency of the state.

Thus is resolved what could appear to be a doctrinal contradiction, or at least a practical antinomy, of neoliberalism, between the downsizing of public authority on the economic flank and its upsizing on that of the enforcement of social and moral order. If the same people who champion a minimal state in order to "free" the "creative forces" of the market and submit the dispossessed to the sting of competition do not hesitate to erect a maximal state to ensure everyday "security," it is because *the poverty of the social state against the backdrop of deregulation elicits and necessitates the grandeur of the penal state.* And because this causal and functional linkage between the two sectors of the bureaucratic field gets all the stronger as the state more completely sheds all economic responsibility and tolerates a high level of poverty as well as a wide opening of the compass of inequalities.*

*Proof is the fact that the inverse correlation established between the incarceration rate and the level of welfare support across the fifty states has increased over the past two decades. Katherine Beckett and Bruce Western, "Governing Social Marginality: Welfare, Incarceration, and the Transformation of State Policy," *Punishment & Society* 3, no. 1 (January 2001): 43–59. Additional evidence is provided by going comparative and mapping the trajectory of punishment in Second-World countries combining

But the interest in excavating the economic underpinnings and the socioracial incubation of carceral bulimia in the New World is not merely archeological or limited to the sole domain of American studies. For to dissect the penal state in the United States is to offer indispensable materials for a historical anthropology of the *invention of neoliberalism in action*. Since the rupture of the mid-1970s, this country has been the theoretical and practical motor for the elaboration and planetary dissemination of a political project that aims to subordinate all human activities to the tutelage of the market. Far from being an incidental or teratological development, the hypertrophic expansion of the penal sector of the bureaucratic field is an essential element of its new anatomy in the age of economic neo-Darwinism. To journey across the US carceral archipelago, then, is not only to travel to the "extreme limits of European civilization," to use the words of Alexis de Tocqueville. It is also to discover the possible, nay probable, contours of the future landscape of the police, justice, and prison in European and Latin American countries that have embarked onto the path of "liberating" the economy and reconstructing the state blazed by the American leader.[38] In this perspective, the United States appears as a sort of historical alembic in which one can observe on a real scale, and anticipate by way of structural transposition (and, emphatically, not replication), the social, political, and cultural consequences of the advent of neoliberal penality in a society submitted to the joint empire of the commodity form and moralizing individualism.

A "European Road" to the Penal State?

By retracing the making, in the United States, of this new government of social insecurity that weds the "invisible hand" of the deregulated labor market and contractualized public aid to the "iron fist" of the punitive state, this book takes us into the living laboratory of the neoliberal revolution. In so doing, it brings to light the springs and reason for the diffusion of the "one-way security-think" (*pensée unique sécuritaire*) that is taking hold everywhere today in Europe, and particularly in France since 2001. For the United States has not been content to be the forge and locomotive of the neoliberal project on the level of the economy and welfare; over the past decade, it has also become the premier global exporter of "theories," slogans, and measures on the crime and

---

swift economic liberalization with extreme inequalities, such as postauthoritarian Argentina and Chile, post-Soviet Russia, and postapartheid South Africa.

safety front.[39] In her panorama of carceral evolution around the planet, Vivien Stern stresses that "a major influence on penal policy in Britain and other Western European countries has been the policy direction taken in the United States,"[40] an influence to which she attributes "the complete reversal of the consensus prevailing in the postwar developed world and expressed in UN documents and international conventions" that "deprivation of liberty should be used sparingly," and the general discrediting of the ideal of "the rehabilitation and social reintegration of the offender."*

The fourth part of the book ("European Declinations") analyzes how France's state nobility has fallen—or, rather, has enthusiastically thrown itself—into the law-and-order trap set from the other side of the Atlantic. Seduced by the "scholarly myths" that dress it in rational garb (chapter 8), France has rallied to the "Washington consensus" in matters of crime fighting, to the point that it is currently experiencing a gust of carceral inflation comparable to that posted by the United States twenty years ago at the acme of its correctional boom (chapter 9). Besides, we need do no more than examine the main provisions of the so-called Perben II Law on Crime, promulgated by French parliament in the spring of 2004—but this demonstration would hold mutatis mutandis for the Everyday Security Act, called the Vaillant Law, passed on 15 November 2001 at the initiative of a Socialist government—to detect the clear and deleterious influence of the US model, based on the intensification of police activity, the escalation of judicial sanction, the reduction of professional discretion, the subservience of penal authorities to political fad, and the relentless extension of the scope of imprisonment.

This controversial law, which, uniquely in the annals of French justice, triggered a near-unanimous strike by the judicial professions,

*Vivien Stern, "Mass Incarceration: 'A Sin Against the Future'?" *European Journal of Criminal Policy and Research* 3 (October 1996): 14. Yet, in a chapter published a few years later in a volume aimed at an activist audience in the United States, Stern curiously contradicts her own diagnosis. In a futile effort to shock and shame US readers, she presents the evolution of the criminal justice system of their country as "an inexplicable deformity" that "arouses incredulity and incomprehension" overseas. Disregarding the growing fascination of European elites for, and accelerating transatlantic importation of, US penal discourse and policies, she blithely asserts that these policies "have been seen as an aberration and have been met with resistance" in other Western societies. Vivien Stern, "The International Impact of US Policies," in *Invisible Punishment*, ed. Marc Mauer and Meda Chesney-Lind, 279–92 (New York: New Press, 2002), citation on 280 and 279. For demonstrations of how and why the English, Italian, and French governments have actively emulated US police and punishment policies over the past decade, see the studies listed in endnote 4.

highlighted by solemn street demonstrations held by judges walking out in their robes and ermines, effects the fifteenth reform of the penal code in ten years on the pretext of adapting judicial procedures to the evolution of delinquency—but, curiously, it omits white-collar and official criminality, in spite of their spectacular growth in recent years. It increases the powers and prerogatives of the police through a set of measures, such as authorizing nocturnal searches and video recording in private places, extending provisional detention (*garde à vue*) without charges from 48 to 96 hours, providing monthly remuneration for police informants and creating the legal status of "repentant," exempting from penalty any criminal who would identify his accomplices, a practice directly inspired by American programs that have normalized the use of denunciation and "snitches" in police operations in the black ghetto.[41] Perben II enlarges the definition of "organized crime" and increases the penalties set for a whole series of infractions (extortion, corruption of minors, weapons manufacturing, etc.), as the United States has already done. It institutes a "guilty plea" procedure copied after American plea bargaining that authorizes a defendant to receive a reduced sentence (typically one year in prison for offenses punishable by five) in exchange for dispensing with a trial, allowing the courts to economize on prosecution costs.* It extends to some fifty new offenses the application of *composition pénale*, whereby a prosecutor can impose a fine, suspend a driver's license, or assign a stint of community service to the presumed perpetrator of a misdemeanor who admits to the facts. It creates a national database with the files of sex offenders, which, in addition to abolishing the traditional "right to oblivion" for this category of convicts, includes the genetic fingerprints of minors, of individuals who have been found innocent, and of persons suspected of but not charged with infractions of a sexual nature, and this measure also requires former sex offenders to register with the police—awaiting the day when they will be obliged to publicize their presence, on the pattern of Megan's Law in the United States, the ins and outs of which we examine in chapter 7. Finally, the Perben II Law extends post-penal-control by generalizing furloughs into community facilities and release under electronic supervision for those leaving prison, which will not fail to increase the rate of return to custody. By normalizing measures of

*However, the French *plaider coupable* is hardly a conforming copy of the US plea bargain, since in France the detainee has access neither to his file nor to counsel, unlike with its American counterpart. This measure is thus more akin to judicial blackmail than with "bargaining," and it is guaranteed to further exacerbate the already sharp ethnic and class bias that affects its use in the United States. See Thierry Lévy, "L'empoisonnement progressif," *Dedans Dehors* 41 (January–February 2004): 21.

exception, accelerating procedures, hardening penalties, and extending the perimeter of judicial supervision, this renovation of the penal code encourages the use of confinement for all (those shorn of economic and cultural capital) and facilitates a slaughterhouse approach to justice to cope with the predictable inrush of inmates.

In its motives as well as its architecture and anticipated effects, Perben II is emblematic of the *de-autonomization of the penal field* and its growing subordination to demands issued from the political and media fields. In this, it vividly illustrates the Americanization of criminal justice in France.* As for the "automatic baseline sentences" for "habitual offenders" that Interior Minister Nicolas Sarkozy promised to establish during the regional election campaign of winter 2004, to the delight of audiences reveling in the public vituperation of criminals, and which promises to be a staple of the political debate over criminal justice for years to come, it is also a French imitation of the "mandatory minimums" that have engorged America's prisons with petty offenders serving terms of imprisonment running into the decades. The fact that the transplantation of this mechanism is impossible in France—since the automaticity of penal sentences is contrary to constitutional texts—does not prevent it from serving the law-and-order guignol.**

Whether through importation or inspiration, the alignment or convergence of penal policies never entails the deployment of identical replicas. No more than other European countries with a strong statist tradition, Catholic or social-democratic, the adjustment that France is effecting in its politics of poverty does not imply a mechanical duplication of the US pattern, with a sharp contraction of welfare as well as a clear and brutal swing from the social to the penal treatment of urban marginality leading to hyperincarceration. The deep roots of the social state in the framework of the bureaucratic field as well as in the national mental structures, the weaker hold of the individualist and utilitarian ideology that undergirds the sacralization of the market, and the absence of a sharp ethnoracial divide explain that the countries of the European continent are unlikely to shift rapidly to an all-out punitive strategy. Each must clear its own path toward the new government of

*In this regard, the current outburst of penal activism contrasts sharply with the previous lurch toward penalization in France during the decade prior to 1997, when increased recourse to confinement was accompanied by the growing professional latitude and public authority gained by judges. Antoine Garapon and Denis Salas, *La République pénalisée* (Paris: Hachette, 1996).

**In his time, Daniel Vaillant, the last interior minister of the Plural Left government of Jospin, had also proposed instituting automatic prison terms for recidivists, with full knowledge that the measure could not be adopted.

social insecurity in accordance with its specific national history, social configurations, and political traditions. Nonetheless, one can sketch a provisional characterization of a "European road" to the penal state (with French, Dutch, Italian, etc., variants) that is gradually coming into being before our eyes through a *double and conjoint accentuation of the social and penal regulation of marginal categories.*

Thus, during the past decade, the French authorities have stepped up both welfare and justice interventions—even if their "social" action has been increasingly stamped with the coin of punitive moralism. On the one side, they have multiplied assistance programs (public utility work with Contrats Emploi-Solidarité, subsidized youth employment, training schemes, the TRACE program, etc.), raised the various "social minima" (targeted government aid to various destitute categories), established the Universal Medical Cover, and broadened access to the Revenu Minimum d'Insertion (RMI, the guaranteed minimum income grant). On the other, they have created special surveillance units (*cellules de veille*) and nested riot police squads inside the "sensitive zones" of the urban periphery, replaced street educators with magistrates to issue warnings to occasional youth delinquents, passed municipal decrees outlawing begging and vagrancy (decrees which are perfectly illegal), multiplied "crackdown" operations and sweeps inside low-income housing projects and routinized the use of *comparution immédiate* (a fast-track judicial procedure whereby an offender caught in the act is brought before a judge and sentenced within hours), increased penalties for repeated offenses, restricted parole release and speeded up the deportation of convicted foreign offenders, and threatened the parents of juvenile delinquents or children guilty of school truancy with withholding family benefits, etc.

A second contrast between the United States and France, and the countries of continental Europe more generally: the penalization of poverty *à l'européenne* is effected mainly through *the agency of the police and the courts rather than the prison.*[42] It still obeys (but for how much longer?) a predominantly panoptic logic, rather than a segregative and retributive rationale. The correlate is that social services play an active part in this criminalizing process, since they possess the administrative and human means to exercise a close-up supervision of so-called problem populations. But the simultaneous deployment of the social and penal treatments of urban disorders should not hide the fact that the former often functions as a bureaucratic fig-leaf for the latter, and that it is ever more directly subordinated to it in practice. Encouraging state social assistance, health, and education services to collaborate with the police and judicial system turns them into extensions of the penal apparatus, instituting a *social panopticism* which, under cover of promoting the well-being of deprived households, submits them to an ever-more precise and penetrating form of punitive surveillance.

The Police to the Rescue of "Youths Having Trouble Integrating"

One finds a concrete and caricatural illustration of this at the beginning of 2000 in the southern French city of Nîmes. The regional daily *Le Midi Libre* confirmed a public rumor according to which the local police had, on order of the prefect, compiled in complete illegality a database of individual files on 179 youths with whom its services had had run-ins. In blatant violation of laws protecting privacy, this data bank combined personal information collected on these youths by the national education authority, the Protection Judiciaire de la Jeunesse (juvenile justice bureau), the Agence Nationale Pour l'Emploi (ANPE, the national employment agency), the Mission Locale d'Insertion (a state job-placement program), Jeunesse et les sports (the antenna of the ministry of sports), and the local social welfare services. These youths (19 of whom were under age sixteen) all came from only five "sensitive neighborhoods"; 83 percent of them had North-African-sounding surnames and most of the others Gypsy surnames. The alphabetic listing produced by the prefecture within the framework of the Commission d'Accès à la Citoyenneté (an administrative council charged with facilitating access to rights among the low-income immigrant population) included the youth's name, date of birth, and the neighborhood they lived in, followed by annotations supplied by the various services involved: the regional police headquarters (Direction Départementale des Services de Police) indicated those who were "DDSP priorities" and "repeat offender minors"; the school district director summarized their academic trajectory over eight columns; the ANPE detailed their experience in the area of employment according to ten variables; as for the Mission Locale d'Insertion, it listed the "first contact," "last contact," and in some cases measures taken for the youth considered ("vocational degree in painting," "ANPE" "Absent. entr. indiv." [Truancy, individual interview], etc.).

The fact that the chief of staff of the prefect of Gard (the district containing Nîmes) dared to publicly justify this flagrant violation of the national legislation on privacy* he was supposed to enforce by invoking—perhaps even sincerely—his desire to help a "panel" of "youths having trouble integrating" speaks volumes

*The law "Informatics and Liberties" of 6 January 1978, modified in July 2004, protects the privacy of personal data on French citizens and residents. It established a national agency, the Commission nationale Informatique et Libertés, that strictly regulates the production, storage, and access to computerized data files containing nominal information by public and private bureaucracies.

about the normalization of recourse to the penal apparatus to regulate marginal categories: "In practical terms, and once again in a republican spirit, it is necessary to work on concrete cases to wage the fight against exclusion."[43] The assurance and even pride with which the chief of staff for the interior minister then defended the appropriateness of this operation before the civil service unions who questioned its justification as "an extension of the decisions made in the *conseils de sécurité intérieure* [periodic cabinet-level meetings supposed to help coordinate different ministries in 'security' matters and meant to signal to the electorate that the government is actively fighting crime]" show the extent to which the equivalence between "youths in a situation of marginality" or "having trouble integrating" and youths accused by the police is taken for granted in the minds of state managers.* This incident, which is but the tip of an immense iceberg of invisible administrative practices crossing the border of legality, shows well how the activities of educational and social services can be annexed, even subordinated, to a police and punitive logic contrary to their basic philosophy.

It remains to be seen whether this "European road" to liberal paternalism is a genuine alternative to penalization in the mold of the United States or merely an intermediate stage or detour leading, in the end, to sustained increases in incarceration. If neighborhoods of relegation are saturated with police without enhancing employment opportunities and life chances in them, and if partnerships between the criminal justice system and other state services are multiplied, there is bound to be an increase in the detection of unlawful conduct and an increased volume of arrests and convictions in criminal court. Who can say today where and when the ballooning of the jails and penitentiaries visible in nearly all the European countries will stop? The case of the Netherlands, which has shifted from a humanist to a managerial penal philosophy and gone from laggard to leader in incarceration among the original fifteen members of the European Union, is instructive and worrisome in this regard.[44]

*According to this senior ministry official, the approach of the prefect of Gard aimed to "make the action of state services toward youth in serious difficulty more coherent and more pertinent and to arrive at an expert evaluation, on their behalf, of the effectiveness of the public programs mobilized to help them," so that they could "reach the point of making real life choices" and "fully exercise their citizenship." And he concluded that "it is to the credit of the Republic when it mobilizes such an effort for its most underprivileged children" (Letter by Jean-Paul Proust, staff director for the minister of the interior, to the president of the SNPES-FSU union for the judicial protection of youth, Gard section, dated 19 January 2000). But then what grounds are there to reserve such generous intention for these 179 youths from the most notorious neighborhoods of the town singled out by the police?

It bears stressing here that, in Western Europe at least, the social regression toward flexible employment, "freed" from the administrative restrictions and legal protections erected through a century and a half of working-class and trade-union struggles, does not entail a simple return to the government of poverty characteristic of the savage capitalism of the close of the nineteenth century, founded on the naked violence of industrial relations of power, local solidarities, and state charity.* There are four major reasons for this. Firstly, the rolling out of the penal state is limited by the fact that, unlike their counterparts of a century ago, the poor citizens and assorted marginal categories circulating in the lower regions of social and urban space enjoy an extensive array of well-established social, economic, and civil rights, and the minimal organizational means to see those respected to some degree. This is true even of nonresident foreigners, who nowadays benefit from a range of legal and administrative protections afforded by human rights statutes and conventions as well as by the diffusion of more inclusive conceptions of membership.[45] Secondly, the resurgence of conditions of employment worthy of Dickens is taking place against the backdrop of collective enrichment and sustained prosperity for the majority of the population. This renders all the more incongruous and unacceptable the crumbling of living standards and the sudden shrinking of the life space and possibilities visited upon the new urban (sub)proletariat.[46]

Next, casualization comes up against the dike constituted by the continual elevation of collective expectations of dignity, produced in particular by the universalization of secondary education and the institutionalization of social rights independent of labor performance, which soften if not practically contradict the sanction of the market. Witness, on the one side, the pressure from business and the international institutions colonized by corporations (such as the OECD [Organisation for Economic Cooperation and Development] or the European Commission) to pare or eliminate "social minima," and, on the other side, the multiplication of legal and activist challenges mounted before public bureaucracies by recipients swindled of their benefits by the permanent recomposition of assistance or employment programs (e.g., in France the annual demonstrations staged every December by the unemployed for a "Christmas bonus," or the successful court action against Unédic launched in spring 2004 by France's first wave of workfare recipients).

*Contrary to the suggestion of Balibar, for whom the reduction of the state to its repressive functions "seems to take us back to a 'primitive' stage in the constitution of the public sphere in bourgeois societies." Etienne Balibar, "Sûreté, sécurité, sécuritaire," *Cahiers marxistes* 200 (1995): 193.

To wit also the persistent public demand for the protective and corrective action of the welfare-state throughout the developed world, in spite of the vigorous media and political campaigns aimed at stifling it.[47] Finally, the generalization of wage-labor instability has itself spawned novel forms of mobilization and transversal solidarities, illustrated by the burgeoning of associations to defend the dispossessed and the sudden spread of labile alliances (called *coordinations*) among precarious workers (thus, in France recently, among the staff of McDonald's, Pizza Hut, and Go Sports, but also FNAC, Arcade, Maxi-Livres, etc.). These solidarities are rooted in the possession of a cultural capital devalorized by the fragmentation of positions, tasks, and work schedules, as well as in the refusal of the docile deference commonly demanded in face-to-face relations with clients in personal commercial services.[48]

There is, however, a major difference on the penal side that pushes in the opposite direction. The state of the dawn of the third millennium is endowed with budgetary, human, and technological resources without equivalent in history for their volume, reach, and degree of rationalization, which bestow upon it a bureaucratic capacity for quadrillage and control that its industrial-era predecessors could never have imagined. Nowadays a suspect or convict can be detected, spotted, tracked at a distance, and captured virtually at any time and in any location, owing to the interconnection of a plethora of instruments of quasi-instantaneous identification and surveillance (video cameras, electronic cards, global positioning devices, satellite-relayed telecommunications, administrative and commercial databases, background checks by employers and realtors, etc.) that cover the most remote corners of a given country,[49] whereas at the end of the nineteenth century it sufficed for an individual to change his name and move to a different city or region and melt into the surrounding landscape for the authorities to lose track of him. Indeed, as the state disengages itself from the economy and defaults on its mission of social protection, its "infrastructural power"—that is, its ability to penetrate the populations under its aegis and rule over their behaviors[50]—operates increasingly through the networks woven by its repressive apparatus, which thus become one of the main vectors of unification of its territory at the national or supranational level (as with Europe's Schengen space). Besides, the dispossessed categories that are the favorite prey of criminal justice are already placed right in the sights of the bureaucracies of public assistance that supervise their ordinary conducts and even their intimate life with neither scruples nor respite.[51]

The Penalization of Precariousness as Production of Reality

Just as the emergence of a new government of the social insecurity diffused by the neoliberal revolution does not mark a historical reversion to a familiar organizational configuration but heralds a genuine *political innovation*, similarly the deployment of the penal state cannot be grasped under the narrow rubric of repression. In point of fact, the repressive trope is a central ingredient in the discursive fog that enshrouds and masks the sweeping makeover of the means, ends, and justifications of public authority at century's close. The leftist activists who rail against the "punishment machine" on both sides of the Atlantic—castigating the chimerical "prison-industrial complex" in America and denouncing a diabolical "*programme sécuritaire*" in France—mistake the wrapping for the package. They fail to see that crime fighting is but a convenient pretext and propitious platform for a broader redrawing of the perimeter of responsibility of the state operating simultaneously on the economic, social welfare, and penal fronts.

In this regard, I emphatically reject the conspiratorial view of history that would attribute the rise of the punitive apparatus in advanced society to a deliberate plan pursued by omniscient and omnipotent rulers, whether they be political decision-makers, corporate heads, or the gamut of profiteers who benefit from the increased scope and intensity of punishment and related supervisory programs trained on the urban castoffs of deregulation.* Such a vision not only confuses the objective convergence of a welter of disparate public policies, each driven by its own set of protagonists and stakes, with the subjective intentions of state managers. It also fails to heed Foucault's advice that we forsake the "repressive hypothesis" and treat power as a fertilizing force that remakes the very landscape it traverses.[52] Interestingly, this is an insight that one finds in Karl Marx's erstwhile dispersed remarks on crime, which suggest that the advent of "liberal paternalism" is best construed under the generative category of *production*:

> The criminal produces an impression now moral, now tragic, and renders a "service" by arousing the moral and aesthetic sentiments of the public. He produces not only textbooks on criminal law, the criminal law itself,

*If the notion of dominant class is invoked on occasion in this book, it is only as a stenographic designation pointing to the balance of patterned struggles over the remaking of the state going on within the *field of power*—which, analytically speaking, is the pertinent category. This point is developed in Pierre Bourdieu and Loïc Wacquant, "From Ruling Class to Field of Power," *Theory, Culture & Society* 10, no. 1 (August 1993): 19–44.

> and thus legislators, but also art, literature, novels and the tragic drama. . . . The criminal interrupts the monotony and security of bourgeois life. Thus he protects it from stagnation and brings forth that restless tension, that mobility of spirit without which the stimulus of competition would itself be blunted.[53]

In other words, Marx himself invites us to break out of the materialist register of a strict economic model to take account of the moral effects of crime and the symbolic import of punishment and assorted societal responses to offending—concerns conventionally associated with his chief theoretical rival, Émile Durkheim. Pursuing this insight reveals that the transition from the social management to the penal treatment of the disorders induced by the fragmentation of wage labor is indeed eminently productive. First, it has created *new categories* of public perception and state action. The transition from the social management to the penal treatment of the disorders induced by the fragmentation of wage labor is indeed eminently productive. Echoing the alleged discovery of "underclass areas" in the United States, in the closing decade of the twentieth century Europe has witnessed the invention of the "*quartier sensible*" in France,[54] the "sink estate" in the United Kingdom, the "*Problemquartier*" in Germany, the "*krottenwijk*" in the Netherlands, etc., so many bureaucratic euphemisms to designate the nether sections of the city turned into a social and economic fallow by the state, and for that very reason subjected to reinforced police oversight and correctional penetration.

The same goes with the bureaucratic notion of "*violences urbaines*" (plural), coined in France by the minister of the interior to amalgamate offensive behaviors of widely divergent nature and motives—mean looks and rude language, graffiti and low-grade vandalism, vehicle theft for joy riding, brawls between youths, threats to teachers, drug dealing or fencing, and collective confrontations with the police—so as to promote a punitive approach to the social problems besetting declining working-class districts by depoliticizing them.[55] In her candid recounting of its accidental birth, the police press officer (and former philosophy high-school teacher) who elaborated it reveals that the jumbled category of *violences urbaines* and the new police department devoted to its promotion and measurement were forged in direct response to the multiplying *banlieues* upheavals of 1990–91. Its purpose was to "give their due to grassroots police staff" and help exculpate them from accusations of ethnic discrimination in dispossessed areas; prevent the "contagion" of collective disturbances in the same; and ward off "the risk of a drift towards an Americanization of our neighborhoods" by pointing police suppression onto the "small handful of deviant youths" deemed responsible for the spreading riots, due to their virulent "refusal of authority" which "very simply reflects a total absence of social bonds" as well as "a system of thought stamped by affectivity" fostering "irrationality."* The category has since assumed an epicentral role in the public discourse and policy on crime and safety in France as well as in urban planning.

New *social types* are another byproduct of the emerging social-insecurity regime. The irruption of "superpredators" in the United States, "feral youth" and "yobs" in the United Kingdom, or "*sauvageons*" (wildings, a social-paternalistic variant of a racial insult scoffing at the alleged deculturation of the lower classes) in France has been used to justify the reopening or the expansion of custodial centers for juveniles, even though all existing studies deplore their noxious effects. Not to forget the "sexual predator" or maverick pedophile, who, as we shall discover in chapter 7, stands as the vilified embodiment of every threat to the integrity of the family, and who is all the more feared as the latter is more submitted to the strains induced by the casualization of labor. To these can be added the renovation of classic types such as the "career recidivist," the latest avatar of the *uomo delinquente* invented in 1884 by Cesare Lombroso, whose distinctive psychophysiological and anthropometric characteristics are now being researched by experts in criminal "profiling"[56] as well as guiding the gigantic bureaucratic-cum-scholarly enterprise of "risk assessment" for the release of sensitive categories of inmates.

For the policy of penalization of social insecurity is also the bearer of new bodies of knowledge about the city and its troubles, broadcast by an unprecedented range of "experts" and, in their wake, journalists, bureaucrats, the managers of activist organizations, and elected officials perched at the bedside of the "neighborhoods of all dangers."[57] These alleged facts and specialist discourses about criminal insecurity are given form and put into wide circulation by hybrid institutions, supposedly neutral, situated at the intersection of the bureaucratic, academic, and journalistic fields, which ape research to provide the appearance of a scientific warrant for lowering the police and penal

*Lucienne Bui-Trong, *Violences urbaines, des vérités qui dérangent* (Paris: Bayard, 2000), 15–16, 18–19, 23, 27, 30, 42–43, and 52. It is worth noting that the incubation of the notion, which manages to be at once illogical and tautological, was informed early by a "training mission" to the United States (in Chicago and Hartford, Connecticut) in spring of 1991 to study street gangs and relied "especially on publications by the police departments of the major US cities."

boom on neighborhoods of relegation. This is the case, in France, with the Institut des hautes études de la sécurité intérieure, an agency created by the Socialist minister of the interior Pierre Joxe in 1989 and then developed by his neo-Gaullist successor Charles Pasqua. This institute, "placed under the direct authority of the minister of the interior" in order to promote "rational thinking about domestic security," irrigates the country with the latest novelties in "crime control" imported from America.* It is assisted in this enterprise by the Institut de criminologie de Paris, an *officine* in law-and-order propaganda which has this remarkable characteristic that it does not number a single criminologist among its distinguished members.

Two Official Organs of Law-and-Order Propaganda

Staffed by some sixty "police officers, gendarmes, customs officers, academics, and judges" but bereft of credentialed researchers, the IHESI (Institut des hautes études sur la sécurité intérieure, Institute for Higher Studies in Domestic Security) is the main platform for diffusing the new law-and-order *doxa* within the state apparatus and the mainstream media in France. Its priorities are "to train security actors" and to supply technical assistance to "partners within the societal body who wage a difficult struggle against insecurity on a daily basis or who are its privileged witnesses," but also and more broadly to "sensitize" the political, economic, and intellectual elites through the training and pedagogical action of its network of graduates (numbering in excess of 1,300 at the end of 2003).

Notwithstanding a resolutely technicist and ostensibly neutral approach, the instructors of the IHESI cannot conceal their fascination with the policing and penal "experiments" of the United States, a country "where imagination is at work" and whose law-and-order boldness demonstrates that "it is possible to push down real delinquency and the subjective feeling of insecurity."** Thus the

*In July of 2004, the IHESI was replaced by the INHES (Institut national des hautes études de sécurité), a very similar outfit presented by interior minister Nicolas Sarkozy as "the elite school of security that France needs." Its board of overseers features not a single researcher.

**According to Frédéric Ocqueteau, in his edited volume *Community Policing et Zero Tolerance à New York et Chicago. En finir avec les mythes*, La sécurité aujourd'hui (Paris: La Documentation française, 2003). Hired by the Institute in 1990 on the basis of a doctorate in law, Ocqueteau is editor-in-chief of the in-house journal of the IHESI. He is the author of *Défis de la sécurité privée* (Paris: L'Harmattan, 1997) and *Vigilance et sécurité dans les grandes surfaces* (Paris: L'Harmattan, 1995), a survey of supermarket managers that describes how their "services of vigilance" ensure the "protection of goods and customers, and thus commercial peace." (Releasing a book

institute published in its internal journal, *Les Cahiers de la sécurité intérieure*, a French translation of the "foundational" article by James Q. Wilson and George Kelling on the American "theory of the broken window" (but none of the critiques that demolished it on the US side of the Atlantic, as we shall discover in chapter 8). IHESI has produced and distributed countless technical reports on "*police de proximité*," inspired by the recent experience of "community policing" in Chicago, and (without fear of contradiction) it hails "zero tolerance," as incarnated by that of New York City, in the practical dossiers it publishes to guide elected officials in establishing Local Security Contracts with the central state. It is in the classrooms of this institute that Socialist deputy and future interior minister Daniel Vaillant took "courses" that convinced him, along with others (Gérard Le Gall, Bruno Le Roux, Julien Dray, and Alain Bauer, CEO of Alain Bauer Associates, a leading firm in "urban security" consulting), to push his party to openly assume its punitive turn by recognizing that "security" is "a republican value" and is "neither of the Right nor of the Left."[58]

Housed by the University of Panthéon-Assas (Paris 2), since 1998, the Institut de criminologie de Paris has offered a postgraduate degree in the "analysis of *menaces criminelles contemporaines*" (MCC, contemporary criminal threats), which easily rivals the doctorate in "astro-sociology" granted in 2001 to Elizabeth Tessier by the neighboring University of Paris 5-Sorbonne.* Set up with the collaboration of senior police officials reconverted into the juicy sector of security "consulting" for business and local government, this degree program is codirected by Xavier Raufer, the author of numerous works on security co-signed with Alain Bauer and Stéphane Quéré (the documentarian of Alain Bauer Associates, misleadingly presented on the back cover of books as a "criminologist").** A former activist of

with L'Harmattan, a low-grade house that requires authors to shoulder the full cost of production and famously grants royalties of zero percent, is tantamount to self-publication.) He is also the sole "academic" member of the Conseil de l'Observatoire de la délinquance established by Interior Minister Sarkozy in November 2003 and placed under the stewardship of the omnipresent Alain Bauer.

*In April 2001, the astrologist and television celebrity Elizabeth Tessier (famous for being the personal "astral counsellor" of President Mitterrand) was granted a doctorate in sociology by the University of Paris-Sorbonne, under the direction of Michel Maffesoli, for a "thesis" advocating the scientific validity of astrology and the primacy of astral over social causality. The scientific community mobilized to get the degree rescinded, but without success.

**The peddlers in law-and-order ideology and services are fond of decking themselves out in academic titles and posts that they do not have, with the complicity of the journalists and publicists who promote them. For example, the publisher of *La Guerre ne fait que commencer* (*The War Has Just Begun*) (Paris: Jean-Claude Lattès, 2002), a work warning that "virulent forms of urban violence" in the French urban periphery "could soon evolve toward terrorism pure and simple," joining up with "the global war" that opened with the September 11 attack on America, writes about its authors:

the extreme right-wing group Occident, close to US intelligence services, Raufer (whose real name is Christian de Bongain) is a journalist specializing in terrorism. He became a "security consultant" on the basis of his political contacts, which he parlayed into being named editor of the "International Criminality" series at Presses Universitaires de France (he was hired there by Pascal Gauchon, the leader of the extreme-right Parti des Forces Nouvelles) and then as an adjunct "lecturer in methodology" (sic) at Paris 2-Assas.[59] His criminological oeuvre comprises 165 short articles that appeared in the weekly news magazine *L'Express* and writings published internally in the *Notes & Etudes de l'Institut de Criminologie*; it does not include a single scholarly publication.

The MCC Department, whose program of "Études" is directed by Raufer, has made its mission to describe, detect, and prevent the "chaotic, rapid, and volatile dangers" born of the "hybridization of criminalities stimulated by globalization."[60] The faculty in charge of the seemingly academic "training" it delivers includes a divisional police commissioner, a senior customs official, the security director of the Alcatel telecommunications multinational, a retired prefect, novelists, directors of "security firms" (among them the inevitable Alain Bauer and the CEO of Fichet-Bauche, a leading lock and armored-door company), a reporter for the news weekly *Le Point*, an infantry officer from Malta, and a Colombian journalist. The supervision of the students' theses leading to the granting of the MCC diploma at the end of a single semester of biweekly, two-hour courses is entrusted to an "entrepreneur, holder of the MCC degree." The lucky recipients of this "education" include student officers from the gendarmerie, who undergo 200 hours of courses bearing in particular on "urban violences," "trafficking," and "fanaticisms" (sic).

It would take pages to list the full roster of all the agents and devices that contribute, each on its level, to the collective work of *material and symbolic construction of the penal state* henceforth charged with reestablishing the state's grip over the populations pushed into the cracks and the ditches of urban space, from private firms of "safety consultants" to "*adjoints de sécurité*" (assistant police officers, hired as part of a state plan to fight unemployment in low-income areas, and entrusted with police chores outside of law enforcement), to publish-

---

"Professor of Criminology at the Sorbonne, specialist in geopolitics and terrorism, for this book Xavier Raufer has joined Alain Bauer, who, aside from his very high duties at the masonic Grand Orient, is a globally recognized expert on security for multinationals." Bauer is regularly presented by the press as a "teacher," a "criminologist," and even "professor at the Sorbonne" or the Institut d'études politiques in Paris (he is none of these).

ing houses eager to peddle books on this hot topic (among whom a special mention must go to L'Harmattan and Presses Universitaires de France), the "*citoyens relais*" (volunteers who anonymously tip the police about law-enforcement problems in their neighborhoods), and a whole series of judicial innovations—*rappel à la loi* (formal legal warning by a magistrate for a petty offense), *juges de proximité* (adjunct community judges), *composition pénale* (a variant of plea bargaining for misdemeanors), and so on, which, on the pretext of bureaucratic efficiency, establish a differential justice according to class and place of residence. In sum, *the penalization of precariousness creates new realities*, and realities tailor-made to legitimize the extension of the prerogatives of the punitive state according to the principle of the self-fulfilling prophecy.

A brief illustration: by treating jostling in the school corridors, rudeness in the classroom, or playground ruckus not as matters of discipline pertaining to pedagogical authority in the establishment but as infractions of the law that must be tallied and centrally compiled via a dedicated computer software (the Signa program) and systematically reported to the local police or magistrates, and by assigning a "police correspondent" (*officier référent*) to every secondary school (rather than a psychologist, nurse, or social worker, who are direly lacking in lower-class districts), the authorities have redefined ordinary school troubles as matters of law and order and fabricated an epidemic of "school violence," even as surveys of students consistently show that over 90 percent of them feel completely safe at school. With the help of mass-media amplification, this "explosion" of "violence" serves in turn to justify the "school-police partnership" that produced it in the first place, and validates the enrollment of teaching staff in the declining neighborhoods of the urban periphery in the police missions of surveillance and punishment. Besides, the staging of "school violence" allows state managers to avoid confronting the professional devaluation and bureaucratic dilemmas created within the educational sphere by the near-universalization of access to secondary schooling, the growing submission of the school system to the logic of competition, and the imperatives of the "culture of results" imported from the corporate world.[61]

Finally, let us note for the benefit of readers who might be surprised that a work on the penal state in America does not address the question of the death penalty that this omission is deliberate.[62] It arises from the conviction, acquired through historical and comparative observation, that the capital sentence does not constitute a major cog in the contemporary economy of punishment in this country. To be sure, the spectacular resurgence of judicial executions after the quasi-abolitionist interlude of 1966 to 1983 (during which the United States did away with only fourteen convicts, and killed none between 1968 and 1976) does partake on its own level of the ascent of punitive populism that gradually seized the country after the mid-1970s as the social, urban, and penal policies of the state were revamped with a view to anchoring the diffusion of desocialized wage labor and containing the repercussions of the crumbling of the black ghettos. And it is endowed with a particular emotive charge that has led it to be commonly depicted as the emblem of US judicial rigor or cruelty, by its supporters as well as its detractors, especially abroad—two scholars of judicial cultures attest that "over the past 25 years the death penalty has become one of the main stumbling blocks in the dialogue between the two versions of Western civilization, the European and the North American."[63]

Moreover, it is not by chance that the United States is the sole Western democracy that not only routinely applies capital punishment, but also the only one which, under the hold of a narrow legalism wedded to unrestrained moral individualism and tenacious racial contempt, inflicts it upon minors, women, the mentally handicapped, and convicts sentenced for nonviolent crimes,* in spite of the social biases and procedural failings that have been amply documented in its implementation. Yet, for all its symbolic salience, the death penalty remains structurally marginal and functionally superfluous.

Indeed, although capital punishment figures in the penal code of 38 states and the federal government, only 13 of them applied it in 2002 and two-thirds of the 820 executions carried out since 1977 have taken place in just five jurisdictions: Texas (with 289 judicial killings), Virginia (87), Missouri (59), Oklahoma (55), and Florida (54).** If tomorrow the federal Supreme Court (the only instance empowered to pronounce at the national level on the constitutionality of a penal sanction whose application falls under the authority of the fifty members of the

*At the end of the 1990s, only 19 of 38 states that applied the death penalty excluded the mentally handicapped from its field of application; sixteen authorized its use in the case of minors (including seven that do not specify any minimum age). Roger Hood, "Capital Punishment," in *The Handbook of Crime and Punishment*, ed. Michael Tonry, 739–75 (New York: Oxford University Press, 1998).

**Thomas Bonczar and Tracy L. Snell, *Capital Punishment, 2002* (Washington: Bureau of Justice Statistics, 2003). The number of judicial executions since 1977 passed the 900 mark in February of 2004. In 2003, the United States put to death 65 convicts, compared to 64 in Vietnam, 108 in Iran, and 726 in China (according to the official figure, which is vastly inferior to the estimates from the best scholars on the question, which range from 10,000 to 15,000 per year if extrajudicial executions are included).

Union and their legislatures) were to render the ultimate penalty unlawful or legally impracticable, as it did between 1972 and 1976 with the *Furman v. Georgia* decision, such a measure would certainly ease the psychological torture inflicted upon the 3,560 convicts currently rotting on death row. And it would save the lives of the several dozens of them who are put to death every year by lethal injection or electrocution (over the past decade, the members of the Union have executed between 31 and 98 convicts per year).

But legal or de facto abolition would diminish neither the immense scope of the US carceral archipelago nor the tightening material and symbolic hold that the penal apparatus exerts on the societal body. It would change nothing about the fates of the other 2,262,700 adults stacked in the country's correctional establishments at the start of 2003 and the roughly 4,748,000 of their compatriots placed under criminal justice supervision outside their walls at that time. It would leave untouched the prevalence of confinement and its extreme concentration on the populations situated at the very bottom of the ethnic and class hierarchy, which ensures that one black American citizen in six is doing or has done hard time and one in three is destined to serve a sentence of imprisonment in the future.* The *practical disconnection between hyperincarceration and capital punishment* is amply demonstrated by the recent experience of California: the Golden State held 614 convicts on death row among its 200,000 jail and prison inmates in 2002, but it executed only one of them that year. Such a disjunction confirms that the question of the implementation or extinction of capital punishment in America pertains to the register of the debate on civic morals and political philosophy more than to the sociology of the penal state.

*This figure is an estimate of the cumulative probability of being sentenced to at least one year of imprisonment over the course of a lifetime, calculated on the basis of the national rate of incarceration in a state or federal establishment for 2001. Thomas P. Bonczar, *Prevalence of Imprisonment in the U.S. Population, 1974–2001* (Washington: Bureau of Justice Statistics, 2003), 1 and 5.

I. POVERTY OF THE SOCIAL STATE

Any permanent, regular, administrative system whose aim would be to provide for the needs of the poor will breed more miseries than it can relieve, deprave the population it seeks to help and comfort, in time reduce the rich to no more than farmers of the poor, dry up the sources of savings, stop the accumulation of capital, curtail the growth of trade, sap human activity and industry, and culminate by bringing about a violent revolution in the State.

—ALEXIS DE TOCQUEVILLE, *Mémoire sur le paupérisme*, 1835*

*Alexis de Tocqueville, *Memoir on Pauperism*, introduced by Gertrude Himmelfarb (Chicago: Ivan R. Dee Publishers, 1997), 37. My translation.

2

The Criminalization of Poverty in the Post–Civil Rights Era

In his lecture course on socialism, Émile Durkheim contends that the state is "not an enormous coercive power, but a vast and conscious organization" capable "of an action at once unified and varied, supple and extensive."* Historical experience shows that these two aspects are by no means incompatible, and that a state apparatus can very well be both at the same time. Such is the case at the dawn of the twenty-first century with the United States, where, notwithstanding the virulently antistatist ambient discourse, public force understood *in the strict sense* plays an increasingly decisive role in the patterning and conduct of national life.

Over the past three decades, that is, since the race riots that shook the ghettos of its big cities and marked the closing of the Civil Rights revolution, America has launched into a social and political experiment without precedent or equivalent in the societies of the postwar West: the gradual replacement of a (semi-) welfare state by a police and penal state for which the criminalization of marginality and the punitive containment of dispossessed categories serve as social policy at the lower end of the class and ethnic order. To be sure, this welfare state was, as we shall note shortly, notably underdeveloped compared to its European counterparts. For a number of well-known historical reasons, the sphere of citizenship is particularly constricted in the United States, and the ability of subordinate categories to make themselves heard, severely circumscribed.** Rather than of a welfare state, one should

*Émile Durkheim, *Socialism*, ed. and intro. Alvin W. Gouldner, pref. Marcel Mauss (New York: Collier, 1962), 43. My translation. This neo-Hegelian conception is further elaborated in a set of little-known papers on the state gathered in *Textes*, vol. 3, *Fonctions sociales et institutions*, ed. Victor Karady (Paris: Editions de Minuit, 1975), chap. 2, in which Durkheim argues that the modern state must increasingly orient its action toward the legal regulation of societal life, thus joining through a normative route with Max Weber's positive view of the pivotal place of the law in contemporary political rule.

**Among these reasons, which are closely intertwined, figure the rigid ethnoracial division inherited from the era of slavery, the "frontier" tradition and the pervasiveness of moral individualism, the decentralization of the political and bureaucratic fields, and the fierce suppression of unions fostered by the strong integration of the capital-

speak here of a *charitable state* inasmuch as the programs aimed at vulnerable populations have at all times been limited, fragmentary, and isolated from other state activities, informed as they are by a moralistic and moralizing conception of poverty as a product of the individual failings of the poor.[1] The guiding principle of public action in this domain is not solidarity but *compassion*; its goal is not to reinforce social bonds, and still less to reduce inequalities, but at best to relieve the most glaring destitution and to demonstrate society's moral sympathy for its deprived yet deserving members.

Moreover, the hypertrophied penal state that is bit by bit replacing the rump social-welfare state at the bottom of the class structure—or supplementing it according to a gendered division of labor—is itself incomplete, incoherent, and often incompetent, so that it can fulfill neither the unrealistic expectations that have given birth to it nor the social functions that it has as its mission to shore up. And it is hard to see how its development could go unchecked indefinitely, since in the medium run it threatens to bankrupt the large states that lead the pack in the frantic race to hyperincarceration, such as California, New York, Texas, and Florida.[2] Lastly, notwithstanding the thundering proclamations of politicians from all sides about the necessity to "end the era of Big government"—the cheery chorus of Clinton's State of the Union address in 1996—the US government continues to provide many kinds of guarantees and support to corporations as well as to the middle and upper classes, starting, for example, with homeownership assistance: almost half of the $64 billion in fiscal deductions for mortgage interest payments and real estate taxes granted in 1994 by Washington (amounting to nearly three times the budget for public housing) went to the 5 percent of American households earning more than $100,000 that year; and 16 percent of that sum went to the top 1 percent of taxpayers with incomes exceeding $200,000. Over seven in ten families in the top 1 percent received mortgage subsidies (averaging $8,457) as against fewer than 3 percent of the families below the $30,000 mark (for a paltry $486 each).[3] This fiscal subsidy of $64 billion to wealthy home owners dwarfed the national outlay for welfare ($17 billion), food stamps ($25 million), and child nutrition assistance ($7.5 billion).

It is the thesis of this book that the United States is groping its way

ist class as early as the end of the nineteenth century. For a comparative perspective, see Gøsta Esping-Andersen, *The Three Worlds of Welfare Capitalism* (Princeton, N.J.: Princeton University Press, 1990); and Maurice Roche, *Rethinking Citizenship: Welfare, Ideology, and Change in Modern Society* (Cambridge: Polity, 1992).

toward a new kind of hybrid state, neither a "protector" state, in the Old World sense of the term, nor a "minimalist" and noninterventionist state, conforming to the ideological tale spun by zealots of the market. Its social side and the benefits it dispenses are increasingly secured by the privileged, especially through the "fiscalization" of public support (for education, health insurance, and housing),* while its disciplinary vocation is upheld mainly in its relation to the lower class and subordinate ethnic categories. This *centaur state*, guided by a liberal head mounted upon an authoritarian body, applies the doctrine of "laissez-faire et laissez passer" upstream, when it comes to social inequalities and the mechanisms that generate them (the free play of capital, dereliction of labor law and deregulation of employment, retraction or removal of collective protections), but it turns out to be brutally paternalistic and punitive downstream, when it comes to coping with their consequences on a daily level.

This chapter provides a preliminary sketch of the twofold shift that has *tipped the balance of the US bureaucratic field from its protective to its punitive pole* when it comes to managing poor populations and territories.[4] It argues that the downsizing of the social-welfare sector of the state and the concurrent upsizing of its penal arm are functionally linked, forming, as it were, the two sides of the same coin of state restructuring in the nether regions of social and urban space in the age of ascending neoliberalism. The gradual rolling back of the social safety net commenced in the early 1970s as part of the backlash against the progressive movements of the previous decade and culminated in 1996 with the conversion of the right to "welfare" into the obligation of "workfare," designed to dramatize and enforce the work ethic at the bottom of employment ladder. We shall show in the next chapter that the new punitive organization of welfare programs operates in the manner of a labor parole program designed to push its "beneficiaries" into the subpoverty jobs that have proliferated after the discarding of the Fordist-Keynesian compromise. The diffusing social insecurity and escalating life disorders caused by the desocialization of wage labor and

*In *The Hidden Welfare State: Tax Expenditures and Social Policy in the United States* (Princeton, N.J.: Princeton University Press, 1997), Christopher Howard shows that the social spending of the federal government is increasingly effected in a concealed manner, by way of fiscal arrangements that systematically favor business and wealthier households and effectively bypass the poor. In 1995, tax expenditures with social welfare objectives (such as deductions for home mortgage interest and employer-provided pensions) exceeded $450 billion, more than ten times the budget for AFDC and food stamps put together. Nine-tenths of these expenditures benefited the middle and upper classes (compared with two-thirds for official social spending).

the correlative curtailment of social protection, in turn, were curbed by the stupendous expansion of the penal apparatus that has propelled the United States to the rank of world leader in incarceration. This abrupt rolling out of the penal state will be mapped out in detail in the second part of the book.

Some Distinctive Properties of the American State

To grasp the nature and means of this political mutation, it is indispensable first to identify the distinctive structural and functional properties of what political scientist Alan Wolfe nicely calls America's "franchise state."[5] Here I will briefly emphasize five.

1. *A "society without a state," a society against the state*

The first distinctive trait of the state in America has to do with the representation it is given in the national *doxa*. Just as France has, until recently, thought of itself as a "nation without immigrants," even as its industrial, urban, and cultural history has been decisively stamped by the influx of foreign populations since the end of the nineteenth century, the reigning civic ideology of the United States has it that it is "a society without a state."[6]

From the Pilgrim fathers to the Bush dynasty, Americans have always viewed themselves as an autonomous people fundamentally rebellious to any suprasocial authority—save for that of God. This is attested by the many articles in the Constitution that disperse and curb public powers, regarded *ex hypothesi* as potentially tyrannical, and the venomous antistatism of the national political culture. The 1996 campaign for the presidential nomination offered a translucent illustration of this streak: all the candidates claimed that they wanted to "clean up Washington" and the federal government was characteristically presented as a foreign force, if not as the enemy of the people, by those who were its very servants. During the 2000 campaign, Albert Gore Jr., the sitting vice president for eight years, insisted on locating his campaign headquarters in Tennessee in order to stage his alleged closeness to the "people" and distance from "government elites," even though, as the son of a senator, he had spent his entire life and career in the corridors of power in Washington. Another indicator: Americans were likelier to blame the federal government (79 percent), and then "American workers themselves" (75 percent) and their fast-flagging unions

(62 percent), than they were Wall Street (50 percent) for the massive destruction of jobs that marked the beginning of the 1990s.[7]

2. *Bureaucratic fragmentation and dysfunctions*

The American state is a decentralized network of loosely coordinated agencies whose powers are limited by the very fragmentation of the bureaucratic field and the disproportionate power the latter grants to local authorities. The sharing of budgetary responsibilities and attributions among the various levels of government (federal, state, county, and municipal) is a source of constant dissension and distortion. The result is that there is often an abyss between the policies promulgated "on paper" in Washington and in state legislatures and the services actually delivered on the ground by street-level bureaucracies.[8]

The related absence of a tradition of public service and of stable channels for the recruitment and oversight of civil servants, especially in higher offices, means that the administrative apparatus is directly subjected to the forces of money, on the one hand, and to the brute demands of "electoral patrimonialism," on the other. Thence the bureaucratic incoherence and ineptitude that often preside over the design and implementation of national and local policies.[9] It also helps account for the extreme porosity of the public-private divide: according to a century-old tradition, updated by the "War on poverty" during the 1960s, a large share of social programs aimed at the lower class (such as the "Head Start" preschool plan or support for orphans and child protective services) is subcontracted to private and nonprofit agencies, which distribute and administer them in the name of the national collectivity. The historically entrenched pattern of reliance on the commercial and third sectors for carrying out many welfare duties of the state has created a vast and intricate mesh of organizations and interest groups "dedicated to preserving the private tilt of US social policy,"[10] which further complicates the landscape of large-scale public provision and creates an institutional terrain very propitious to efforts at further privatization of its activities.

3. *A dual state, or the great institutional-cum-ideological bifurcation*

Since the foundational era of the New Deal, the social action of the US state has been split into two hermetically sealed domains that are sharply distinguished by the composition and political weight of their respective "clienteles" as well as by their ideological charge.[11] The first strand, under the heading of "social insurance," is responsible for the collective management of the life-risks of wage earners—unemployment, sickness, and retirement. In principle, everyone with a stable job is entitled to participate in these programs and enjoys benefits construed as the just counterpart to their contributions (but we shall see shortly that this principle is in practice routinely violated in the lower tiers of the job market). The second plank, designated by the loathsome idiom of "welfare,"[12] concerns only assistance to dependent and distressed individuals and households. Its recipients are submitted to draconian conditions (of income, assets, marital and familial status, residence, etc.) and are placed under a harsh tutelage that clearly demarcates them from the rest of society and effectively makes them second-class citizens, on grounds that the support they receive is granted without an offsetting contribution on their part, and thus threatens to undermine their "work ethic."

Historically, the main beneficiaries of the "social insurance" side of the US social state, such as the Social Security retirement fund, have been men (as full-time workers and heads of households), whites (who have long cornered the lion's share of stable jobs in the industrial and service sectors), and the families of the labor aristocracy and the middle and upper classes. Although public assistance programs such as Aid to Families with Dependent Children (AFDC, income and in-kind grants to destitute single mothers with young children) reach a broad public that is majority white—more than one American household in four was on the "welfare" rolls at some point during the 1980s[13]—in the popular imagination their clientele is essentially made up of urban minorities and dissolute women living off the nation in the manner of social parasites.

4. *A residual welfare state*

The American state is the prototype of the "residual welfare state"[14] to the extent that it offers support only in response to the cumulative failures of the labor market and the family, by intervening on a case-by-case basis through programs strictly reserved for vulnerable categories that are deemed "worthy": ex-workers temporarily pushed out of the wage-labor market, the handicapped and severely disabled, and, subject to varying restrictive conditions, destitute mothers of young children.[15] Its official clientele is thus composed of "dependents" from working-class backgrounds, low-pay workers, the unemployed, and families of color, who have no influence upon the political system and, by the same token, no means of protecting their meager prerogatives.

The United States thus presents the paradox of a nation that venerates children but has no family support or education policy, so that one child in four (one black child in two) lives under the official "poverty line"; a country that spends vastly more than any of its competitors on healthcare as a percentage of its GDP, yet leaves some 45 million people (including 12 million children) without medical coverage at any one time; a society that sacralizes work, yet has no national framework for training or supporting employment worthy of the name. All because "state charity" has for its primary objective bolstering the mechanisms of the market and especially imposing the tough discipline of deskilled wage labor upon marginal populations.[16]

5. *A racial state*

Finally, the United States sports the highly distinctive property of being endowed with a *racial state* in the sense that, much like Nazi Germany and South Africa until the abolition of apartheid, the structure and functioning of the bureaucratic field are thoroughly traversed by the imperious necessity of expressing and preserving the impassable social and symbolic border between "whites" and "blacks," incubated during the age of slavery and subsequently perpetuated by the segregationist system of the agrarian South and the ghetto of the Northern industrial metropolis.* The pervasiveness and potency of this denegated form of ethnicity called "race" as a principle of social vision and division that effaces, ideologically and practically, the insuperable contradiction between the democratic ideal founded on the doctrine of the natural

*We return, in the third part of this book (chapter 6), to the historical sequence of "peculiar institutions" that, since chattel slavery, have kept blacks in a marginal and dependent position and there discover that the task of defining, containing, and controlling the casualized fractions of the African-American proletariat now befalls in part to the prison.

The theoretical and empirical relevance of the parallelism between the United States, Nazi Germany, and South Africa, which might shock gentle souls raised in the Tocquevillian tradition, is immediately evident upon reading Michael Burleigh and Wolfgang Wipperman, *The Racial State: Germany 1933–1945* (Cambridge: Cambridge University Press, 1991); George M. Fredrickson, *White Supremacy: A Comparative Study in American and South African History* (Oxford: Oxford University Press, 1981); and Joel Williamson, *The Crucible of Race* (New York: Oxford University Press, 1986). In this perspective, the trajectory and operation of the US Leviathan differs sharply from the modal path of the Western bureaucratic state, contrary to the thesis advanced by Goldberg that makes the modern state and race coeval and virtually coextensive with each other. David Theo Goldberg, *The Racial State* (Malden, Mass.: Blackwell, 2002).

rights of the individual and the persistence of a caste regime, is essential to understanding the initial atrophy and accelerating decay of the American social state in the recent period on the one hand, and the stupefying ease and speed with which the penal state arose on its ruins on the other.

Indeed, the originary caesura of the national social space into two communities perceived as congenitally disjoint and inherently unequal, between which the other components of the US ethnic mosaic are inserted (Latinos, Asians, and Native Americans, according to the official taxonomy), overdetermines the design and implementation of public policy in all domains. The white-black cleavage infects the national political culture and distorts the electoral and legislative game at the local as well as the federal level, from campaign fund-raising to the drawing of districts, the rhetoric of candidates for office, the formation of legislative factions and alliances, to the manufacturing of legislation.[17] From its origins, this rigid partition has also thwarted the unification and organization of the working class. Together with the strong integration of the capitalist class at the onset of industrialization, it accounts for the absence of union mobilization of an oppositional kind and, by the same token, for the feeble political oversight of the markets for labor, capital, and public goods.[18]

Lastly, through the intercession of regional cleavages, racial division anchors the teratological development of a welfare state split into two blocs, one turned toward whites and the middle and upper classes, the other aimed at blacks and the unskilled working class during the foundational era of the New Deal no less than during the expansionary period of the 1960s; and it underpins the tilting, over the ensuing two decades, from the assistantial to the penal management of poverty, misperceived as a problem affecting blacks first and foremost.[19] The ethnic division of the proletariat and the structural dualism of the semiwelfare state contribute to perpetuating the racialization of politics, which in turn feeds the retreat from civic participation, facilitating the stranglehold of corporations and wealthy funders on the electoral system.

Rolling Back the Charitable State

These distinctive characteristics explain why, although social inequality and economic insecurity increased sharply during the closing three decades of the twentieth century,[20] the American charitable state has steadfastly reduced its perimeter of operation and squeezed its modest budgets so as to allow for the explosive increase in military spending

Table 1. Decrease in welfare payments to poor single mothers (AFDC)*, 1975–95

	1970	1975	1980	1985	1990	1995
Current dollars	221	264	350	399	432	435
Constant dollars	221	190	165	144	128	119
Change	100	86	75	65	58	49.8

*Median payment for a family of four

SOURCE: Committee on Ways and Means, US House of Representatives, *1996 Green Book* (Washington, D.C.: U.S. Government Printing Office, 1997), 443–45, 449.

and the extensive redistribution of income from wage earners toward firms and the affluent fractions of the upper class. So much so that the "War on poverty" has given way to a simile *war against the poor*, made into the scapegoats of all the major ills of the country[21] and now summoned to care for themselves lest they be hit by a volley of punitive and humiliating measures intended, if not to put them back onto the narrow path of precarious employment, then at least to minimize their social demands and thus their fiscal burden.

Impaired by the administrative and ideological split between "welfare" and "social insurance," stigmatized by their close association with the demands of the black political movement, and tarnished by the notorious inefficiency of the agencies responsible for implementing them, programs targeted at the poor were the first victims of the sociopolitical reaction that carried Reagan to power in 1980 and then fostered the success of Clinton's "New Democrats."[22] Although the cost of AFDC never reached 1 percent of the federal budget, every government since Jimmy Carter has promoted its reduction as a top priority. And they have very largely succeeded at the level of recipients (see table 1): in 1970, the median AFDC payment for a family of four without any other source of income was $221 per month; in 1990, this sum reached $432 in current dollars, or $128 adjusting for inflation, corresponding to a net decline in purchasing power of 42 percent. By 1995, on the eve of its elimination, the AFDC package came to a paltry $435, or $110 in 1970 dollars, representing a real drop of more than one-half.

Moreover, these nationwide statistics conceal sharp regional disparities (see table 2). Social assistance was always significantly higher in the urban and industrial Midwest and Northeast, the historic cradle of both the working class and the black ghetto, than in the South, where poverty is more prevalent still and the social safety net virtually nonexistent. Thus, in 1996 the maximum monthly allowance for a family of three came to $577 in New York and $565 in Boston, as against a

Table 2. Maximum AFDC payment for a family of three in selected states, 1970–96*

	1970	1980	1990	1996	% change in real value, 1970–96
New York (City)	279	394	577	577	−48
Michigan (Detroit)	219	425	516	459	−48
Pennsylvania	265	332	421	421	−60
Illinois	232	288	367	377	−59
Texas	148	116	184	188	−68
Mississippi	56	96	120	120	−46

*In dollars per month

SOURCE: Committee on Ways and Means, U.S. House of Representatives, *1996 Green Book* (Washington, D.C.: US Government Printing Office, 1997), 459, 861, 921.

mere $120 in Mississippi, $185 in Albert Gore's Tennessee, and $188 in George W. Bush's Texas. But the decline in real terms was catastrophic everywhere, ranging from one-half in Michigan to two-thirds in Texas. In 1970, the AFDC package covered a national average of 84 percent of the "minimal needs" officially entitling one to public assistance; by 1996, this figure had fallen to 68 percent; in Texas, this ratio had plummeted to 25 percent (compared to 75 percent a quarter-century earlier).

Yet impoverished families must first succeed in receiving the meager assistance to which they are legally entitled. The second technique for shrinking the charitable state is not budgetary but administrative: it consists in multiplying the bureaucratic obstacles and requirements imposed on applicants with the aim of discouraging them or striking them off the recipient rolls (be it only temporarily). Under the cover of ferreting out abuses and turning up the heat on "welfare cheats," public aid offices have multiplied forms to be filled out, the number of documents to be supplied, the frequency of checks, and the criteria for periodically reviewing files. Between 1972 and 1984, the number of "administrative denials" on "procedural grounds" increased by almost one million, two-thirds of them directed against families who were fully within their rights.[23] This practice of bureaucratic harassment has even acquired a name well known among specialists, "churning," and it has given rise to elaborate statistics tracking the number of eligible claimants on assistance whose demands were unduly rejected for each program category. Thus, whereas 81 percent of poor children were covered by AFDC in 1973, over 40 percent did not receive the financial aid to which they were entitled fifteen years later. In 1996, at welfare's burial, it was estimated that every other poor household in America did not receive benefits for which it was eligible.

Finally, there remains the third and most brutal technique, which consists of simply eliminating public aid programs, on grounds that their recipients must be snatched from their culpable torpor by the sting of necessity. To hear the chief ideologues of American sociopolitical reaction, Charles Murray, Lawrence Mead, and Daniel Patrick Moynihan, the pathological "dependency" of the poor stems from their moral dereliction. Absent an urgent and muscular intervention by the state to check it, the growth of "nonworking poverty" threatens to bring about nothing less than "the end of Western civilization."[24] At the start of the 1990s, several formerly industrial states with high unemployment and urban poverty rates, such as Pennsylvania, Ohio, Illinois, and Michigan, unilaterally put an end to General Assistance, a locally funded program of last resort for the indigent—overnight in Michigan, after a brief transition period in Pennsylvania. This resulted in the dumping of one million aid recipients nationwide.

In 1991, Republican John Engler became governor of the predominantly Democratic state of Michigan by running on an aggressive antiwelfare platform. He immediately ordered that the Department of Social Services be renamed the Family Independence Agency and AFDC retitled the Family Independence Program. Even though expenditures for General Assistance had already plunged from $342 million in 1985 to $217 million, Engler invoked the need to balance the state budget and to prevent the formation of a permanent class of "able-bodied" scroungers to slash that budget to a meager $37 million in 1992, before abruptly terminating the program in 1993.[25] By contrast, that year Michigan spent $1.32 *billion* to incarcerate 44,000 convicts, and each prisoner was estimated to cost eleven times the average allowance given to a welfare recipient.

The suppression of General Assistance instantly cut from all assistance some 82,000 adults (receiving an average of $226 a month), half of them indigent blacks living in the collapsing city of Detroit. Some 7,700 recipients were then discreetly transferred to a newly created program called State Family Assistance and another 4,500 to State Disability Assistance, while others fought to try and gain access to other governmental support, forced to play a cruel game of "welfare musical chairs" to subsist. So-called "dependency" receded but hardship remained largely untouched, with 34 percent of African Americans in the state living under the official poverty line three years later.[26] Engler then parlayed his image as a tough "reformer" (i.e., cutter) of public aid into reelection and an acclaimed nomination on President Clinton's bipartisan advisory panel on welfare reform. He joined governor Tommy Thompson of Wisconsin as a national champion in the political crusade to dismantle welfare.

Out on the West Coast, Los Angeles County combined all three major strategies for downsizing the welfare state in response to booming need and rising public expenditures: cutting the value of aid packages, springing new administrative hurdles to ration services, and eliminating programs. In the 1980s, quality control campaigns, the punctilious micromanagement of cases, and the consolidation of offices across neighborhoods combined to produce rising rates of bureaucratic disentitlement. In 1993, the County deleted General Assistance, and by 1997 all remaining programs had been rolled up under workfare (called CalWorks) with reduced payments and strict time limits, producing a new "local regulatory" apparatus for the management of disruptive poverty, wedding "the convolution of Franz Kafka with the misery of Charles Dickens."[27]

The downsizing of America's charitable state has proceeded across a broad front and has not spared the privileged domain of social protection. In 1975, the unemployment insurance scheme established by the Social Security Act of 1935 covered 76 percent of wage earners who lost their jobs. By 1980 that figure had fallen to one in two due to state-mandated administrative restrictions and the proliferation of "contingent" jobs; and in 1995 it approached one worker in three. While coverage shrank, for twenty years the real average value of unemployment benefits stagnated at $185 per week (in constant dollars of 1995), disbursed for a meager fifteen weeks, giving most jobless people "on the dole" incomes putting them far below the poverty line.[28]

The same trend applies to occupational disability, for which the rate of coverage dropped from 7.1 workers per thousand in 1975 to 4.5 per thousand in 1991. Likewise for housing: in 1991, according to official figures, one in three American families was "housing poor," that is, unable to cover both basic needs and housing costs, while the homeless population numbered between 600,000 and 4 million. Meanwhile, the federal budget for social housing plummeted from $32 billion in 1978 to less than $10 billion a decade later in current dollars, amounting to a cut of 80 percent in real dollars.[29] At the same time, Washington eliminated funding for general revenue sharing, local public works, and urban development grants, as well as drastically pared most programs aimed at reintegrating the unemployed. When the Comprehensive Education and Training Act (CETA) program was terminated in 1984, over 400,000 public jobs for unskilled people disappeared. In 1975, the federal government devoted $3 billion to providing job training to 1.1 million poor Americans; by 1996, this figure had fallen to $800 million (in constant dollars), barely enough to cover 329,000 trainees. Meantime, budgets allocated to financing "summer jobs" for underprivileged youth were cut by one-third and the number of their beneficiaries by one-half.[30]

But it is at the municipal level that the concerted attack on urban and social policy was most ferocious. Using the pretext of the fiscal crisis triggered by the exodus of white families, middle-class revolts against taxation, and the drying up of federal subsidies, American cities sacrificed public services essential to poor neighborhoods and their inhabitants—housing, sanitation, transportation, and fire protection, as well as social assistance, health, and education. They diverted a growing share of public monies toward the support of private commercial and residential projects that promised to attract the new service-based corporations and the affluent classes.[31] This shift was justified by invocation of the alleged efficiency of market mechanisms in the allocation of city resources and federal funds. And it was greatly facilitated by the rigid racial segregation of the American metropolis, which sapped the collective capacity of poor residents by fracturing them along the color line. A single example suffices to indicate the devastating effects of this turnaround: while the costs and profits of free-market medicine soared, in Chicago the number of community hospitals (i.e., those accessible to people without private medical coverage) slumped from 90 in 1972 to 67 in 1981 to 42 in 1991. By that year, outside of the dilapidated and overcrowded Cook County Hospital, no health center in the entire city provided prenatal support to mothers without private insurance. In 1990, the director of Chicago's hospitals announced that the public health system was a "non-system on the brink of collapse," fundamentally incapable of fulfilling its mandate. That this declaration elicited no response from city and state officials and administrators speaks volumes about the indifference with which the rights and well-being of the urban poor are regarded.[32] The fact that the dispossessed families of Chicago are disproportionately black and Latino (from Mexican and Puerto Rican parentage) is key to explaining their civic invisibility.

The consequences of the withdrawal of the charitable state are not hard to guess. At the end of 1994, despite two years of solid economic growth, the Census Bureau announced that the official number of poor people in the United States had surpassed forty million, or 15 percent of the country's population—the highest rate in a decade. In total, one white family in ten and one African-American household in three lived below the federal "poverty line." This figure conceals the depth and intensity of their dereliction inasmuch as this threshold, calculated according to an arbitrary bureaucratic formula dating from 1963 (based on family consumption data from 1955), does not take into account the actual cost of living and the changing mix of essential goods, and it has been drawn ever lower over the years: in 1965 the poverty line stood at about one-half of the national median family income; thirty years later it did not reach one-third.* Comparative analysis reveals that, despite a notably lower official unemployment rate, "poverty in the United States is not only more widespread and more persistent, but also more severe than in the countries of continental Europe."[33] In 1991, 14 percent of American households received less than 40 percent of the median national income, as against 6 percent in France and 3 percent in Germany. These gaps were considerably more pronounced among families with children (18 percent in the United States versus 5 percent in France and 3 percent for its neighbor across the Rhine), not to mention single-parent families (45 percent in the United States, 11 percent in France, and 13 percent in Germany). This is hardly surprising when the minimum hourly wage is set so low that an employee working full-time year-round earned $700 per month in 1995, putting him 20 percent below the poverty line for a household of three, and when public aid is calculated to fall well below that wage rate in order to avoid creating "disincentives" to work:[34] the maximum AFDC cash payment in the median state in 1994 came barely to 38 percent of the poverty line and reached only 69 percent when combined with the value of food stamps and other in-kind support.

The degradation of employment conditions, shortening of job tenures, drop in real wages, and shrinking of collective protections for the US working class over the past quarter-century have been brought about and accompanied by a surge in precarious wage work. The numbers of on-call staff and day laborers, "guest" workers (brought in through state-sponsored programs of seasonal importation of agricultural laborers from Mexico or the Caribbean, for instance), office- or service-workers operating as subcontractors, compulsory part-timers, and casual staff hired through specialized "temp" agencies have all increased much more quickly than other occupational categories since

*For years, US social scientists have called for an overhaul of this flawed definition of poverty, finding it in turn outdated, unreliable, and invalid. In 1995, the Panel on Income and Family Assistance of the National Research Council officially recommended its revamping, but to no avail. For a provocative discussion of the theoretical and methodological issues involved in designing a multidimensional index of poverty understood as civic (in)capacity sensitive to historical and comparative variations and able to capture the depth of deprivation and the effects of state transfers, see David Brady, "Rethinking the Sociological Measurement of Poverty," *Social Forces* 81, no. 3 (March 2003): 715–52.

the mid-1970s—with temporary help leading the pack at a yearly clip of 11 percent. Today *one in three Americans in the labor force is a non-standard wage earner*: such insecure work must clearly be understood as a perennial form of subemployment solidly rooted in the new socio-economic landscape of the country and destined to grow.[35]

Drawing on field observations and in-depth interviews with the directors and staff of temp agencies, Robert Parker has deciphered the process of *normalization of precarious wage labor in the United States* recorded by longitudinal aggregate data through a detailed anatomy of the temporary employment sector. His study goes by the revealing title of "Flesh Peddlers and Warm Bodies."[36] This sector of the employment market has been booming: its turnover went from $547 million in 1970 to $3.1 billion in 1980 to $16.8 billion twelve years later, while the number of temporary employees increased tenfold to reach 1.5 million in 1993. Thus, the country's largest employer is no longer General Motors (the world's largest company in terms of revenue) but Manpower Incorporated, a multinational temp agency that hires out the services of 500,000 people in 34 countries and whose 1,400 outlets saw revenues grow by an average of 7 percent per year in the 1980s. Nowadays "normalized" insecurity can be found throughout the US economy: in the major corporations of the leading sectors like finance and real estate, in insurance and hospitals, agriculture and computers, nuclear power and office cleaning, not to mention retail trade, transportation, universities (one-half of the teaching staff in higher education work part-time or on temporary contracts), and even at the heart of public bureaucracies.[37]

The expansion of contingent employment is not a cyclical or conjunctural phenomenon linked to the adaptation of firms to a context of crisis, since it can be observed during periods of recovery as well as in recessions. Far from being the product of an impersonal process, inexorably connected to technological changes, business mergers, and the internationalization of economic competition, as the dominant media and the political vision would have it, it is the result of a *new employer strategy of externalization of the workforce and its costs*—a strategy encouraged by public authorities and powerfully reinforced by the active marketing of temporary employment agencies. Its impulse comes neither from global competition nor the labor market but mainly from domestic supply.[38] The business restructuring of the 1980s and early 1990s was aimed above all at the maximum "flexibilization" of the workforce by compressing the unit cost of labor and eliminating workers' rights in order to give (back) to firms fuller control over the parameters of employment, henceforth treated as "adjustment variables" in the quest for short-term financial returns. American corporations have thus consistently used the threat of layoffs, rather than improved wages and benefits, as a means of motivating their increasingly insecure workforce and extracting labor concessions.[39]

Not surprisingly, the casualization of jobs affects first and foremost women, the youngest and oldest workers, and finally unskilled blacks and Latinos living in the inner cities, for whom it has translated into an unprecedented social regression: a draconian cut in incomes and decline in living standards (a temporary worker typically earns around one-third of the wages of a permanent employee), a reduction of social and medical coverage to a bare minimum (when they still exist), a severe narrowing of the temporal and occupational horizon, a fraying of social relations at work, the deskilling of jobs, and an almost total loss of control over one's activity. By fragmenting the workforce, the institutionalization of job insecurity also thwarts traditional forms of collective action and thus serves as a battering ram to further assault the social benefits of workers who are still protected.[40] This means that insecurity eventually promises to seriously affect not only temporary employees but all wage earners, including the middle managers who currently defend it and are implementing it with zeal.

The United States boasts an official unemployment rate markedly lower than those of the major European countries: in July 1996, as Congress voted to delete welfare, it stood at 5.4 percent, half the average for the continent. But this artifice of social accounting—the US Labor Department uses one of the most restrictive definitions of unemployment, regarding any job-seeker who worked a single hour or more in the course of the previous month as "employed" and overlooking jobless workers deemed "discouraged"*—cannot conceal the fact that, over the past fifteen years, *three out of four Americans experienced or were directly touched by the social ignominy of layoffs*: 20 percent personally lost a permanent job, 14 percent saw this fate strike a member of their household, and 38 percent a parent, friend, or neighbor. Moreover, 14 percent changed jobs for fear that their post might get eliminated. The result is that fully one-half of Americans worry that unemployment will befall them, and 37 percent feel that their job situation is insecure. How could they not when 3.4 million employees were laid off in 1994 alone, amid the return of prosperity, as against 2.6 million during the recession of 1982? And while working-class families remain the main victims of ongoing economic restructuring, it is among the middle classes that the anxiety—and shame—over downward mobility reaches its apex.

*Thus, in October 1993, the Bureau of Labor Statistics estimated that the effective number of jobless Americans to be 17 million, whereas the official unemployment rate published by the Labor Department (based on the computations of the self-same Bureau of Labor Statistics) came to only 8.8 million. Massimo Calabresi, "Jobs in an Age of Insecurity," *Time Magazine*, 22 November 1993.

During the 1980s and 1990s, mass layoffs became a privileged instrument for the short-term financial management of US firms,[41] so that the country's middle and managerial classes made the bitter discovery of job insecurity during a period of sturdy growth. The return of economic prosperity to the United States was thus built on a spectacular degradation of the terms and conditions of employment: between 1980 and 1995, 41 percent of "downsized" employees were not covered by unemployment insurance and two-thirds of those who managed to find new work had to accept a position with lower wages. In 1996, 82 percent of Americans said that they were prepared to work longer hours to save their jobs; 71 percent would consent to fewer holidays, 53 percent to reduced benefits, and 44 percent to a cut in pay.[42] The absence of collective action in the face of stock-market-driven layoffs is explained by the congenital weakness of unions, the lock that corporate financiers have placed on the electoral system, and the power of the ethos of meritocratic individualism, according to which each wage earner is responsible for his or her own fate.

Failing a language that could gather the dispersed fragments of personal experiences into a meaningful collective configuration, the diffuse frustration and anxiety generated by the disorganization of the established reproduction strategies of the American middle classes have been redirected *against the state*, on the one side, which was accused of weighing on the social body like a yoke as stifling as it is useless, and, on the other, *against categories held to be "undeserving,"* or suspected of benefiting from programs of affirmative action, henceforth perceived as handouts violating the very principle of equity they claim to advance. The former tendency expressed itself in the pseudo-populist tone of electoral campaigns during the closing decade of the century, in which politicians near-unanimously directed a denunciatory and revanchist discourse against Washington's technocrats and other bureaucratic "elites"—of which they are typically full-fledged members—and public services—whose personnel and budgets they promised to "trim." The second tendency is evident in the fact that 62 percent of Americans are opposed to affirmative action for blacks and 66 percent are against affirmative action for women, even in those cases where it is proven that those helped were targets of discrimination, while two Americans in three wish to curtail immigration, even as 55 percent concede that immigrants take jobs nationals do not want (precisely because they are overexploitative).[43] This is the logic according to which in 1996, confirming its historic role as the nation's bellwether, California abolished the promotion of "minorities" in higher education and excluded so-called illegal immigrants from all public services, including schools and hospitals.

Whence, finally, the national hysteria around the problem of "welfare" that led to the public aid "reform" of 1996, which we shall analyze in some detail in the next chapter. Hypocritically entitled the "Personal Responsibility and Work Opportunity Act," it amounted to abolishing the right to assistance and instituted forced deskilled wage labor as the sole means of support on the pretext of setting the indigent back onto the road to "independence." Sacrificing the poor—and especially the black urban subproletariat, incarnation and scapegoat of all the country's ills—to exorcise the worries of the middle and working classes over their future is once again to ask those who are the living negation of the "American dream" to suffer for their alleged alterity so that, in spite of everything, the country may uphold its faith in the national myth of prosperity available to all.

Rolling Out the Penal State

How to stem the mounting tide of dispossessed families, street derelicts, alienated jobless youth, and the despair and violence that intensify and accumulate in the neighborhoods of relegation of the big cities? At all three levels of the bureaucratic field, county, state, and federal, the American authorities have responded to the rise of urban dislocations—for which, paradoxically, they are largely responsible—by developing their penal functions to the point of hypertrophy. As the social safety net of the charitable state unraveled, the dragnet of the punitive state was called upon to replace it. Its disciplinary mesh was flung throughout the nether regions of US social space so as to contain the disarray and turmoil spawned by the intensification of social insecurity and marginality. A causal chain and functional interlock was thus set into motion, whereby economic deregulation required and begat social welfare retrenchment, and the gradual makeover of welfare into workfare, in turn, called for and fed the expansion of the penal apparatus.

The deployment of this *state policy of criminalization of the consequences of state-sponsored poverty* operates according to two main modalities. The first and least visible one—except to those directly affected by it—consists in *reorganizing social services into an instrument of surveillance* and control of the categories indocile to the new economic and moral order. Witness the wave of reforms adopted between 1988 and 1995 in the wake of the Family Support Act by some three dozen states that have restricted access to public aid and made it conditional upon upholding certain behavioral norms (economic, sexual, familial, educational, etc.) and upon performing onerous and humiliating bureaucratic obligations. The most common of these requirements stipulate that the recipient must accept any job or assimilated activity offered to her, whatever the pay and working conditions, on pain of forsaking the right to assistance ("workfare"). Others index the amount of assistance received by the families to the school attendance record of their children or teenage recipient ("learnfare"), or peg them on enrollment in pseudo-training programs that offer few if any skills and job prospects.[44] Yet others establish a ceiling on the cash value of aid or set a maximum duration after which no support will be accorded. In New Jersey in the mid-1990s, for instance, AFDC benefits were terminated if an unmarried teen mother did not reside with her parents (even in cases where the latter had thrown her out), and the amount she received was capped if she begat additional children.

The insufficiency and inefficiency of forced-work programs are as glaring as their punitive character. While such programs are periodically vaunted as the miracle cure for the epidemic of "dependency" said to afflict the American poor, none of them has ever allowed more than a handful of participants to escape destitution. The reasons for their failure are several: the jobs proposed or imposed are too precarious and ill paid to offer a platform for economic autonomy; they do not provide medical coverage or child care assistance, making employment both risky and prohibitively costly for mothers with young offspring; the workplaces are physically and emotionally degrading; and a majority of "welfare mothers" already work while receiving aid in the first place.[45] At best, such programs replace "dependency" on means-tested state programs with "dependency" on superexploitative employers at the margins of the labor market, supplemented by fragile family networks, and illegal street commerce where accessible, a combination that nearly guarantees continued poverty. But precisely: it will be shown in the next chapter that workfare policy does not aim to reduce *poverty* but seeks only to diminish the *visibility of the poor in the civic landscape* and to "dramatize" the imperative of wage labor by issuing "a warning to all Americans who were working more and earning less, if they were working at all. There is a fate worse, and a status lower, than hard and unrewarding work."[46]

The long train of welfare reform measures also extols and embodies the new paternalist conception of the role of the state in respect to the poor, according to which the conduct of dispossessed and dependent citizens must be closely supervised and, whenever necessary, corrected through rigorous protocols of surveillance, deterrence, and sanction,

Table 3. Number of inmates in federal and state prisons, 1970–95 (in thousands)

	1970	1980	1990	1995	change 1970–95 (%)
Total	199	320	743	1078	442
Annual growth in preceding decade (%)	*−1.2*	*6.1*	*13.2*	*9*	
Blacks	81	168	366	542	569
Annual growth for blacks (%)	*−0.7*	*10.8*	*17.9*	*9.7*	

SOURCE: Bureau of Justice Statistics, *Historical Corrections Statistics in the United States, 1850–1984* (Washington, D.C.: Government Printing Office, 1986); idem., *Prisoners in 1996* (Washington, D.C.: Government Printing Office, 1997).

very much like those routinely applied to offenders under criminal justice supervision. The shift "from carrots to sticks," from voluntary programs supplying resources to mandatory programs enforcing compliance with behavioral rules by means of fines, reductions of benefits, and termination of recipiency irrespective of need, that is, programs treating the poor as *cultural similes of criminals* who have violated the civic law of wage work, is meant to both dissuade the lower fractions of the working class from making claims on state resources and to forcibly instill conventional morality into their members.* And it is instrumental in embellishing the statistics of public aid offices by "dressing up" recipients as workers while trapping the assisted population in the urban wastelands set aside for them.

The second component of the policy of punitive containment of the poor is *massive and systematic recourse to incarceration* (see table 3). Confinement is the other technique through which the nagging problem of persistent marginality rooted in unemployment, subemployment, and precarious work is made to shrink on—if not disappear from—the public scene. After decreasing by 12 percent during the

*This moral agenda is frankly laid out by the ideologues of state paternalism: "The social problems associated with long-term welfare dependency cannot be addressed without first putting the brakes on the downward spirals of dysfunctional behavior common among so many recipients. . . . Character is built by the constant repetition of diverse good acts. These new behavior-related welfare rules are an attempt, long overdue in the minds of many, to build habits of responsible behavior among long-term recipients; that is, to legislate virtue." Douglas J. Besharov and Karen N. Gardiner, "Paternalism and Welfare Reform," *The Public Interest* 122 (winter 1996): 70–84, citation p. 84.

1960s, the population condemned to serve time in state prisons and federal penitentiaries (excluding detainees held in city and county jails, awaiting judgment or sanctioned with short custodial sentences) exploded after the mid-seventies, jumping from under 200,000 in 1970 to nearly one million in 1995—an increase of 442 percent in a quarter-century never before witnessed in a democratic society. Like the social disengagement of the state, imprisonment has hit urban blacks especially hard: the number of African-American convicts increased sevenfold between 1970 and 1995, after falling 7 percent during the previous decade (even though crime rose rapidly during the 1960s). In each period, the growth rate of the black convict population far exceeded that of their white compatriots. In the 1980s, the United States added an average of 20,000 African Americans to its total prisoner stock *every year* (over one-third the total carceral stock of France). And, for the first time in the twentieth century, the country's penitentiaries held more blacks than whites: African Americans made up 12 percent of the national population but supplied 53 percent of the prison inmates in 1995, as against 38 percent a quarter-century earlier. The rate of incarceration for blacks *tripled in only a dozen years* to reach 1,895 per 100,000 in 1993—amounting to nearly seven times the rate for whites (293 per 100,000) and twenty times the rates recorded in the main European countries at that time.[47]

We will track down the sources and modalities of this astronomical increase in the prison population in detail in chapter 4 and demonstrate in particular that it is utterly disconnected from crime trends. In chapter 6, we will moreover show how the sudden growth of the prison relates to the crumbling of the urban ghetto as physical container for undesirable dark bodies. Here we want simply to note that a major engine behind carceral growth in the United States has been the "War on drugs"—an ill-named policy since it refers in reality to a guerilla campaign of penal harassment of low-level street dealers and poor consumers, aimed primarily at young men in the collapsing inner city for whom the retail trade of narcotics has provided the most accessible and reliable source of gainful employment in the wake of the twofold retrenchment of the labor market and the welfare state.[48] It is a "war" that the authorities had no reason to declare in 1983, considering that marijuana and cocaine use had been declining steadily since 1977–79 and that the supply-reduction approach to drug consumption has a long and distinguished history of failure in America.* And it was fully

*"The Reagan administration's declaration of a war on drugs resembles Argentina's declaration of war against Nazi Germany in March 1945. It was late and beside the

predictable that this policy would disproportionately strike lower-class African Americans insofar as it was directly targeted on dispossessed neighborhoods in the decaying urban core.

The rationale for this narrow spatial aiming of a nationwide penal drive is easy to disclose: the dark ghetto is the stigmatized territory where the fearsome "underclass," mired in immorality and welfare dependency, was said to have coalesced under the press of deindustrialization and social isolation to become one of the country's most urgent topics of public worry.[49] But it is also the area where police presence is particularly dense, illegal trafficking is easy to spot, high concentrations of young men saddled with criminal justice records offer easy judicial prey, and the powerlessness of the residents gives broad latitude to repressive action. It is not the War on drugs per se, then, but the timing and selective deployment of that policy in a restricted quadrant located at the very bottom of social and urban space that has contributed to filling America's cells to bursting and has quickly "darkened" their occupants.

One indicator of volume: in 1975 one federal inmate in four was behind bars on a narcotics conviction; twenty years later, that figure had reached 61 percent. Meanwhile, the population confined by the Federal Bureau of Prisons had quadrupled to approach 90,000, making it one of the largest correctional systems in the world when it had been a minor auxiliary to the US carceral apparatus until Reagan entered the White House (see table 4).

One indicator of racial disparity: the ratio of black to white arrest rates for drug-related offenses was 2 to 1 in 1975; fifteen years later it had zoomed to 5 to 1, even though the relative propensity of blacks and whites to use drugs had not changed. More shockingly, the arrest rate of white juveniles for drug infractions, which had been dropping steadily from a high of 310 arrests per 100,000 since 1975, continued to sag on the same slope after the launching of the War on drugs to reach a low of 80 per 100,000 in 1991—meaning that white teenagers were left *entirely untouched* by that aggressive penal campaign. By contrast, the drug arrest rate for black minors, which had dropped parallel to that of whites from 250 per 100,000 in 1979 to some 185 in 1981, made an abrupt U-turn in 1983 and rocketed to pass 460 per 100,000 by 1989, at the height of the so-called war.[50] Clearly, young black men from the ghetto were the prime quarry of the aggressive rolling out

point. . . . It was well known among public officials and drug policy scholars that drug use was in steep decline. . . . Only the willfully blind could have failed to know that no war was needed." Michael Tonry, *Malign Neglect: Race, Class, and Punishment in America* (New York: Oxford University Press, 1995), 83 and 91.

Table 4. Inmates in federal prisons convicted of drug offenses, 1975–95

	1975	1980	1985	1990	1995
Number	23,566	24,252	40,505	57,331	89,564
Share (%)	27	25	34	52	61

SOURCE: Federal Bureau of Prisons, *Quick Facts 1998* (Washington, D.C.: Government Printing Office, 1998).

of the penal state after the Civil Rights Revolution, just like young black women receiving public aid were the choice figure at the center of the whirling debate around "welfare reform."

In light of the objectives set by its strategists, the War on drugs has been a spectacular failure—so say some 80 percent of the country's heads of police polled by the Annual Survey of Police Chiefs and Sheriffs after 1995. Since it was declared, the retail price of cocaine has declined continually, the quantities of narcotics in circulation on the streets have increased year after year, and the number of black convicts for drug crimes has swollen without interruption. But it has served well to point the spear of the penal state onto the most wretched segments of the country's urban subproletariat and to erect a public stage onto which politicians could display themselves in the act of delivering an essential service to the hard-working citizenry: virile protection from street thugs.

Yet, the doubling of the carceral population in ten years, and its tripling in twenty years after the mid-1970s, seriously underestimates the real weight of penal authority in the new apparatus for treating urban poverty and its correlates. For those held behind bars represent only a quarter of the population under criminal justice supervision (see table 5). If one takes account of individuals placed on probation and ex-convicts released on parole, more than five million Americans, amounting to 2.5 percent of the country's adult population, fell under penal oversight by 1995. In many cities and regions, the correctional administration and its extensions are the main if not the sole point of contact between the state and young black men from the deskilled lower class: as early as 1990, 40 percent of African American males age 18 to 35 in California were behind bars or on probation and parole; this rate reached 42 percent in Washington, D.C., and topped 56 percent in Baltimore.[51] Thus, during the same period when the US state was withdrawing the protective net of welfare programs and fostering the generalization of subpoverty jobs at the bottom of the employment ladder, the authorities were extending a reinforced carceral mesh reaching deep into lower-class communities of color.

Table 5. Populations under criminal justice supervision, 1980–95 (in thousands)

	1980	1985	1990	1995	% Change
Probation	1,118	1,969	2,670	3,078	175
Jail	184	257	405	507	142
State and federal prison	320	488	743	851	176
Parole	220	300	531	679	209
Total	1,842	3,013	4,350	5,343	190

SOURCE: Bureau of Justice Statistics, *Correctional Populations in the United States, 1995* (Washington, D.C.: Government Printing Office, 1997).

The financial translation of this "great confinement" of marginality is not hard to imagine. As will be documented fully in chapter 5, to implement its policy of penalization of social insecurity at the bottom of the socioracial structure, the United States massively enlarged the budget and personnel devoted to confinement, in effect ushering in the era of "carceral big government" just as it was decreasing its commitment to the social support of the poor. While the share of national expenditures allocated to public assistance declined steeply relative to need, federal funds for criminal justice multiplied by 5.4 between 1972 and 1990, jumping from less than $2 billion to more than $10 billion, while monies allotted to corrections proper increased elevenfold. The financial voracity of the penal state was even more unbridled at the state level. Taken together, the fifty states and the District of Columbia spent $28 billion on criminal justice in 1990, 8.4 times more than in 1972; during this stretch, their budgets for corrections increased twelvefold, while the cost of criminal defense for the indigent (who make up a rising share of those charged in court) grew by a factor of 24. To enforce the Violent Crime Control and Law Enforcement Act of 1994, which envisaged boosting the national carceral population from 925,000 to some 2.26 million over a decade, the US Congress forecast expenditures of $351 billion, including $100 billion just for building new custodial facilities—nearly twenty times the AFDC budget that year.[52] We shall see in chapter 4 that these predictions turned out to be rather accurate: a decade later the country had doubled its population under lock, and budgets for corrections were pushing counties and states deep into debt.

Incarceration in America thus expanded to reach an industrial scale heretofore unknown in a democratic society, and, in so doing, it spawned a fast-growing commercial sector for operators helping the state enlarge its capacity to confine, by supplying food and cleaning services, medical goods and care, transportation, or the gamut of activities needed to run a penal facility day-to-day. The policy of hyperincarceration even stimulated the resurgence and exponential expansion of *jails and prisons constructed and/or managed by private operators*, to which public authorities perpetually strapped for cells turned to extract a better yield out of their correctional budgets. Incarceration for profit concerned 1,345 inmates in 1985; ten years later, it covered 49,154 beds, equal to the entire confined population of France. The firms that house these inmates receive public monies against the promise of miser's savings, on the order of a few cents per capita per day, but multiplied by hundreds of thousands of bodies, these savings are put forth as justification for the partial privatization of one of the state's core regalian functions.[53] By the late 1990s, an import-export trade in inmates was flourishing among different members of the Union: every year Texas brings in several thousands convicts from neighboring states but also from jurisdictions as far away as the District of Columbia, Indiana, and Hawaii, in utter disregard of family visiting rights, and later returns them to their county of origin where they will be consigned on parole at the end of their sentence.

Now, to turn the penal apparatus into an organizational contraption suitable for curbing and containing social disorders (as opposed to responding to crime) in decaying lower-class and ghetto neighborhoods ravaged by economic deregulation and welfare curtailment required two transformations. First its processing and warehousing capacities had to be vastly expanded. Second, it had to be remade into a flexible, muscular, and efficacious instrument for the tracking and confinement of troubled and troublesome persons caught in the cracks of the dualized urban order. Increased reach was achieved by implementing four major penal planks:

1. *"Determinate Sentencing"*: under the sanctioning regime known as "indeterminate sentencing," put in place across the United States from the 1920s onward, the court condemned an offender to a custodial sentence defined by a broad bracket (e.g., from two to ten years, or "fifteen to life"); the effective duration of confinement was set later by a parole board, based on the behavior of the convict and his progress toward "rehabilitation." Under the new "determinate sentencing" regime, introduced around 1978–84, punishment is set once for all in court by the judge within a narrow range defined by the application of a quasi-mathematical formula: each convict is assigned a number of points, converted into months of reclusion, computed on the basis of scores corresponding to the seriousness of his

crime, the circumstances of its commission, and his criminal background. At century's turn, twenty-two states applied determinate sentencing and another twenty-two a mixed regime. The main effect of this drastic reduction of judicial and correctional discretion has been to lengthen the sentences handed down by judges at conviction.

2. *"Truth in Sentencing"*: this policy, applied after 1984 in response to the perceived leniency and inequity of the regime of indeterminate sentencing, stipulates that every convict shall serve a minimum portion of his sentence before he becomes eligible for parole. The threshold is set at 75 percent in four states, 85 percent in thirty states, and 100 percent in four others (Wisconsin even supplements custodial sentences with an automatic period of judicial supervision after release equal to one-fourth of the time spent behind bars). Its implementation entails the amputation of time deducted for "good behavior" and the elimination of parole for violent offenders in four states as well as for all convicts in fourteen states. It primary effect: an automatic lengthening of the sentences effectively served.

3. *"Mandatory Minimums"*: this federal legislation, voted in 1986 for drug crimes, establishes a plank of compulsory and irreducible sanctions for specific offenses, without regard for the injuriousness of the crime, the justice background of the convict, and the circumstances of his actions. In the case of narcotics offenders, for instance, the sanction is set by the amount of drugs involved (measured in grams or feet). Thus the same automatic punishment of a minimum of five years of imprisonment without the possibility of early release on parole is given in federal court for simple possession of one hundred plants of marijuana, one hundred grams of heroin, ten grams of methamphetamine, five grams of cocaine in solid form (crack) or five hundred grams in powder form, and one gram of LSD. In 1988, Congress extended this statute to a long list of crimes committed with a firearm. Its main consequence has been to widen the use of imprisonment and to sharply increase sentences both pronounced and served.

4. *"Three Strikes and You're Out"*: borrowed from the "national pastime" of baseball (a sport in which the batter who swings and misses the ball thrown at him three times is "out" and loses his turn at bat), this expression refers to the drastic and mechanical enhancement of sanctions inflicted in cases of recidivism and the implementation of life sentences (or "twenty-five to life") when the accused has committed three serious or specially designated felonies. Such laws were adopted by two dozen states and the federal government in the 1990s. They vary greatly by jurisdiction, with California enforcing a particularly brutal version in which over five hundred offenses (including minor misdeeds such as a simple theft in a store) qualify as "third strikes" mandating lifetime imprisonment, and Georgia applying "two strikes and you're out" for seven violent crimes.

These four trains of judicial measures illustrate well the flexible, double-sided rationale of penal policy discussed in the prologue, which spans the material and symbolic orders. Thus truth-in-sentencing and mandatory-minimums statutes have primarily the *material* effects of reducing systemic discretion and enlarging as well as extending the confinement of whole categories of offenders by sweeping ever-larger numbers of low-level offenders into the carceral system for longer periods. By contrast, "Three Strikes and You're Out" and similarly vengeful laws play essentially the *symbolic* role of communicating the intense sentiments of public outrage and state severity toward criminals, as in practice their application is sharply limited, and they fail to generate significant numbers of additional incarcerations (except in California, where the very idiosyncratic manner in which the law was drafted and voted has resulted in its "biting louder than it barks," but in that regard it is highly atypical).[54] As for the determinate sentencing regime, it may be viewed as fulfilling a mix of instrumental and expressive missions: it curtails judicial discretion and escalates the intensity of punishment, bringing the mass of convicts under stiffer correctional control, at the same time as it signifies a newfound collective commitment to moral austerity and judicial fortitude.

Whereas the rolling back of welfare was effected through blanket retraction and affected all recipients and would-be recipients indiscriminately, without regard to their needs, options, and location, penal rigor was delivered very selectively in social space. *Class and ethnic selectiveness was achieved primarily by the targeting of certain geographic zones,* which guaranteed that the categories composing their residents would be the primary if not exclusive "beneficiaries" of the newfound policing zeal and penal largesse of the state. It was further enhanced by the multiplication of new law-enforcement tactics and special measures designed for, and deployed specifically in, declining lower-class districts, such as order-maintenance policing (known as "zero tolerance" in its New York variant, dissected in chapter 8), antigang loitering ordinances, intensive police sweeps through public housing or public schools, and youth curfews.[55]

The establishment of *curfews,* aimed at keeping minors off the streets after nightfall and applied essentially in and around the hyperghetto and poor barrios, is emblematic of the increased propensity of the American state to fling its police and punishment dragnet wider only in those very regions of social space where it is retracting its safety net. Pointing to a rise in violent crime attributable (or reflexively attributed) to gangs, 59 of the 77 largest cities in the country have instituted such prohibitions, half of them between 1990 and 1994. In Chicago, a municipal ordinance forbids people under age sixteen from being outdoors without proper authorization between 10:30 at night (11:30 on weekends) and 6:00 in the morning. Criminologists William Ruefle and Kenneth Reynolds observe that this raging epidemic of curfews was "a leap into the unknown," since no one had documented whether these measures reduce delinquency rather than simply displace it.[56] Since the mid-1990s, numerous studies have indeed found that juvenile curfews have no suppressive effect on street crime or juvenile offending and even have serious criminogenic consequences of their own.[57] What is certain is that these curfews significantly increase chances of incarceration for the young residents of poor urban areas. According to FBI data, some 75,000 youths were arrested on this basis in 1992, twice as many as for theft (excluding car theft) that year. And the rate of juvenile arrests for loitering and curfew violations more than doubled between 1992 and 1997, when it peaked at 700 per 100,000 juveniles.[58] The ability to modulate their implementation at ground level according to the geographic, class, and ethnic origins of those caught by them gives curfews a privileged place in the panoply of new techniques for the punitive containment of young men from the neighborhoods of relegation gutted by the neoliberal restructuring of market and state. Other techniques include "boot camps," the electronic surveillance of offenders, and the increasing diversion of juvenile cases into adult court.

The explosive swelling of the population behind bars, the retraction of vocational and educational programs within prisons, the massive recourse to the most diverse forms of pre- and postcustodial control, and the multiplication of instruments of surveillance up and down the penal chain, the "new penology" being put in place does not aim at "rehabilitating" criminals, but rather at "managing costs and controlling dangerous populations"[59] and, short of this goal, at warehousing them in isolation to make up for the indigence of social and medical services that are neither willing nor able to care for them. The rise of the American penal state thus responds not to rising crime—which was first stagnant and then declined during these three pivotal decades, as we will show in chapter 4—but to the social dislocations caused by the desocialization of wage labor and the retrenchment of the charitable state. And it tends to become its own justification inasmuch as its criminogenic effects contribute powerfully to the insecurity and violence it is supposed to remedy.

The same congenital properties that inclined the American state to treat the poor in an increasingly stingy manner on the social welfare front after the mid-1970s also predisposed it to behave in generous ways on the penal front. The same overlapping divisions between lower class and middle class, black and white, and deserving versus undeserving citizen, inscribed in the deep structure and routine functioning of the bureaucratic field, conditioned it to distribute ever meager welfare benefits and to mete out ever larger doses of punishment at the bottom of the class and ethnic order as a means of reasserting the civic imperative of work. The temporal coincidence of these two complementary shifts with each other and with the reversal of labor and social trends toward deepening inequality, their convergence onto the same populations trapped in dilapidated urban enclaves, their joint invocation of the ethics of individual responsibility and (de)merit, and their shared punitive ethos constitute powerful prima facie evidence that restrictive social welfare reforms and expansive criminal justice policies are twinned state responses to the generalization of social insecurity in the nether regions of US social space and that they must therefore be analyzed together.

The Gaols of the Subproletariat: An Experimental Verification

It suffices, to discern the extrapenological functions served by the outsized extension of the US carceral apparatus *even as crime plummeted* for over a decade,[60] to sketch in broad strokes the sociological profile of the "clientele" it accommodates at its entry point. Whence it turns out that the half-million detainees who glut the country's 3,300-odd jails on any one day—and the fourteen million bodies that pass through their gates in the course of a typical year—are essentially drawn from the most marginalized fractions of the working class, and especially from the subproletarian families of color in the segregated cities ravaged by the conjoint transformation of wage labor and social protection.* Thus, recovering its historical mission of origin, incarceration

*The statistics in this section are taken from a survey, conducted by the federal Department of Justice from October 1995 to March 1996, of a representative sample of 6,000 detainees in 431 county jails. Caroline Wolf Harlow, *Profile of Inmates 1996* (Washington, D.C.: Bureau of Justice Statistics, 1998). For comparisons over time, these earlier studies were relied upon: *Profile of Jail Inmates, 1989* and *Profile of Jail Inmates: Socio-Demographic Findings from the 1978 Survey of Inmates of Local Jails* (Washington, D.C.: Government Printing Office, 1991 and 1980, respectively), while various Census Bureau publications were used for comparisons with the national population. Statistical data of this kind have a high coefficient of uncertainty owing to the conditions under which the interviews are conducted, the characteristics of the

serves above all to regulate, if not to perpetuate, poverty and to warehouse the human rejects of the market. In this regard, the gargantuan operation of punishment houses converges with and complements the aggressive rolling out of workfare programs.

Indeed, six in ten occupants of county jails are black or Latino (41 percent and 19 percent, respectively), as against 48 percent in 1978, whereas these two communities put together represent barely one-fifth of the national population. Just under *one-half held a full-time job* at the time of arrest (49 percent), while 15 percent worked "part-time or occasionally" and the remainder were looking for work (20 percent) or economically inactive (16 percent). This astronomical jobless rate is hardly surprising considering the educational level of this population: one-half had not graduated from high school, even though this requires no examination, and barely 13 percent said that they had pursued vocational, technical, or academic postsecondary education (compared to one-half of this age category in the country as a whole).

As a result of their marginal position on the deskilled labor market, two-thirds of detainees lived in a household with under $1,000 in income per month (and 45 percent in households with under $600), corresponding to *less than half the official poverty line* for a family of three that year—although two-thirds said that they had received wages. This indicates that the vast majority of the occupants of county jails do come from the ranks of the "working poor," that fraction of the working class that does not manage to escape poverty *although they work*, but who are largely ineligible for social protection *because they work* at poverty-level jobs.* Thus, despite their penury, barely 14 percent received public aid (payments to single parents, food stamps, food assistance for children) on the eve of their arraignment. If we include the 7 percent receiving disability or retirement benefits and the 3 percent on the unemployment rolls, it turns out that less than one-quarter of jail detainees received some government support. The twofold exclusion from stable

---

population questioned, the sensitivity of some of the items asked, and a lack of precision in the coding of responses. However, the orders of magnitude they establish in the respects that interest us here are sufficiently clear that we can treat them as reliable, especially since other, local investigations suggest that this study tends to *underestimate* the material insecurity and sociocultural destitution of the carceral population.

*On the one hand, these jobs generally provide neither medical insurance nor social coverage (which depends on the goodwill of the employer). On the other, having a job, and thus an income, however meager, disqualifies them from public assistance and medical coverage for indigent households (public benefits which, in any case, are now very hard to obtain and provide only for strictly limited periods, as we shall document in the next chapter).

wage work and public assistance that affects widening sections of the American proletariat explains the lengthening of careers in the illegal economy, and thus the pronounced aging of the jail population: in 1996 one detainee in three was older than 35, twice as many as in 1978. This aging directly parallels that of persistent offenders and the entrenching of criminal commerce in the inner city, where established street gangs have taken an entrepreneurial turn and included more members in their thirties and forties as opportunities in the regular economy dried up.[61]

The material insecurity of detainees in American jails is matched only by their *social denudement*: only 40 percent grew up with both parents (as against a national average of 77 percent) and fully 14 percent spent their childhood in an orphanage or group home. Nearly half were raised in households receiving public assistance, and over one-quarter grew up living in public housing—the most reviled sector of the urban housing market due to its extreme dilapidation, dangerousness, and the double class and caste segregation that stamps it.[62] Moreover, more than one-third of jail inmates confided to having a parent or guardian who is an alcoholic (30 percent) or drug addict (8 percent). Confirming the fragility of their social ties, a bare 16 percent of them were married, compared to 58 percent for men in their age bracket nationwide.

Besides, incarceration is quite familiar to detainees in the strict sense that *more than half of them have or had a close relative in prison* (a brother, 30 percent; their father, 16 percent; a sister or mother, 10 percent). The same goes for physical violence and especially gun-related violence. One in nine men and one in three women said that they had suffered physical or sexual abuse during their childhood; three percent of men and one woman in three reported being raped as adults. Everything suggests that these percentages are low estimates, especially for the men, since most inmates have already done time behind bars and homosexual rape is quite common in American houses of detention, where it is estimated that as many as one inmate in four is subject to serious sexual abuse every year.[63] According to a 1994 survey carried out by the head physician at the Cook County Department of Corrections, half of the men admitted to Chicago's jail had previously been hospitalized as a result of an assault and one in four had been wounded by gunshots at least once. In addition, 60 percent of shooting victims had personally witnessed shootings during their childhood.[64] A germane study of detainees entering the jails of Washington, D.C., in 1997 found that one in four had suffered serious injuries unrelated to their incarceration. In-depth interviews with a subsample of these men found that 83 percent had been at the scene of a shooting incident;

46 percent had had a family member killed with a gun (in most cases during a robbery, assault, or crossfire); and 40 percent still carried some disability related to a earlier gunshot wound.[65]

Material insecurity, cultural deprivation, social denudement, physical violence—the *deplorable health* of the denizens of America's jails is in tune with their degraded class position and condition: more than one-third (37 percent, compared to one-fifth of the general population) report that they suffer from physical, psychic, or emotional problems serious enough to curtail their ability to work. This diagnosis is confirmed by the fact that half of the new entrants into the carceral system had to receive treatment upon admission, aside from the superficial medical examination to which all "fish" are subjected during the procedures initiating them to their detainee status.* (To this percentage one can add the 13 percent of jail inmates injured while behind bars as a result of assaults, riots, and accidents.) And detainees are not only more likely to *be* in ill health upon being put under lock; they are also at inordinately high risk of *becoming* ill while there, as America's jails and prisons have become gigantic incubators for infectious diseases, with prevalence rates of the major afflictions far exceeding those of the general population. It is estimated that 20 to 26 percent of all persons infected with HIV-AIDS in the United States, 29 to 43 percent of those detected with the hepatitis C virus, and 40 percent of all those struck by tuberculosis in 1997 had passed through a correctional facility.[66]

It is moreover well established that American jails have become the shelters of first resort for the mentally ill who were thrown onto the streets by hospitals in the wake of the massive "deinstitutionalization" campaign of the 1960s and 1970s and for those who simply cannot access a grossly defective public health system. It is hardly surprising then that over one-quarter of jail inmates have been treated for mental health problems, while 10 percent have been previously admitted to a psychiatric facility.** This is consistent with clinical studies conducted by medical researchers reporting that 6 to 15 percent of the clientele of

*The mass processing of detainees at the Los Angeles County jail is depicted in the two ethnographic vignettes of jail intake (drawn from fieldwork carried out in the summer of 1998) offered in chapters 4 and 5 (pages 146–50 and 186–91).

**The proportion of inmates identified as suffering from mental afflictions during admission is deliberately lowered in keeping with the lack of resources available to treat them. As one psychiatrist working at the clinic of the Twin Towers, the reception center of the Los Angeles jail system, explained to me: "We have an instrument [a psychological test] that gives us 6 to 10 percent of serious cases, but the percentage diagnosed really depends on how many beds we have. If we had the room and the staff, we could easily up that figure to 15, 20, or 30 percent."

city and county jails suffer from *severe* mental illness (rates for convicts in prison range from 10 to 15 percent), and this rate has increased over the past two decades as a result of the downsizing of the medical sector of the state, more rigid criteria for civil commitments, and increasingly negative attitudes among the public and the police.[67] The disproportionate rate of street arrests of mentally ill persons combines in turn with the explosive growth of computerized criminal records (analyzed in chapter 5) to fortify the tendency of the authorities to divert their treatment from the public health to the penal wing of the Leviathan.

As they come almost exclusively from the most precarious strata of the urban proletariat, the denizens of American jails are also, by (socio)logical implication, "regulars" of the carceral system: 59 percent have already experienced detention, and 14 percent were previously put on probation, leaving just under one-quarter who are "novices" to the jailhouse. For, as shall be discussed shortly, the carceral institution has grown more *autophagous*. This is attested by the rising share of inmates who have been repeatedly convicted: fewer than one detainee in four had served three custodial sentences in 1989; seven years later, that figure reached one-third. Finally, it is significant that 80 percent of those sentenced to at least one year of prison time were defended—if one can call it that—by public defenders. Only half of the detainees shorn of the means to hire their own lawyer were able to speak with counsel within two weeks of being locked up.[68] In fact, it is routine for public defenders to meet their clients for the first time a few minutes before they hastily appear together before a judge, since state-appointed lawyers are typically in charge of hundreds of cases at a time. Thus in Connecticut members of the public attorney's office, who officiate in three-quarters of the state's felony trials, each handle an average of 1,045 cases in the course of a year. As in many other jurisdictions, they have filed suit against the agency that employs them in order to compel the state to disburse the funds needed to meet its constitutional mandate to provide all the accused with minimal means of defense in criminal court.[69] Over the past decade, the costs of indigent defense services have ballooned out of control, exacerbating the chronic crisis of legal services for the poor, due not only to the multiplication of punitive statutes such as mandatory minimum sentences and long narcotics-related sanctions, but also to "an overall increase in criminal filings and a larger percentage of defendants found to be indigent." This confirms that the penal state is more aggressively raking the very bottom layers of social and urban space.[70]

The profile in urban marginality drawn from this national survey of jail inmates is fully corroborated by a two-year field study conducted by sociologist—and ex-convict—John Irwin, combining direct observation and in-depth interviews with the "fresh fish" caught in the net of the San Francisco jail. Irwin emphasizes that "the persons who fill the jails in the big cities are largely members of the rabble class, that is, persons who are poorly integrated into society and who are seen as disreputable": hustlers and hoodlums, derelicts and the mentally ill, drug addicts, illegal immigrants, and "corner boys" (working-class youths who hang out in cliques in public places and consort in taverns in low-income neighborhoods). But, more importantly, their arrest and detention, and even their conviction and sentencing to prison, are explained largely by "offensiveness, as much or more than [by] crime seriousness." Worse still, the police and carceral management of social insecurity certainly has the effect of controlling members of the "rabble" that soil the city streets in the short run, but over time it also "confirms their status and continually replenishes their ranks." Aside from the fact that "jail is the primary institution of socialization into rabble existence," the recent campaign of penal harassment of the poor in public space contributes to aggravating the feeling of insecurity and impunity insofar as it "blurs the distinction between actual crime and what is merely bothersome or offensive."[71] And it is well suited to diverting public attention from white-collar and corporate crime, whose human damage and economic costs are vastly greater and more insidious than those of street delinquency.

Considering that jail detainees form a more diverse and less deprived population than the convicts of state prison, it is clear that, when we are tracking the carceral stock of the United States, we are indeed dealing overwhelmingly with the most precarious and stigmatized segments of the urban working class, disproportionately nonwhite, and in a regular if fractious relationship with various public aid programs targeted at the poor, from orphanages and housing to health and income support. Whatever offenses they may have committed, their trajectory cannot be mapped out and explained within the compass of a "classless criminology."[72] And, whatever behavioral foibles threw them into the clutches of criminal justice, they issue from and remain an integral part of the core population that is the traditional focus of public assistance schemes. This suggests that analysts of the welfare state in America cannot continue to ignore the vast and growing sections of the urban (sub)proletariat that are churning through the penal system, and they must imperatively bring the prison into the picture of the determinants and correlates of marginality and inequality in the age of economic deregulation. Integrating the analysis of penal policy and social policy is all the more urgent when the welfare rug is being pulled from under the feet of the urban poor to be replaced by a trampoline toward low-wage work and the illegal economy of the street—which is what the great "welfare reform" of 1996 entailed. It is to an analysis of this "reform" and how it embodies and accelerates the establishment of the new government of social insecurity that we turn in the next chapter.

3

Welfare "Reform" as Poor Discipline and Statecraft

> If people stay on welfare for prolonged periods of time, it administers a narcotic to the spirit. This dependence on welfare undermines their humanity and makes them wards of the state.—FRANKLIN DELANO ROOSEVELT, 1935

> This is an incredible day in the history of this country. [It] has to go down as Independence Day for those who have been trapped in a system that has been left dormant and left to allow people to actually decay on the layers of intergenerational welfare which has corrupted their souls and stolen their future. —E. CLAY SHAW JR., 1996 *U.S. Representative from Florida, coauthor of the "Personal Responsibility and Work Opportunity Reconciliation Act"*

The welfare "reform" passed by the US Congress and signed into law with great fanfare by William Jefferson Clinton in August of 1996 caused a big stir on both sides of the Atlantic. On American shores, the President's decision to endorse a set of measures concocted by the reactionary fringe of the Republican Party, throwing by the wayside some of the most precious social advances of the New Deal and the War on poverty of the 1960s, could not fail to trouble the Democratic establishment and to shake up its traditional allies. Numerous voices rose even from within the government to denounce this political turnaround and the renunciation it implied.

A True-False Reform

Several high-ranking officials in the federal Department of Health and Human Services, among them the director of its research arm, tendered their resignation in protest on grounds that, according to the projections done by their staff, the said "reform" would result in a significant increase in hardship for the most impoverished Americans and especially their children.* (In point of fact, Clinton had refused

*One catches the flavor of the intense emotional and political turmoil caused by Clinton's endorsement of the bill among US liberal circles in the scathing obituary-

to communicate the results of these studies to Congress, fearing the negative publicity that would result.) The head of the Children's Defense Fund, a close personal friend of the Clintons, publicly broke with the presidential couple before calling the decision of the leader of the New Democrats "an outrage."[1] Religious organizations, trade unions, liberal politicians and academics, and welfare rights activists unanimously condemned it. Even centrist senator Daniel Patrick Moynihan, who had spearheaded the previous wave of welfare refurbishing, resulting in the passage of the Family Support Act of 1988, denounced it as a sure recipe for "increasing poverty and destitution." And his colleague Paul Simon, a long-time supporter of Clinton, chimed in that signing the welfare package into law would forever tarnish the president's legacy.[2] Hugh Price, the head of the Urban League, an outfit devoted to black advocacy usually noted for its genteel moderation, summed up the standpoint of mainline progressive organizations thus: "The bill is an abomination for America's most vulnerable mothers and children. It appears that Congress has wearied of the war on poverty and decided to wage war against poor people instead."[3]

But the debate was quickly smothered by electoral imperatives: one had to take care to not interfere with the president's reelection campaign. Indeed, having positioned himself mid-way between the ruling Republicans and the congressional Democrats in the wake of the crushing defeat of his camp in the 1994 elections, Clinton did not hesitate to use this law as one last instrument of blackmail against the left wing of his own party, in effect arguing: hush up and send me back to the White House since I am the only one who can soften the most nefarious effects of this "reform." Then there was the strong approval of the citizenry: polls showed that Americans supported "welfare reform" by huge margins of three-fourths and more—although a CBS and New York Times poll conducted around the time of the vote also revealed that 44 percent of the public admitted not knowing much if anything about its actual contents, only that it would "end welfare as we know it," the singsong moniker of the law, coined by Clinton in a campaign pledge of October 1991 intended to establish his credentials as a New Democrat.[4] As for the country's conservative forces, they could only rejoice at seeing the president rallying to their positions and endorsing a legislative plank similar in nearly every major respect to the two bills that he had vetoed just a few months earlier (but that was before the

---

like piece written by the former assistant secretary for planning and evaluation in his welfare administration. Peter Edelman, "The Worst Thing Bill Clinton Has Done," *Atlantic Monthly* 279, no. 3 (March 1997): 43–51.

opening of the electoral season).* Thus the US Chamber of Commerce, the nation's main employers' association, exulted that Clinton would thus reaffirm "America's work ethic," while Newt Gingrich, the leader of the Republicans in Congress, waxed lyrical in evoking "a historic moment where we are working together to do something very good for America."[5]

In Europe, and especially in England, Germany, and France, there was no shortage of popular and policy commentators, as hurried as they were ill informed, to present the measure as the courageous step forward of a "Left" president aiming at a necessary "adaptation" of social welfare schemes to the new economic realities. According to this vision, in which sheer ignorance of US realities rivals ideological bad faith, Clinton showed the way forward to the sclerotic societies of the Old World. He taught them that remaking "welfare" into "workfare" is the price to pay to achieve efficiency and success in the pitiless capitalist competition that now spans the globe. And that, although the transition is not painless, the poor will be the ultimate beneficiaries of this bold and broad policy innovation because it opens the gates of employment to them.[6]

In reality, the so-called reform of public aid was nothing of the sort. First, it was not a reform but a counterrevolutionary measure, since it essentially *abolished the right to assistance* for the country's most destitute children, which had required a half-century of struggles to fully establish, and replaced it with *the obligation of unskilled and underpaid wage labor* for their mothers in the short run. Second, it was not broad at all: it affected only a small sector of American social spending—the outlays targeted at dispossessed families, the disabled, and the indigent—while sparing much larger programs benefiting the middle and upper classes—usually gathered under the term "social insurance" in opposition to the reviled label of "welfare." The narrowness of the target of Clinton's move was widely overlooked by policy observers and pundits in Europe. This is a particular case of the *allodoxia* fostered by the uncontrolled reinterpretation (more often than not unconscious) to which a term of sociopolitical debates is subjected when it crosses over from one national framework to another or across the Atlantic. Thus European commentators translated "welfare" as "*État-*

*Political advisor and pollster Dick Morris counseled Clinton that a third veto of a "welfare reform" bill so close to the election would look like "presidential obstructionism" and might cost him his reelection by turning a fifteen-point lead over Bob Dole into a three-point deficit at the voting booth. R. Kent Weaver, *Ending Welfare As We Know It* (Washington, D.C.: Brookings Institution, 2000), 328.

providence" (*Wohlfarstaat, stato sociale, estado de bien-estar*), a term referring to the totality of government schemes of social protection and transfers with a universalist ambit, whereas Americans put under this label only means-tested programs reserved for populations eligible for state charity.

Finally, "welfare reform" was not bold: far from introducing novelty, it merely recycled remedies issued straight out of the country's colonial era even as these had amply demonstrated their ineffectiveness in the past:[7] namely, drawing a sharp demarcation between the "worthy" and the "unworthy" poor so as to force the latter into the inferior segments of the job market (irrespective of the availability and parameters of employment), and "correcting" the supposedly deviant and devious behaviors believed to cause persistent poverty in the first place. Under cover of a "reform" intended to benefit the poor, the Personal Responsibility and Work Opportunity Reconciliation Act of 1996 (PRWORA) instituted one of the most regressive social programs promulgated by a democratic government in the twentieth century. Its passage confirmed and accelerated the gradual replacement of a protective (semi-)welfare state by a disciplinary state mating the stinging goad of workfare with the dull hammer of prisonfare, for which the close monitoring and the punitive containment of derelict categories stand in for social policy toward the dispossessed.

The aim of this chapter is not to dissect the ins and outs of this latest avatar of the reorganization of American public relief per se, a task best left to the legions of scholars who have addressed the topic from myriad angles.[8] It is to spotlight selected aspects of this latest revamping of assistance in the United States that converge to treat—and in turn constitute—the dependent poor as a troublesome population to be subdued and "corrected" through stern behavioral controls and paternalistic sanctions, thus fostering a programmatic convergence with penal policy. I focus on the explicit intentions and the tacit missions of "welfare reform" as formulated in the debates, provisions, and initial implementation of the 1996 law. Several features of the overhaul of public aid at century's close both mirror and complement the workings of penal institutions: the narrow aiming of state action at the bottom of the class and caste hierarchies; the built-in gender slant; the practical presumption that recipients of welfare are "guilty until proven innocent" and that their conduct must be closely supervised as well as rectified by restrictive and coercive measures; and the deployment of deterrence and stigma to achieve behavioral modification. In the age of deregulated and underpaid labor, this law effectively assimilates welfare beneficiaries to *civic felons* for whom workfare will serve as an analogon of probation fit to ensure that they abide by the reaffirmed national norms of wage work and family morality, on pain of being effectively kept out of the citizenry.

Women and Children First, with Blacks as the New Villains

The proclaimed objective of PRWORA was to reduce not *poverty* but the alleged *dependency* of families on public aid, which means to trim the rolls and budgets of the programs devoted to supporting the most vulnerable members of American society: the women and children of the precarious fractions of the proletariat,[9] and secondarily the indigent elderly and recent immigrants (in keeping with the built-in class duality and other peculiarities of the US bureaucratic field outlined in chapter 2).

Indeed, the 1996 "reform" left untouched Medicare, the health coverage for retired wage earners, and Social Security, the national retirement fund, even though these programs are far and away the two largest items on the social spending ledger of the US state, with $143 billion and $419 billion respectively in 1994. It bore exclusively on targeted programs reserved for poor people receiving direct income or in-kind support: Aid to Families with Dependent Children (AFDC), Supplemental Security Income (SSI, benefits granted to the indigent, or disabled elderly), and Food Stamps. Now, these programs covered only a fraction of the population officially classified as deprived: in 1996, 39 million Americans lived below the federal "poverty line" (about $16,000 per year for a family of four), but fewer than 13 million (among them 9 million children) received AFDC payments.* In 1992, only 43 percent of the families officially designated as poor received income assistance, 51 percent garnered food stamps, and a mere 18 percent benefited from housing assistance.[10] It is the recipients of AFDC and food stamps who bore the costs of the "reform," even though these programs were twelve times less costly than those directed mostly at the middle and upper classes, with $22 billion going to AFDC (combining federal and local spending) and $23 billion to food stamps. For the 1996 law planned to save $56 billion over five years by reducing payments, capping disbursements, and excluding millions from entitlements—among them a majority of children and elderly people without means.

*In addition, 69 million Americans, including 6 million full-time workers and 5.5 million part-time wage earners, lived in households posting annual incomes coming to less than 150 percent of the poverty threshold.

How does a society in which every other lone mother and one child in four (over 13 million youngsters, including 10 million without any social or medical coverage) lived below the official "poverty line" in 1995 manage to convince itself that the penury that afflicts so many of its most defenseless members is a consequence of their individual failings? The answer to this query is found in the *moral individualism* that undergirds the national ethos and the tenacious ideology of gender and the family that makes poor unwed mothers (and fatherless children) into abnormal, truncated, suspect beings who threaten the moral order and whom the state must therefore place under harsh tutelage.[11]

The poverty of these anomalous families is perceived as a "virus" whose diffusion must be circumscribed if it cannot be stopped, the living precipitate of an indelible and contagious blemish of the self, a foreign "enemy" upon whom one wages "war." The din of endlessly recycled discourses on the imputed immorality of single mothers is matched only by the resounding silence on the steep class inequalities, abiding sex discrimination, and perverse demands of a paternalistic bureaucracy that conspire to keep them in a situation of persistent social insecurity and marginality.

Historian Linda Gordon has described how, since the dawn of the twentieth century, the dilemma of single mothers has been conceived as a clinical problem: they are "morally bad for themselves as well as for their children and for society" because of their inner deficiencies.[12] In her book *Lives on the Edge*, Valerie Polakow traces the trajectories of fifteen young single mothers in Michigan and recounts narratives of their children's daily lives at school to show how these century-old representations and the assistance programs they inform entangle these women in an administrative snare that turns the myth of the bad mother into a self-fulfilling prophecy. Bad mothers they are if they work since they then violate the patriarchal norm that designates the household as the natural sphere of women and sacrifice the care of their offspring to the pursuit of a meager income outside the home. Bad mothers they are if they do not work since then they "live off the state" and, in so doing, inculcate in their little ones the habits of the social parasite.[13] The 1996 public assistance "reform" cut through this alternative by resolutely favoring the second reading, giving clear priority to the imperative of wage labor (or its surrogates and similes: training programs, apprenticeships, or volunteer work in the not-for-profit sector that will count administratively as make-work or mock-work) over the maternal duty of raising children, based in part on the doctrine of "gender sameness" favored by middle-class women.*

*This latter point is stressed by Ann Orloff, "Explaining US Welfare Reform: Power, Gender, Race and the US Policy Legacy," *Critical Social Policy* 22, no. 2 (February

> But above all, whether they turn to the state or the market, dispossessed women in the United States find themselves condemned to chronic poverty. In 1990, every other single mother received no financial support from the father of her children due to the laxity and disorganization of social services; and those who did receive alimony had to make do with a bare average of $2,100 per year. A wage worker toiling full-time, year-round at the minimum wage earned a mere $700 per month, coming 20 percent below the poverty line for a family of three. A mother who opted for AFDC so that her children would at least have medical coverage received a national average of $367 per month, an amount coming by design to less than 55 percent of the "poverty line." Far from relieving it, then, America's charitable state bears primary responsibility for the feminization and infantilization of poverty in that country: it actively perpetuates both its brute realities and its enduring myths, the material foundations upon which it rests and the warped representations in which it lives.

These draconian measures are popular with the core electorate—of the white working and middle classes—because "welfare" is perceived as essentially benefiting lower-class blacks, that is, coddling a population of shady civic standing owing to its alleged flaws in the twofold register of the work ethic and family values.[14] It matters little that a plurality of public aid beneficiaries at any one time (and a majority over time) are actually of European descent: 39 percent of the "stock" of AFDC recipients in 1995 were white, as against 35 percent African American and 18 percent Hispanic; and that the proportion of black recipients decreased steadily from 1969 (when it peaked at 45 percent) to 1996. The country's *idée fixe* remains that assistance to the poor serves mostly to keep inner-city mothers mired in idleness and vice, and to encourage among them the "antisocial behaviors" denoted and denounced by the semischolarly tale of the loathsome "underclass."[15]

This collective perception is a late ethnic reversal of the twentieth-century pattern and a direct fallout of the surging black mobilization against caste rule leading to the race riots that shook America's big cities in the mid-1960s. Prior to 1964, African-American deprivation had been nearly invisible on the national stage. Thus the central characters of Michael Harrington's *The Other America*, the 1962 book conventionally credited with catalyzing the policy debate that culminated with

---

2002), 96–118. A different diagnosis spotlighting the unresolved tension between the "Work Plan" and the "Family Plan" coexisting in tension inside the workfare agenda is given by Sharon Hays, *Flat Broke with Children: Women in the Age of Welfare Reform* (New York: Oxford University Press, 2003), esp. 18–24 and 32–93.

the declaration of the ill-named War on poverty, were not urban blacks but rural whites of the Appalachian hollows.[16] Right after the Watts uprising and the wave of ghetto upheavals it ushered, however, poverty came to be consistently painted with a black face in the mass media. As the poor grew darker in the collective conscience, they were also cast in an increasingly unsympathetic and lurid light, as irresponsible, profligate, and dissolute. And public assistance was swiftly depicted as a "welfare mess" steadily worsening into the insuperable "welfare crisis" of the 1990s calling for an authoritarian makeover of social policy. In news magazines for instance, the share of blacks in major stories on poverty between 1967 and 1995 came to 62 percent, double their share in stories of the 1950s as well as double their weight in the national population living under the poverty line.[17]

The close association between categorical assistance programs and race in the public mind rendered these programs especially vulnerable on the political front. It made it possible to mobilize against this sector of the charitable state the force of racial animus and class prejudice which, in combination, turn the ghetto poor into social leeches, if not veritable "enemies" of American society.[18] Indeed, as the image of poverty got blacker on television and in the press, white hostility toward welfare surged. It should be noted here that this racial dimension of welfare "reform," thinly euphemized but ubiquitous in American political debate—at the media ceremony on the White House lawn marking the signing of the bill into law, President Clinton was flanked by a matronly black recipient of AFDC—went completely unnoticed by European commentators.* Moreover, the racial connection reveals a direct causal parallelism and chronological coincidence between the changing symbolic construction of problem populations at the bottom of the socioracial order and the punitive turn taken by the US state on both the social and penal fronts. Following the ghetto mutinies of the 1960s, the diffusion of racialized images of urban destitution went hand in hand with rising resentment toward public aid which bolstered (white) demand for *restrictive* welfare measures centered on deterrence and compulsion. During the same period, the spread of blackened images of crime—even as the share of African Americans in the offending population was decreasing—fed mounting animosity toward

*It is telling, *a contrario*, that Rebecca Blank lists the fact that "racial issues are becoming more prominent in Europe" due to postcolonial immigration among the factors that (should) make "welfare reform" more useful, attractive, and applicable in Old-World nations. Rebecca Blank, "U.S. Welfare Reform: What's Relevant for Europe?" *Economic Studies* 49, no. 1 (January 2003): 49–74, at 69.

criminals and fostered (white) support for *expansive* prison policies narrowly aimed at retribution and neutralization.[19]

The primary justification for the steep cuts in public aid proffered by PRWORA was that welfare support is too generous, that it saps the will to work of its beneficiaries, and sustains a "culture of dependency" as harmful to them as it is to the country, and that this culture in turn explains the rise of out-of-wedlock births and the string of pathologies that allegedly come with them. This justification has been reiterated with minor inflections throughout the past century each time the question of poverty relief has surged onto the national political scene—some analysts trace it all the way back to the colonial founding of the country and even earlier, in Edwardian England wracked by the problem of vagrancy.[20] In the debate leading to the 1996 "reform," four racialized figures coalesced into a new controlling image of the issue by offering vivid incarnations of "dependency" and its corrosive consequences: (i) the "welfare queen," a wily and fecund black matriarch who shirks employment, cheats the public aid bureaucracy, and spends her assistance check high on drugs and liquor, leaving her many children in appalling neglect; (ii) the African-American teenage mother, a "baby having babies" often raised on welfare herself, whose immaturity is matched only by her moral depravity and dissolute sexuality; (iii) the lower-class "deadbeat dad," typically black and unemployed, who impregnates women left and right and flippantly abandons them and his offspring to the care of taxpayers; (iv) and the elderly immigrant from the Third World who slips into the United States to manipulate welfare into a cost-free high-class retirement.[21] This caricatural quartet, orchestrated by an endless stream of journalistic, political, and scholarly reports, was presented as living proof of the fundamentally corrupting nature of public assistance.*

In reality, as we pointed out in the preceding chapter, the real value of AFDC payments declined by one-half over the quarter-century leading to the deletion of the program, melting from a national average of \$676 per month in 1970 to some \$342 in 1995 (in constant dollars of 1995), a sum coming to less than half the poverty line. This means that the households which received welfare could hardly "depend" on it and

*The obsessive focus on these four figures, led by the flamboyant "welfare queen," is also instrumental in obfuscating the fact that AFDC beneficiaries are overwhelmingly *children and not adults* (8.8 million as against 3.9 million in 1996). This means that the negative consequences of welfare reform would be borne, not by wastrels who shirk their moral duties, but primarily by minors who can hardly be held accountable to norms of work, sexuality, and matrimony (and made to pay for the putative errant conduct of their parents).

were forced to tap other sources of income to subsist. In point of fact, a majority of AFDC recipients were engaged in some paid activity, legal or illegal, formal or informal, and they toiled hard to make ends meet in the 1990s.[22] In a detailed study of the budgets and income-generating strategies of 379 women receiving AFDC in four cities in 1994, Edin and Stein found that 39 percent worked off the books in the regular economy, and 8 percent toiled in underground trades, while fully 77 percent received unreported income from kin and partners, both absent and cohabiting with them sub rosa.[23] In short, all relied on welfare but none could depend on it. And, as meager as welfare was, unskilled single mothers who moved into the job market often did worse than on public aid due to the added costs in transportation, child care, apparel, and health care occasioned by joining the unprotected labor force. What is more, over half of welfare recipients nationwide left the program within a year of getting on the rolls, and two-thirds exited it within two years. This is because the vast majority of recipients intensely dislike receiving aid, disapprove of members of their family doing so, and find the material deprivation, social burdens, and cultural stigma associated with being on the rolls simply unbearable. Similarly, the prevalent notion that most children who grow up on welfare land on the assistance rolls as adults is empirically unfounded: only 20 percent of daughters raised in a highly dependent household (e.g., drawing over one-fourth of its income from welfare payments) became reliant on public aid at some point in adulthood, and they did so not because they got habituated to welfare but because, like their parents, they faced a closed opportunity structure.[24] So much to say that AFDC was hardly a "way of life," transmitted across generations in the manner of a genetic disease, as alleged by neoconservative ideologues and their epigones among the New Democrats.

On paper, the "reform" endorsed by Clinton aimed at "moving people from welfare to work." But, to begin with, most mothers on assistance were already engaged in gainful activity, albeit on the margins of the workforce. Next—and this is revealing of the intentions of the legislators—*the law had absolutely no jobs component.* Not one of its eight titles addressed economic issues.* Not a single measure in the law was aimed at improving the employment options and conditions faced by

*These titles concern: (1) the establishment of TANF, (2) restrictions on SSI, (3) the enforcement of child support, (4) the exclusion of aliens from public benefits, (5) child protective services, (6) child nutrition programs, (7) food stamps and hunger prevention, and (8) a grab bag of miscellaneous measures, including drug testing of recipients, the elimination of assistance to drug offenders, and abstinence education.

welfare recipients. No budget for job training and job creation figured in it. State governments were given pecuniary incentives to devise plans to meet preset quotas of caseload reduction and work participation, but such plans would center entirely on the "personal reformation" of dispossessed single mothers through "readiness workshops" designed to teach them mainstream cultural norms and work submissiveness, as if poverty and joblessness were caused by "fear of failing, dependency, bad attitude, a sense of entitlement, the victim mentality, and low self-esteem."[25]

Advocates of PRWORA have weighed in exclusively on the "push" side of the transition from assistance to earnings without concern for the absence of "pull" from the work side. The new legislation never addresses the dearth of jobs, the subpoverty wages, the instability of employment, and the lack of protection and ancillary supports such as transportation at the bottom of the labor market. It concentrates on making public aid beneficiaries "work ready" while disregarding the fact that the jobs that single mothers find or need are themselves not "mother ready."[26] The $3.8 billion in subsidies for child care (spread out over six years) penciled in the law were little more than a drop in the ocean of needs in this regard. The "work opportunity" to which the legislators made copious reference, enshrined in the title of the act, was left entirely to the benevolence of employers. During the final phase of the 1996 presidential campaign, Clinton made a resounding appeal to the civic conscience of corporations, churches, and philanthropic organizations so that they would "create the jobs necessary for the reform to succeed," arguing that employers who ceaselessly complain about welfare have a moral obligation to hire its (former) clients. But it is hard to see how and why businesses would suddenly rush to employ en masse a sorely underqualified population—one-half of AFDC recipients did not graduate from high school, and only 1 percent held a university degree—that is moreover severely stigmatized when the market was already awash with cheap labor.[27]

Based on telephone interviews with a representative sample of 800 employers in each of four metropolitan areas chosen to control for regional and demographic variations (Atlanta, Boston, Detroit, and Los Angeles), economist Harry Holzer analyzed the volume and tenor of the jobs offered to low-education workers, their spatial distribution (downtown, inner city, suburbs near to, or far from, the city center), the type of skills required by firms which hire, and the starting wages of the employees recruited.[28] The results of his study, published in March 1996, just as the final phase of the welfare debate was gearing up, show that blacks residing in the ghettoized districts of the metropolis cumulate all possible obstacles. Not only are there fewer jobs in the central city than at its periphery, but 80 percent of these jobs are in the service sectors requiring a level of education that far exceeds their own. Most of these job vacancies are filled through informal channels via personal recommendation and trustworthy connections—which the inner-city poor typically lack. Moreover, employers tend to screen out applicants with a spotty employment history or a criminal justice record (an issue we revisit in chapter 5). Finally, racial discrimination persists to the detriment of young black men in particular, who are "last hired and first fired" in nearly all sectors of the economy and whose pay rates remain abysmally low (generally well below the official poverty line).[29] Before bill HR 3734 turned into PRWORA, then, one could clearly foresee the bleak socioeconomic future that awaited welfare recipients forcibly pushed into the inferior segments of the precarious and underpaid job market which they would enter with every handicap.

A comprehensive report prepared for the US Department of Health and Human Services under the Bush administration in May of 2004 would later confirm that somber picture. Its major findings are that the employers prepared to tap the new labor pool constituted by recipients of TANF (Temporary Assistance to Needy Families, the aptly named successor to Aid to Families with Dependent Children) are "concentrated in specific types of firms," namely, large companies in the urban service sector looking for employees "to fill jobs with irregular work hours, low pay and benefits, and nonstandard job arrangements."

These firms hire welfare leavers "primarily to meet business objectives, not to provide a public service" and they "are skeptical of TANF recipients' 'soft skills,'" that is, the "positive outlook, conscientiousness, teamwork, and ability to adapt to workplace norms" that workfare programs concentrate on drilling into their clients. Employers "worry that recipients face significant barriers—such as poor academic preparation, transportation and child care problems, and mental illness and substance abuse—that limit their on-the-job effectiveness and increase the chance of job turnover."[30] And they have no intention to tackle these obstacles themselves for the simple reason that the low-wage labor pool is copious, and they can simply keep recruiting more laborers as they turn over. This means that, absent massive state support and continuing services to help the poor hanging on to the margins of the employment market, they will keep churning in and out of the workforce without ever gaining a firm foothold in the regular economy and thus be in a position to stabilize their household.

The new law was similarly careful to avoid confronting the economic causes of poverty: the stagnation of the median household income and the uninterrupted decline of the real value of the minimum wage over the previous two decades (from $6.50 in 1978 to $4.25 in 1996 in constant dollars of 1996); the explosive growth of so-called contingent jobs, which make up over one-quarter of the country's labor force at century's close; the erosion of social and medical coverage for low-skill workers; the persistence of astronomical unemployment rates in the neighborhoods of relegation of the big cities as well as in remote rural counties; and the pronounced reluctance of employers to hire ghetto residents and deskilled welfare recipients.[31] It is more expedient, and more profitable electorally, to pitch vituperative portrayals of the poor that alternately feed and tap the resentment of the electorate toward those who receive "handouts" from the state.

Bringing the Poor to Heel

The ponderous brick of more than 251 pages composed in 913 sections, signed into law by President Clinton in August 1996, whose architecture is so byzantine that no one can fully master its logic or grasp all of its ramifications, is based on four principles which, together, cast persistent poverty as an outlaw status to be dealt with through paternalist supervision and deterrence, and effectively shift the burden of coping with destitution onto the most deprived individuals and their families.

First, the law *abrogates the right to assistance* enjoyed by lone mothers with young children under the Social Security Act of 1935.* In its stead, it stipulates the obligation for parents on assistance to work within two years as well as sets a lifetime cap of five years of support. Once this personal "quota" is reached, a mother without resources whose children are over five years old no longer has access to assistance from the state: she has to accept whatever job is available or to turn to family support, begging, criminal activities, or the informal economy of the

*The law is crystal clear on this point. Section 433 of PRWORA specifies in its paragraph (a), article 1: "Nothing in this title may be construed as an entitlement or a determination of an individual's eligibility or fulfillment of the requisite requirements for any Federal, State, or local governmental program, assistance, or benefits." Personal Responsibility and Work Reconciliation Act of 1996, 171. The full text of the law is available online at the Library of Congress site: http://thomas.loc.gov/cgi-bin/query/z?c104:H.R.3734.ENR:htm.

street.* By eliminating welfare as an entitlement, PRWORA reversed a major plank of the "legal rights revolution" of the 1960s that had enabled poor Americans to call on the federal courts to extract the delivery of minimal public goods from state and local bureaucracies. This legal regression on the social welfare front parallels the mounting legislative restrictions enacted in the 1990s on inmates' use of the judicial system to obtain the enforcement of their fundamental rights behind bars. Not coincidentally, it was also in 1996 that Congress passed the Prison Litigation Reform Act that sharply curtailed convicts' access to the federal courts (it cut the number of cases by 40 percent in six years even as the inmate population kept growing).[32]

Secondly, *the federal government devolves responsibility for assistance* to the fifty states and, through them, to the 3,034 counties entrusted with setting eligibility criteria, disbursing payments, and establishing the job search and support programs necessary to "move people to work" (inasmuch as they come up with the funds necessary to underwrite them). Within this decentralized framework, states and counties have all latitude to impose more restrictive conditions than those stipulated by the federal law. A number of them hastened to use it to lower lifetime eligibility from five to two years and to delete various categories of benefits. A few weeks after the passage of the Personal Responsibility Act, Governor Engler of Michigan, who yearned to make his state a "national model for welfare reform," proposed cutting all assistance to poor mothers who would not work within six weeks of giving birth and to reduce benefits by 25 percent for all participants who would fail to be gainfully employed within two months of getting on the rolls. This is hardly surprising, since the law sets up an elaborate system of financial rewards and penalties that encourages states to use all means necessary to cut the number of recipients, 25 percent of whom had to be "put to work" in the year following passage of the law and 50 percent by 2002. The definition of "work" entailed here (wage labor in the private sector, a subsidized public job, attending a training program, etc.) remains hazy and is to be determined by each state within the framework of a contractual agreement with the federal government. The minimum number of hours worked per week was set at twenty during the first year and thirty afterward.

*Remarkably, the device of lifetime limits on public aid receipt was first proposed, not by right-wing detractors of the welfare state, but by liberal intellectuals smitten with the notion of "individual responsibility": Columbia social work professor Irwin Garfinkel, Princeton sociologist Sarah McLanahan, and Harvard economist David Ellwood all advocated it in the 1980s. Joel F. Handler, *The Poverty of Welfare Reform* (New Haven, Conn.: Yale University Press, 1995), 3 and 153.

Now, the public aid budgets of the states were already falling fast by the time welfare "reform" came through, and everything indicated that they would continue to decline in real terms.[33] The possibility of turning a portion of welfare payments into subsidies for employers who agree to hire recipients resolves nothing. It only shifts what meager public monies circulate from the pockets of the poor to the coffers of firms. This also guarantees that, for fear of attracting welfare recipients from neighboring areas as well as to satisfy the fiscal and moral rigorism of their electorate, states will follow the lead of the least generous of them, and further pare their programs for the dispossessed (whose voice in public debate is muted as they scarcely vote). Those who would doubt this reasoning can ponder this precedent: when responsibility for psychiatric hospitals was transferred from Washington to the states in the 1970s, local governments hastened to close them down and turn their patients out onto the street, swelling the flood of the homeless and human flotsam who have been haunting America's cities ever since. A decade later, it was estimated that 80 percent of the country's homeless had gone through an establishment for mental health care.[34] When it comes to programs for the poor, devolution implies bureaucratic retrenchment leading to the reduction of services from the social wing of the state, which in turn necessitates an extension of those services provided by its penal wing to "mop up" the ensuing public troubles.

"The patients we examine in jails are the same ones we used to examine in psychiatric hospitals" twenty years ago, explains a former head of the psychiatric ward of the clinic of Men's Central Jail in Los Angeles (the largest in the country).[35] In the wake of the policy of closure of large public hospitals, the number of patients in the country's asylums plummeted from 559,000 in 1955 to 69,000 forty years later. In theory, these patients were to receive ambulatory care from community health centers.[36] But the local clinics expected to replace the asylums never materialized due to the absence of public funding, while the existing health centers withered away as private insurance balked at picking up the slack and the federal medical net was reduced—just as the number of Americans stripped of health coverage rose to record highs.

The *"deinstitutionalization" of the mentally ill in the medical sector* of the state thus translated into their *"reinstitutionalization" in the criminal justice sector*, after they had transitioned through more or less extended periods of homelessness. Indeed, the majority of infractions for which they are put under lock are public order offenses that are little more than the practical manifestation of their psychological impairment.[37] Mentally ill persons have thus filled the bottom rung of the overgrown carceral system, creating insuperable dilemmas for the managers of custodial establishments who have to cope as best they can with the consequences of the shift from the medical to the penal treatment of mental afflictions in the nether regions of social space.

Thirdly—and this is at once the most anodyne and the most consequential mechanism in the medium run—after 1996 welfare budgets are set, not as a function of the needs of the populations served, but by *fixed endowments* called "block grants." The amount allotted to TANF for the country as a whole was pegged at $16.3 billion per year until 2002. This means that federal welfare outlays can no longer play a countercyclical role. If unemployment and poverty rise suddenly, due for instance to a recession or swift demographic changes, states must face rising demand for assistance with stagnant means—or reduced means since the computation of TANF allocations also does not take inflation into account. This technical device, whose purpose is to cap the level of public assistance outlays irrespective of external pressures to raise it, is bound to sharpen the tensions between the counties and cities of a state confronted with a resurgence of visible poverty without the resources to meet it. And so it cannot but reinforce the tendency toward "defensive localism," which is one of the main causes of the extreme concentration of destitution in the American metropolis.[38]

Finally, the new public assistance law squarely *excludes from the welfare rolls*, including medical assistance to the indigent, an assortment of categories shorn of the means of exerting political pressure: foreign residents who arrived within the preceding six years (even when they pay taxes and social premiums), persons convicted of narcotics offenses under federal law, poor children suffering from disabilities (315,000 of them would lose all benefits in the six years following the passage of the law), and teen mothers who refuse to live with their parents. On the pretext of promoting marriage, PRWORA allows states to deny aid to unwed mothers under eighteen and to children born while their parents were on welfare. It also rolls back payments to mothers receiving assistance who decline to identify the father of one of their children and prohibits adults with neither resources nor offspring from receiving food stamps for more than six cumulative months over a period of three years. And these are only the most visible elements of a vast web of "disentitlement strategies" aimed at occluding the channels for distributing assistance.[39] One such strategy consists in redefining medical conditions that qualify as disability in a restrictive manner: such was the jolly task undertaken by the public aid offices of two dozen states after passage of the law, with the goal of "reclassifying" thousands of disabled people as fit for work, and therefore barred from assistance.

The Personal Responsibility and Work Opportunity Reconciliation Act came on line in July 1997 but did not begin to exercise its full effects until the fall of 2002, when the five-year cut-off period was reached by the first wave of recipients, many of whom found themselves stripped of all support. Its provisions are so numerous, complex, and contradictory that it is difficult to this day to ascertain exactly how and at what pace they have been applied and with what effects. All the more so since states were granted considerable leeway in adapting them (and in escaping some of them through "opt-out clauses"). Welfare rights organizations as well as the mayors of big cities penalized by the exclusion of immigrants from assistance also enrolled the judicial apparatus to thwart the implementation of the act. Thus the Republican mayor of New York, Rudolph Giuliani—who waged a merciless campaign against the poor of his own municipality during his two terms in office[40]—rose up against the measure in 1996, arguing stridently that it violates the federal constitution. He opposed the federal law because it threatened to throw tens of thousands of New Yorkers of foreign origin onto the street while New York State law obligates counties (including that of New York City over which he presided) to provide assistance to "persons in distress." The behavior of the poor and their families, public bureaucracies, charitable organizations, and private firms have all changed in myriad ways to adjust to the new system of incentives and constraints created by the "reform" of welfare. It is well established that, when it comes to social policy, projections are not predictions.[41] Nevertheless, it was not hard to anticipate the main effects of the law, *ceteris paribus*—and especially holding constant the state of the labor market.

It was expected at the time of its passing that PRWORA would, first of all, cause a further drop in the living standards of the poorest American families, since the law dictated a reduction in the real value and accessibility of assistance. According to projections drawn up by the Department of Health and Human Services, 2.5 to 3.5 million indigent children would be denied support by 2002 solely through the enforcement of the five-year lifetime cap, even as the United States already sports the highest child poverty rate in the Western world: one child in four—and one black child in two—grows up below the "poverty line" in America, as against 6 percent in France, Germany, and Italy, and 3 percent in Scandinavian countries.[42] On January 1, 1997, half-a-million foreign residents were slated to lose the modest assistance they had hitherto received, the "Supplemental Security Income" check of $420 per month granted to the disabled or blind elderly. A study by the Center on Budget and Policy Priorities computed that households subsisting below *one-half of the poverty line* (that is, making do with less than $7,800 per year for four people) would bear half of the cuts to the food stamp program ($23 billion over six years) and that some 300,000 immigrant children would thereby lose their nutrition assistance.

By throwing hundreds of thousands of readily exploitable new applicants onto the peripheral segments of the labor market, welfare "reform" promised to further depress the level of wages for unskilled workers, thus swelling the ranks of the "working poor."[43] The informal economy of the street was bound to experience a growth spurt, and with it the criminality and insecurity that eat away at the fabric of daily life in the collapsing ghetto. The ranks of homeless persons and families was set to swell, as was the number of indigents and sick people left without care, since the new law prohibits hospitals from offering free medical treatment to drug addicts or prenatal care to women convicted of narcotics possession or sale, among other restrictions. Cities would be in a position to weaken the last trade unions to retain a modicum of influence, those of municipal employees, by threatening to replace local functionaries in low-level positions with the free person-power provided by the forced-work programs that welfare recipients would be required to join.

Eight years after its passage, the results of welfare "reform" are as contrasting as they are controversial.[44] Neither the providential prophecies of work and dignity for all Americans proffered by the advocates of PRWORA, nor the catastrophic predictions of explosive poverty swamping America's cities made by the opponents of the law have come true. This was foreseeable, to the degree that both sides exaggerated the "dependency" of AFDC recipients on state support, the former better to indict welfare and the latter better to salvage it. In reality, as we stressed above, no indigent family could rely on an assistance program that, by design, was woefully insufficient to provide it with minimal material security. But several additional factors have combined to derail both of these antipodean previsions.

First of all, the effects of the new law have been scrambled and submerged by five years of economic prosperity without precedent in recent U.S. history. The stupendous rise in national income driven by the real estate and stock-market boom between 1996 and 2000 (the average income reported by taxpayers jumped from $43,000 in 1995 to $55,700 in 2000 in constant dollars of 2004) and the resulting tightening of the labor market (the official unemployment rate approached 3 percent in 1999) improved the lot of lower-class Americans and accelerated the ongoing reduction of welfare outlays and rolls, *independently of any modification of that policy.** Next, a number of states had already, on their own initiative, undertaken for many years experiments similar to the federal measures enshrined into law in 1996, on the one hand, and some fifteen states chose to remain outside the framework of the new legislation until 2002, on the other. At the end of 2003, Kansas, Massachusetts, Montana, Nebraska, and Oregon, as well as South Carolina, Tennessee, Virginia, and Hawaii, continued to be exempt from many of the stipulations of PRWORA. Moreover, due to the general prosperity, 28 of the 50 members of the Union elected to use their own funds to extend benefits beyond the sixty months authorized by TANF, while two more eliminated time limits on aid entirely, thus softening the harshest provisions of the new regime.[45] In 1997 Congress voted to raise the minimum wage from $4.25 to $5.15. It also improved child support enforcement and collection, doubling the share of poor single mothers receiving income from absent fathers over a decade. Finally and most importantly, the sudden economic boom and the unexpected budget surpluses it generated made it possible for states to increase subsidies for childcare and transportation, and to extend state-sponsored medical coverage and income support in the peripheral sectors of the job market: the Earned Income Tax Credit was expanded to where it subsidized the earnings of a low-income parent by up to 40 percent by 2003.[46] This means that the United States surreptitiously implemented an *active labor market policy*, paradoxically, at the very moment when it was swinging "from welfare to workfare" during a phase of general prosperity.

Disregarding the exceptionally favorable conjuncture in which it was launched and the many ways in which its early implementation flouted its core principles, advocates of the new disciplinary policy of social assistance have gloated over its evident "success" by pointing to *one and only one statistic* (revealing of its singular objective): the spectacular decline in the number of recipients. From this Malthusian perspective, the triumph of welfare "reform" is incontrovertible, as that figure

*The respective causal weights of economic trends and policy reform in accounting for the sharp decline in public aid receipt is a matter of dispute, but early research gives a decisive edge to the economy. Of nine major econometric studies conducted by 2000, three concluded that welfare changes had virtually no impact (due to a pattern of sluggish caseload adjustment), with the economy explaining 80 percent of the drop in the rolls; the six that granted reform an influence estimated that it accounted for only 15–35 percent of the outcome, compared to 25–50 percent for the economy. Stephen Bell, *Why Are Welfare Caseloads Falling?* New Federalism Discussion Paper (Washington, D.C.: The Urban Institute, 2001).

plunged from 12.7 million in 1996 to 6.5 million in 2001, barely 2.3 percent of the national population (the lowest share recorded since 1969), and down to 5 million by mid-2003. But what became of the 2.7 million adults and 5 million children who previously received assistance?

One need only follow their trajectories after they "exited" the welfare rolls to realize that the springboard of workfare hardly enabled them to escape material poverty and social insecurity. In 2003, over 40 percent of the household heads leaving TANF had not found work and were forced to turn to kin support, the informal economy or criminal endeavors to subsist. Among the 60 percent who had found a job thanks to the economic bang of the late 1990s, the vast majority worked part-time, most lacked medical and social insurance, and they earned an average of seven dollars an hour[47]—keeping them well below the federal poverty line.* What is more, a large share of Americans pushed off of welfare lost their access to Medicaid and food stamps, even though they continued to be entitled to them in principle: eight in ten families living with an income less than half the poverty line received all the assistance for which they were eligible in 1995; this proportion had dropped to one in two five years later. Reforming welfare clearly succeeded in sharply increasing disentitlement. Thus it was estimated that in 2002 around one-third of the welfare population had left the rolls due to bureaucratic sanctions and discouragement in the face of a tedious and abusive process. A field study reports that out of every 100 persons walking through the door of the new-style welfare office to apply for aid, 25 are diverted at entry; of the 75 filling an application, 25 will be discouraged or evicted within weeks, leaving only 50 pursuing the process.[48]

Finally and most importantly, former welfare recipients pushed toward compulsory work display "profiles in hardship" virtually identical to those of their compatriots who had received or still receive assistance. In 1997, 34 percent of TANF recipients experienced "critical situations" in terms of housing, food, and access to healthcare; this was the case for 35 percent of those who had recently "exited" the welfare rolls and for 30 percent of former recipients thrust back onto the deskilled labor market more than one year earlier.[49] That same year, as

*An hourly wage of seven dollars yields a gross annual income of $14,000, 22 percent below the poverty line for a family with two children after deductions and before taxes ($14,348 in 2002). Note, moreover, that the said line is abysmally low since current consumption needs put the minimal budget for a household of two adults with two children at $33,511. Heather Boushey, Chauna Brocht, Bethney Gundersen, and Jared Bernstein, *Hardship in America: The Real Story of Working Families* (Washington, D.C.: EPI Books, 2001), 8–17 and 52–55.

Republican and Democratic politicians joined in the chorus singing the praises of welfare "reform," one-quarter of former AFDC beneficiaries who had ended up with part-time work were forced to skip meals regularly, 57 percent worried about not being able to feed their families, and 21 percent had to forego urgent medical care. The situation of ex-recipients who had found *full-time* work was scarcely less precarious, since 30 percent did not earn an income sufficient to cover their rent, 46 percent worried about getting enough food, and 11 percent had had their phones cut off for failing to pay their bills.[50]

A series of evaluation studies conducted by the Urban Institute confirms that, contrary to the dominant discourse, America's subproletarians are far from moving smoothly from "welfare as a way of life" to the world of work as vector of material security, personal betterment, and social dignity. By 2002, only 40 percent of those "leaving" TANF held a job—down from 50 percent in 1999, at the height of the boom. Over one-quarter returned to the TANF rolls within a year, while 14 percent were listed as "disconnected" (without a job, assistance, or any other means of survival identified by the study). The others remained in situations of definite dependency or insecurity: 8 percent had a spouse who was employed (most often at the bottom of the occupational ladder); 7 percent were unemployed or had recently worked; and 4 percent were receiving SSI payments for the disabled and the blind. Moreover, the percentage of those "returning to assistance" within a year after their alleged transition to work increased by one-fourth between 1999 and 2002. This prompted the Urban Institute to remark coyly that "the early employment success of welfare reform is moderating."[51] It would be more accurate to say that the 1996 law failed to break the long-established pattern of cycling in and out of public assistance, except that now the cycle will eventually end due to lifetime limits.

Among the recipients who had "successfully" joined the labor market, over one-third held a part-time job; one-quarter worked nights, weekends, or irregular hours; and one in nine were working at least two jobs to make ends meet, while two-thirds had no medical coverage. The gross median wage of former welfare recipients on payrolls was $8.06 per hour, barely above the hourly minimum and far below the wage rate needed to lift a family of three above the poverty line (around $11 per hour). Lastly, it should be stressed that it is an administrative artifice—and a political abuse—to describe those "leaving" TANF as no longer dependent on public assistance, since in 2002 two-thirds of them, including those employed, continued to rely on Medicaid for their children, and 48 percent were on Medicaid for themselves, while 35 percent received food stamps (more than in 1999, when these rates were 57, 40, and 28 percent, respectively).[52]

As for the former beneficiaries reported as "disconnected," 55 percent of whom had not finished high school and 41 percent suffered from serious physical or mental disabilities, seven in ten worried about not being able to cover their food expenses and half about paying rent while 63 percent did not have enough cash left to feed their families at the end of the month. This pattern of acute socioeconomic marginality is confirmed by soup kitchens, which have witnessed an explosive growth in demand since 1996: the Salvation Army served 51 million free meals in 1997; this figure was nearing 65 million by 2003. A recent research report focusing on households pushed off public assistance notes charitably: "Helping disconnected families poses a difficult challenge. Welfare offices may not even know who these families are, since offices do not necessarily follow up on those that leave welfare. Some families may have lost benefits because of mental or physical problems that render them unable to navigate the system. Misinformation and administrative hassles may have prevented other families from regaining benefits."[53]

One truly remarkable fact stands out in the sea of statistics generated by studies of the fallout of welfare "reform": while the number of aid recipients dropped dramatically, *the national poverty rate has remained nearly unchanged.* The percentage of Americans living below the federal poverty line dipped slightly from 13.7 percent in 1996 to 11.3 percent in 2000 before climbing back to 12.7 in 2004, following closely the curve of national economic trends—as it did before the "reform" of public aid endorsed by Clinton.[54] And while the overall *level* of poverty has stagnated despite the boom and the alleged success of welfare "reform," the *intensity* of poverty has *increased*: in 2002, the gap between the average income of poor households and the federal poverty line (taking into account housing support, food stamps, and in-kind assistance) came to $2,813, which is 23 percent *more* than in 1996 in constant dollars.[55] This intensification is corroborated by the detectible rise in the ranks of the homeless and users of soup kitchens in big cities across the country. It is hardly surprising that new-style public aid remedies a declining share of the deepest poverty in the country considering that funding for TANF has remained fixed (at $15.6 billion per year) throughout this period as mandated by the 1996 law, which translated into a net decrease of 20.4 percent after inflation by 2004, and given that only one dollar in three was distributed in the form of direct income transfer to recipients, with the rest covering administrative costs and programs supporting transportation, childcare, and employment preparation.[56]

So much to say that, instead of being "dependent" on state assistance and thus reliant on collective redistribution, the more insecure fractions of the American proletariat are now *dependent on poverty-level wage labor, the brittle social economy centered on the family, and the parallel circuits* of informal and criminal enterprise. We find numerical confirmation of this in the fact that wage earners represented 9.6 percent of all Americans officially classified as poor in 1996 as against 11.2 percent in 2002.[57] The poor in the United States are just as numerous and more deprived after welfare "reform" as they were before. But the forced transition to workfare has made it possible to reassert in dramatic fashion the imperative of wage labor as a requisite of full membership in the civic community. And, by deflating the welfare rolls, it has helped *invisibilize urban marginality* by transferring it from the public domain to the private sphere of the family and the market. By the same token, it has converted poverty into a matter of the individual responsibility of each poor person—much like the justice apparatus treats criminal conduct as a matter of the personal culpability of each offender.

Knitting the Assistantial-Correctional Mesh

Probing the gestation, operant philosophy, and early results of the welfare "reform" of 1996 highlights three developments fostering the penalization of public aid and thence its emergent coupling with the penal wing of the state. First, in both the political debate leading to the passage of the law and the body of the legislative text itself, poor single mothers have been aggressively *typecast not as deprived but as deviant*, a problem population whose civic probity is by definition suspect and whose alleged work-avoiding "behaviors" must be urgently rectified by means of preclusion, duress, and shaming, three techniques typical of crime control. The shift to workfare accentuates their status, not as citizens participating in a community of equals, but as subjects saddled with abridged rights and expanded obligations until such time as they will have demonstrated their full commitment to the values of work and family by their reformed conduct.[58] This makes them sociological similes of convicts released on parole who, having served most of their custodial sentence, recover their membership only after a protracted period of surveillance and testing establishing that they have mended their errant ways.

Second, the social silhouette of AFDC beneficiaries turns out to be a *near-exact replica of the profile of jail inmates* save for the gender inversion. Nearly all of them live below half of the federal poverty line (the threshold of eligibility), as do two-thirds of detainees, owing to their shared peripheral status on the low-wage labor market. They are 37 percent black and 18 percent Hispanic, just like jail denizens (41 percent and 19 percent respectively). Fully one-half did not finish high school, the same proportion as those entering the carceral system; and they are seldom married (25 percent compared to 16 percent for inmates). Welfare recipients and jail inmates are also both intimately acquainted with violence (60 percent of the former suffered an assault in their life, as did 50 percent of the latter). And both are saddled with serious physical and mental health disabilities interfering with their participation in the workforce (44 percent of AFDC mothers as against 37 percent for jail inmates).[59]

This verifies that the primary clients of the assistantial and carceral wings of the neoliberal state are essentially the two gender sides of the same population coin drawn from the marginalized fractions of the postindustrial working class. The state regulates the troublesome behaviors of these women (and their children) through workfare and those of the men in their lives (that is, their partners as well as sons, brothers, cousins, and fathers) through criminal justice supervision.* The fact that PRWORA makes ineligible for aid recipients who commit a range of minor offenses (such as those involving narcotics) typical of street illegality and stipulates an array of new criminal sanctions for errant conditions or conducts that were previously dealt with by administrative penalties[60] reinforces our contention that one cannot analyze the implementation of welfare policy at ground level without taking into account the overlapping operations of the penal institution. Conversely, it suggests that one cannot ferret out the causes, modalities, and effects of carceral hyperinflation without linking developments on the justice front with shifts in social policy.

Third, the process of "construction of the target population" of wel-

*This is confirmed by a field study of workfare in a Southeastern city, where the absent fathers of children receiving aid were found to be overwhelmingly poor men, frequently unemployed or underemployed, saddled with enormous debt for child support, of whom the local caseworkers estimated that 10–20 percent were in jail or prison. Hays, *Flat Broke with Children*, 80–81. A median rate of 15 percent currently under lock—a reasonable figure coming to twice the national figure for all black men in 2000—implies that some 45 percent of these men were likely under criminal justice supervision (adding parole and probation to custody). This, in turn, means that upward of two-thirds of these fathers would serve time for a felony conviction over the course of their lives (using rough multiplier ratios for the overall black male population of the United States). This prevalence fits the gendered division of the labor of state control we have postulated, with the women under workfare watch while *their men* are behind bars (and not just men from the same socioeconomic and ethnic milieu).

fare reform turns out to be analogous to that of the carving of the primary clientele of the penal state in the era of hyperincarceration. In both cases, *public vilification, racial accentuation and even inversion, and moral individualization* work in tandem to make punitive programs the policy tool of choice and censorious condemnation the central public rationale for rolling out these programs. In both cases, in keeping with the theoretical model elaborated by political scientists Anne Schneider and Helen Ingram, the benefits supplied by the state have been curtailed and remain undersubscribed while the burdens stipulated by the authorities are increasing and oversubscribed.[61] Lastly, as with criminal justice, the mutation of welfare policy in the 1990s resulted, not from a novel policy move by the Right, but from the espousal of paternalistic measures by the Left, that is, the conversion of (neo-)democratic politicians to the neoliberal vision stressing the need *for the state to diligently enforce the "individual responsibility" and civic obligations* of the poor on both the welfare and the crime front.[62]

As with penal policy, it is indispensable to hold together the material and the symbolic moments of welfare "reform" to fully grasp its logic, import, and impact. Studies that attend exclusively to the one or the other, reducing the new law to a blunt instrument to push welfare beneficiaries onto the low-wage labor market, on the one hand, or to a swirl of public discourses and bureaucratic rituals communicating to lower-class Americans the new cultural rules of the game of work and family, on the other, are not just needlessly one-sided and analytically imbalanced; they truncate the empirical phenomenon itself. For the efficacy of welfare "reform" resides precisely in its ability to weld these dimensions and to operate in the instrumental and expressive registers simultaneously. This allows it to cumulate the support of (economic) "realists" who would design public policy on grounds of *rationality* as well as of (cultural) "idealists" for whom *signification* and the exemplification of shared values is paramount.

At the level of cultural categories and representations, the public debate and legislative battle climaxing with the 1996 law have refurbished the most hackneyed Malthusian caricatures of the "undeserving poor." Effacing the polarizing class structure and the multisided role of the state in molding marginality, they have powerfully reasserted the fiction according to which poverty is a matter of individual deed and will, and that it would suffice to stoke the matrimonial fire and zeal for work of those on assistance by means of material constraint and moral suasion to defeat the culpable "dependency" they evince.[63] The new law has made this fiction more plausible than ever before by replacing a categorical entitlement with an individual contract between recipient and state, and by redefining the core assignment and reorganizing the day-to-day activities of the line staff of welfare offices accordingly—as illustrated by the frequent renaming of welfare administrations as the "Department of Family Independence" and their local agencies as "Job Centers."[64] These moralistic stereotypes are tailor-made for legitimizing the new politics of poverty, in which the state responds to the rise of the social dislocations that it has itself generated by deregulating labor and thinning the social safety net, first, by turning welfare into a funnel toward insecure employment and, next, by tightening the mesh of the penal dragnet in the lower tier of the social and spatial structure.

But the heavy symbolic charge of the welfare reform saga should not blind us to its material mission. The so-called reform was not just "an experiment in legislating in family values and the work ethic," as Sharon Hays suggests when she argues that "the cultural message of reform has always been more important than its practical efficacy."[65] The revamping of welfare in the fin-de-siècle United States partakes of a revolutionary makeover impinging on both market and state in concrete ways that redraw their material configuration and connections. It is true that the shift to workfare has failed to dent the aggregate poverty rate and was even accompanied by an intensification of destitution in the nether regions of the national social space. But PRWORA was never meant to fight poverty and alleviate social insecurity; on the contrary, it was *intended to normalize them*, that is, to inscribe them as modal experience and accepted standards of life and labor for the new service proletariat of the dualizing metropolis, a task which is indivisibly material and symbolic. It was the culmination of a train of measures deployed over the preceding two decades whereby the American state has turned away from passively protecting the poor toward actively making them into *compliant workers fit or forced to fill the peripheral slots* of the deregulated labor market.

In that regard, welfare "reform" was a forceful intervention into the economy, and one may argue that it has worked to the degree that it has (1) reshaped the dispositions of recipients through intensive "moral rearmament," implying a concurrent and mutually reinforcing degradation of the recipient self and glorification of the working self; (2) transmogrified the categories of perception through which welfare and work are perceived and evaluated so as to (re)sacralize labor and elevate it to the rank of absolute civic duty—as in the slogan, posted on the walls of countless welfare offices, "All Jobs Are Good Jobs"[66]; and (3) pressed the poor into the substandard slots of the unskilled labor market, thereby increasing the supply of pliable workers, accelerating the churning at the bottom of the employment pool, and intensifying the desocialization of wage work, in keeping with the core mission of the "workfare state" all over the capitalist world.* And, to do so, welfare offices have borrowed the stock-and-trade techniques of the correctional institution: a behaviorist philosophy of action à la Skinner, constant close-up monitoring, strict spatial assignments and time constraints, intensive record-keeping and case management, periodic interrogation and reporting, and a rigid system of graduated sanctions for failing to perform properly.[67]

The penalization of public aid extends even to its material setting and ambiance. The physical resemblance of the post-reform welfare office to a correctional facility is striking: "It's not just the gates, the guards, and the warning signs, or even the orange plastic waiting room chairs and the floors of a dirty-gray institutional linoleum tile. It's also the overcrowded conditions, the signs commanding 'Wait Here,' 'Take a Number for Service,' and 'Authorized Personnel Only,' and the voice coming over the intercom announcing the name of the next customer to be served or calling on this or that caseworker. This office additionally has something of a prison feel engendered by the seemingly endless rows of locking doors, each with its own number, leading into the tiny rooms where caseworkers conduct eligibility interviews with welfare clients."[68]

The mandatory activities purported to instill the work ethic in welfare recipients and the string of incentives (modulated provision of support services, income disregards) and especially penalties (escalating benefit cuts, eventually leading to permanent ineligibility) look like a first cousin of intensive supervision programs for probationers and parolees, or other "intermediate sanctions." Classes such as the "job readiness" and "life skills" workshops are redolent of the contents-empty rehabilitation courses given to convicts behind bars. As with a prison, the atmosphere of the public aid office is saturated with distrust, confusion, and fear. Relations between recipients and their caseworkers were surely adversarial and riven with suspicion before welfare "reform," but the new law has eliminated legal guarantees, magnified the authority and severity of caseworkers (whose continued employment hinges on pushing a preset share of clients into jobs, or simply off the rolls), and dramatically increased the stakes of compliance as well as the probability of detection of violation, and with them the level of anxiety. And, no matter how docile one is, the "welfare clock" is inevitably ticking

*"Stripped down to its labor-regulatory essence, workfare is not about creating jobs for people who don't have them: it is about creating workers for jobs that nobody wants. In a Foucauldian sense, it is seeking to make 'docile bodies' for the new economy: flexible, self-reliant, and self-disciplining." Jamie Peck, *Workfare States* (New York: Guilford, 2001), 6.

> toward termination due to lifetime limits. So much so that Sharon Hays concludes her description of the new workfare regime at ground level by stressing that "the Work Plan of welfare is more effective as a form of punishment than it is a positive strategy for independence."[69]

The material mission of welfare "reform," moreover, does not stop at promoting labor flexibility. Indeed, the central thesis of this book is that, like the relentless growth and glorification of the penal apparatus after the mid-1970s that we are about to examine in the next two chapters, the shrinking of welfare and its paternalist conversion into workfare in the United States is *not* a mechanical response to economic changes so much as an *exercise in state crafting* aimed at producing—and then adapting to—these very changes.* In other words, like its "prisonfare" counterpart, the workfare revolution is a *specifically political project* aimed at remaking not only the market but also, and above all, the state itself. The effect of PRWORA in this regard is to recalibrate public authority at three levels: its internal organization (bureaucratic segmentation and differentiation through devolution), its external boundary (redrawing the division of labor between the public and private sectors), and its functional loading (via the penalization of welfare and the shift from the assistantial to the penal treatment of the more disruptive correlates of poverty).

The 1996 *workfare revolution has reshaped the internal makeup of the state* by discursively decoupling the questions of welfare and work while practically remaking the former as an institutional support for the latter. It has elevated the notion that "welfare dependency" is a problem unto itself, unconnected to the (wretched) condition of unskilled labor, to the rank of doxic tenet of social policy. In so doing, it has accentuated the structural properties of the US bureaucratic field (highlighted in the preceding chapter, pages 44–48) that facilitate neoliberal restructuring by further curtailing the political capacity and muffling the collective voice of the urban (sub)proletariat: namely,

*As statecraft, welfare reform necessarily fuses the material and the symbolic. It entails, first, a reorganization of the public bureaucracies in charge of the oversight of dependent populations. Second, it involves the production and diffusion of new official categories of perception and appreciation that provide a language for depicting and justifying the actions of state functionaries as well as shaping the subjectivity of citizens. This duality of the state as monopolistic manipulator of public goods and maker of efficient mental schemata is discussed by Pierre Bourdieu, "Rethinking the State: On the Genesis and Structure of the Bureaucratic Field," *Sociological Theory* 12, no. 1 (March 1994 [1993]): 1–18.

administrative fragmentation, the class dualism of aid programs and clienteles, the residual character of public assistance, and the racial "filtering" of policy. As for the devolution of welfare provision to states and counties, it has amputated the effective citizenship of the poor by rendering this provision variable and contingent on local budgets and local balances of political and bureaucratic power.

A second major material consequence of the law on Personal Responsibility and Work Opportunity has been to redraw the state-market boundary by accelerating the commodification of public aid. Historian Michael Katz reminds us that America's charitable state has a long tradition of contracting to the private and philanthropic sectors, going all the way back to the colonial period.[70] Since its expansion of the 1960s, a majority share of the goods and services provided to the poor by the American state have been distributed through the mediation of nonprofit agencies and commercial outfits. In 1980 already, 40 percent of the social expenditures of states were allotted through the former and 20 percent through the latter, leaving only 40 percent to pass through the channels of public bureaucracies.[71] The 1996 "reform" has vastly expanded the market for social services, not so much out of an ideological commitment to privatization under the catchy slogan of "reinventing government" as for the simple reason that *the US state does not possess the administrative capacities required* to implement its new politics of social insecurity on the social welfare side. Indeed, we shall discover in chapter 5 that a similar bottleneck emerged on the penal side, leading to a similar outcome: the resurgence and stupendous growth of private correctional operators as adjuncts of the state.

To enforce the five-year lifetime "cap" on assistance or to authorize the allocation of food stamps requires detailed and comprehensive data on the full welfare trajectory of applicants. To date, no state or county has all this information at its disposal. The administrative records available at the onset of PRWRA contained only dispersed and fragmentary data, which were typically erased after a few months. Moreover, these records were neither standardized nor compatible from one county to the next (in many rural areas, the files of recipients were still being processed manually using paper forms). According to political scientist Henry Brady, who was commissioned by the American Academy of Arts and Sciences to report on this thorny issue, creating the information systems needed to implement the new welfare law would require a colossal administrative and financial effort over many years, on a scale comparable to that which accompanied the creation of Social Security during the New Deal. But the welfare "reform" of 1996 neither provided a budget nor assigned the federal government the task of coordinating state and county endeavors on this front.[72]

Short of a mammoth expansion of public bureaucracies that would visibly defeat the goal of shrinking the welfare state, there was only one solution to implement the revamping of public aid into a springboard toward low-wage work: to resort massively to private operators in both the for-profit and the nonprofit sectors. The welfare revolution of 1996 thus opened a new era in the marketization of social services, as states and counties scrambled to outsource workfare activities in order to meet the mandated targets of placing one-quarter of their recipients into jobs by 1997 and one-half by 2002 on pain of losing federal funds. Within five years of the passage of PRWORA, all but one state had outsourced their TANF obligations, a market estimated at $1.5 billion with nearly one-third of state contracts going to commercial operators.[73]

As noted above, privatization of public goods and services is not a novel development in the United States. It has grown in spurts at each major stage in the historical trajectory of domestic policy—during the Progressive era and the New Deal, in the Great Society years, and under the Reagan presidency—and it has advanced during phases of both expansion and contraction in state activities.[74] But welfare "reform" has reconfigured the landscape of privatization after 1996 in dramatic and unprecedented ways in terms of scale and dynamics. PRWORA has hugely increased the size of the pie and the prospects for growth and profit-taking on the social welfare front, with a market potential estimated at $15 billion of the $30 billion in state and local services.[75] It has extended the principle of competitive bidding to all contractors, including nonprofit providers who used to get government missions on account of their community standing. And it has authorized private operators to bid for the full gamut of services, including welfare intake and the determination of eligibility (two sensitive operations strictly reserved to public entities under AFDC).[76] This has attracted for the first time large firms specializing in data systems and information management that possess the size and technological means to capture the more lucrative end of the spectrum of social services.*

*For example, Lockheed Martin Information Management Services, a unit of the $30-billion Lockheed Martin Corporation, created in 1984, launched a Welfare Reform Division centered on "self-sufficiency" in 1996. It provides a range of government services, from child support and employment preparation to ticket enforcement to truck registration and inspection. The new workfare market made it the fastest growing subdivision of the entire corporation: by 2001, it had garnered 26 TANF contracts in 8 states, worth about $108 million. Mary Bryna Sanger, *The Welfare Marketplace:*

The corporate giants Lockheed Information Services (a subsidiary of the military behemoth Lockheed Martin), Electronic Data Systems (run by Texas billionaire Ross Perot), Andersen Consulting, IBM, DynCorp, and Unisys have thus joined the fray to vie with historically established firms such as Maximus, Curtis & Associates, and America Works, and benevolent associations delivering services to the poor.[77] Some companies active in the booming private incarceration market on the justice side have also jumped in to offer turnkey information systems and the administrative supervision necessary to enforce the workfare law. Yet expanded competitive contracting has not merely created new opportunities for profiteering; it has profoundly altered the entire organizational ecology of welfare provision by changing the strategies of, and relations among, public, nonprofit, and for-profit operators. Accelerating commodification has significantly increased administrative complexity and unpredictability, deepening the fragmentation and opacity of the bureaucratic field. It has destabilized nonprofit agencies by eroding their traditional role as self-professed protectors of the poor. And it has weakened government by draining experienced managers away from public bureaucracies just when the state needs to augment administrative oversight over contracts to guarantee basic accountability.[78]

For a fee, these companies take over the supervision of new-style welfare recipients who, much like (ex-)convicts, find themselves the object of extensive record-keeping, constant testing, and close-up surveillance, allowing for the multiplication of points of restraint and sanction. In so doing, they not only enlarge governmental capacity to "train" the urban poor for their appointed place in the new economic and civic division of labor, in Michel Foucault's expansive sense of *dressage*, joining the notions of taming, enskilling, and inuring. Situated at the meeting point between the social and the penal strands of state activity, the workfare firms specializing in the oversight of the poor (as well as, for some of them, prisoners who were poor on the outside and will become so again upon release) are key agents knitting together an *assistantial-correctional mesh without precedent or equivalent* in the Western world—and not a "corrections commercial complex" as some criminologists have proposed.[79] For the novel institutional nexus now constituting a single organizational contraption for the management of problem populations does not join the state and the market, and even less so prison and industry (as with the militant myth of the "prison-industrial complex"). It spans the welfare and the correctional sectors

---

Privatization and Welfare Reform (Washington, D.C.: Brookings Institution, 2003), 74.

of the bureaucratic field. In keeping with the American political tradition, this composite organizational ensemble in the making is characterized by the interpenetration of the public and private sectors as well as by the fusion of the state functions of cultural branding, moral amendment, and social control.

In his book *The Poverty of Welfare Reform*, published a year before the vote of PRWORA, Joel Handler observed that "criminal justice and welfare reform have an eerie similarity today."[80] The legislative developments of the summer of 1996 and policy deployments since have demonstrated that this similarity goes far beyond superficial resemblance at the level of discourse and mood, to extend deep into bureaucratic philosophy, administrative structures, and managerial strategies. By shifting from "an emphasis on economics and entitlement" to "efforts to control the lifestyle of the adult recipients" of welfare,[81] by making coercion, behavioral supervision, and deterrence central elements of public aid, and by accentuating the taint of welfare so as to drive (sub)proletarian women into the peripheral segments of the low-wage labor market (or into the crevices of the social structure so that they are made invisible), the 1996 legislation heralding "the end of welfare as we know it" has fostered the interweaving of social policy and penal policy at the bottom of the polarizing class structure. It has placed public aid programs under the same punitive ethos of administrative compulsion and punitive behaviorism that have traditionally organized criminal justice operations.*

It would be a serious mistake, then, to see in the assent given by William Jefferson Clinton to the overturning of US social policy toward the poor an "electoralist" decision, even if it was also that—at the time, the *New York Times* thought it discerned in it a "masterful campaign move." Nor was it an accidental development provoked by the accumulation of tactical blunders followed by an unforeseen redrawing of the political landscape, as economist David Ellwood, the architect of the original Clinton reform plan, tried to convince himself after returning to his academic haunts at Harvard University to contemplate (at a distance) the human disaster that he had helped set off.[82] For the

*There is an irony here that will not have escaped students of penality: the revamped welfare wing of the state is importing the prospective, person-centered philosophy of rehabilitation just when that philosophy has been discredited and jettisoned in the correctional realm, to be replaced by a retrospective, offense-centered philosophy of neutralization and "just deserts." Relatedly, workfare is proclaiming and projecting the positive power of the state to change behavior for the good through coercion, a power that is shrilly denounced as abusive, ineffective and/or counterproductive when it is invoked for the regulation of the economy.

abolition of AFDC is part and parcel of a deep and broad movement of *reconstruction of the American charitable state* aimed at compressing and revamping the sphere of social citizenship in a paternalistic and punitive direction while expanding the prerogatives of private operators at the very heart of public action. The penal revamping of welfare emerges as a core component of the new state apparatus joining workfare and prisonfare into a single institutional mesh entrusted with the *double regulation of poverty* on the work and crime fronts.

A note of caution is in order here, as an echo of our methodological warning in the prologue: we must beware of exaggerating the coherence and functionality of workfare policy, as this summary analysis tends to do for reasons of analytic focus and space. Much like the criminal justice "system," which is systematic only on paper, the emerging workfare apparatus is a loose assemblage of organizations, programs, and principles that do not form a fully coherent ensemble. Jamie Peck is right to insist that "the landscape of workfare is a fluid one. . . . Workfare is not some *deus ex machina* lowered into place spontaneously to solve the contradictions of welfarism, flexible labor markets, and urban social dislocations. Rather, workfare ideologies and strategies have emerged unevenly and iteratively, as the outcome of years of institutional experimentation, policy reform, and political struggle," and so workfarism as a regime of regulation "remains unstable and contradictory."[83] The same can be said about the emerging nexus of workfare and prisonfare, since cultural instability and organizational looseness are redoubled by their coupling.

The aim of the latest avatar of welfare "reform"—to discipline the poor and, failing this, to "disappear" them—conforms well with the history of public assistance in the United States over the *longue durée*, as well as with the history of the prison at its birth.[84] It must not, however, obfuscate the function that the transition from welfare to workfare also fulfills in the current conjuncture for more fortunate Americans. Émile Durkheim taught us that punishment is a communicative device, a "language" delivering messages not so much to offenders as to the witnessing public—in this case the *working* citizenry.[85] For the latter, the punitive makeover of social policy signifies without equivocation that nobody can opt out of wage labor without exposing themselves to a material and symbolic degradation worse than the most demeaning job. And it reminds all that you must count on no one but yourself in this "war of all against all" that is life in a society subordinated to the market. Throwing the poor to the wolves thus allows state elites to reaffirm the ideological primacy of meritocratic individualism at the very moment when the generalization of social insecurity, by reaching deep into the middle class, threatens to unsettle their practical belief in the national myth of "the American dream."[86]

Conservative political scientist Lawrence Mead, who, as chief ideologist of US political paternalism, has his finger on the pulse of the new Leviathan *in statu nascendi,* was right when he proposed that "today's welfare reform is an exercise, not in economic transfer, but in state building."[87] Only, building the neoliberal state involves two construction sites, not just one: while it was converting welfare into workfare, the United States was also busy bolstering and broadening the carceral arm of the state. And so we must now turn to probing the dizzying ascent of the penal institution in America after the close of the Fordist-Keynesian era.

II. GRANDEUR OF THE PENAL STATE

As a daily witness to these wonders, the American sees nothing astonishing in them. This unbelievable destruction, this still more stunning growth seems to him the habitual course of events. He accustoms himself to them as to the immutable order of nature.

—ALEXIS DE TOCQUEVILLE, "Quinze jours au désert," 1831*

*Alexis de Tocqueville, "Fortnight in the Wilderness," in George Wilson Pierson, *Tocqueville in America* (Baltimore: The Johns Hopkins University Press, 1996), 232. My translation.

4

The Great Confinement of the Fin de Siècle

It is in 1973, in the immediate aftermath of the Attica riot, in which forty-three prisoners and guards held hostage were massacred in the assault launched by the national guard, that the carceral population of the United States reached its postwar low.[1] That year, the National Advisory Commission on Criminal Justice Standards and Goals, a group of experts charged with evaluating the state of the judicial system, submitted a report to President Nixon that recommended closing down juvenile detention centers and freezing prison construction for a decade. This governmental commission noted, on the one hand, that far from curbing insecurity, imprisonment feeds it through its criminogenic action, while, on the other hand, the existing number of beds in the country's custodial institutions "[was] more than enough to meet the needs of the foreseeable future."* And it called for the vigorous development of job training and education programs aimed at the reintegration of convicts.

It is true that the imprisoned population had declined steadily since the beginning of the 1960s, by about 1 percent per year. Penologists were then debating opening the carceral environment, developing alternative or "community" sentences, and moving toward general "decarceration." Breaking with their wait-and-see attitude, the courts extended the protection of constitutional rights to inmates and, for the first time, attacked the rampant illegality that plagued correctional administrations. The American Correctional Association, the main professional body bringing together the various incarceration trades, established an "accreditation program" aiming to upgrade and harmonize detention norms across the country. One seriously envisaged reserving custody for the hard-core minority of "dangerous predators" whom criminology had just discovered commit the vast majority of

*National Advisory Commission on Criminal Justice Standards and Goals, *Task Force Report on Corrections* (Washington, D.C.: U.S. Government Printing Office, 1973), 349. The commission emphasized in its conclusions that "the prison, the reformatory, and the jail have achieved a shocking record of failure. There is overwhelming evidence that these institutions create crime rather than prevent it" (597).

violent crimes.[2] Research on imprisonment levels focused on the so-called homeostatic theory of Alfred Blumstein, according to which each society has a "normal" threshold of punishment, determining a rate of incarceration stable over the long term. And the revisionist history of the penal question inaugurated by David Rothman and canonized by Michel Foucault heralded the irreversible decline of the prison: whereas it had held a central place in the disciplinary framework of industrial capitalism, it was now said to be destined to play a minor role in advanced societies, in which forms of social control at once more subtle and more diffuse were being invented and deployed.[3]

Hyperinflation and Overpopulation

The about-turn of US carceral demographics after 1973 proved to be as sudden as it was spectacular. Contrary to all expectations, the country's confined population took to growing at a vertiginous speed such that, in a development without precedent in the history of democratic societies, *it doubled in ten years and quadrupled in twenty*. Starting from less than 380,000 in 1975, the number of people held behind bars approached 500,000 in 1980 before leaping beyond 1 million in 1990 (see table 6). It continued to expand at an infernal rate of 8 percent per year on average—corresponding to 2,000 net additional inmates every week—during the 1990s, until on June 30, 2000, America officially sported 1,931,850 under lock, including over 620,000 held in county jails (more than the population of Washington, D.C.) and 1.31 million confined in federal and state prisons.* If it were a city, the carceral system of the United Sates would be the country's fourth-largest metropolis, behind Chicago.

> The US carceral system is organized into three distinct levels. The first is made up of some 3,300 municipal or county jails in which are confined persons held by the police, awaiting trial, or sentenced to terms of custody with less than one year remaining. The second comprises state prisons (which number 1,450, including 309

*Unless otherwise specified, all the penal statistics in the text are taken from various publications from the Bureau of Justice Statistics of the US Department of Justice, which compiles them on the basis of data collected by state correctional administrations and county sheriff's offices. They exclude 3,000 individuals confined in the country's 28 military prisons as well as some 110,000 minors locked up in juvenile detention centers and several tens of thousands held at any given time in police lockups around 2000.

Table 6. The carceral boom in the United States, 1975–2000

	1975	1980	1985	1990	1995	2000
City and county jails	138,800	182,288	256,615	405,320	507,044	621,149
State and federal prisons	240,593	315,974	480,568	739,980	1,078,357	1,310,710
Total incarcerated	379,393	498,262	737,183	1,145,300	1,585,401	1,931,850
Cumulative increase	100	131	194	302	418	509
Annual rate of growth (%)	—	6	10	11	8	4

SOURCE: Bureau of Justice Statistics, *Historical Corrections Statistics in the United States, 1850–1984* (Washington, D.C.: Government Printing Office, 1986); idem., *Prison and Jail Inmates at Midyear 2000* (Washington, D.C.: Government Printing Office, 2001).

The carceral archipelago, fourth-largest "city" in the United States

1. New York City	7,380,906
2. Los Angeles	3,555,638
3. Chicago	2,721,547
4. *Jails and prisons*	*1,931,850*
5. Houston	1,744,058
6. Philadelphia	1,478,002
7. Phoenix	1,159,014
8. San Diego	1,171,121
9. Dallas	1,053,292
10. Detroit	1,000,272

SOURCE: Deirde Gaugin and Mark S. Littman, *1998 County and City Extra: Annual Metropolitan, City, and County Data Book* (Lanham, Md.: Bernan, 1998).

"maximum security" facilities), which hold convicts sentenced to more than one year, called "felons" (a felony is any criminal offense punishable by a prison term exceeding one year). In addition to these two types of institutions, there are 125 federal prisons, facilities placed under the authority of Washington, for individuals prosecuted and convicted for infractions of the federal penal code—covering mainly white-collar offenses, narcotics violations, and organized crime.[4] In thirty years, the number of penal establishments in the country tripled to surpass 4,800 (by comparison, mainland France currently has 180 penal establishments, compared to 169 in 1975), so that the states leading the race to hyperincarceration are now literally carpeted with jails and prisons.

This carceral mesh is a remarkably diversified and heterogeneous ensemble. Facilities vary widely according to their age and size, architecture and amenities, internal organization and disciplinary regime, level of security and surveillance technologies, programs on offer and inmate profile. Some prisoners spend twenty-three hours a day alone in a steel cage under continuous electronic supervision with scant human contact for years (in the case of reinforced security centers called "Supermax," which have proliferated in the past decade). Others are packed into rundown gaols where, rather than isolation and sensory deprivation, they suffer above all from forced promiscuity and ambient insalubrity. Still others serve their time in work camps in the countryside or in "weekend prisons" without fences or bars, which they are authorized to leave during the week to attend to their regular jobs. Some establishments deploy the latest electronic and computer technologies; others are more akin to the reformatories of the nineteenth century in their functioning and atmosphere. Beyond this dispersion, the modal experience of penal confinement is that of the denizens of large state facilities that are satellites to the cities, for whom prison is a "place of deadening routine punctuated by bursts of fear and violence," perpetuated by forced idleness and endemic overcrowding.[5]

It is necessary to stress that *penitential trajectories and carceral experiences are powerfully stratified* according to a series of social and juridical factors, the former comprising class position, gender, and ethnoracial identity, and the latter the nature of the offense and length of sentence, access to legal resources, jurisdiction, possibility of recourse to external agents, etc. The effects of the judicial factors tend to reinforce those of the social factors, since the former often do little more than retranslate the latter into the categories and practices proper to the penal field.* Thus, in the US case, the bulk of white-collar criminals, who are overwhelmingly whites of higher social origins, serve their sentences in so-called open facilities (with neither bars nor fences), where they enjoy better supervision and a level of comfort and services (work, training, health, food, fitness, recreation) that cannot compare to the austere and oppressive regime of the "big houses," wherein rot the vast majority of "street" criminals, essentially drawn from the marginal sectors of working class blacks and Latinos (as previously demonstrated in chapter 2).

The curve displaying the evolution over a half-century of the confinement rate for convicts sentenced to more than one year in federal or state prison (thus excluding those in jails on remand detention and struck by short sentences) spotlights a sharp opposition between two carceral regimes (see figure 1). During the three decades following the

*The mechanisms that ensure that "the 'poor' in prison experience a more rigorous incarceration than the 'rich,' and all the more so as the [specific] establishment itself is poorer" are described by Anne-Marie Marchetti in *Pauvretés en prison* (Ramonville Saint-Ange: Cérès, 1997). Remarks to the same effect can be found in the beautiful article by Michael Pollak analyzing how class (and, secondarily, gender) competencies determine chances of survival even within this radically leveling institution that is the concentration camp. Michael Pollak, "Des mots qui tuent," *Actes de la recherche en sciences sociales* 41 (September 1982): 29–45.

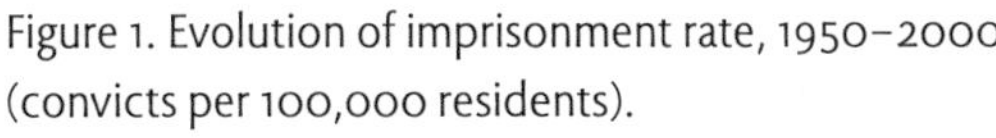

Figure 1. Evolution of imprisonment rate, 1950–2000 (convicts per 100,000 residents).

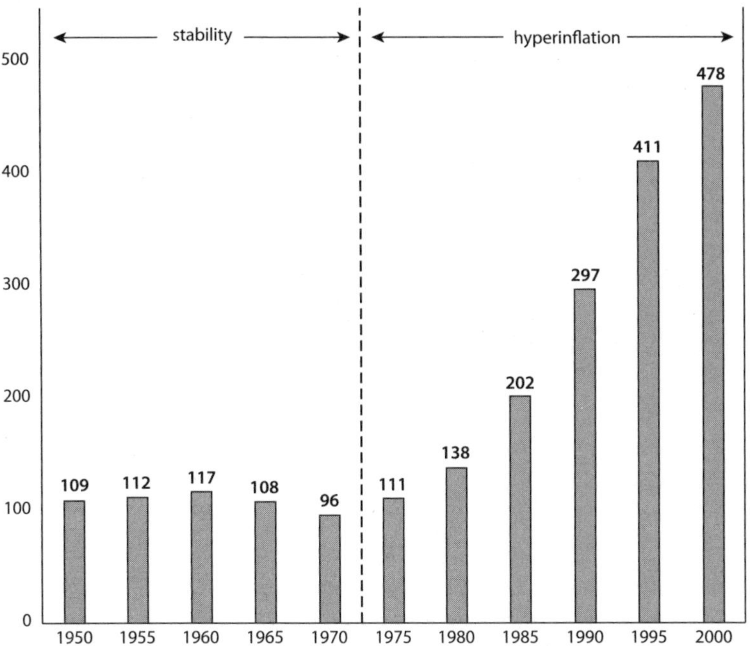

SOURCE: Bureau of Justice Statistics, *Sourcebook of Criminal Justice Statistics 2000* (Washington D.C.: US Government Printing Office, 2002), 634.

Second World War, as during the interwar period, that is, from the New Deal to the forsaking of the Keynesian compromise and the crisis of the black ghetto, this rate fluctuated within a narrow band between 90 and 115 prisoners per 100,000 inhabitants. It is this "impressive stability" that led Alfred Blumstein to formulate his homeostatic theory of the incarceration level. However, as the eminent criminologist conceded, this theory was made obsolete in the mid-1970s[6] by the shift to an unprecedented *regime of permanent and accelerating carceral inflation.* After 1973, the imprisonment rate increased continually and exponentially to cross the 200-mark in 1985 and the 480-bar in 2000. If we include the population confined in city and county jails, on the threshold of the third millennium, the US incarceration rate stood at 702 prisoners per 100,000 inhabitants, five times its level of the mid-1970s.

Carceral hyperinflation affects all the jurisdictions that make up the nation's territory. Thus, with the exception of Maine and Kansas, all members of the Union posted a correctional population increase

Table 7. States leading carceral inflation in 1996*

Population imprisoned		Imprisonment rate		% Growth 1991–96	
California	147,712	Texas	686	Texas	156
Texas	132,383	Louisiana	615	Wisconsin	64
Federal prisons	105,544	Oklahoma	591	North Carolina	62
New York State	69,709	South Carolina	532	Mississippi	60
Florida	63,763	Nevada	502	Iowa	53
Ohio	46,174	Mississippi	498	New Mexico	52
Michigan	42,349	Alabama	492	South Dakota	50
Illinois	38,352	Arizona	481	Utah	50
Georgia	35,139	Georgia	462	Hawaii	49
Pennsylvania	34,537	California	451	Minnesota	49
(number of convicts)		(convicts per 100,000)			

*Figures exclude inmates convicted to sentences of less than one year and inmates awaiting trial in city and county jails.

SOURCE: Christopher Mumola and Allen Beck, *Prisoners in 1996* (Washington, D.C.: Government Printing Office, 1997), 4 and 5.

exceeding 50 percent between 1986 and 1996; half of them recorded a doubling of the number behind bars during this period; Texas and Colorado did even better, with a tripling in ten years.[7] Twenty-five different states figure on the roster of the top ten leaders in penal confinement according to three criteria—number of inmates, imprisonment rate, and increase of prison population (excluding jails) between 1991 and 1996 (see table 7).

All these figures converge to indicate that a new type of relation has been forged between American society and its prisons during the past quarter-century. For, as we shall see below, this stupendous increase in the numbers under lock occurred during a period in which crime was first stagnant and then rapidly decreasing. A detailed statistical analysis of correctional evolution in the fifty states of the Union reveals moreover that carceral inflation is *a deep-seated national trend* that asserts itself independently of the individual characteristics of states, their crime level, and the political color of the local executive branch.[8]

Indeed, no democratic nation has ever experienced such carceral bulimia—even in times of acute social crisis or military conflagration. As a result, the United States now caracoles far ahead of the other postindustrial countries when it comes to confinement. The US incarceration rate is six to twelve times that of the members of the European Union, whereas it was only one to three times their rate only thirty years ago

Figure 2. Incarceration rate in the United States and European Union, 1997 (inmates per 100,00 residents in bold; total number of inmates in thousands in parentheses).

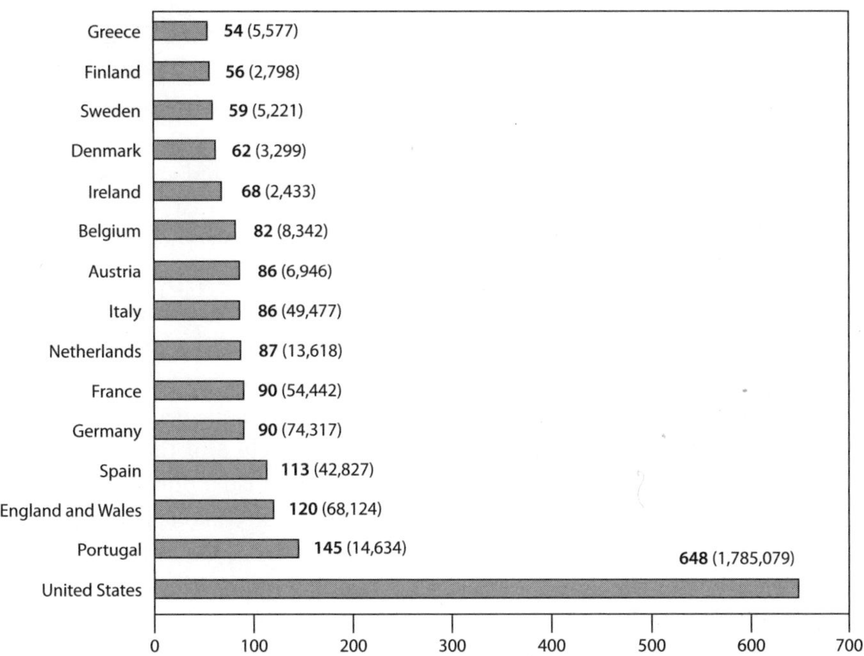

SOURCE: Bureau of Justice Statistics, *Prison and Jail Inmates at Midyear 1997* (Washington D.C.: Government Printing Office, 1998); Pierre Tournier, *Statistique pénale annuelle du conseil de l'Europe* (Strasbourg: European Council, 1999).

(see figure 2). On the cusp of the new century, America locked up seven times more than France, Germany, or Italy and ten times more than Sweden or Denmark, even though these countries have levels of crime (outside of homicide) similar to that of the US (as we shall see in chapter 8). The fifteen EU countries sported a total of 351,000 inmates for 370 million inhabitants, one-fifth the confined population of the US for 267 million inhabitants.

Even South Africa at the close of the civil war against apartheid, with 369 inmates per 100,000 inhabitants in 1993, imprisoned *half as many people* proportionately as the prosperous America of President Clinton. Today only Russia, which went in a short decade from dying Sovietism to savage capitalism, is in a position to vie with the United States on this front, as its incarceration rate doubled since 1989 to perch around 740 inmates per 100,000 inhabitants in 1999, just ahead of the American rate.* The other republics born out of the collapse of the Soviet empire also post astronomical incarceration rates, but these are nevertheless well below that of the United States: 246 for Latvia, 351 for Lithuania, 385 for Ukraine, and 500 for Belarus. The great victor of the Cold War, sole superpower to survive the arms race, self-proclaimed policeman of the planet, America has raised itself in two short decades to the rank of world leader in imprisonment.

The most palpable consequence of this unprecedented carceral hyperinflation is that, despite their proliferation, America's custodial establishments are literally bursting at the seams. Overcrowding is so extreme that most cities and states have been compelled by the courts to release criminals by the thousands after having been prohibited from locking up more in an effort to prevent further deterioration in conditions of confinement. In 1999, thirty-three members of the Union were under court supervision for this reason. Nine had seen their entire carceral system declared in violation of Article 8 of the Constitution, which protects citizens from "cruel and unusual punishment." Only three states, Minnesota, New Jersey, and North Dakota, had managed to shelter their correctional administration from the wrath of the judges. One in five jails is currently subject to a *numerus clausus* imposed by a county court. And fewer than half of state prison systems meet the minimum norms necessary to be "accredited" by the American Correctional Association.[9]

In 1995 the official occupancy rate of state penitentiaries exceeded 133 percent as a national average, with peaks above 150 percent in six states, including Ohio (177 percent), Illinois (166 percent), and California (161 percent), where it neared 200 percent by 2003. And yet these figures are low estimates. The occupancy rate is commonly manipulated by correctional authorities to conceal the real overpopulation and thereby avoid possible judicial troubles—courts can inflict on them stiff fines by the day for seriously and repeatedly exceeding their housing capacity.** One example: New York State (which held 69,709 prisoners

*In 1997 President Boris Yeltsin proposed—in vain—to amnesty a half-million convicts in order to bring the conditions of custody in Russian prisons closer to the international norm. See Nils Christie, "Eléments de géographie pénale," *Actes de la recherche en sciences sociales* 124 (September 1998): 68–74. By 2003, an active policy of decarceration for those awaiting trial had allowed Russia to fall below 600 inmates per 100,000 inhabitants.

**As the Bureau of Justice Statistics coyly notes: "The extent of prison crowding is difficult to determine because of the absence of uniform measures for defining ca-in its penitentiaries in 1996) has 53,366 beds according to its "design capacity," 65,700 in terms of "operational capacity," and a "rated capacity" of no fewer than 68,996—yielding an occupancy rate ranging from 101 to 131 percent. The difference between these figures is explained by the fact that everywhere, gymnasia, libraries, bathrooms, classrooms, closets, and recreation halls have been hastily converted into extra cells and dormitories. In a majority of jurisdictions, the number of beds has been doubled by setting up bunk beds ("double bunking") and even tripled by adding a mattress stored under the bed or leaned against the wall during the day ("triple celling"). Despite this, at the end of 1996, 27 states were forced to confine some 30,000 inmates with long sentences in municipal jails for lack of space in their penitentiaries. And another 15 rented 7,000 "outsourced" beds in public or private facilities located outside their borders.

As the first rampart against social disorders and point of entry into the carceral network, county jails have become huge storage and sorting facilities for poor and precarious populations that churn millions of bodies—and soak in billions of dollars—every year. Thirteen cities each hold over 5,000 in their jails at any given time (equal to the carceral stock of Sweden)*: at the top of the list as of June 1998 came the Los Angeles jail, with a total of 21,000 inmates, followed by New York City (17,500); Cook County, for Chicago and its vicinity (9,300); Harris County, home of Houston, and Dallas (with 7,800 and 7,100 respectively); and finally Dade County, seat of Miami (7,100).[10] As early as 1993, 76 municipal jails held more than one thousand inmates each and 23 housed over two thousand. Jails are generally less overcrowded than state prisons because they have increased their capacity more under pressure from the courts. Moreover, they enjoy greater latitude to periodically offload an excessive surplus of bodies by releasing detainees awaiting trial under judicial supervision or accelerating early releases. Yet this did not prevent occupancy rates from reaching 151 percent in Los Angeles, 146 percent in Dallas, and 113 percent in Chicago in 1999.

---

pacity." Christopher Mumola and Allen Back, *Prisoners in 1996* (Washington, D.C.: Bureau of Justice Statistics, 1997), 7.

*It should be noted that these figures fluctuate perceptibly from publication to publication for the same dates according to the time of year when the population is counted. In effect, in winter carceral establishments fill up with the homeless who get arrested voluntarily in order to find shelter. The director of Cook County Jail confessed to me in an interview that his inmate count increases quasi-mechanically five to ten percent when the rigors of the Chicago winter set in.

Everywhere city gaols are buckling under the mountains of bodies poured onto them by a police and judicial apparatus seized by a voracious appetite. This gives rise to astonishing, even surreal, scenes. New York City renewed an old London tradition extinct since the mid-nineteenth century: it turned barges moored on the docks of the Hudson River into "floating prisons" to warehouse its overflow of inmates. In Chicago, the residents of Cook County Jail slept by the thousands on mattresses strewn on the floor, even on mere blankets thrown onto the concrete ground, and, for some, packed into the bathrooms, even as the courts periodically ordered the automatic release of thousands of detainees awaiting trial. In Los Angeles, the jail discretely resorted to using dozens of buses to "stretch" its housing capacity by keeping entire loads of inmates in them overnight: the buses drove around the city or simply parked at the entrance of the jail's admission center and waited in the lot for hours on end for cells to be freed up. In Nashville, Tennessee, 200 detainees slept in the underground tunnel connecting the local jail to the courthouse, without showers or bathrooms, because the facility, designed for 300 inmates, held 1,100, including several hundred pressed like sardines onto the gymnasium floor.

In Phoenix, the sheriff of Maricopa county, Joe Arpaio, set up an outdoor camp of army tents and bunk beds (with surplus wares from the Korean War) in the middle of the Arizona desert—where the temperature nears 120°F in the shade—surrounded by chain link fences and concertina wire, and rounded up some 2000 inmates in it. At the entrance, he hung a blinking neon sign flashing "Vacancy," similar to the one used by motels to signal that they have rooms available. This stratagem and a few others, such as issuing striped uniforms, distributing pink jail underwear, and using leg-irons on chain gangs, and making detainees pay for their meals (Arpaio was proud to point out that feeding detainees cost only 90 cents per day compared to $1.10 for guard dogs), quickly made him a national, and then an international, media star. And turned Arpaio's carceral dormitory under the stars into a mandatory stop for politicians eager to burnish their image of "crime fighters."*

In Silicon Valley, the onrush of detainees was so strong that the jail of Santa Clara (seat of San Jose, California's second largest city) had ATM kiosks installed at its gates so that people brought in for minor offenses (drunk driving, vandalism,

*The flap cover text gives a good idea of the pitch of Joe Arpaio's autobiography: "America's Toughest Sheriff is an unfiltered account of Sheriff Joe's 'get smart and get tough' approach to jail. Tents are only the beginning. Green bologna, pink boxer shorts, and chain gangs are all part of his philosophy that jail should be punishment, period. He believes that criminals should never live better in jail than they do on the outside." The tome's front cover bears the urgent endorsement of extreme-right-wing talk-show host Rush Limbaugh: "This book demands to be read." Joe Arpaio and Len Sherman, *America's Toughest Sheriff: How We Can Win the War against Crime* (Phoenix: Summit Publishing Group, 1996).

or possession of small quantities of narcotics) having a credit card could withdraw the 10-percent payment required to go free on bail—to the hew and cry of the bond agencies, which complained loudly about unfair competition. The authorities hoped thereby to free up a dozen beds in their cells each weekend. "That may seem like a little, but over the course of a year that's a benefit to us," explained the jail spokesperson. "We're looking for any way to give us flexibility to deal with crowding issues."[11]

Far removed from academic debates about the purposes of incarceration—to punish, neutralize, deter, or rehabilitate—the primordial concern of the managers of these gigantic warehouses for the undesirables that American jails have become is pragmatic and functional: to "process" the endless torrent of arrestees and convicts as quickly as possible through "the system" so as to minimize costs and reduce incidents linked to the packing and mixing of disparate, difficult, and often (mutually) hostile populations. But this managerial approach is powerless to stem the deterioration of accommodations and access to basic services—hygiene, health care, exercise, visiting rooms, and lawyers, not to mention education, vocational training, and work, which have been elevated to the rank of luxuries.

In point of fact, conditions of detention in big-city jails are so punishing that the majority of those remanded in them rush to plead guilty and negotiate a reduced sentence with the prosecutor responsible for their case in exchange for dispensing with a trial, so as to be either immediately released on probation or quickly transferred to a state penitentiary, where the regimen is typically less erratic and stressful. Anything rather than vegetate in the promiscuity and dull violence of jail for months on end waiting to come before a judge. So much so that one may consider that one of the main functions of the jail in the hypertrophic penal apparatus the United States has developed is to *extort a guilty plea from its denizens* and allow the judicial system to realize mammoth savings by cutting out the costly trial phase: in the country's 75 largest urban counties, 92 percent of those sentenced to more than one year in prison in the twelve months after being placed in detention do so following a barter of this kind.[12] For the vast majority of the urban poor sent behind bars, a trial has become a judicial oddity they encounter only on television shows such as "Law and Order."

The Saga of the New York Penal Barges

In January 1992, on the docks of the South Bronx not far from the Hunts Point fish market, the New York City authorities inaugurated a ship unlike any other: a flatbed barge made entirely of steel, 600-feet long and 150-feet wide, custom-built for $161 million on the Mississippi by a Louisiana shipyard. The *Vernon C. Bain* was then the latest addition to the city's carceral facilities. Its four lower decks accommodate a cluster of dormitories with a total of 700 bunk beds, a clinic, a law library, a church, a refectory, and kitchens. The bridge is occupied by a span of individual cells that can house some hundred detainees and an exercise yard surrounded by fences topped with concertina wire. The carceral ship can, if need be, function in autarky: it is endowed with a powerful electrical generator, a water desalinator, an industrial-capacity laundry, and it has its own sewage system.

If New York turned to this rather unusual device, it is because in six short years, between 1986 and 1992, the population crammed into its eighteen jails doubled to more than 21,500 (equivalent to the total carceral stock of Scandinavia and the Benelux countries put together). At the high point of use of these "floating detention centers"—as the local correctional administration likes to call them—the city confined 2,000 people on five barges, including two old Staten Island ferries refitted for this purpose and two British troop transport ships retired after having seen duty in the Falklands War. But they had no sooner been put in service than their wardens sought to decommission these warehouse-vessels, owing to their prohibitive maintenance costs and the ease with which detainees could hide in their innumerable nooks and crannies (two vessels were still in service at the end of 1999, at the piers of Rikers Island, where they moored to absorb the chronic overflow of residents).

In 1993, San Francisco studied the possible purchase of the penal barges New York no longer wanted. Like all major American cities, the metropolis that inspired Jack Kerouac was battling with a serious shortage of cells, forcing it to rent 350 beds on the other side of the bay, in the jail of neighboring Oakland, for a daily tab of $20,000. In spite of which, in a single year, San Francisco had had to pay $2 million in fines inflicted by the county court for repeatedly exceeding the numerus clausus imposed on its correctional administration. It was a complicated and delicate project, since it would require first towing these barges through the Panama Canal, then ferrying them to the northern California coast, and, after passing under the Golden Gate Bridge, finding an anchor location that would not raise too virulent an opposition from the local population. And so the attempt failed.

In March 1997, one of these barges, the *Bibby Resolution*, completed a 3,000-kilometer journey to dock at Portland Harbor, near Weymouth in Cornwall, where it was promptly rebaptized Her Majesty's *Prison Weare*: the former British troop transport vessel had been purchased back by the UK prison service to serve as a floating dormitory for 500 "low-security" inmates, in spite of protests by the representatives and inhabitants of its new port of call. This is because, having acceded to the rank of showpiece and pilot of the "Americanization" of penal policy in Europe, England was experiencing unprecedented carceral hyperinflation—its confined population had leaped 50 percent in just four years to reach 62,000 that year—and it no longer knew where to store its convicts. The return of the *Bibby Resolution* to its original homeland was a boon to the European shipping company that had bought it from New York City for less than one million dollars and resold it to the British government for eight million. But the real turkey of this maritime-cum-penal farce was the City of New York, which had acquired and outfitted the barge for a total exceeding $41 million.

The "Penal Net" Tightens and Widens

This sudden inversion of the curve of carceral demography followed by a seemingly unstoppable takeoff is all the more remarkable for having occurred during a period in which *crime was stagnant and then declining.* Indeed, contrary to the assertions of the prevailing political and media discourse, the incidence of the main categories of criminal offenses did not change fundamentally in the two decades following the mid-1970s.[13] The national homicide rate was confined to between 8 and 10 per 100,000 inhabitants from 1975 to 1995, while the frequency of robbery oscillated between 200 and 250 per 100,000 without displaying a particular trend in one direction or the other (by themselves, these two crimes account for one-quarter of the population confined in state prisons). The rate for simple assault remained stable throughout the period, at around 30 per 100,000, while the frequency of aggravated assault declined from 12 to 9 per 100,000, its lowest level in a third of a century. As for property crimes, they declined markedly: the aggregate rate of victimization for theft and burglary fell from 550 per 100,000 in 1975 to less than 300 twenty years later. And, since 1995, the incidence of all categories of crimes and misdemeanors have been heading down.

The quadrupling of the US carceral population in two decades cannot be explained by the rise of violent crime. It results from *the extension of recourse to confinement for* a range of *street* crimes and misdemeanors that did not previously lead to a custodial sanction, especially minor drug infractions and behaviors described as public disorders and nuisances, as well as from the *continual stiffening of sentences* incurred. After the mid-1970s and even more so after 1983, when the federal government declared its "War on drugs," incarceration has been applied with growing frequency and increased severity to the gamut of offenders, be they career criminals or occasional lawbreakers, big-time bandits or small-time hoodlums, the violent and the nonviolent.[14] The only exception to this punitive pattern was economic crimes and misdemeanors that are the preserve of the privileged classes and corporations: fraud, embezzlement, breach of trust, insider trading, credit or insurance fraud, check fraud, money laundering, violations of the commerce or labor codes. Despite a slight toughening at the end of the period, these "crimes in the suites" were treated with a leniency increasingly out of harmony with the atmosphere of extreme penal severity prevailing at the bottom of the class structure. "Class advantage" à la Sutherland, rooted in the sociocultural affinity of justice officials with bourgeois offenders, an edge in juridical resources available to corporate scofflaws, and laws promulgating restrictive definitions of economic crime and favoring civil remedies for them, have combined with the inherent complexity and furtiveness of white-collar crime as violations of trust in complex chains of agency to shield corporate criminals from the renewed zeal of the penal state.[15]

"White-collar" offenders are, first of all, much less likely to be detected, prosecuted, and sentenced in criminal court than street scofflaws. Next, when they are convicted, the penalties meted out for the most part exclude custodial sanctions. Finally, in the exceptional cases where white-collar convicts are incarcerated, the sentences they serve are considerably shorter than those inflicted upon the run-of-the-mill offenders. For example, at the beginning of the 1980s, 96 percent of those convicted of robbery were punished by a prison sentence averaging 60 months (for burglary, it was 82 percent for an average of 26 months), whereas only 31 percent of those convicted of embezzlement were sent to prison, and the minority who were served an average of 11 months.[16]

Thus, the same decade that saw small-time drug dealers and consumers from poor neighborhoods thrown by the hundreds of thousands behind bars for sentences measured in years (nay decades) and the homeless overfill jails on the sole ground that they engaged in panhandling or inconvenienced storeowners on "Main Street" was also the decade when "collective embezzlement," the typical crime of finance-driven capitalism, proliferated, and fraud reached its acme on "Wall Street" with near-total impunity.[17] A detailed study of the policing of the stock market by the New York Securities and Exchange Commission reveals that only 12 percent of operators who committed proven fraud were dispatched before a criminal court, a mere 6 percent were charged, and just 3 percent were eventually sent to prison.[18] The 2,500 bank directors and managers convicted after the biggest financial scandal in national history, the fraudulent bankruptcy in 1992 of thousands of Savings and Loan associations with funds guaranteed by the federal government, leaving

American taxpayers with a mop-up bill estimated at one *trillion* dollars, were sanctioned by 18 months imprisonment on average (compared to a mean of 38 months for motor vehicle theft, 54 months for burglary, and 64 months for narcotics violations with no priors meted out by federal courts during the same period). And this after the FBI had, for want of sufficient funds (Congress having refused to pass the supplemental appropriation required), dropped a full three-quarters of the 95,045 complaints registered by the federal office responsible for regulating this banking sector. Even the small minority of executives successfully prosecuted and sent to prison served but a fraction of their sentences after these were systematically reduced by judges in the closing phases of the procedure (typically, from fifteen to 2 years). The restitution of $355 million and fines of $11 million ordered by the courts came to only 4% and 0.13% respectively of the losses of $8.2 billion incurred in the debacle; and only $26 million of the restitution was actually recovered (less than 0.5% of the fines and restitution stipulated for the top 100 referrals were paid).[19] Many of the most notorious defendants never spent a single night in jail, including Arthur Kick, CEO of the North Chicago Federal Savings and Loan, who was sentenced to three years of probation for having embezzled $1.2 million, or Ted Musacchio, CEO of Columbus Marin Savings and Loan, who received five years probation for having stolen $9.3 million.

Michael Milken, the junk-bond king responsible for billions of dollars in illegal stock maneuvers on Wall Street, served the longest prison sentence in the country's history for "insider trading" as of 2000: a total of 22 months in a semi-open work center (according to inflated press reports, he had faced "up to 520 years of prison"). After paying a record fine of $1.1 billion, his personal fortune was estimated at $150 million (and that of his wife and children at $325 million). He was no sooner released than he became a star lecturer at the UCLA School of Management, a high-powered "strategic consultant," a director of Knowledge Universe (along with Rupert Murdoch), a leading firm in the new "educational services industry," the head of a large charitable foundation devoted to the fight against cancer (he survived prostate cancer), and a hero to the business press.[20]

Proof for this shift in penal attitude is the continual and accelerating increase of the ratio of the number of convicts over the volume of offenses committed during the corresponding year during the past three decades (see table 8). This index of "punitiveness" rose from 21 prisoners per thousand crimes in 1975 to 37 per 1,000 in 1985 to 75 in 1995, before jumping to 113 in 2000. In short, controlling for crime shows that *the United States has become nearly six times more punitive over this quarter-century*. The fact that the growth of this indicator is markedly superior to the parallel increase in the imprisonment index for *violent crimes alone* (438 percent versus 299 percent) confirms that

Table 8. Escalating punitiveness of penal authorities, 1975–2000

Number of inmates per 1,000 crimes	1975	1980	1985	1990	1995	2000	% increase
Punitiveness for "index crimes"	21	23	37	49	75	113	438
Punitiveness "index crimes" lagged 5 years	*29*	*27*	*35*	*57*	*71*	*95*	*227*
Punitiveness for "violent crimes"	231	227	350	392	577	922	299
Punitiveness "violent crimes" lagged 5 years	*326*	*292*	*347*	*536*	*570*	*732*	*125*

Index crimes: murder and nonnegligent manslaughter, forcible rape, robbery, aggravated assault, burglary, larceny-theft, motor vehicle theft, arson.
Violent crimes: murder and nonnegligent manslaughter, forcible rape, robbery, aggravated assault.

SOURCE: Bureau of Justice Statistics, *Sourcebook of Criminal Justice Statistics 2000* (Washington, D.C.: Government Printing Office, 2001), 528; Federal Bureau of Investigation, *Uniform Crime Reports* (Washington, D.C.: Government Printing Office, various years).

the greater severity of the American state has been directed primarily, not at the "predators" who threaten bodily mayhem, but at run-of-the-mill delinquents who commit nonviolent offenses, the overwhelming majority of whom are dredged from the lower strata of the urban proletariat, and especially its black and Hispanic components.* A lagged index of punitiveness dividing the number of inmates by the volume of crimes committed five years earlier (to take account of the delay in police action, judicial processing, and media echo) yields essentially the same result, save for a dip in the years 1975–80. Indeed, the overall increase in punitiveness is similar for the simultaneous and lagged indicators when the lagged period is shifted to cover the quarter-century from 1980 to 2005: the rise in the lagged index reaches 355% for all crimes and 244% for violent crimes. The trough observed in 1975–80 confirms that it is the penal treatment of crime after the mid-1970s (and not the evolution of the crime rate itself) that has driven the steep rise in incarceration in America.

What changed during this period is not the nature or frequency of criminal activity but the attitude of the public authorities—and the white middle class that makes up the bulk of the active electorate—toward the black proletariat and subproletariat taken to be crime's main hotbed and to whom the penal state took charge to reaffirm the

*Only a feat of intellectual bad faith or sheer ignorance of these elementary facts, which are attested by all data sources, could lead one to speak of the "myth of punitiveness" in the United States and support the bizarre claim that, "rather than being in the ascendancy, punitive and emotive sanctions may in reality be becoming increasingly untenable." Roger Matthews, "The Myth of Punitiveness," *Theoretical Criminology* 9, no. 2 (May 2005): 175–201, citation at 196.

civic imperatives of work and morality with all the more vigor as the growing instability of employment and the withering away of state charity made their situation worse.[21] Reinforced by the class and caste bias of the police and judicial system, penal austerity aims at and strikes the categories most affected by the economic insecurity and social austerity instituted as a response to the "stagflation" of the 1970s. This is to say that *hyperincarceration in the United States does not concern the "dangerous classes" so much as the precarious sectors of the working class*—and by direct implication the black subproletariat of the collapsing ghetto, insofar as it is the living intersection of these two categories. Rediscovering the mission of its historical origins, the carceral institution henceforth serves as a major instrument for managing poverty in the United States.[22]

Indeed, America's carceral hyperinflation has been fed by the concomitant growth in two factors which comparative penology shows rarely vary in the same direction in modern societies, especially with such amplitude, namely the length of detention and the volume of those sentenced to confinement.* *The lengthening of sentences expresses the toughening of judicial policy* in the United States outlined in chapter 2: multiplication of offenses punishable by imprisonment; rise in the quantum inflicted for minor infractions (such as theft, auto theft, and drug possession) as for violent crimes; mandatory minimum sentences for certain categories of law breaking (narcotics and sexual offenses) and automatic lifetime imprisonment for a third conviction (under "Three Strikes and You're Out" statutes); a steep escalation of sentences for repeat offenders; the processing of defendants below the age of sixteen as adults; and the reduction or elimination of parole. Thus, owing especially to "truth in sentencing" measures requiring that at least 85 percent of a sentence be served, inmates in state prisons convicted of offenses against persons served an average of 60 months in 1997, seven months more than in 1990, while those convicted of simple drug possession served 30 months instead of 24. However, for the great mass of prisoners, the lengthening of sentences remains in the end limited due to the swelling share of those convicted for minor offenses and the stubborn dearth of cells to house them in:[23] the average length of effective incarceration for first-time state convicts rose from 20 months in 1985 to 25 months ten years later (compared to eight months in France).**

*Recall that, at any moment in time, the *stock* of inmates (the number of individuals under lock) is the algebraic product of the *flow* of those held in deprivation of liberty (measured by the number of "admissions" to custodial establishments) by the average *length* of their confinement.

**Strong regional disparities should be noted here: the average duration of incar-

Table 9. Flow of convicts entering and leaving state prison, 1980–95 (in thousands)

	1980	1982	1984	1986	1988	1990	1992	1994	1995
Admissions	159	203	218	273	347	461	481	500	522
Releases	144	164	195	234	305	405	430	419	455
Difference	15	39	23	39	42	56	51	81	67

SOURCE: Bureau of Justice Statistics, *Correctional Populations in the United States, 1995* (Washington, D.C.: Government Printing Office, 1997), 13.

If American prisons posted an explosive growth over the past three decades, it is not only because the American penal system "strikes" harder over the years; it is also and primarily because it "rakes" in vastly more bodies. When Reagan began his presidency, the police made some 10.4 million arrests yearly, of which about two-thirds (69 percent) led to placement in custody. Fifteen years later, the annual number of arrests reached 15.2 million, and nearly all of them (94 percent) resulted in jailing. Over the same period, admissions to state penitentiaries quadrupled, jumping from 159,000 in 1980 to 522,000 in 1995 and 665,000 in 1997 (see table 9). And the gap between admissions and exits deepened by about 50,000, the equivalent of the carceral population of France or Italy.

From this angle, America's carceral evolution diverges strikingly from that of Western European countries—at least up to the mid-1990s. With some variations, the member states of the European Union have implemented penal policies of "dualization," which consist of punishing crimes considered serious more severely while making greater use of noncustodial sanctions for less serious infractions: suspended sentences, day fines, public service work, intensive parole supervision, and probation. Between 1985 and 1995, at the height of carceral hyperinflation in the United States, the number of annual admissions in jails and prisons remained stable in France (82,917 and 82,860) and in Italy (91,702 and 93,051); it rose slightly in Holland (from 24,980 to 29,232) and in Greece (from 7,054 to 8,889); and diminished elsewhere, slightly in Belgium (from 19,979 to 16,320) and dramatically in Spain (from 73,058 to 53,728). The growth of the confined population in Europe over the past two decades is explained solely by the lengthening of sen-

ceration (measured by the sentence served by prisoners released in 1997) runs from 8 months in Delaware to 62 months in West Virginia. Nineteen states lock people up for over 30 months on average. Camille Graham and George M. Camp, eds., *The Corrections Yearbook 1998* (Middletown, Conn.: Criminal Justice Institute, 1999), 56–57.

tences handed down by the courts.[24] There was no such "dualization" of punishment in the United States, where all scofflaws were subject to an increasingly punitive regime and an ever-larger volume of individuals found themselves in the clutches of the carceral apparatus.

The systematic recourse to the police and judicial institutions to contain the disorders of everyday life in poor neighborhoods and households explains why American prisons today are overfull, not with "violent predators," as the partisans of all-out incarceration drone, but by nonviolent criminals and petty delinquents, most of whom, as we emphasized in chapter 2, are drawn from the most vulnerable fractions of the working class. As can be seen upon reading table 10, the overwhelming majority of the half-million people admitted to state prisons (73 percent) and federal penitentiaries (94 percent) in 1994 were "sent down" for nonviolent offenses. Even grasped from the point of view of stocks, where their weight is necessarily greater insofar as they serve considerably longer sentences, those convicted of crimes of violence (homicide, manslaughter, forcible rape, assault, robbery) represent only 26 percent of the residents of county jails, 13 percent of those confined in federal prisons, and less than one-half of the clients of state facilities. This was also the case with the 110,000 minors incarcerated in 1998, only 15 percent of whom were accused or convicted of crimes against persons.

At the beginning of the 1990s, at the height of the carceral wave sweeping the country, the typical convict entering a state penitentiary in America was an African-American male (54 percent as against 19 percent for whites), under 35 years of age (for three-quarters of them), without a high-school diploma (62 percent), convicted for a nonviolent crime in more than seven of ten cases.[25] The most common offenses committed by the new entrants were possession or sale of narcotics (29 percent), theft or concealing stolen goods (19 percent), burglary (15 percent), and public order violations (8 percent). Barely one-quarter were sent down for violent crimes, including robbery (11 percent), assault (7 percent), sex offenses (5 percent), or murder and kidnapping (4 percent together). And this breakdown does not include the almost one-third of entries who were unsuccessful parolees, many of whom were returned behind bars not as a result of a new court conviction but due to a mere administrative revocation sanctioning a violation of the terms of their conditional release.

Here is another indication that penal confinement serves above all to control the disruptive street "rabble" more than combat the crimes of blood whose specter haunts the media and feeds a thriving cultural industry of fear of the poor, led by such television programs as

Table 10. Share of violent offenders in the flow and stock of inmates, 1995

	Flow Admissions	% violent	% property	% drugs	% public order
Jails	—	—	—	—	—
State prisons	*337,492*	28.8	29.5	30.8	10.2
Federal prisons	*31,805*	6.9	21.1	44.2	27.7

SOURCE: Bureau of Justice Statistics, *Correctional Populations of the United States, 1995* (Washington, D.C.: Government Printing Office, 1997), 12 for flow, and 6–7 for stock in state prisons; 14–15 for flow and 8–9 for stock in federal penitentiaries; Caroline Wolf Harlow, *Profile of Jail Inmates 1996* (Washington, D.C.: Bureau of Justice Statistics, 1998), 5 for jails.

"America's Most Wanted" and "Cops":* the number of convicts held for violent crimes in state prisons increased 86 percent between 1985 and 1995, while the number of their comrades locked up for drug and public order offenses grew by 478 percent and 187 percent, respectively. The former accounted for 39 percent of the increase of the population under lock during this period, the latter for 43 percent. Similarly, the share of those convicted of narcotics possession or distribution in federal prisons went from one-third in 1985 to 60 percent ten years later. By themselves, violators of drug laws accounted for 71 percent of the population growth in these establishments.[26]

Based on in-depth interviews with a representative sample of prisoners in Illinois and Nevada allowing them to go beyond the rough aggregate figures of correctional statistics, John Irwin and James Austin demonstrated that over half of the clients of state penitentiaries were locked up for petty infractions entailing no physical violence and negligible material damages, and thus presenting none of "the features that would cause ordinary citizens to view the crime as particularly serious."[27] A detailed examination of their social and judicial trajectories reveals that six in ten prisoners are occasional criminals who committed their misdeed by association, impulsively, or because they were cast adrift. Far from being "vicious predators" (the term consecrated by the mainstream media and politicians), 60 percent of "habitual of-

*These programs broadcast in prime time videos of real police interventions, typically in dispossessed black and Latino neighborhoods, in utter disregard of the rights of those arrested and humiliated on camera. Aron Doyle, "'Cops': Television Policing as Policing Reality," in *Entertaining Crime: Television Reality Programs*, ed. Mark Fishman and Gray Cavender, 95–116 (New York: Aldine, 1998).

Stock Population	% violent	% property	% drugs	% public order
507,026	26.3	26.9	22.0	24.3
989,005	46.5	22.9	21.5	8.7
88,101	13.1	8.7	59.9	18.3

fenders" are low-level "disorganized offenders without skills or discipline who rarely committed acts of violence" and who turned to crime by default, as it were, due to their inability to find a stable and durable occupational footing. "Their crimes are petty and pathetic. These are drunken car thieves who fall asleep in their victim's car, shoplifters being caught in a clumsy attempt to brazenly walk out of a store with a shopping cart full of stolen goods, and crack-heads selling $2 rocks to undercover agents. They are, in many respects, aging offenders who know no other way to live."[28]

Impressive as they may be, carceral statistics nonetheless seriously understate the hold that judicial institutions have on the populations consigned to the nether regions of American social space. For they do not take into account the spectacular expansion of indirect modes of surveillance and control which the authorities have evolved to regulate the deskilled fractions of the working class in the age of the generalization of precarious wage labor and the retraction of the protections offered by the state.

First of all, the mass of people under "criminal justice supervision" at any moment is composed not of inmates but of persons placed on *probation* and former prisoners released on *parole* after having served the greater share of their sentence (see figure 3). The number of offenders on probation grew from 1.12 million in 1980 to some 3.84 million twenty years later, while the population on parole took off from 220,000 to nearly 726,000.[29] In total, *the stock of Americans under penal oversight grew by more than four and a half million in twenty years*: starting from 1.84 million in 1980, it rose to 4.35 million in 1990 and reached 6.47 million in 2000, a figure that represents 3 percent of the country's adult population, corresponding to one adult male in twenty and one

Figure 3. 6.5 million Americans under criminal justice supervision in 2000

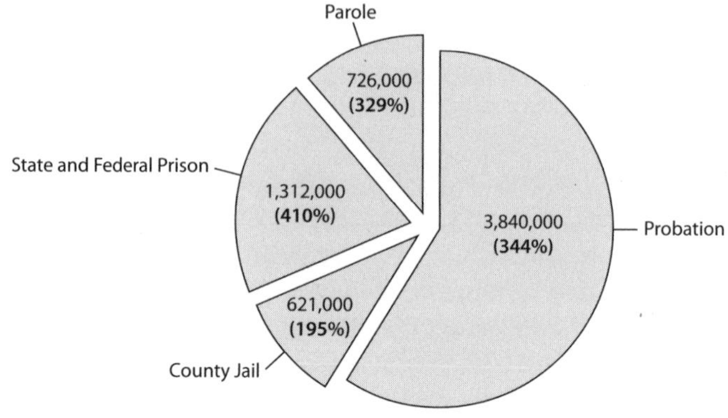

SOURCE: Bureau of Justice Statistics, *Sourcebook of Criminal Justice Statistics 2000* (Washington, D.C.: US Government Printing Office, 2002), 145.

black man in ten. In 1998, eleven states each held in excess of 100,000 probationers under their heel; that is more than France holds (87,000). By themselves, Texas (with 429,000 convicts on probation), California (287,000), Florida (237,000), and New York State (174,000) controlled more than one million. Aside from the sheer volume of convicts outside the walls and its continual growth, what must be noted is that the four and a half million people kept in the shadow of the prison were in an eminently precarious judicial position since they had a good chance of landing in it (again): two in five probationers and six in ten parolees who exited this status in 1997 were thrown behind bars, either because they committed a new offense or because they violated one or another administrative condition of their release (by failing an alcohol test or failing to hold a job, missing an appointment, leaving their county of assignment, etc.).

Next, the extension of judicial supervision itself does not fully capture the multiform processes by which the mesh of the penal net has been at once reinforced and expanded—a process that criminologists designate by the visually evocative concepts of "net strengthening" and "net widening."[30] Thus, in addition to the deployment of "intermediate sanctions" such as house arrest and boot camps, "intensive supervision," day reporting, community service, and telephone or electronic surveillance (with the help of bracelets and assorted technological gadgets), the grasp of the American judicial system has been considerably enlarged thanks to the proliferation of criminal databanks and the multiplication of the means and points of control-at-a-distance they authorize.

Identify, Test, (Re)capture

In *The Justice Juggernaut*, Diana Gordon shows how, alongside its "capture" function, in the 1970s and 1980s the American state energetically developed its "observation" function regarding populations considered deviant or dangerous.[31] Under the impetus of the Law Enforcement Administration Agency, the federal bureaucracy entrusted with activating the fight against crime in response to the citizen "demand" elicited by the diffusion of the discourse of "law and order" (the LEAA distributed over $8 billion in subsidies during the twenty years of its existence), the police, courts, and correctional administrations of the fifty states have created centralized computerized databanks, which have since proliferated in all directions.

The result is that the country's various police agencies (local, state, and federal) now hold some 55 million "criminal files"—as against 35 million a decade earlier—on about *30 million individuals*, corresponding to nearly *one-third of the nation's adult male population*.[32] Access to these databanks varies by case and jurisdiction. Some can be consulted only by judicial authorities and strictly for judicial purposes. Others are accessible not only to other public bureaucracies, such as the Federal Bureau of Investigation, the Immigration and Naturalization Service, or its successor agencies (responsible for policing foreigners), and welfare services, but also to private persons and organizations via the internet. These "rap sheets" (police reports, court records, and correctional files) are commonly used, for example, by employers to weed out ex-convicts applying for jobs. And it matters little that the information included in them is frequently incorrect, out of date, harmless, or sometimes even illegally disseminated: their circulation places not only criminals and those suspected of offenses, but also their families, friends, and neighborhoods, into the sight of the police and penal apparatus.

As of December 31, 1997, the so-called "criminal history" archives of the states (Criminal History Record Information, or CHRI) contained 54,210,800 individual files, 7.4 million of them manual and 46.8 million automated. Some 18 million of these arrest records with fingerprints were also stored in the Interstate Identification Index (III), the computerized national registry containing the profiles of all persons arrested for crimes deemed serious by the country's various police services and which can be consulted online by the 39 states participating in the program.[33] Finally, in 1997 the FBI received and entered 8.6 million new sets of fingerprints into its NFF (National Fingerprint File) databank, 3 million of which were passed on for nonjudicial purposes.

The geometric growth of police and judicial databanks is part of a broader movement of extension and diversification of "undercover" police surveillance, which has become more proactive and diffuse over the years with the growth of the number of agents and agencies involved—and, with them, the number and variety of their targets.[34] The absence of national legislation regulating the use of this information and the massive (although relatively late) recourse to computers in effect make it possible to expand, routinize, and automate the collection and circulation of data harvested by the forces of order, the courts, and correctional administrations and their satellites. And there is still plenty of room for growth: only half of the states have contributed more than 70 percent of their arrest records accumulated over the past five years to the CHRI; the entry or exit of inmates is systematically recorded in only thirty states in the case of prison convicts and in fifteen for jail detainees.

This is well illustrated by the proliferation of electronic databanks on juvenile delinquents—or those thought to be such. During the 1980s, with the support of the federal Department of Justice, most big American cities established computerized registries called "SHODI youths" (the acronym means "serious and habitual offender/drug infraction"), which catalog teenagers believed to be real or potential delinquents—a convenient pretext for placing segregated neighborhoods and their residents under reinforced police and penal surveillance. As a result, in 1993 the Denver police had garnered files on some 6,500 youths "suspected" of being gang members, even as, according to their own estimates, there were fewer than 500 gang members in the entire city. This is because, to figure in these files, it sufficed to be arrested at the same time as a (presumed) gang member, to wear (supposed) gang colors, to be reputed to know an (alleged) gang member, or simply to have been seen in his company. By virtue of this loose definition, over nine youths in ten on this list were African American (57 percent) or Latino (33 percent), although the population of Denver was 80 percent white. One understands the intermingled furor and fury of the black community at discovering that no fewer than 3,691 of its youth, amounting to fully two-thirds of African Americans ages 12 to 24 residing in the city, were considered suspect if not guilty on principle by the authorities.[35] The judicial fuzziness and flagrant ethnic bias that affect the compiling of such lists do not prevent the police from relying on them to target their patrols and arrests and prosecutors from impeaching those included on them with redoubled severity.

In 1997, Illinois put the files of all its current and recent inmates on the internet site of its corrections administration and made them freely accessible. With a few mouse-clicks, and without any justification or the slightest control, anyone can read or download the profiles of all of the state's prisoners—name, date of birth, social security number (normally held secret), "race," height and weight, intimate distinctive markings ("a description of each mark, scar, tattoo worn by the inmate, including its physical description and location")—as well as a summary of their judicial records comprising an enumeration of their convictions (nature, category, and number of infractions, some of which can go back twenty or thirty years, and place of judgment). Anyone can also find out when and where such and such an inmate was incarcerated, their anticipated (or effective) date of release and of the ending of supervision. Thanks to "Look Up an Inmate," every employer or landlord can, before hiring or renting, check that the applicant in question has no criminal background, and thus discriminate at will on the basis of his judicial record. As the spokesperson of the Illinois Department of Corrections explained with a tone of self-evidence, "these are criminals, after all, surely people have the right to have this information to protect themselves. It's the same as seeing them on television, it's in the public domain."[36]

The Texas Department of Public Safety—as the correctional administration of that state is called—is more cautious: its site records the identity of the internet inquirer (but one can easily provide fanciful information to get through) and warns that the data made available to the public may be incomplete, incorrect, or deceptive, if only because they have been systematically collected only since 1994 and many convicts are listed in it under borrowed names, and so these data cannot engage the responsibility of the state. It is more interested, too, since one has to pay to consult the registry of convicts, which comprises 2 million files: $3.15 per request, plus a connection fee of 57 cents. The information provided is less rich, since it does not include the distinctive physical markings born by the convict (on the other hand, it contains hair and eye color, which after all are more immediately discernable than private tattoos), but it allows more elaborate searches by combining variables: for example, in May 1999 a query about "John Wilson" brought up 216 files, which fell to 69 if one specified "black," then 7 if one added "B" as middle initial (including 4 individuals for whom this was an alias). A similar search for "Robert Smith" in the databank reserved for sex offenders delivered more than 50 files.

> But it is Florida that is the pacesetter in the race to disseminate the personal data and criminal history of convicts "in the interest of public safety": the "Corrections Offender Network" rubric on the web site of its correctional administration, which has received over 12 million visitors since its inauguration in March 1998, offered the usual private and carceral information, a large-format color photograph, as well as the address at which recently released convicts were presumed to reside.

The relentless growth of official criminal databases is dwarfed by the unregulated proliferation of private companies offering criminal background checks and commercial information banks amassed by the "data mining" industry, which dredges, sifts, compiles, buys, and resells information drawn from a vast array of public and private registries (rolls of voters, holders of drivers licenses, civil records, real estate transactions and property taxes, census data, credit ratings, medical records, military personnel receiving a "dishonorable discharge," war veterans committed to psychiatric hospitals, etc.), all of which can be connected to judicial files culled from court reports and correctional records. In 2004, 472 companies offered databases to ascertain the criminal justice background of individuals for the entire United States.[37] Such verification has become routine because advanced digital technologies and online services allow firms to obtain immediate checks at a very low cost. For instance, the company InstantCriminalChecks.com offers online criminal background verification for $19.95 for one state, $39.95 for three states, and $45.95 for the entire country. It promises its "customers the best criminal data, the easiest ordering process, and the most detailed criminal reports INSTANTLY." The "criminal check" purchased contains the name, Social Security number, and profile of the offender; the offense type, code, and disposition; custody and case information, as well as jail and probation data.* In reaction to an increasingly litigious work environment and the shock of the 9/11 attacks, the proportion of companies running such criminal

*The firm vaunts its services thus: "Performing a comprehensive criminal background check before you hire a new employee can save your company from big headaches including monetary and legal costs. With repeat criminal offenders applying for work, you need to keep your company and your employees as safe as you can. Conducting a criminal background check with InstantCriminalChecks.com is easy, fast and affordable." In addition to employment decisions, verification is encouraged for "self checks, nanny checks, babysitter criminal background checks, and private investigations." A list of legal disclaimers follows, including the concession that "users should not assume that this data provides a complete or accurate history of any person's criminal history."

checks on applicants prior to hiring jumped from 30 percent in 1996 to 80 percent in 2004, making the verification of judicial background as common as checking prior work history. According to a study by the Society for Human Resource Management, one-half of those firms, big and small, also verify education transcripts and motor vehicle records and 35% of them even run checks on the credit history of job applicants (up from 19% a decade earlier).

The diffusion of criminal justice files through internet sites or private agencies specializing in "background checks" on employees cannot but drastically reduce the occupational chances of people placed under, or having gone through, judicial supervision, given the demonstrated reluctance of employers to hire them. A study of a representative sample of 800 businesses employing unskilled labor in Atlanta, Boston, Detroit, and Los Angeles reveals that these firms tend to reject applicants who have either an intermittent employment record or a criminal background, with ex-convicts coming way at the end of the "queue" of desirable candidates. Thus 68 percent of firms said that they are open to hiring a person who has been unemployed for over a year, and one-half would employ an individual who has only worked temporary jobs, but *two-thirds would refuse on principle to hire any applicant sentenced to prison or jail*. Now, almost half of businesses in the service sectors—those where employment is growing and unskilled former inmates are most likely to seek a job—check the criminal background of applicants.[38] Moreover, in a number of states ex-convicts are required by law to inform their employer of their judicial status under pain of having their release revoked. It is, all the same, very difficult for those on conditional release to conceal their status from their employer since their parole officer will routinely check up on them at their place of work (according to inmates from San Quentin state prison questioned on the subject, this is the most humiliating aspect of being put under supervision, since it instantly makes them lepers among their fellow employees).

A questionnaire survey of 300 employers in Dallas and Houston representative of the local economy deliver still more discouraging results with barely 12 percent of them stating that they would be prepared to hire an ex-convict.[39] The percentage rises to just 22 percent for former prisoners who followed a job training program while in custody and falls to less than 5 percent in the case of those convicted of violent crimes or sex offenses. To be sure, the rate of welcoming businesses approaches one-third in the case of ex-convicts who obtained a college degree while behind bars, but this is a highly improbable scenario since the US Congress cut off all public funding for higher education in prison in 1994. This places former prisoners before this impossible choice: either admit their criminal background and thus be immediately excluded from the pool of viable job applicants, or falsify their application form at the risk of being sent back to prison later (by the correctional administration) or fired for having lied on their application when the firm proceeds to a routine background check of the judicial status of its employees.* As a result, "those who have (or are suspected of having) criminal records or checkered work histories will have difficulty getting hired in even the lowest-wage jobs and least skill-intensive sectors of the economy."[40] The virulent ostracism to which "ex-cons" are subjected on the job market explains why a stint behind bars cuts their average length of employment by half (as measured by the number of hours worked annually) and consequently their income. For African-American convicts returning to life outside, the negative effect of incarceration is even more pronounced, with their postimprisonment income reaching an average of only 44 percent what it was before.[41] And everything indicates that this ostracism is being reinforced by the broader diffusion of personalized criminal data, on the one hand, and the crystallization of a genuine public culture of loathing of prisoners, on the other.

What is more, the same techniques of digital fingerprinting deployed to supervise convicts released on parole are used to "downsize" the welfare rolls and prevent public aid fraud. In winter 1996 the governor of New York State boasted that compulsory identification by "finger imaging" (the optical reading of fingerprints) had allowed the "weeding out" of more than 25,000 public aid recipients during the program's first year. "I am confident that my plan to reform welfare by replacing the aid check with a paycheck will be as great a success as our fingerprinting program."[42] In one year, the welfare administration submitted 747,000 people to digitalized checks and excluded 35,000 from its rolls,

*In order to safeguard against possible lawsuits in a business environment getting ever-more litigious, a growing number of firms systematically check the "criminal background" of their employees, not only upon hiring (by means of a written questionnaire and during the individual hiring interview) but also periodically, by having the list of their employees scoured annually by a specialized agency. There were about 600 "background checking" companies in the United States, 71 of which posted earnings in excess of one million dollars in 1999. The leaders of this booming market (especially for checking backgrounds for drug use) are Medtox Scientific Incorporated and Bayshore Clinical Labs (with annual revenue approaching $50 million that year), Records Services Inc. and Occupational Health Services (between $10 million and $20 million), and Avert Inc., Borg Warner Information Services, Worksigns, and Blue River Services (between $5 and $10 million each). *American Business Database of 10,000,000 Public and Private Companies in the United States* (CD-ROM, 1999).

amounting to 5 percent of their "clients" (according to the official terminology), for having failed to register their fingerprints in the state's computer databank. Ten thousand of them had their rights restored later, but only after losing their benefits for several months. Among the files purged, 16,000 received "home relief," a program for single indigent adults that paid out $350 per month to 271,000 people. The director of social services celebrated these results: "The high rate of permanent file closure shows that digital fingerprinting deters people who would otherwise use multiple identities to defraud welfare."

In any case, all these "old-style" files, manually put together from rough records based on physical fingerprints and mugs shots, are themselves in the process of being superseded by infinitely larger, more precise, and more powerful databanks containing the *genetic fingerprints* of the individuals caught in the police and penal dragnet. Forty-eight states have already used some variant of "biological filing" for several years, done by means of a blood sample taken at release of certain sensitive categories of prisoners such as murderers and sex offenders (as well as prostitutes in Connecticut, or all juvenile offenders as in Virginia).* But a new era of penal panopticism opened in the United States in 1994 when Congress passed the DNA Identification Act, releasing $25 million to facilitate the systematization of computerized criminal files and their countrywide interconnection through the creation of a common source registry, the CODIS (Combined DNA Information System). Enthusiasm for genetic filing has since spread like wildfire from Savannah to Seattle and El Paso to Chicago. Some even present it as the miracle cure that will finally allow America to rid itself of the plague of criminal violence by effectively isolating the supposed "hard core" of incorrigible criminals.

On October 13, 1998, the FBI officially put in operation its national genetic databank containing the DNA profile of 25,000 felons as well as the "forensic data" for 4,600 unresolved criminal cases. Since this milestone date, the states that wish to can connect to this central registry to transfer their own genetic samples and get access to the samples

*The existing legal frameworks vary widely. For example, Colorado stipulates that any prisoner convicted for sexual assault must supply a DNA sample before being released on parole. Kansas authorizes "the collection of blood and saliva samples for all those sentenced to prison for more than one year [felons] due to an illegal sexual act, first or second degree murder, incest, aggravated incest, or child abuse." Ohio uses genetic fingerprinting for those convicted of murder, kidnapping, forcible rape, and sexual assault, but excludes theft. Florida, to the contrary, includes theft with violence, assault, and carjacking. Alaska extends this practice to any person implicated in a natural disaster; Maine to juvenile offenders. And so on.

collected by the others. The number of prints already amassed by the different correctional administrations waiting to enter into the FBI databank was then estimated at 350,000, and the cost of the operation at $22 million. For example, California's correctional genetic databank alone contained some 100,000 saliva and blood samples taken from convicts for sexual offenses, homicide, and kidnapping.[43] A national competition immediately started to see which state would solve the most crimes by a simple check of its genetic databank: in April 1999, Florida claimed to have scored 155 "cold hits," but all envied Great Britain, which proudly posted 30,000 cases solved thanks to DNA identification. By 2004, according to an FBI brochure, the CODIS databank contained just over 2 million offender profiles, including 94,000 forensic profiles (DNA prints developed from crime scene evidence such as blood or stains), which had allowed 13,800 "offender hits" nationwide.

The forces aiming to check the vertiginous expansion of genetic databanks in police and penal matters—as elsewhere in the field of health and life insurance, employment, and civil disputes such as paternity suits—are fighting a rear-guard battle that seems lost in advance, so great is the fascination for this new technique of identification and surveillance. It appears indeed to marry legal rigor, moral neutrality, financial frugality, and scientific infallibility. And it benefits to the full from the predilection that Americans have for technological solutions to social problems.[44] Finally, its advocates can emphasize the possibility it affords of proving the innocence of those falsely convicted: the country's major newspapers are suddenly teeming with moving stories about prisoners freed after years of unwarranted confinement thanks to a simple DNA test,* as if to counterbalance the usual dismal and alarming daily coverage of violent crimes and gruesome trials.

In December 1998 the New York City chief of police, always on the lookout for gadgets liable to help him to uphold his city's planetary reputation as the Mecca of law enforcement, proposed taking the genetic fingerprints of all individuals apprehended by the city's police

*Sixty-two prisoners had been retroactively cleared by this means as of spring of 1999 ("DNA Tests are Freeing Scores of Prison Inmates," *New York Times*, 19 April 1999), a figure which nearly doubled by 2005. A populist plea for genetic testing as a means for exonerating the wrongfully convicted typical of a new genre of books on the topic is Harlan Levy, *And the Blood Cried Out: A Prosecutor's Spellbinding Account of DNA's Power to Free or Convict* (New York: Avon, 1997). For a narrative account of how devious interrogation tactics, faulty identification, overaggressive prosecutors, and incompetent defenders routinely combine to produce wrongful convictions, see Dave Eggers, Lola Vollen, and Scott Turow, *Surviving Justice: America's Wrongfully Convicted and Exonerated* (Boston: McSweeney, 2005).

by having an officer armed with a cotton swab collect a saliva sample at booking. Meanwhile, Louisiana and North Carolina were discussing bills going in the same direction, and several weeks later, the annual national convention of police chiefs offered enthusiastic support for adopting such a measure.[45] In spring of 1999, in response to this groundswell, a group of government experts, the National Commission for the Future of DNA Evidence, was directed by attorney general Janet Reno to examine the legal and technical problems posed by the establishment of a national megabank of genetic identification data concerning not only criminals convicted of violent or sexual offenses, nor even all those convicted by the courts, but *all those arrested* by the various police services, amounting to a dozen million Americans every year. Such a system of systematic mass police filing could very quickly become reality, considering the combined progress of biotechnology and computers as well as the economies of scale that the generalization of this technique of identification would offer: experts predict that it will be possible within a few years to collect, store, and analyze a DNA sample for under ten dollars. The recent development of a portable "DNA mini-laboratory" the size of a briefcase allowing for the analysis of blood, saliva, hair, or fingernail samples *in situ* and the deciphering of the genetic code of individuals present at crime scenes within a half-hour cannot fail to encourage this practice.

In theory, genetic fingerprinting and data collection is intended to enable the authorities to train the sights of the penal system on "career" criminals and hardened multirecidivists and, in the process, reduce its "collateral impact." In practice, their generalization translates into an unprecedented widening of surveillance and indirect control as well as their indefinite extension in time:[46] an individual recorded in CODIS or the genetic databank of his city police will be in it for life. He will thus be liable to being identified and apprehended even for minor infractions committed years or decades earlier following a routine police check, a simple arrest functioning in the manner of an instantaneous minitrial. There is no more "right to oblivion" for the Americans caught in the trap of the police and penal apparatus that is gradually replacing the remnants of the welfare state in the lower regions of the national social space: they have already entered into a society of continual and perpetual punitive surveillance.

One last transformation, at once qualitative and quantitative, completes the tightening of the penal noose around the fractions of the working class destabilized by the rise of precarious wage labor and the withering away of social protection: the drying out of early release and the mutation of parole into a policing program devoted, not to helping convicts reintegrate into society (to the degree they were ever "integrated"), but to recapturing the greatest possible number by subjecting them to intensive surveillance and punctilious discipline, especially by means of drug testing (which has become the main activity of probation and parole services in many jurisdictions). Each year, half a million convicts are released from state prisons; the vast majority (around 85 percent) are then placed under the supervision of a parole officer for a period averaging 23 months. In the three years following their release, 60 percent will find themselves back behind bars, most for committing minor offenses such as causing a public disturbance, theft, or a drug infraction. The "springboard" of parole has become a "trapdoor": between 1985 and 1997, the rate of parolees who successfully completed their period of "community supervision" dropped from 70 percent to 44 percent. And the share of recaptured parolees among prison admissions doubled nationwide in two decades, going from 16 percent of new entries in 1980 to 34 percent in 1997.[47]

In California, the number of parolees sent back behind bars—which the state correctional administration refers to by the acronym PVRC ("Parole Violators Returned to Custody")—exploded from 2,995 in 1980 to 75,400 in 1996, 58,000 of them following a simple administrative revocation.* According to the latest figures from the California Department of Corrections (CDC), 85 percent of the state's parolees suffer from chronic alcohol or drug dependency, 10 percent are without a regular home (that rate exceeds one-half for inmates from Los Angeles), more than half are functionally illiterate, and 70–90 percent are unemployed when they come out. Upon release, the correctional administration gives them $200 in pocket-money and a bus ticket to the county in which they lived at the time of their arrest (they are legally required to reside there so long as they are under supervision of the criminal justice system), without any assistance or preparation for release in more than nine out of ten cases. Thus, the CDC has 200 beds in shelters for 10,000 homeless parolees, four clinics for 18,000 parolees in need of serious psychiatric care, and 750 beds in detoxification wards while 85,000 ex-convicts on parole suffer from known drug addiction or alcoholism.

*For comparison, with a national population double that of California, France's correctional administration sported 525 revocations of parole release in 1996, corresponding to 11 percent of those supervised under this status: 233 were returned behind bars following a new conviction, 186 for failing to fulfill the terms of their parole, and 40 for "notorious misconduct." Administration pénitentiaire, *Rapport annuel d'activité 1996* (Paris: Ministère de la justice, 1997).

This change of parole procedures and outcomes is the product of the jettisoning of the ideal of rehabilitation in the wake of the converging criticisms of the Right and the Left during the 1970s. Rehabilitation was effectively replaced by a managerialist philosophy that is content to handle flows and contain costs by carefully eluding the question of the causes and consequences of hyperincarceration, and that turns away from the social fate of the inmate once his sentence has been served. In this perspective, the prison serves to isolate and neutralize deviant or dangerous categories through standardized surveillance and the stochastic management of risks, according to a logic more akin to operational research or the processing of "social waste" than to social work.[48] Indeed, thirty years ago parole officers graduated from schools of social work and studied the basics of sociology and psychology. Today, while their caseload has doubled, they are trained in schools of criminal justice where they learn police techniques and the handling of firearms. The new panoptic philosophy that guides them is confirmed by this semantic slide: parole programs have recently been renamed "controlled release" in Florida, "community control" in Minnesota, and even "community detention" in Washington State.[49] For, under the new liberal-paternalist regime, the parolee is less an ex-convict returned to freedom than a quasi-inmate waiting to be sent back behind bars.

The new-style parole programs exhibit a pronounced penchant for drug testing (and secondarily alcohol detection) verging on obsession. This obsession would be incomprehensible, if not for the fact that this permanent checking allows the authorities to dramatize their determination to crack down and draw a sharp dividing line between good and bad parolees, those who behave in accordance with the law (and public morality) and those who continue to violate it, be it in a discrete and harmless way. They reveal how a punitive logic has now openly superseded therapeutic treatment even in the case of offenses that pertain at least partly to the medical register. A recent survey of 22 parole administrations across the country emphasizes that only 7 offer detoxification programs (and only 14 jobs programs), whereas all of them without exception make intensive use of drug testing.[50]

In 1998 Maryland allocated $5 million for a drug-testing program called "Breaking the Cycle," which aimed to impose "forced abstinence" on its 15,000 probationers and parolees by subjecting them to two mandatory drug tests every week. "Stay clean, or stay in jail": to implement this slogan in seven counties, Maryland increased the annual number of tests from 40,000 to one million by subcontracting them to a specialized firm.[51] The professed objective of this heightened surveillance campaign for convicts on the outside is not to heal a drug-addicted population but to improve the "quality of life" of "law-abiding citizens" by reducing the nuisances, panhandling, and petty crime connected to narcotics trafficking on the street, and to reaffirm the principle of inflexible intolerance toward all drugs by enlisting medical personnel as auxiliaries to the forces of order. "Therapists are policemen," a clinical psychologist charged with administering a version of this program in Michigan said proudly.

Subjected to conditions of release ever more numerous and difficult to satisfy while supervision is bolstered and focused on technical violations, and caught in the pincers of a reduction of support and a rise in public intolerance for any failure owing to the media stir around crimes committed by ex-convicts, the majority of parolees "remain dependent on others or the state, drift back and forth from petty crime to subsistence, menial, dependent living, or gravitate to the new permanent underclass—the 'homeless'"—unless they die prematurely of illness, drug overdose, or violent crime.[52] They are condemned to survive by hook or by crook, flushed from under the protective wing of the welfare state, in direct reach of the punitive arm of the penal state.

"Controlled Chaos" in the Leading Penal Colony of the Free World

Since the end of the 1980s, the Los Angeles County Jail (LACJ) has held the title of largest penal colony in the Western world, edging out its rival in New York—the county sheriff's office boasts about it on its web site. In 2000, its seven establishments in operation held around 23,000 detainees, as against fewer than 9,000 in 1980 (by comparison, the largest prison in Western Europe, Fleury-Mérogis, twenty miles south of Paris, holds 3,900).

As one would expect, the bulk of the jail's clients come from the lower reaches of Angelino social space: 46 percent are Latino and 33 percent black, as against only 18 percent white, whereas whites make up 51 percent of the population in the county. One-half are between 18 and 29 years old and seven in ten did not complete high school. Much like the country's other big jails, three perennial problems afflict the LACJ: overpopulation, violence, and ethnic conflict.

The network of Angelino gaols holds 11,000 more detainees than it officially has beds, since its establishments were designed to accommodate 12,000. Worse, if judges were to enforce all of the prison sentences they inflict on the 120,000-odd persons placed under the county's penal supervision, they would contain 39,000! But space is sorely lacking, with the result that, despite the suffocating political climate of penal rigor, a large majority of individuals arrested for minor misdemeanors are released without oversight while the others serve only a fraction of their sentences. Due to overpopulation, a conviction by the criminal court of the county of Los Angeles to one year of custody translates on average into 83 days of effective detention.

The challenge the LACJ confronts daily consists in receiving, sorting, and "processing" the detainees as quickly as possible "through the system"—in the manner of a treatment center for social waste—in order to avoid bottlenecks and violent incidents, which still result in the death of around twenty inmates annually.* Considering that between a quarter and a third of a million people pass through the gates of the LACJ in the course of a year, one understands easily why its managers describe its operation by the expression "controlled chaos" (the other expression that frequently comes to their lips is "zoo").

The arrestees and convicts who pour in at the rate of one thousand per day are steered to the "selection center" of the Twin Towers, on the edge of downtown, before being distributed among the various establishments located on the city's periphery. In theory, they are divided into 40 categories according to the nature of their offenses, their criminal record, and their propensity to violence. In reality, "there exists no systematic procedure for segregating inmates according to their level of violence or escape risk."** For the mere identification of an arrestee presents a mind-boggling challenge: it requires consulting five different databanks in which the same individual may figure (or not) under various aliases. Los Angeles County recently put in service a computerized system for "digital recognition," but the neighboring counties do not have it; nor is there a truly reliable and complete criminal database on a national level.

In any case, the available resources of cells and staff do not always allow for properly separating dangerous convicts from common-law detainees, blacks from Latinos, members of the Crips street gang from their rivals of the Bloods, sexual offenders from their fellow jailees intent on brutalizing them (as is the custom in almost all the prisons in the world). Whence the violence that wracks the

*In 1997 the Los Angeles County Jail officially recorded the deaths of 47 inmates, including 38 from "natural causes," three from the consequences of AIDS, and one by homicide, for a mortality rate of 2.3 per thousand, significantly higher than the national average for big-city jails: it came to double the figure for Phoenix and triple that for Detroit, Oakland, and Seattle; but Baltimore and Philadelphia posted the same mortality rate. Graham and Camp, *Corrections Yearbook 1998*, 230.

**According to the periodic evaluation of the commission appointed by the county court to supervise the reform of the operations of the Sheriff's Office in response to a series of lawsuits filed by inmates' rights associations in the 1980s. Los Angeles County Sheriff's Department, *Fifth Semiannual Report by Special Counsel Merrick J. Bobb and Staff*, February 1996, mimeograph, 14.

gaols of the City of Angels, where, as even the authorities admit, "confrontations between ethnic and racial groups, between gangs, and between sub-gangs, are endemic."[53] Rumor among the residents of the LACJ has it that in the Pitchess East and Pitchess West facilities, located about thirty miles from downtown on the edge of the Sierra, there is "a race riot every day." Officially, in 1996 there were 61 incidents in these two jails that pitted hostile groups against one another and required the use of firearms by the staff or the intervention of special operations forces, which explains why detainees and guards alike are openly fearful of being sent out there. When they learn that they are to be transferred to "the Ranch" (the nickname of these two outlying detention centers), some inmates do not hesitate to tear off their identity bracelet in the hope that their sudden anonymity will postpone the inevitable, even though they know that this act will be punished by an automatic lengthening of their sojourn behind bars.

To the violence between residents one must add the violence that the guards wield upon them, whether it be to enforce discipline and safety within the legal framework of their office or by incompetence or abuse of authority, as when certain "screws" deem it incumbent upon themselves to ensure a level of penal rigor in their establishment higher than that stipulated by its regulations. Such was the case with a secret "posse" of "enforcers" formed by a dozen Twin Towers guards, eight of whom were relieved of their duties in September 1998 for having visited organized and aggravated violence on the inmates of the psychiatric ward, whom they considered to be overly "pampered." "When these screws beat you up," recounted a jail veteran preparing to leave on furlough under electronic supervision, "you can read the brand of their flashlight on your body" (the LA carceral argot calls this "getting the flashlight treatment").

Violence is sustained by the glaring imbalance between the number of guards and the number guarded. With 2,530 uniformed deputies, the gaol of Los Angeles County has by far the lowest officer-to-inmate ratio of any big American city: Houston has as many guards for 60 percent fewer jailees, and New York has four times as many for a slightly smaller carceral population. Every year, the county disburses millions of dollars in damages to detainees injured or crippled by rubber bullets, tear gas grenades, interventions by "extraction squads" (responsible for subjugating obstreperous inmates who refuse to leave their cells), or following medical maltreatment.* One detainee at the Pitchess East center had this lapidary formula for describing the daily existence of his ilk: "Everybody will tell you that living in the Los Angeles County Jail is like living in hell."[54]

A large share of the resources of the LACJ, as in all the country's major jails, is

*In the spring of 1998, several guards from the Twin Towers were charged for having, over several months, identified the new "fish" arrested for sex offenses against children to the other detainees and then letting these detainees beat them without intervening. One of the alleged child molesters thus attacked died from his injuries.

absorbed by organizing the transport of defendants and convicts before the judicial authorities.* Every day, over 1,100 inmates (250 of them women) are transferred from the LACJ's reception center alone to the courts of Los Angeles and neighboring counties. The volume of movements is so large that the Twin Towers' transportation and dispatch office (called the "court line") starts collecting the individuals involved as early as 3:30 in the morning. Blacks are kept in one transfer cell, Latinos in another, and whites and youths under eighteen in a third (whites are assimilated de facto to minors in this setting where they are the "minority," and Asians are currently grouped with Euro-Americans to protect them from possible assaults). "Often, we get so many detainees at once that *we just don't have enough chains to transport everyone.* So sometimes some of them get ready to go to court, they wait in the cell here, but we can't send them off, even if we tie them three to a chain," the officer printing the badges to identify jailees in transit explained to me with a chagrined air.

At nine at night, when the buses return from the courts packed to the gills with their human cargo, the clogging of holding cells forces the staff to use the hallways as a storage area. "It's really *hopping in the evening.* Sometimes we got five or six buses coming in at the same time [with 250 to 300 jailees], and we don't have enough room to handle them, so what you do is, *you pack them in as fast as you can,* you process them as fast as you can." Or else they leave the detainees to stew in their bus for hours on end until space finally opens up in the holding cells. (Each bus holds between 48 and 53 detainees, all tied in chains and isolated in pairs in wire cages, except for the "high-powered inmates," who are chained in individual cages. This manner of prison on wheels is handled by two deputies, the one driving and the other standing guard. Both are armed and separated from the passengers seated in their cages by a heavy metal grate, and they are in constant radio contact with the jail's transportation center.) At eleven at night come some 250 convicts transferred daily to state penitentiaries ("in-custody releases") via the Chino and Delano reception centers, which assign them to one of 30-odd establishments under the authority of the California Department of Corrections—which the City of Angels alone supplies with more than one-third of its residents. "This place is jam-packed. All of these cells are full to the ceiling, with guys crammed who urinate on themselves, because there's no toilets so they can't get rid of drugs or weapons" they might have hidden on them before the search.

The human tide that rushes without letup through the LACJ network is such that, despite the 200 officers assigned to "admissions" who handle some 6000 administrative documents per day, slip-ups are numerous and costly. In 1997, 700

*A city adjoining Los Angeles resolved (or at least significantly reduced) the thorny problem of transporting detainees by building its criminal court within the confines of its main jail.

prisoners were held under lock for an average of 6.9 days after their official release date (one of them was illegally incarcerated for 260 days and two others for 90 days each). In total, that year the county paid out almost $200,000 in damages to 548 detainees kept in arbitrary detention for a total of 3,694 days.* On the other side, every year the jails of Los Angeles mistakenly release dozens of prisoners who should be kept securely behind bars: this was the case with 32 detainees in 1996, among whom six were accused of homicide.

*These data are taken from an administrative note by Captain David Betkey addressed to his superiors and obtained from the Information Service of the Los Angeles County Sheriff's Office through the Freedom of Information Act. In November 1996, Cook County (Chicago) agreed to pay $5.85 million in damages to settle a class action suit filed on behalf of 65,000 inmates who had been arbitrarily held at least ten hours past their legal date of release, corresponding to $90 per plaintiff. "$5.85 Million Accord Reached in Jail Lawsuit," *Chicago Sun Times*, 27 November 1996.

5

The Coming of Carceral "Big Government"

You favor a political revolution. You want to replace the welfare state with an opportunity society. You favor workfare over welfare. You want to lock prisoners up and you're actually prepared to give up some political pork barrel to build as many prisons as you need.—REPRESENTATIVE NEWT GINGRICH, 1996*

In the climate of social and racial revenge that set in after the reelection of Richard Nixon in 1972 in response to the advances of black mobilization and the popular claims surging in its wake, the battle against crime was to serve as alibi to thwart the demand for an expansion of the social state. The discourse of "law and order," coined by politicians from the segregationist South to disqualify Martin Luther King's civil rights movement, fed the conflation of public assistance, immorality, and criminality: the poor take to crime because the state, by lending them a helping hand with excessive eagerness, maintains them in idleness and vice, thereby condemning them to the worst of "dependencies," that which turns them into "welfare addicts."**

Such a discourse, which we noted in chapter 2 returned to the forefront of the public scene during the debate around welfare "reform" in 1996, is tailor-made to legitimize the recentering of the missions of the state on order maintenance and the control of populations deemed dispossessed, deviant, and dangerous—chief among them the black (sub)proletariat of the big cities, whose specter has haunted the country

*Newt Gingrich, GOPAC training tape, in PBS's *Frontline*, "The Long March of Newt Gingrich," 1996.

**The moralistic notion of "dependency" with regard to public aid ("welfare dependency")—an inherently pejorative notion in a national culture that sacralizes "independence," virtual synonym for freedom and therefore Americanness—is so pervasive that it is used, not only by state officials and people in everyday life, but also by scholars specializing in the study of poverty. The expression "narcotic of welfare" is commonly invoked by politicians, Democrats as well as Republicans. For a critical analysis of representations of assistance to the poor in US culture and social science, read Sanford Schram, *Words of Welfare: The Poverty of Social Science and the Social Science of Poverty* (Minneapolis: University of Minnesota Press, 1995).

since the wave of urban riots which, from Watts to Harlem, shook the white order to its foundations. The law-and-order policy of the United States was then built on the basis of a triple reduction: from the outset, it has focused only on the visible delinquency of the lower class ("crime in the streets"), as opposed to the veiled criminality of the well-to-do ("crime in the suites"), even though the latter is much more costly to the country and reaching new heights.* Among lower-class offenses, it has targeted first and foremost the retail sales and consumption of drugs in segregated black and Latino neighborhoods, where this trade anchors the informal economy that has filled the void created by the withdrawal of the wage economy. Finally, it has treated drugs as a problem of public order, susceptible to a strictly police and judicial solution, rather than as a public health challenge requiring an expanded range of preventive and therapeutic interventions.[1]

As a consequence, the prison has returned to the institutional forefront inasmuch as it offers a simple and direct means for restoring order—inseparably economic, ethnoracial, and moral—and for curbing all manners of "social problems" that the dominant vision perceives and projects as resulting from the excessive "liberalization" of the sixties: drugs, drifting, violence, the contestation of white hegemony, the familial and social disintegration of the ghetto, the despair of youths from poor neighborhoods faced with decrepit public schools and a continually worsening job market. Under Reagan's presidency, as caste and class inequalities deepened again under the combined effect of  deindustrialization, the erosion of unions, and the retrenchment of the social welfare state,[2] incarceration confirmed its role as the all-purpose remedy for the rise of social insecurity and the string of "urban pathologies" associated with it. "Lock 'em up and throw away the key" became the leitmotif of modish politicians, official criminologists, and media eager to exploit the fear of violent crime and the loathing of the (black) criminal to expand their markets.[3]

Third-Largest Employer in the Nation

The mad race to incarcerate into which America threw itself inevitably translated into a spectacular expansion of the penal sector within

*As revealed by the unprecedented string of corporate scandals that accompanied the bursting of the speculative financial bubble of the late 1990s, involving such leading firms such as Enron, Arthur Andersen, Tyco, Adelphia, WorldCom, Qwest, Healthsouth, Global Crossing, etc.

federal and local bureaucracies. Of all the items that make up public expenditures at the three levels of US political organization, the county, the states, and the federal government, "corrections" is that which posted the fastest expansion from 1975 to today—and by a wide margin. This growth of the budgets and personnel of the carceral sector is all the more remarkable for having occurred *during a period in which the weight of the state was continually shrinking* in the economic and social life of the country and when direct spending for vulnerable populations suffered drastic cuts. Thus, we noted in chapter 2 that the main public aid package for the poor (AFDC) lost 48 percent of its real value between 1970 and 1995, while its coverage dropped to only one-half the population living under the official "poverty line." During the same period, the percentage of jobless covered by unemployment insurance plunged from an annual average of 76 percent to 36 percent. And federal expenditures for job creation and training fell from $18 billion in 1980 to a paltry $6.7 billion thirteen years later (in constant 1993 dollars).[4]

In his 1996 State of the Union address, President Clinton trumpeted: "We know big government does not have all the answers. We know there's not a program for every problem. We have worked to give the American people a smaller, less bureaucratic government in Washington. And we have to give the American people one that lives within its means. The era of big government is over."[5] But the principle of "small government," sacrosanct when it comes to employment and social protection, does not apply to the penal sector—quite the opposite. Thus, under Clinton's presidency, the Federal Bureau of Prisons saw its expenditures leap from $1.6 billion in 1992 to $3.4 billion in 2000 and its personnel balloon from 24,000 to 34,000—the largest decennial increase in the history of the department. The same occurred at the state level: between 1982 and 1997, correctional budgets increased 383 percent, while the sums allocated to criminal justice as a whole grew 262 percent, and total state spending rose by only 150 percent (see table 11). At the end of this period, America spent one-half more for its jails and prisons than for its judicial arm ($43 billion versus $28 billion), whereas budgetary allocations to these two administrations were similar at the beginning (around $8 billion each). The carceral function now absorbs over one-third of the justice budget, as against one-quarter at the beginning of the 1980s. The sums disbursed by the country just on building penitentiaries and jails exploded between 1979 and 1989: plus 612 percent, or three times the rate of increase in military spending, which enjoyed particular favor under the presidencies of Ronald Reagan and George Bush Sr. Carceral construction experienced such a boom that numerous counties and states found themselves short of funds to hire the staff necessary to open the establishments they were building! So it was in 1996 in South Carolina, where two "high-tech" penitentiaries could not come on line for lack of funds required to cover their operating costs, or in Los Angeles, where the "jail of the twenty-first century" stood empty for over a year after its construction had been completed.

As early as 1992, four states devoted more than a billion dollars just to the operations of their prisons (that is, outside of building): California (3.2 billion), New York State (2.1), Texas (1.3), and Florida (1.1). And Michigan and Illinois were not far behind.[6] The share of corrections in Michigan's public expenditures leapt from 6 percent to 15 percent between 1986 and 1996. The budget of the California Department of Corrections (CDC) stagnated around $300 million at the beginning of the 1980s; by 1999 it had swollen to $4.3 billion, more than the total municipal budget for San Francisco or the funds allotted to the four-year campuses of the California university system, long regarded as the state's jewel. The CDC boasts of having conducted "the largest prison construction program in history" during the 1980s. And rightly so: California inaugurated 12 penitentiaries between 1852 and 1965, and then built none between 1965 and 1984. Since then, it has opened 23 new facilities, including six reserved for housing new mother-inmates with their children. In a single decade, the Golden State gulped $5.3 billion to build and renovate cells, and took on over $10 billion in debt to do so. Each new establishment costs on average a hefty $200 million for 4000 inmates and requires the hiring of 1000 employees, among them the best-paid guards in the country, thanks to their superpowerful union. One understands better how, whereas it had led all the other states on the educational front at the beginning of the 1970s, today California is well back behind the pack in schooling but stands among the country's leaders on the carceral front.[7]

California at the Cutting Edge

The policy of confinement of the categories deemed superfluous, dangerous, or disruptive, into which California threw itself head first has translated into an exponential growth of its correctional system, unprecedented in history, which has made it the *first penal colony* of the democratic era and its correctional administration the avant-garde of the emerging penal state that "liberal paternalism" reserves for the dispossessed of the new economic and moral order.

The California Department of Corrections, CDC to the initiated, is a veritable empire within the state, and its staff constitutes one of California's most influential lobbies. With a budget surpassing $4 billion (exceeding 8 percent of public expenditures, just ahead of spending on universities), this administration employs 45,000 and manages a network of 33 prisons, six specialized centers for inmate mothers, and 38 "boot camps" for young offenders.* In December 1998 these establishments accommodated 159,706 inmates, of whom 31.5 percent were black, 34 percent Latino, and 29.6 percent white, whereas these categories weighed 7, 26, and 59 percent of California's population, respectively.

According to official forecasts set out by the "Master Plan 1995–2000," the population held in state prisons was expected to grow by 15,000 per year to reach 210,000 inmates in June 2000, corresponding to *ten times the 1977 figure*, and more than France, Germany, Italy, and England combined. In light of this projection, the CDC recommended the immediate building of fifteen new penitentiaries to dam this human flood on the basis of two inmates per cell designed for one person in 90 percent of its establishments.[8]

With five prisons already under construction, building cost estimates came to $1.7 billion for 1995 alone ($2.1 billion if one takes into account the emergency plan aimed to absorb the overflow of convicts already in the system). Along the way, the CDC institutionalized carceral overpopulation by establishing a "standard of overoccupancy" presented as "tolerable in the long term" (two or three inmates held in cells built for one), allowing it to reduce the investment required to face the predicted takeoff of its carceral stock by a full $5 billion over five years.

This is a way for the CDC to display its budgetary frugality at a moment when California's political class balks at disbursing the extravagant sums required by its policy of criminalization of poverty. In the year 1994 alone, the Sacramento Assembly promulgated over one hundred new laws expanding the use of prison or extending the length of sentences. Republicans and Democrats joined to vote overwhelmingly (85 percent) for Assembly Bill 971, called "Three Strikes and You're Out" (automatic life sentence for double recidivism), a measure locked in by way of referendum in November 1994 thanks to the approval of 72 percent of the state's voters.** A sister law, nicknamed "One Strike and You're Out," establishes life imprisonment for first-time offenders committing certain sexual crimes and mandates a scaling back of sentence reductions granted for good behavior.

*In these camps, the juvenile inmates are initiated into the rudiments of firefighting and then sent to the front in the battle against forest fires during the summer months. This is a way of instilling them with a sense of discipline while making substantial budget savings when it comes to civil protection personnel, which cannot but please the electorate.

**The endorsement of "Three Strikes and You're Out" by popular initiative after it was passed by the state legislature means that the law, now codified as Penal Code section 1170.12, can be amended or repealed only by a supermajority of two-thirds in the California assembly and senate or by a new ballot measure.

Since 1977, when the state's prison population was perched at 20,600 inmates, the California Assembly has voted more than one thousand laws extending and toughening prison sentences.

The union of state prison guards, the California Correctional Peace Officers Association (CCPOA), is without contest the country's most powerful outfit in this sector. Its rolls soared from 4000 to 24,000 within a decade (1985–95). It has at its disposal over $10 million in annual dues, which enable it to be among the largest purveyors of funds for local political campaigns. The California corrections union thus allocates one million dollars per electoral cycle to the support of candidates who favor the expansion of prisons. Its political "donations" during the 1992 gubernatorial race amounted to twice those of the California teachers' union, which has ten times as many members. This mobilization was decisive for the 1994 reelection of ultraconservative governor Pete Wilson,[9] as it was for that of Democrat Gray Davis in 2002. Aside from politicians smitten with "law and order," the CCPOA actively supports "victims' rights" organizations, such as Crime Victims United of California and the Doris Tate Crime Victims Bureau, which are among the most virulent advocates of the extension and lengthening of custodial sentences. The union generously allocates $40,000 in start-up money to any new chapter of this type of organization and helps them gain influence with key operators in the political field. In 1994, the CCPOA was the second largest donor to the campaign supporting the referendum on "Three Strikes," with $100,000. And each year it sponsors the "March of Crime Victims on the Capitol," which takes place in Sacramento every April, in which the gamut of organizations pushing for punitive criminal policies parade to put pressure on the state assembly.

The organized support that the prison guard union lends to well-chosen politicians in turn enables its members to enjoy particularly advantageous work conditions, remuneration, and pensions.[10] The average yearly wages of a California correctional officer was $14,400 in 1980; by 2000, it topped $55,000, 60 percent above the national average for guards and one-quarter more than an assistant professor at the University of California, although it requires only six weeks of training beyond a high school diploma. It will come as no surprise that the turnover rate among prison guards has fallen from 25 percent to 8 percent over the past decade and that the job constantly attracts new blood: every year, hundreds of primary and secondary school teachers figure among its recruits, who turn in their school robes to put on a guard's uniform.

The stupendous growth of correctional employment further confirms that, while it has pursued an aggressive policy of "downsizing" on the social welfare front, America has fully stepped into the *era of carceral "Big Government."* Between 1980 and 1997, the workforce in corrections

Table 11. Growth of criminal justice budgets and personnel, 1980–97

	1980	1982	1984	1986	1988	1990	1992	1994	1997
Expenditures (in billions of dollars)									
Police	15.1	19.0	22.7	26.2	31.0	35.9	41.3	56.4	57.7
Justice	—	7.8	9.4	11.5	14.0	17.4	21.0	22.6	28.5
Corrections	6.9	9.0	11.8	15.8	20.3	26.1	31.5	34.9	43.5
Total	—	35.8	43.9	53.5	65.3	79.4	93.8	103.5	129.8
Personnel (in thousands of employees—FTE)									
Police	715	724	747	772	805	825	858	890	951
Justice	—	248	278	300	324	351	374	391	419
Corrections	271	299	349	392	455	534	567	621	708
Total	—	1,270	1,373	1,466	1,584	1,710	1,798	1,902	2,078

SOURCE: Bureau of Justice Statistics, *Sourcebook of Criminal Justice Statistics* (Washington, D.C.: Government Printing Office, 2001), 3–4, 25–26.

increased 2.6 times to exceed 700,000, while the staff working for the courts increased by one-half and those of the police by one-third to reach 950,000 and 420,000, respectively, for a total of two million public employees in the penal sector (see table 11). Sixteen states saw their guards rolls double over the past decade, while most of them reduced their overall public employment. Taking account of temporary employment agencies—whose sudden climb to the apex of American corporations[11] is functionally connected to the frenetic development of incarceration through the mediation of the increased casualization of wage work—state and county correctional administrations, taken together, have elevated themselves to the rank of *third-largest employer in the land*, just behind Manpower Incorporated and the national retail chain Wal-Mart, and ahead of the automobile behemoth General Motors, the world's largest company as measured by sales in 1998 (see table 12). The US carceral system now employs four times as many people as McDonald's and seven times more staff than IBM. The California correctional administration alone has twice as many employees (45,000) as Microsoft, the world leader in computer software (22,200).

And this policy of expansion of the penal sector of the state is by no means the prerogative of Republicans. Between 1993 and 1998, while Bill Clinton proclaimed to the four corners of the country his pride in overseeing "the smallest federal bureaucracy in thirty years" and that, under the leadership of his aspiring successor, Albert Gore, the Commission for Government Reform pruned 200,000 public jobs, 213 new prisons opened their doors—a figure that excludes private estab-

Table 12. Corrections, third-largest employer in the land

1. Manpower Inc. (temporary employment)	1,610,200
2. Wal-Mart Stores Inc. (retail trade)	728,000
3. Incarceration (county, state, and federal)	708,200*
4. Kelly Services Inc. (temporary employment)	669,800
5. General Motors Corp. (automobile)	646,000
6. Interim Services Inc. (temporary employment)	414,000
7. Ford Motor Company (automobile)	371,700
8. United Parcel Service (package delivery)	336,000
9. Sears Roebuck (retail trade)	335,000
10. Tricon Global Restaurants (food and beverages)	334,000

*1997 figure, excluding employment in private facilities and juvenile services

SOURCE: Largest businesses by number of employees from *Dunn and Bradstreet Rankings*, 1998.

lishments, which, we shall see below, proliferated with the explosive growth of a lucrative market in for-profit incarceration.

Charity or Chastisement

In times of fiscal dearth caused by the sharp decrease in effective taxation rates on corporations and the wealthy, the increase of the means devoted to incarceration would not have been possible without cutting into the social assistance budgets and squeezing those allotted to public health and education. Thus, between 1976 and 1989 correctional spending by the states nearly doubled (plus 95 percent) in constant dollars, while funds allocated to hospitals grew by only 5 percent, and monies for school and universities decreased (by 2 and 6 percent, respectively) in the face of continual increases in enrollment. During this period, the total welfare budget sank by 41 percent, taking into account inflation and the jettisoning of programs.[12] Another way of gauging the country's budgetary priorities: between 1977 and 1995, US carceral expenditures rose by 823 percent in current dollars to exceed $35 billion (outside of construction), as against a 374 percent increase for higher education. In Texas, the growth rate of the correctional budget was six times that of the university budget, and it reached twice the latter in twenty other states, including California, Florida, and Pennsylvania as well as Arizona, Colorado, Arkansas, Ohio, Hawaii, and Alaska.

The comparative evolution of correctional budgets with funds devoted to the two main programs of assistance to the poor, AFDC (for

Table 13. Comparative evolution of correctional and public aid budgets, 1980–95 (in billions of current dollars)

	1980	1982	1984	1986	1988	1990	1992	1993	1995
Corrections	6.9	9.0	11.8	15.8	20.3	26.1	31.5	31.9	46.2
AFDC	10.9	12.1	13.4	14.3	15.5	17.1	20.4	20.3	19.9
Food Stamps	9.6	11.7	13.3	13.5	14.4	17.7	24.9	26.3	27.4

SOURCE: Kathleen Maguire and Ann L. Pastore (dir.), *Sourcebook of Criminal Justice Statistics 1996* (Washington, D.C.: Bureau of Justice Statistics, 1997), 3; Lea Gifford, *Justice Expenditures and Employment in the United States, 1995* (Washington, D.C.: Bureau of Justice Statistics, 1999), 8; and Committee on Ways and Means, *1996 Green Book* (Washington, D.C.: Government Printing Office, 1997), 459, 861, 921.

destitute single mothers) and food stamps (nutritional assistance to households living below the "poverty line"), confirms the swing of the American state's priorities from the social to the penal front (see table 13). Between 1980 and 1995, the country increased its carceral expenditures sevenfold in current dollars, while the AFDC budget stayed well below the inflation rate, with a 285 percent increase. At the beginning of this period, the United States spent 50 percent more on AFDC than on jails and prisons ($11 billion versus $7 billion); by 1993 it was the reverse ($20 billion versus $32 billion); and in 1995 corrections cost 2.3 times more than assistance to destitute mothers. The year 1985 marks a milestone in the historical transition from the assistantial to the carceral treatment of poverty, since this was the year that annual allocations to correctional administrations definitively surpassed those for AFDC and food stamps.

Similarly, when Reagan entered the White House, the United States devoted $6.9 billion to operating its penal establishments as against $27.4 billion for public housing. Ten years later, the amounts for these two budget items had nearly reversed: $19 billion more went to prisons, for a total of $26.1 billion, while $17 billion had been subtracted from public housing, leaving a meager funding of $10.6 billion, insufficient to maintain an increasingly decrepit public housing stock (see figure 4).*

*The public-housing stock has deteriorated to such a point that, under Clinton's second presidency, the federal government undertook a policy of massive demolition of large housing projects ostensibly aimed at dispersing their residents onto the private rental market by means of vouchers and facilitating the gentrification of inner-city areas made valuable by the return of upper-class households to the city. This policy, codified by the Quality Housing and Work Responsibility Act of 1998 is "broadly consonant with those of welfare reform wherein the 'workfare' system helps to bolster and

Figure 4. A decade of trade-off between public housing and corrections

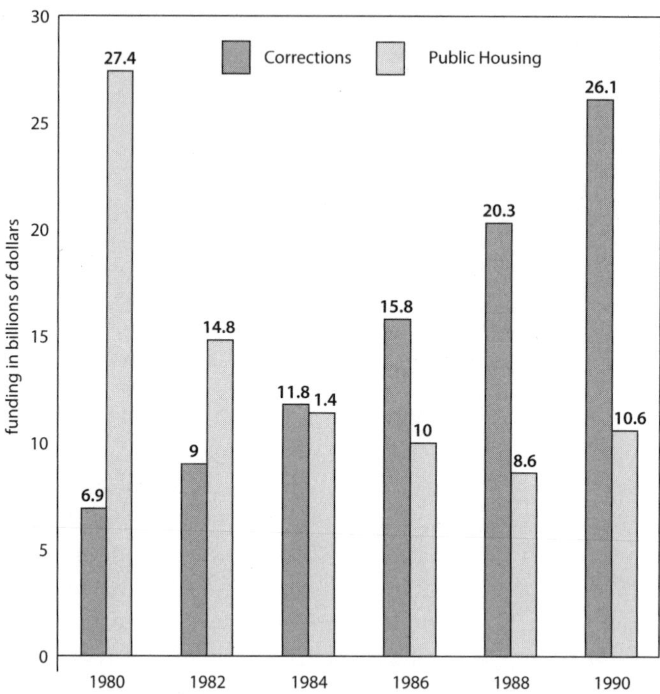

SOURCE: Committee on Ways and Means, *Green Book 1996* (Washington D.C.: Government Printing Office, 1997), 921; Kathleen Maguire and Ann L. Pastore (dir.), *Sourcebook of Criminal Justice Statistics 1996* (Washington D. C.: Bureau of Justice Statistics, 1997), 3.

From these inverse criss-crossing budgetary trends, one can conclude indifferently that the American state has ceased to support housing for the dispossessed and left them to be dumped onto the streets (as attested by the spectacular rise in the ranks of the homeless)[13] and into prisons, or, considering the sums poured in as well as the class profile of inmates sketched in chapter 2, that *the construction of prisons has effectively become the country's main public housing program.* Besides, since 1995 it has also overtaken the construction budget for university buildings across the land.

This infernal trade-off between charity and chastisement was posed

produce the emergence of contingent low-wage urban labor markets." Jeff R. Crump, "The End of Public Housing As We Know It: Public Housing Policy, Labor Regulation and the US City," *International Journal of Urban and Regional Research* 27, no. 1 (March 2003): 179–87.

in particularly stark terms in Los Angeles in September 1996, when the executive branch of the county planned to cut the budget for emergency assistance to the indigent by $19 million in order to finance the wages of the staff needed to open the Twin Towers detention center, which was standing empty a year after construction had been completed due to a lack of funds to cover its operating costs. After a stormy debate, the proposal was rejected by a bare margin, but the incident remains symptomatic of the pressure to replace the assistantial treatment of poverty by its carceral management. Locking up the poor offers the great benefit of being "legible" by the electorate. The results of the operation are tangible and easily measured: so many more inmates and, as a bonus, so many recipients off the welfare rolls (since inmates lose all rights to public assistance or government transfers sixty days after being put behind bars). Its costs are badly measured and poorly understood, and still less often subject to public debate—when they are not squarely presented wholesale as benefits thanks to the "savings" in crime that incarceration is supposed to effect, crimes whose incidence and price the authorities strive *a contrario* to exaggerate.[14] The penal management of poverty is moreover endowed with a positive moral charge, whereas the question of welfare is irremediably sullied by immorality. The former is "paternalist" and suggests rigor, and therefore moral and social uprightness; the latter is "maternalist" and for this reason suspected from the outset of perpetuating indolence as well as economic, ethical, and sexual laxity (the modal welfare recipient in the dominant public representation is a black teenage mother, designated by the stigmatizing term of "teenage welfare mother").[15] This Los Angeles episode is in any case an "indicator of the rise" of the carceral reflex, notes Jackie Walker, spokesperson for the National Project on Prisons of the American Civil Liberties Union, an organization that intervened in this debate to defend the rights of the indigent. "Many cities are faced with the same dilemma: either pay for the construction and operation of prisons, or provide for social needs. In California, prison construction siphons money away from education."[16]

It is a fact that, between the penitentiary and the university, the Golden State has made its choice. In 1979, the budget for California prisons consumed 3 percent of public resources and that for the University of California and California State University, pride of the state, topped 18 percent. By 1984, these figures were 6 percent and 10 percent respectively. Another ten years later, prison expenditures had caught up with and then surpassed those for higher education (delivering the BA and above), with 8 percent.[17] During this decade, California opened only one university campus, despite a 50-percent increase in student enrollment, while building 19 new penal establishments—the preparatory documents for the vote on the "Three Strikes and You're Out" law passed in 1994 recommended the opening of 34 new prisons in the period 1995–2000 alone, three times as many as the state possessed in 1984. In his budget proposal for 1994–95, governor Pete Wilson (who never missed an opportunity to congratulate the California Department of Corrections for "conducting the biggest prison construction program in the history of our nation") sought to cut teaching positions in higher education by 968 in order to create 2,879 new positions on the carceral ledger, while at the same time the number of state employees outside the penal sector would decline by 3,058. The budget was not carried out due to the acute financial crisis caused by the recession of the region's economy, but the direction and magnitude of the budgetary trade-offs involved clearly indicate the priority the California executive placed on the state's penal function. In point of fact, between 1984 and 1994 the correctional administration alone absorbed 45 percent of all new state personnel.[18] The result of this reversal: annual tuition at the University of California, which stood under $1,000 in 1980, topped $4,300 in 1994, the year when for the first time the prison population exceeded the number of graduating BA students.

But it is the city-state of Washington, D.C., seat of the federal government and *sanctum* of US democracy, that best illustrates, by pushing it to the point of paroxysm, the involutive process whereby the penal state tends, for the categories confined to the lower reaches of the social and spatial structure, to replace the social state; its police, judicial, and correctional functions undermining its educational and assistantial missions by devouring their budgets and stealing their staff. The result is that today young Washingtonians from the lower class, who are nearly all black and who depend entirely on crumbling public institutions, have a higher chance of finding themselves behind bars than behind the desks of a university lecture hall—as for the children of the middle and upper classes, they have the means needed to take refuge in the dozen private universities in the city and neighboring states.

Capital rhymes here with caricature: when Ronald Reagan moved into 1600 Pennsylvania Avenue, Washington had 15,000 students enrolled at the University of the District of Columbia (UDC, the city's sole public university, inaugurated in 1976 on the occasion of the Bicentennial) as against fewer than 3000 inmates, even though the District had already long been the jurisdiction with the highest confinement rate in the country. When Bill Clinton arrived in 1992, the city's carceral population was on the brink of catching up with its campus rolls, which were in free fall as a result of draconian budget cuts to higher

Table 14. Evolution of staff and enrollment at the prison and the public university of the District of Columbia, 1980–97

	1980	1990	1997
Students enrolled at UDC*	15,340	11,161	4,729
Inmates	*2,873*	*9,632*	*12,745*
Primary and secondary teachers	7,719	7,120	5,800
University teachers	804	587	454
Social workers	2,367	1,861	1,187
Jail and prison staff	*229*	*1,974*	*1,984*

*University of the District of Columbia (the sole public university); full- and part-time students.

SOURCE: Bureau of the Census, *Public Employment in 1980, Public Employment in 1990, Statistical Abstracts of the US 1998, Detailed Population Characteristics, District of Columbia, 1980 Census*; Bureau of Justice Statistics, *Source Book of Criminal Justice Statistics* 1981, 1991, 1997 (Washington, D.C.: Government Printing Office).

education during this period of public financing famine—the city was bankrupt and its administration would soon be placed under federal receivership. This occurred in 1994. In the interim, the probability of being enrolled at UDC among blacks from the District sank one-third, while their rate of incarceration *quadrupled* to reach the stupendous figure of 3000 inmates per 100,000 (as against 84 per 100,000 for white residents, whose rate increased 84 percent[19]).* As a result, by 1997 the ratio of students to inmates had reversed: the carceral population of the District—whose motto is *Justitia omnibus*, "justice for all"—closed in on 13,000 prisoners, practically *three times* the number enrolled in its university, which had fallen to under 4,700 (see table 14).

The fact is that, in the meanwhile, the capital of the United States blazed the trail for the rest of the country: in a little over a decade, to purvey for the "War on drugs" raging inside the black ghetto adjoining the White House, it multiplied the number of guards eightfold while slashing social welfare staff and positions at the public university by one-half. In 1980, the district employed four higher-education teachers for every correctional worker (804 versus 229); in 1997 it was the reverse: 454 versus 2,000, or twice as many as the personnel for welfare and, for a city of only 530,000 inhabitants, more guards than were employed by smaller European countries like Norway, Portugal, or Greece. But the inflow of inmates was such that, despite this outpouring of means, the

*For France, this incarceration rate would yield a population under lock of 1.8 million (the actual figure is 58,000).

District no longer knew where to store its convicts, so that, after 1994, it found itself forced to export its surplus to private prisons in Kentucky and Ohio. And to sell its largest penitentiary to the Corrections Corporation of America in order to generate the cash flow needed . . . to rent it back from that very same company on a leasing agreement.

Less than two miles from the glitz of Capitol Hill, but out of sight and physically separated from it by the double physical barrier composed of Interstate 395 and the river that gives it its name, the neighborhood of Anacostia is one of the most impoverished in the United States.* The historic home of the black abolitionist Frederick Douglass houses one-quarter of the city's population; its residents are 94 percent black. Streets lined with abandoned buildings, boarded-up storefronts, and vacant lots, crumbling schools and a run-down infrastructure, pervasive insecurity and the collective demoralization of the residents tell better than any statistic the effects of the public policy of *social dumping* on the Washingtonians from below. Half of Anacostia's young men are without work and almost two-thirds are under the supervision of the criminal justice system.[20] Irony has it that the main job creation program launched by (the black) Mayor Marion Barry—who lost his office in 1990 after being convicted of possession of cocaine and was re-elected in 1994 after a six-month sojourn behind bars—is the building of a 2,200-bed private prison by Corrections Corporation of America. In point of fact, when the construction contract was announced, a city councilman expressed the wish that the prison would have a high-quality school behind bars, "since that's where 'our youth' seem to be going."[21] To be sure, the carceral facility will hardly be out of place in this ghost-neighborhood, whose two largest employers are a water treatment plant and St. Elizabeth Hospital, one of the country's largest psychiatric hospitals (the one described by Erving Goffman in his book *Asylums*). It is no doubt better to fulfill its calling as the city's social dumpster that Washington's new (black) mayor proposed in March 1999 to transfer what was left of the University of the District of Columbia from its current site at the heart of an upscale white neighborhood in the north of the city to Anacostia, on the pretext of "better serving" the area's families and on the grounds that proceeds from the sale of the campus would provide funds to ensure the coming "renewal" of the university.

*The invisibility of poor African Americans to official Washington finds a paradigmatic and literal illustration in the book of photographs by George W. Kousoulas, *Washington: Portrait of a City*, intro. Senator Daniel Patrick Moynihan (New York: Norfleet Press, 2001), which contains not a single poor black face.

"The Proud Face of America"

A report on the state of public schools in America's poor neighborhoods

> [We must] renew our great Capital City to make it the finest place to learn, to work, to live; to make it once again the proud face America shows to the world. This is a city of truly remarkable strengths. . . . We see it in the eyes of our children. They deserve the best future we can give them, and we can give them a better future.—WILLIAM JEFFERSON CLINTON, remarks at the District of Columbia College Reading Tutor Announcement, February 21, 1997[22]

Not too long ago, the basement cafeteria was flooded [in the main elementary school in Anacostia]. Rain poured into the school and rats appeared. Someone telephoned the mayor: "You've got dead rats here in the cafeteria." . . . The school is on a road that runs past several boarded buildings. Gregory tells me they are called "pipe" houses. "Go by there one day—it be vacant. Next day, they bring sofas, chairs, day after that, you see the junkies going in." . . . A teacher sitting with us says, "At eight years old, some of the boys are running drugs and holding money for the dealers. By 28, they're going to be dead." . . .

"The little ones come into school on Monday," says the teacher, "and they're hungry. A five year-old. Her laces are undone. She says, 'I had to dress myself this morning'. I ask her why. She says, 'They took my mother off to jail'. Their stomachs hurt. They don't know why." . . .

A child named Monique goes back to something we discussed before: "If I had a lot of money, I would give it to poor children." The statement surprises me. I ask her if the children in this neighborhood are poor. Several children answer, "No." Tunisia (after a long pause): "We are all poor people in this school."

The bell rings, although it isn't three o'clock. The children get up and say goodbye and start to head off to the stairs that lead up from the basement to the first floor. The principal later tells me he released the children early. He had been advised that there would be a shooting in the street this afternoon.

I tell him how much I liked the children and he's obviously pleased. Tunisia, he tells me, lives in the Capital City Inn—the city's largest homeless shelter. She has been homeless for a year, he says; he thinks that this may be one reason she is reflective and mature.[23]

The Price and Spoils of Hyperincarceration

Whereas the budgetary burden of social assistance programs was a leitmotif in the national debate over "welfare," the question of the cost of hyperincarceration, which concerns more or less the same precarious population on the other side of the gender line, is almost never posed as such in the national public sphere—except to rehash the received idea, whose self-evidence has been imposed by the ideological sapping work of neoconservative think tanks, according to which "prison works" (without it ever being said according to precisely what criteria).* Three tenacious myths, manufactured and spread by these institutes with the active support of the US Department of Justice, dominated the debate on criminal violence in America at century's turn: the first has it that the country's penal policy sins by its perennial laxity; the second affirms that repression is a successful policy, whereas in the social domain the state proves congenitally impotent (unless it adopts the same punitive outlook); the third maintains that in the end incarceration is less expensive than the sum of the crimes it prevents through its neutralizing effects.[24] Yet a summary examination of the question suffices to indicate that the policy of penal enclosure of the poor implemented by America is digging a bottomless financial pit.

Outside of food and health care (these services are generally accounted for separately as they come out of other budgets or are subcontracted to private operators), the average cost of custody in a state penitentiary is estimated at $22,000 per inmate per year, three times the annual income tax paid by the average US household.[25] This national average, however, conceals wide regional variations: the yearly cost of a prisoner ranges from $8,000 in Alabama to $37,800 in Minnesota.[26] In Illinois, for example, just to cover the operational costs of corrections in 1993, each inmate absorbed five times the maximum aid disbursed by AFDC to a mother with three children. The building cost of a cell nationwide came to $54,000 on paper, but in reality it exceeded twice that amount when one includes indirect expenditures (infrastructure improvement, insurance, legal costs, etc.) and financial charges—most states issue twenty-year bonds to expand their carceral capacity. Not to mention the opportunity costs of imprisonment that are never tallied

*It is revealing that one of the main documents supporting the policy canard according to which incarceration is an efficient means of reducing offending since "career felons who are in prison cells rather than on the streets do not commit crimes" was produced in Wisconsin, the state spearheading the shift from welfare to workfare (under the gleeful eye of neopaternalist advocate Lawrence Mead), by the same private think tank which led the crusade to curtail public assistance (George A. Mitchell, *Prison Works* [Milwaukee: Wisconsin Policy Research Institute, 1995]). Conveniently, this argument omits the rampant crime committed behind bars, substitution effects among the criminal population, and the criminogenic effects of imprisonment as well as less costly alternatives to penal confinement. The same fuzzy reasoning is at work in the widely cited editorial by Princeton political scientist John J. DiIulio Jr., "Prisons Are a Bargain, by Any Measure," *The New York Times*, 16 January 1996.

as such, such as the economic output and the taxes lost due to the idleness of inmates, as well as the supplementary collective expenditures occasioned by their banishment. One illustration: it is estimated that 200,000 children have a mother behind bars and 1.6 million a father; the direct cost to child welfare services of caring for these children is assessed at one billion dollars per year.[27]

A comprehensive assessment of the burden of hyperincarceration would moreover require taking account of the financial impact of its deleterious effects on the social structure and culture of the communities the prisoners come from: interrupted academic and occupational trajectories, destabilized households and aborted marital careers, children subtracted from parental custody, income curtailed and diverted toward support for those incarcerated, the stigmatization and distortion of social life in neighborhoods where the intrusive ubiquity of the police and penal apparatus makes judicial intervention commonplace and feeds defiance toward an authority perceived as arbitrary and abusive—all contributing to entrenching delinquency and fueling recidivism.[28] We know that, by prematurely and repeatedly throwing them behind bars for longer and longer sojourns, the state contributes to closing down the two main avenues out of delinquency for young men from the precarious fractions of the working class caught in the net of its repressive apparatus: finding a stable job and getting married. It thereby increases the chances that criminality will be perpetuated across the lifecycle as well as across the generations.[29]

Medical care alone absorbs a disproportionate and growing share of resources allocated to confinement, owing first of all to the poor physical state of the carceral population: 31 percent of state prisoners report having a learning or speech disability, a hearing or vision problem, or a mental or physical condition, including 12 percent who suffer a physical impairment (this rate rises to one-quarter among inmates older than 40); one in eight receives therapy or counseling; and one-third of inmates will be injured during their first two years of confinement, half of them during an assault or a fight.[30] The second major cause behind the take-off of medical costs is the resurgence, within penal facilities, of virulent epidemics of tuberculosis (as early as 1992, half a million cases were recorded behind bars, where the incidence of this disease is six times greater than on the outside) and the spread of the HIV virus (the rate of HIV-positive prisoners is seven times the national average and the rate of AIDS fourteen times).[31] As a result, in 1996, for example, the Texas correctional administration spent $230 million to care for its inmates, corresponding to 12 percent of its overall budget, while its counterpart in Florida disbursed $200 million (15 percent of $1.32

billion).[32] Nonetheless, in the medium term it is the accelerated aging of the inmate population that presents the greatest financial challenge: by mid-2000, US jails and prisons housed 54,000 residents over 55, for whom the average cost of detention exceeds $75,000 a year, almost twice the annual income of the median US household, due in particular to the "over-aging" caused by reclusion (the health profile of a prisoner in his fifties is akin to that of a free man a dozen years older). Now, the number of elderly prisoners is about to explode due to the multiplication of long sentences and the implementation of automatic lifetime sanctions for the third crime. Just in the state of California, the stock of inmates over 55 is forecast to soar from 5,000 in 1994 to as much as 126,400 in 2020.[33]

The dilemma is that even as they vote overwhelming in favor of the so-called War on crime that has driven the quadrupling of the country's carceral population in twenty years, the American electorate refuses to shoulder the exorbitant cost of the swing from the social state to the penal state. This has pushed the authorities toward a solution in keeping with the ideology of commodification that already guides the retrenchment and hardening of social programs aimed at the destitute: *appeal to the private sector.* Banned in 1925 following a series of scandals around the abuse of the captive workforce in the South and the growing opposition of unions and industrialists in the North, private prisons have made a smashing return onto the US penal scene.[34] It is in 1983 that construction on the country's first for-profit prison began in Chattanooga, Tennessee, at the behest of the Immigration and Naturalization Service (INS), within the framework of a campaign for all-around privatization launched by the Reagan administration and encouraged conjointly by neoconservative think tanks and big Wall Street brokerage houses, such as Merrill Lynch, Prudential-Bache, and Shearson Lehman Brothers, which saw in it a goldmine of fantastic profits. In 1988 a Heritage Foundation report presented private imprisonment as a "new economic and technological frontier" and predicted—the better to produce—the imminent engagement of the country's largest firms on this new business front.[35] Resort to the commercial sector appeared then as the best if not the only way to stem the furious tide of inmates and to curb the vertiginous increases in state carceral budgets. For, at the rate America was locking people up, it would have to open *a new one-thousand-bed prison every five days,* which no government had either the financial means or the administrative capacity to do. A private operator, by contrast, could deliver a turnkey prison in 18 months (as against three to four years for the public sector), trim the wages and cut the "benefits" (medical coverage, retirement, paid vacation) of its staff, and introduce new technologies and the latest management techniques so as to increase the productivity of surveillance work. Whence the promise of savings that the advocates of privatization did not hesitate to value at the outset at over 20 percent for establishments built by a commercial firm and between 5 and 10 percent for those managed by a for-profit corporation.[36]

Since then the number of beds housed by private establishments of custody has grown at an explosive clip: from 3,100 in 1987, it leapt to 20,700 five years later before zooming past 145,000 in 1999 (including 15,700 beds abroad by the end of this period). In 1997, a study by the Private Corrections Project at the University of Florida at Gainesville—financed by carceral firms and whose author struggles to conceal his partisan and pecuniary commitment in favor of privatization—projected that this figure would double every two years to reach 276,000 beds in 2001. From 5 percent, the share of the commercial sector would then exceed one-quarter of the US carceral stock a decade later (see figure 5).[37] These performative predictions did not come true due to the multiplication of well-publicized scandals tainting private establishments, the delivery of a large volume of public beds, and the stock market crash of 2000. A victim of the bursting of the "speculative bubble" of the fin de siècle, private incarceration is no longer featured along with the internet or biotechnology among the star investments of Wall Street, as was the case around 1996, when Corrections Corporation of America ranked among the country's five most profitable companies.

This did not prevent for-profit operators from furnishing fully one-quarter of the beds coming on line at the end of the 1990s. Inconceivable just twenty years ago, the private prison is an inescapable component of the US penal landscape of today. Better yet, its presence has profoundly changed the behavior of correctional administrations, by goading them into a frantic competition to offer cheap "beds" to rent out to neighboring jurisdictions running out of cells. Moreover, firms specializing in the construction and management of custodial facilities are not the only ones to profit from American carceral hyperinflation. All sectors of activity liable to furnish goods and services to custodial institutions are concerned, from insurance and food to architecture, transportation, telecommunications, and technologies for identification and surveillance. This is particularly the case with health care, which represents a market estimated at $4 billion in 2003 and growing at 25 percent per year, of which one billion has already been cornered by private operators (as against $300 million in 1994).[38]

Seventeen firms, fifteen American and two British, offer the "full-scale management" of custodial facilities. Seven of them are listed

Figure 5. The explosive growth of private imprisonment, 1987–99

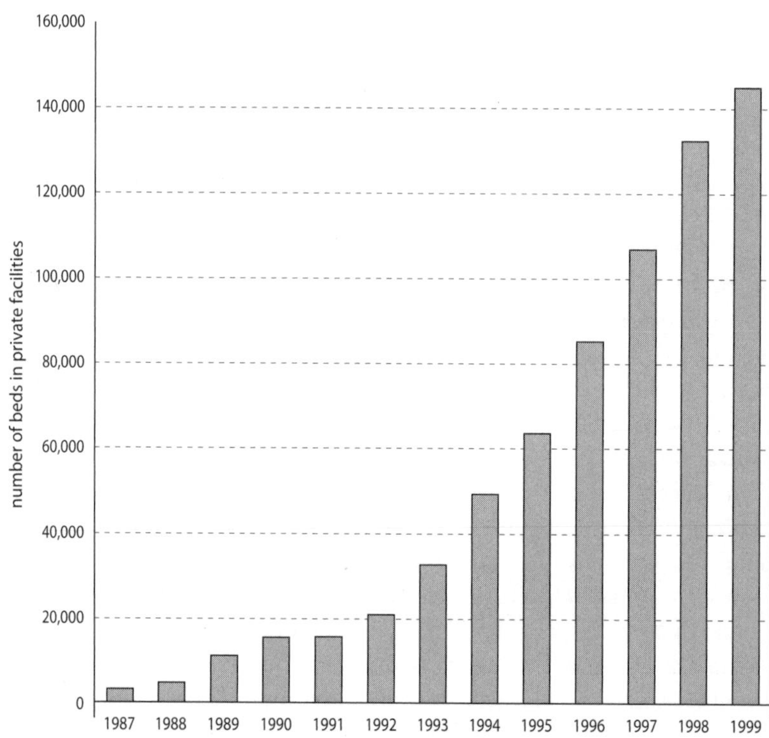

SOURCE: Charles W. Thomas, Dianne Bolinger, and John L. Badlamenti, *Private Adult Correctional Facilities Census*, 10th ed. (Gainesville: Center for Studies in Criminology and Law, University of Florida, 1997).

on the stock market, either on the New York Stock Exchange or on NASDAQ: Corrections Corporation of America, Wackenhut, Correctional Services Corporation (formerly Esmor), Cornell Corrections, Avalon Community Services, Correctional System, and Securicor (based in London). At the end of 1998, these seven firms controlled 87 percent of the beds in the commercial sector and had a combined turnover approaching $2 billion.* With 83 establishments for a capacity of 68,300 residents, Corrections Corporation of America had captured 49 percent of the market at the end of 1999. It was followed by Wack-

*This roster covers only "adult" incarceration; it excludes custodial and correctional services companies for juveniles, such as Children's Comprehensive Service and Youth Services International Incorporated, both listed on the NASDAQ technology index (under the acronyms KIDS and YSII, respectively).

enhut, with a 27 percent share and 26,700 beds distributed among 39 facilities, and then by a handful of firms weighing in at 3 to 4 percent of the sector each. With an aggregate growth rate of 45 percent per year between 1986 and 1996, most of these businesses doubled their volume of beds and sales from one year to the next. Several of them also manage custodial centers for juvenile offenders and halfway houses. Indeed, the traditional distinction between the adult and youth markets as well as between service providers in the carceral milieu and imprisonment firms is fast blurring as the leaders of this flourishing industry diversify and use their economies of scale (and their extensive political connections) to absorb their smaller competitors in neighboring activities.

After first focusing on minimum-security facilities, incarceration firms now take charge of the full range of custodial establishments (with the partial exception of "supermax" prisons reserved for the most violent or difficult convicts). Similarly, at their beginnings, carceral companies were content to staff and administer existing penitentiaries that remained the property of the state or county; nowadays they more often combine design, financing, construction, and management: 40 of the 118 new custodial facilities coming on line in 1995 were built and owned by commercial operators.

Originally concentrated in the southern states, which, for historical reasons harking back to the era of slavery, are at once the most restrictive in the social register and the most expansive in the penal realm,[39] the incarceration industry is gradually becoming national. Twenty-seven members of the Union plus the District of Columbia and Puerto Rico presently make use of for-profit jails and prisons. The bulk of the 156 institutions in operation at the end of 1999 (as against 102 three years earlier) were located in Texas (where they contributed 30,000 beds), California (11,500), Oklahoma (10,400), and Georgia (9,500), but also in Tennessee (7,300), Arizona (6,900), Florida (5,500), New Mexico (5,300), and Mississippi (4,700). Lastly, the US imprisonment industry has become internationalized since Wackenhut and Corrections Corporation spread into other Anglo-Saxon countries run by governments with neoliberal orientations: their subsidiaries control two-thirds of the "beds" in fifteen private institutions in Australia (7,500 beds), ten in England (7,200), two in Scotland (500), two in South Africa (6,000), and one each in Surinam and New Zealand (700 and 400 beds, respectively).

A second strategy for reducing the cost of the policy of confinement of poverty consists of *making inmates or their families shoulder a fraction—be it only minimal—of the costs of their incarceration*. Since 1994, a growing number of jurisdictions charge their correctional populations for custodial costs per day, impose fees for access to house services (health clinic, laundry, workshop, etc.), or make automatic deductions from funds put on their commissary accounts to lower the bill for their upkeep. According to a tally made by the National Prison Project of the American Civil Liberties Union in fall 1998, 21 states practiced a variant of "carceral taxation." In September 2000, President Clinton signed a new law, which had passed unopposed in Congress, requiring that federal inmates who have personal funds pay a one-dollar fee for each doctor visit behind bars, thus joining with the 38 states imposing such a co-payment to their convicts. Everything suggests that, for ideological no less than budgetary reasons, the authorities will amplify their efforts in this direction and strive to transfer an increasing share of the financial burden of hyperincarceration onto those who are its target.*

Thus inmates in the high-security penitentiary of Fort Madison, Iowa, who rot 23 hours a day in two-by-three meter concrete cubes, must remit a monthly "rent" of five dollars. Furthermore, since 1996, also in Iowa, a visit to the prison dentist costs three dollars. These sums are by no means modest in light of the miserable incomes of those concerned. The inmates lucky enough to work inside the penitentiary—in the kitchens, the laundry, or in maintenance—receive "wages" ranging from ten to sixty dollars per month. But their earnings are already cut by various deductions, for purposes of restitution to the victims of their misdeeds and to cover the court-ordered support for their children. Moreover, the personal hygiene supplies they need must be bought from the prison "commissary" at prohibitive prices, as do stamps, paper, extra food, and so forth. Seventeen Fort Madison inmates filed a complaint against the Iowa correctional administration and threats of strikes and riots are looming. "You can't get blood out of a turnip," sighed one of the inmates who mobilized against these measures. "The taxpayers want the punishment of incarceration, yet basically they don't want to foot the bills. Perhaps they should consider alternative sentencing then."[40]

Some prison and jail wardens have taken the step of hiring specialized collection agencies to ensure that convicts on parole pay the outstanding "rent" left uncovered at the time of their release. But, due to the growing disproportion between their means and the mass of clients entrusted to them, all correctional administrations have been

*In several states bills have been introduced aiming to make their parents, nay their siblings or extended families, pay for the costs of the confinement of minors. More and more convicts now come out of prison burdened with the debt of high court-processing costs and fees, as well as restitution to victims, whose reimbursement puts additional strain on their precarious economic situation.

forced to resort to a third strategy: *lowering the "living standards" and services within custodial facilities*—within the limits tolerated by the courts. After two decades of tangible improvements following a wave of lawsuits filed by prisoners' rights organizations, the 1980s inaugurated a pronounced hardening of detention regimes and ushered a noticeable deterioration of conditions of confinement in the 1990s:[41] reduced training and increased turnover of the custodial staff, decrease in the funds allocated for "rehabilitation," elimination of in-house law libraries, de facto restriction of inmates' rights to appeal, etc. Budgets for activities directed toward reintegration were the first to be cut, even though they never amounted to more than one-tenth of carceral expenditures. Between 1989 and 1994, sixteen states terminated their literacy and remedial education programs; during 1993–94 alone, over half of the members of the Union reduced or eliminated education behind bars, in violation of the law in the case of juvenile inmates, since the latter continue to fall under the legal obligation to attend school.[42] Cutting expenditures aimed at "rehabilitation" is easier to justify when the prison no longer sports any ambition other than neutralizing its denizens and making them expiate their mistakes in suffering.*

The dominant penal philosophy in the United States at century's turn can be encapsulated by an expression much in vogue among penal professionals: "Make prisoners smell like prisoners." Incarceration must urgently become again what it was at its origin and should never have ceased being: an ordeal (the word punishment comes from *poena*, which means suffering). And the suffering should be as great and long as the crime committed is serious.[43] Whence the popularity of "boot camps," the reintroduction of striped uniforms, and calls to restore corporal punishments (such as caning) and public humiliation in order to instill in candidates for crime the fear, if not the shame, of imprisonment. Whence also the disproportionate media hoopla around measures whose aims are purely symbolic—they often turn out to be juridically impracticable or financially ruinous—such as the use of stocks (to which the disobedient prisoner is attached upright for hours in the broiling sun) and the return of chain gangs (squads of inmates work-

*As Tennessee state Representative Don Bird, a Democrat sponsoring legislation designed to make prison conditions tougher on inmates, explained: "All we are obligated to provide these criminals is a clean place to sleep and decent food—that means corn bread and beans. Neither would I be opposed to bringing back the chain gangs. Give these men a heavy sledge hammer and put them in a rock quarry eight hours a day, six days a week. That will give them calluses on their hands, a sore back and a good night's sleep. They won't need exercise equipment then." Cited in Mark Curriden, "Hard Times," *American Bar Association Journal* 81 (July 1995): 74.

ing with their legs chained together), brutal reminders of the era of slavery, in certain states of the South.[44] In Arizona, the only program allowing incarcerated mothers to remain in contact with their children (by attending "parenting" classes and, for the luckier ones, by occasionally spending between 8 and 72 hours with them in a special housing unit) was eliminated in 1994 on account of the cost of the visits and the risk of lawsuits they occasioned,* but also because "these people are supposed to be punished and part of punishment is being isolated from your family and friends," as explained by Republican representative Susan Gerard, who sponsored this cancellation. "I think families should understand that if you screw up, you lose your kids."[45]

For politicians but also for judges, prosecutors, and sheriffs (whose positions are elective), being "tough on crime" is more than a mandatory campaign theme: it is an article of faith to be sworn on pain of immediate professional death. This sets up a competition between those who would ostentatiously maximize what Gresham Sykes calls "the pains of imprisonment."[46] During every election cycle, candidates vie to vow to eliminate "privileges" that no inmate actually enjoys, with the sole aim of proving that they are driven by the greatest severity toward society's black sheep. Elected on the promise to "put prisoners back into leg iron," Alabama Governor Fob James restored chain gangs in August 1995 and had them parade before a crowd of reporters and camera crews from around the world to signify publicly that "prison isn't what it used to be" and that convicts would henceforth rediscover penal suffering thanks to his program of "shock incarceration": twelve hours a day breaking rocks, with no television and radio, and a strict ban on tobacco, soft drinks, and cookies.[47] During the presidential campaign of 1996, Republican nominee Robert Dole made a point—and a spectacle—of visiting Sheriff Arpaio's "tent-city jail" in the Arizona desert to "show he's a Rambo against crime."[48] On the same campaign tour, he contrived to have himself photographed and filmed for the local and national evening news visiting the death-row unit in San Quentin state penitentiary. During his 1992 nomination campaign, Bill Clinton made a point of interrupting his electoral tour in the northeast to rush back to Arkansas and attend in person the putting to death of Ricky Ray Rector, a deeply mentally impaired convict—his last wish was to have his dessert set aside so that he could eat it after his execution—whom Clinton had refused to save from the gallows as governor. From presiden-

*At the end of 1997, Arizona held 1,677 women in custody, as against 689 ten years earlier; 80 percent of these prisoners had children.

tial contestants to congresspersons to local representatives, national politicians are well attuned to the fact that the electorate clings to a very jaundiced view of the prison and its role: according to a 1995 NBC poll, for instance, 82 percent of Americans believe that "life in prison is too easy" and over 60 percent hold that rehabilitation programs behind bars have utterly failed and should be curtailed. A Time/CNN poll conducted the same year found that 65% of Americans approve of the reintroduction of chain gangs and 51% believe that convicts should be deprived of their TV sets and barbells.[49]

Prison wardens who enjoy a reputation for "toughness" within their professional milieu are aggressively courted and their careers accelerate through lateral mobility. This is famously the case of Michael Moore, the former director of the prison system of Texas—one of the most repressive states of the Union—who was hired to preside over the correctional administration of North Carolina so as to initiate in it a sturdy policy of carceral austerity. His first measures were to eliminate televisions and fans in cells, to close down sporting activities, to impose the wearing of uniforms upon all inmates, as well as to forbid convicts from sporting beards or long hair. The result was a string of riots that cost millions of dollars in damage, during which five guards were stabbed.[50] A law passed in 1998 by the California Assembly prohibits the use of weights and dumbbells, pornographic magazines, cigarettes, and personal clothing, as well as medium-length hair and beards. The same tendency toward the hardening of custodial regimens has asserted itself at the federal level. Thus, the Prison Security Act of 1995  forbids the inmates of federal penitentiaries "from engaging in activities to increase their strength or fighting ability while in prison," thus suppressing weight training, the main pastime of prisoners, for whom "pumping iron" is also a means of preserving a sense of pride in self. The No Frills Prison Act of 1995 similarly reserves federal funds for prison  building to those states that commit to eliminating a battery of "frivolous favors" granted to convicts, among them the reduction of sentences for good behavior, musical instruments, the showing of R-rated movies on television, and in-cell coffee pots. The law goes so far as to stipulate that prison food must not be better than Army "chow." When he introduced the bill in the House in 1995, Dick Zimmer (a Republican from New Jersey) vented the social resentment at the fulcrum of that law: "It is shameful that so many good, hardworking people are struggling just to put food on their table, while criminals serving time in prison have such luxuries as cable TV, [exercise equipment] and prime rib dinners. . . . We should not be using taxpayer dollars to turn prisons into vacation spas."[51] We see here how public pronouncements about penal policy and the corresponding shifts in correctional practices become disconnected from any identifiable penological end to serve as fleet vehicles for stoking, tapping, and targeting collective sentiments of reprobation and bile toward convicts as a conspicuously undeserving category, thereby contrastively valorizing the "hardworking people" to whom they are counterposed.

A 1995 survey of 823 prison wardens confirms the jettisoning of the ideal of "rehabilitation" in favor of the sole function of "neutralization" and the correlative toughening of conditions of confinement.[52] Two-thirds of the interviewees state that they have reduced or eliminated postsecondary education programs in their facilities, while 47 percent have banned tobacco, 40 percent boxing and conjugal visits (where they had been allowed), and one-third the reading of adult magazines, the use of personal clothing and weights, and dental care deemed cosmetic. Moreover, seven in ten wardens wish to limit or eliminate the distribution of contraceptives and the remittance of benefits for physical disability, while one-half advocate restricting inmates' access to legal information and free legal assistance. Comparison with earlier surveys shows that today's prison managers have markedly more punitive orientations than their predecessors.[53]

To make people accept the rapid and endless growth of the numbers under lock and key and thus the continual expansion of their budgets and personnel, the correctional administrations of the states leading the trend to hyperincarceration compete in vaunting the side-benefits that the free citizenry is supposed to draw from plethoric carceral populations. Thus, in March of 1996, Texas governor (and future president) George W. Bush personally announced with great fanfare that the convicts of the Lone Star State would be put to work to embellish the state's natural heritage, in the manner of ecological activists despite themselves: "Prisoners, parolees, and probationers will provide in FY 96 an estimated $4 million worth of labor for 25 parks and Wildlife Management Area (WMA) projects, ranging from building nature trails to expanding handicapped access to mowing, clearing brush, and removing trash. Sixteen projects involving over 700 offenders from 13 prisons are already underway; agreements have been reached for 10 additional projects." Against a backdrop of inmates cleaning gravestones and freshening up the lawns at the Austin state cemetery, the governor proudly declared: "This is a unique way for those who have committed crimes to make some restitution to the citizens of Texas. Prisons should be a place of punishment, where inmates work to repay a debt. This program puts them to work on public improvement projects which all Texans can enjoy when they visit our parks and public lands."[54]

The California Department of Corrections never misses an opportunity to remind the public of the crucial contribution that its denizens make to the fight against summer forest fires in the Sierra and to the emergency reinforcing of dikes during the big winter floods in the valleys. "As of 4:30 pm today, nearly 900 inmate crew members and 46 staff from the California Department of Corrections are at work battling floods throughout northern and central California. About 864 inmates are at work:—Sandbagging tributaries of the Sacramento and Trinity rivers;—Cooking for evacuees and rescue workers at the emergency shelters at Colusa fairgrounds, Yuba and Marysville Community Colleges;—Filling and loading sandbags in 12 counties;—and Providing assistance to other agencies where needed. Additional inmate crews are expected to begin work Friday sandbagging levies in the Sacramento Delta near Isleton." Every announcement ends with this formulaic statement which reflects well its purpose: "It is estimated that by using inmates state and local governments save millions of dollars that otherwise would be paid to accomplish the work inmates perform."[55]

A press release of February 1998 by the correctional administration celebrated the fact that "California inmates [are] donating their hair to sick children who need wigs."[56] Following the implementation of a draconian new set of rules regarding personal grooming expressly forbidding state prisoners from wearing beards, moustaches, and requiring them to cut their hair to military length, the CDC authorized and even encouraged its denizens to send their hair to an association called Locks for Love, based in Fort Lauderdale, Florida, which uses them to make wigs for children suffering from baldness caused by illness. "In this 'everyone wins' [sic] arrangement, the inmates will benefit from knowing they have helped a group of children, and the children will get a hair replacement that allows them to look good and feel good about themselves." And the director of the CDC added: "It's a chance for many of these men and women to do something positive for society, even from their prison cell." A rather limited opportunity, since it turns out that only seven inmates at Calipatria prison and six at Wasco (out of some 160,000) participated in the program, which earned them a personal thank-you note from Locks of Love. True, participating in the program presupposes having hair at least six inches long, and that the latter be washed, dried, braided, and put under special plastic wrapping. The CDC nevertheless assures us that "[a]s more inmates clip their hair to meet the new requirements for short hair, additional donations are expected." And when, for the sixth consecutive year, the inmates of Folsom prison, reputed to be among the toughest convicts in the state, delivered one hundred baskets garnished with treats (donated by the guards) as Halloween gifts to children in the orphanages of El Dorado County, the CDC even put out a video of the prisoners preparing the baskets.[57]

It is also good organizational marketing, when inaugurating a new prison, to insist on the benefits that such an establishment brings to the locality that hosts it.[58] But, for purposes of hyping the profits of imprisonment, nothing beats the money to be had by taking it straight from the prisoners' piggy banks by way of judicial decree. California convicts on whom the courts have inflicted a "restitution fine" must transfer to the state a minimum of 22 percent (with 2 percent going to administrative costs) of all the sums they receive while in custody, whatever their source. For, since 1995, the law authorizes the correctional administration to take a cut not only of its denizens' wages (when they accrue any), but also from the sums deposited by their family onto their "commissary" accounts. Combined with automatic deductions, this law enabled the state to pass the half-million dollars-mark for monthly withholdings from inmates. "With its October check of $445,393, the California Department of Corrections now has contributed more than $10 million to the State Board of Control Crime Victim Compensation Fund," the director of the correctional administration stressed. "Although the money can't erase the devastating impact of a crime on its victims, it can help with the very real costs of medical care, counseling and emergency expenses." And he further insisted: "We can do better. Fewer than half our inmates are paying restitution. I think it should be 100 percent." To which end the CDC director promised that his staff would work diligently: "We are reaching out to district attorneys, chief probation officers and judges. We want everyone in the criminal justice system to realize that we have the laws and the means to hold every inmate financially accountable for his or her criminal actions."[59]

But the ultimate goal of all institutional communication aimed at the general public remains to reaffirm whenever possible the inflexible implementation of the rule of carceral austerity: that time behind bars is not a walk in the park, that inmates pay their dues, and that they enjoy no "privileges" that they do not earn through their obedient, even servile, conduct. Thus the Texas correctional administration makes it a matter of pride to inform the state's citizenry of the draconian living and working conditions it imposes upon its inmates on the FAQ page of its web site. The summary description of the penitential daily round heavily emphasizes the discomfort, absence of privacy and autonomy, and obligation to labor; all characteristics commonly associated with leisure (choice, bodily well-being, the arrangement of one's room at will) are vigorously excluded.* The correctional administration even apologizes for the fact that Texas does not have chain gangs due to the special risks that these would pose for public safety; but it points out that low-security convicts perform "public service projects," supervised by armed guards on horseback. Above all, there is no question of prisoners enjoying services to which ordinary law-abiding citizens do not have access in the "free world," such as free higher education. To be sure, "offenders who have a high school diploma or GED may earn the privilege of taking college courses," but it is carefully specified that "upon release to parole or mandatory supervision, the offenders must reimburse the state for those courses that are offered through a contract arrangement with various junior colleges."

"No Free World Clothing Is Authorized"

Do offenders in prison have color televisions in their cells?
No. Offenders do not have televisions in their cells. There are, however, color televisions available for viewing by offenders who earn the privilege. Televisions are usually located in dayrooms where 60 to 90 offenders may watch one set. Seating is generally on metal benches bolted to the floor. Correctional officers are in charge of the remote controls and only the basic networks, sports, and educational channels are permitted. The televisions are purchased with profits from sales in the offender commissaries (in-prison stores where snack foods, toiletries and approved magazines and books may be purchased). Offenders receive money from their family and friends through deposits to a trust account.

Are the prison units air conditioned?
All Texas prisons have a heating system, but in the summer only the prison hospital and psychiatric units have air conditioning. The other units have forced air systems that keep inside air moving and fresh air coming in.

How do offenders spend their day?
The day starts with wake-up call at 3:30 a.m. and breakfast is served at 4:30 a.m. Offenders report to their work assignments at 6:00 a.m. Every offender who is physically capable has a job in the prison system. Offenders are not paid for their work, but they can earn privileges as a result of good work habits. They also

*In Tennessee, where severe overcrowding triggered a wave of riots that forced to the federal courts to take over the entire prison system in the mid-1980s, the legislature took the trouble to approve a proposal to amend the state constitution so as to drop the word "comfortable" from its legal mandate to run "safe and comfortable prisons." Richard Lacayo, "The Real Hard Cell," *Time Magazine*, 4 September 1995.

learn job skills that can help them find employment when they are released from prison.

Most offenders work in prison support jobs—cooking, cleaning, laundry and maintenance of the system's 107 prison units. About 10,000 inmates work in the system's agriculture jobs which last year produced almost $50 million worth of edible crops, livestock and cotton for the prison system on 139,000 acres of farm and ranch land. Prison units that don't have enough land to be in the agricultural program still produce several million pounds of fresh vegetables each year to donate to local food banks for the needy.

About 8,000 offenders work in the prison industries program, a system of 46 factories that last year produced $100 million worth of products—all offender and Correctional officer clothing, mattresses, cleaning supplies and equipment, furniture, stainless steel, school bus and dump truck repair, license tags, highway signs and microfilming for state agencies, just to name a few. Prison industry products are sold to other state agencies, cities, counties and school districts.

What happens if an offender refuses to work?
Offenders who refuse to work lose their privileges and are placed on "cell restriction." Cell restriction means remaining in the cell 24 hours a day, with no trips to the day room, commissary, or recreation yard. Meals are also eaten in the cell. Personal property is taken away while on cell restriction. . . .

What kind of medical care do offenders receive?
All prison medicine is handled as a managed health care program operated by an agreement between TDCJ, the University of Texas Medical Branch, Texas Tech Health Sciences Center and the University of Houston College of Pharmacy. . . .

Under a new law passed in 1997, offenders who have any money in their trust account must pay a $3 co-pay for a visit to a prison doctor. This "co-pay" system is expected to bring in nearly $1 million a year to help offset the cost of prison health care. . . .

What kind of dress code applies to offenders?
No free world clothing is allowed; all offenders wear prison-made white uniforms. Male offenders are required to have very short haircuts and no facial hair.

Are offenders allowed to make telephone calls?
Offenders who demonstrate good behavior can earn one 5-minute phone call every 90 days. Calls are monitored and may be made only to approved individuals.

What do offenders eat?
Most meals consist of ground beef dishes, chicken, or pork. The ground beef is bought with proceeds from the sale of prison-raised cattle. Although the prisons have more than 250,000 hens, they are used only for egg production. It is less

expensive to buy chicken meat at market. The system raises and serves its own pork products.

What kinds of educational opportunities do offenders have while in prison?
Offenders entering the prison system with less than a seventh grade education are required by law to attend in-prison school and work toward a GED. Those who have higher than a seventh grade education, but do not have a High School diploma, may request to go to school and finish their GED. They will be allowed to attend school only if they earn that privilege through good behavior and satisfactory performance in their prison job. . . .

What does it cost to incarcerate an offender?
The average cost per day to incarcerate an offender in the Texas prison system is $39.50.[60]

Putting Prisoners to Use

"What do I hope to accomplish with this crime bill? I'd like to start by building prisons, but we have to stop building them like Holiday Inns! I'd like to put people in prison so that they work. I don't see why the workers of this country have to pay to keep criminals in prisons while the criminals in prison themselves for the most part do not work."[61] This tirade by senator Phil Gramm of Texas during the congressional debate on the Omnibus Crime law, passed by an overwhelming majority of both US chambers in summer 1994,* Democrats and Republicans joined, points to one last possible method for lightening the crushing bill of hyperincarceration: putting inmates to work and then skimming off their wages so as to make them bear some or all of the financial burden of their own reclusion.

Among the received ideas widely peddled about the US penal system

*The hackneyed penal myth of the "Holiday Inn prison" rose to the level of personal obsession for Senator Gramm, who rarely missed a chance to include it in his public speeches and made it a central theme of his abortive run for the presidency in 1996: "Phil Gramm would replace the Clinton Crime bill and its misguided social programs with policies that grab violent criminals by the throat. A Gramm administration will stop building prisons like Holiday Inns and make prisoners work. 'We don't have to live in a country where we open up the newspaper every morning and read that a robber, or a rapist, or a murderer who has been convicted five or six times is back on the street having killed another child. I know how to fix that. And if I have to string barbed wire on every closed military base in America, I'm going to put those people in jail and keep them there.'" Phil Gramm for President, *Restoring the American Dream*, 1996, campaign brochure available online at www.4president.org.

in recent years—by journalists from the mainstream media as well as by progressive activists opposed to what they improperly call the "prison-industrial complex"—is the thesis according to which prisoners constitute an abundant and docile workforce that is ruthlessly exploited by capitalist firms. On this view, the search for profit is the driving engine of mass imprisonment, and inmates serve as a substitute labor source in sectors such as textiles, furniture, automobiles, and telemarketing, to the point that some union publications believed that they could discern in its use a serious threat to the condition of the working class as a whole.[62] In reality, carceral work concerns only a tiny minority of inmates:[63] in 1996, 80,000 prisoners, less than 7 percent of the clients of federal and state penitentiaries, held a paying job behind bars, and fewer than 5000 of them worked for private businesses, amounting to *0.25 percent of the population under lock.** They produced $1.6 billion worth of merchandise and received $74 million in salaries, a minuscule drop in the ocean of correctional operating expenditures ($40 billion that year).[64] But, precisely, because their use is so minimal, convicts would represent a "goldmine" of manpower, and thus potential revenues that many advocates of penal expansion are eager to develop.

Making prisoners work would reconnect the present to a central thread of the nation's penal history. In the nineteenth century the country's penitentiaries were self-financed by the labor of their occupants and a good number of states (especially those of the South) even made colossal profits by renting out their convict workforce to the large mining, industrial, and agricultural concerns of their region. (Carceral wage labor was eventually banned in the 1940s under union pressure.)[65] Next, work behind bars is prized by prison wardens insofar as it helps them enforce custodial order by reducing idleness and violence. It is also appreciated by the inmates, who as a general rule prefer to engage in some activity than to rot all day long in overcrowded cells, as well as by penologists, who stress its moderating influence upon recidivism after release as it gives convicts a modicum of work experience. Finally, penitentiary employment has the ideological virtue of extending the civic obligation to work to those among impoverished Americans who

*According to the 1993 *Sourcebook of Criminal Justice Statistics* (Washington: Government Printing Office, 1995), that year 7 percent of prisoners worked at a paid job and 4 percent in agricultural production (compared to 16 percent for these two activities in 1984); 41 percent performed various maintenance and upkeep tasks (cooking, laundry, cleaning); 8 percent participated in a job training program, and 1 percent had a job on the outside, leaving 39 percent of inmates without any activity. The idleness rate in jails is considerably higher, close to two-thirds. Moreover, official figures reporting activities are systematically inflated.

are the most recalcitrant to the new hegemonic regime of desocialized wage labor. Thus, throughout the 1990s, scientific studies, administrative reports, legislative bills, and political pronouncements proliferated which aimed to remedy the economic drawbacks, underline the material and moral advantages and remove juridical obstacles to work behind bars, if not to put the country on the road to "carceral full employment."[66] In 1996, the voters of Oregon even passed a constitutional amendment approving compulsory work for the entire correctional population of the state.

In 1990, California voters rejected a referendum on government bonds of $450 million intended to finance the building of two new prisons, but on the same ballot they approved an amendment to the state constitution authorizing carceral industries so long as these do not compete against workers in the corresponding sectors of the economy on the outside. California's Prison Industry Authority (PIA) has since expanded and today manages 65 production units located in 23 state prisons, in which are manufactured flags, shoes, road signs, eyeglasses, gloves, office and printing furniture, license plates, and assorted correctional clothing and equipment.* Half of these products are consumed by the California Department of Corrections itself, and the rest are sold to the captive market of county, state, and federal administrations for an annual gross of $152 million (including $33 million in agricultural and food products, $32 million in textiles, $30 million in paper and other wood-derived products, and $22 million in metal wares). After the mandatory deductions for judicial costs and restitution to victims (20 percent), the PIA inmate-workers receive an hourly wage ranging from 30 to 95 cents, for an average of 57 cents per hour.

According to an econometric study commissioned by the correctional administration, these productive activities do not compete with the state's private companies and even induce a net gain of 560 jobs on the outside.[67] The PIA is said to improve the skills of participating inmates and to be concerned to help them find a job after release by providing them with a certificate of "employability." But, although it is the largest of its kind in the country after that run by Texas, this program employs only 7000 inmates and 700 civilians; and the output of prisons remains negligible for the state economy and budget: it is barely larger than the California chewing gum industry ($133 million) or equivalent to the

*In July 1998 the inmates at Chico prison launched an internet site, set up with the help of students from the nearby university, featuring an "electronic catalogue" allowing one to order online over 24,000 items produced by California's convicts: see the web site of the California Prison Industry Authority, http://catalog.pia.ca.gov/.

average returns on a single film by Steven Spielberg. This is because the well-known advantages of captive labor—permanent availability, docility, a sense of discipline, low wages, absorption of its reproduction costs by the correctional administration—are woefully insufficient to make up for its serious drawbacks: very low skills and therefore low productivity, geographic isolation (large prisons are situated in remote rural areas), environing bureaucratic inertia, calamitous insufficiencies of the infrastructure, and the unavoidable primacy of the imperative of security and the rigid practical constraints it imposes.

Furthermore, upon closer examination, aside from strict spatial confinement, the employment circumstances of convicts are not that divergent from the degraded conditions of unskilled wage earners on the outside after "welfare reform." The shift from welfare to workfare, analyzed in chapter 3, has accelerated the growth and institutionalization of contingent labor markets in which workers cannot but submit to demeaning, authoritarian, and unstable work arrangements delivering subpoverty wages, no health benefits, no pensions, and no vacations.[68] Not to mention that it takes only a spike in the unemployment rate to call into question the legitimacy of carceral wage labor: by what right would a criminal be provided with a guaranteed job when law-abiding Americans cannot find one on the outside? This is to say that it will not suffice to repeal federal and state laws limiting the sale of goods produced in prison, to create marketing offices promoting the use of the carceral workforce, and to stimulate partnerships with the private sector—as the advocates of carceral wage-labor would have us believe—for prisons suddenly to mutate into profitable "factories behind bars" for the state.

Making the inmate or his kin pay, reducing services within custodial establishments to a bare minimum, generalizing unskilled work inside penitentiaries: for now, these measure are pursued less for their financial fallout, which is negligible compared to the pharaonic expenditures demanded by the policy of penalization of poverty, than for the message they send to prisoners and their families as to the rest of the population. They attest to a reversal of the causal connection traditionally postulated by the political economy of punishment: here the communicative function of penal policy trumps its instrumental mission, and symbolic considerations drive material changes, turning penality into a potent engine of moral signification.[69] These measures aim, first of all, to reaffirm the principle of "less eligibility," erstwhile articulated by Jeremy Bentham, according to which the condition of the best-treated inmate must imperatively be inferior to that of the most underprivileged worker on the outside—absent which the latter could be tempted to turn to a life of vice and crime rather than submit to the mandate of work.[70] Besides, how could one justify the fact that a prisoner receives free room and board and medical care from the collectivity when, in spite of renewed prosperity, 45 million Americans (including two-thirds of wage earners grossing less than $15,000 annually) are deprived of medical coverage, 30 million suffer from chronic hunger and malnutrition, and seven million lack housing?[71] This is the argument put forth by Congress in 1994 to exclude inmates from Pell Grants (federal educational subsidies) and in one stroke decimate higher education behind bars, since 17,000 inmates found themselves forced to abandon their studies overnight, even though all existing studies concur that, in addition to helping sustain carceral order day to day, educational programs sharply reduce offending after release.

What matters, next, is to magnify in the eyes of the electorate the fact that prisoners are "paying their debt" to society and, in order to do so, to *accentuate the symbolic boundary that demarcates and isolates them from the citizenry* by dramatizing their suffering in custody and denying them the elementary rights enjoyed by law-abiding citizens. Sheriff Arpaio, who boasts of charging his detainees a dollar a meal and of having eliminated coffee and mayonnaise from his jail, concedes that these measures allowed him to cut only $80,000 and $150,000, respectively, out of an annual operating budget of $70 million. A pittance, but no matter: "This is not just to save money. I'd do it if I could afford steak. They should not like jail, and paying for it helps that." In an interview with *Time Magazine*, "America's toughest sheriff" explained: "I want to make this place so unpleasant that they won't even think about doing something that could bring them back. I want them to suffer."[72] So it is that American inmates are deprived of the right to vote, not only during their detention, but as long as they remain under penal supervision, if not for life—in violation of international conventions pertaining to political rights.* This is why the law voids the meager social rights they could claim and mandates that all public "benefits" (retirement, food stamps, access to social housing, payments to the handicapped, etc.) be

*Thirty-six states deprive convicts released under correctional supervision of their voting rights, while thirteen others take them away permanently. Over 4.2 million Americans are thus excluded from the exercise of so-called universal suffrage, including 1.4 million black men representing 14 percent of the African-American electorate. Jamie Fellner and Marc Mauer, *Losing the Vote: The Impact of Felony Disenfranchisement in the United States* (Washington, D.C.: The Sentencing Project and Human Rights Watch, 1998).

withdrawn from them as well as their families.[73] National solidarity—or government "compassion"—should not be extended to them because they are not properly speaking members of the American civic community.

Struck by a triple stigma at once moral (they have put themselves beyond the pale of citizenry by breaking the law), class (they are poor in a society that venerates wealth and conceives of socioeconomic standing as the result of sole individual effort), and caste (the majority of them are black, and thus issued from a population deprived of "ethnic honor"), inmates are the pariah group among the pariahs, a *sacrificial category* that can be vilified and humiliated with total impunity and to immense symbolic profit. The policy of criminalization of poverty pursued by the American state thus finds its cultural extension in a public discourse of abomination of prisoners, in which the country's highest authorities participate, that makes them the incarnation of absolute evil: the living antithesis of the "American dream" whose banishment serves as collective exorcism.

"The Benchmark for the Jails of the Twenty-First Century"

According to an informational brochure from the Los Angeles County Sheriff's Department, the Twin Towers Correctional Facility, entry-point and hub of the county's web of custodial facilities, embodies the futurist prototype of jails for the new millennium, thanks to its "ultra modern design and state-of-the-art electronics systems." See for yourself.

With its 1.5 million square feet arrayed on ten acres at the intersection of Highway 101 and César Chávez Boulevard, at the very heart of the city, "the world's largest known jail facility" (as its officials like to proclaim) comprises a high-security ward, an inmate admission and sorting center, and a medical wing with 200 beds. At full capacity, it will employ 2,400 people, in the manner of a gigantic factory whose raw materials and finished products would be the bodies of inmates.

The two peach-colored towers, each crowned by a heliport, which bookend the reception center and give the facility its name can house up to 4,200 detainees. The first, some 200 feet high, also houses the administrative and support services for the facility, storage areas, staff locker rooms, dining rooms, and kitchens (capable of serving 17,000 meals daily), as well as meeting and training rooms and even two gymnasiums open 24 hours a day. The second tower houses inmates in need of medical and mental health care, distributed over four floors, cloistered from the rest of the complex. The medical ward has its own analysis and radiological laboratories and employs 60-some nurses (out of 350 employed by the LA County Jail [LACJ]), in addition to 35 physicians and seven dental assistants.

The inmates' quarters take the form of a bare concrete heptagon made of six identical modules of sixteen cells each, arranged in a circle around a control cockpit according to the Benthamite principle of the Panopticon. In addition to its eight cells at ground level and another eight on the mezzanine, each module comprises a common room outfitted with round metallic tables bolted to the floor, where inmates can congregate and talk with their lawyers when the latter visit them. At the center of the heptagon, seated in the safety and comfort of his ergonomic chair, a single guard takes in all 96 cells through their glass doors and closed-circuit television. Ventilation, temperature, lighting, and fire surveillance are regulated by a central computer. The detention heptagons are stacked over five stories, each with its own "yard," an encaged triangular area 50 feet on each side equipped with a basketball hoop, a block bathroom (with toilet and wash-basin), and a wire cage that serves as yard for inmates needing to be isolated from their companions of misfortune (such as "celebrities" and child rapists). All areas are dotted with telephone banks: "It's their umbilical cord to the outside world," notes the nurse who is taking me around the joint.

This spatial layout is designed to avoid having to resort to using inmates as a workforce and to minimize their movements, and thereby to curtail the frequency and type of contacts that they have with one another as well as with the guards (in addition to private toilets, each control booth has a kitchenette). The strict prohibition on smoking and using money likewise aims to reduce materials for contraband and thus opportunities for violent incidents among inmates. The antiseptic and stunningly silent ambiance of the place (the floors, doors, and walls are soundproof), the abundance of natural light, and the absence of bars on openings would almost make you forget that you're inside a jail . . . if not for the uniforms, dull brown for the guards, canvas blue for the inmates (over a screaming yellow t-shirt with "LA County Jail" emblazoned on the back in large dark blue letters), the shut doors and their omnipresent digital codes. And the submissive behavior of the residents, visibly stamped with apprehensive deference.

The Inmate Reception Center spreads its 180,000 square feet over two sparkling floors. Designed to "process" as many as 4,000 clients per day, it currently triages between 700 and 1,500 (around 200 over the course of the day and between 600 and 1,000 in the evening, with a spike around 9:30 p.m.). The maximum is reached in the evenings before the weekend and the minimum at the beginning of the week. The 25 counters for "booking" and 25 others for "classification," lined up perpendicular to a walkway arrayed with waiting rooms, large enough to hold a hundred people each, is strongly evocative of an airport. Seated on a small metal stool, the arrestees give their "horsepower" (identity, height, weight, distinctive markings, address, aliases, and criminal and correctional background) into a microphone connecting them to a registration clerk perched behind a shatterproof glass window. And they wait and wait: three hours here, six hours there, four more hours at the next stage, then two more hours . . .

From the moment they cross the gate of the Inmate Reception Center, it will take the candidates for admission between twelve and twenty-four hours—often more, especially if they demand to be examined by a doctor—to finally reach their "housing unit" (the administrative term by which the LACJ designates their cell). During the interval, they sleep on the concrete ground or on metal benches in the waiting rooms, under bright neon lights and the lurid glow of television sets that are on continuously to "pacify" the "fresh fish" in transit—this is what the guards call the new arrivals filtering through the "holding stations" of the city and neighboring municipalities that purchase their police and detention services from the Los Angeles Sheriff's Bureau. "Most of our clients have come through many times, they know how to play the game. Ninety-nine percent go along with the program. And then, sure enough, you got your one percent that are creating all the trouble": the agitated, the quick tempered, the aggressive, the rebellious, those who are out of control due to medical or mental problems or simply because they are exhausted and exasperated of waiting, gang members who spot a rival in the line, and so on.

The "violent fish" are stored separately in bare concrete "isolation cells" of five by seven feet, outfitted with a small built-in bench and a toilet, if necessary bound in chains. "They'll be shackled, still they bang their heads on the wall, they hit their faces on the walls, then they'll pretend they got hit by a deputy. They'll urinate, defecate on the floor, throw feces at you, they ruin the place, for real: you can see it." Indeed, every visible surface is scratched, dented, and spoiled, with marks that look like a thousand blows on all four walls and on the inside of the metal door. The most recalcitrant are handled by the Emergency Response Team, the shock unit made up of fierce, hulking guards who function as clean-up crews, armored in "extraction suits" and "spit masks," and make it their duty to bend any resistance to the carceral order in a jiffy: "There they get to have their fun with you. But most inmates, they realize it's not in their interest to wind up in there. But you got no choice: you got to fight violence with violence." Each intervention of the ERT, involving "combative inmates," "keep-aways," and "special cases," must be supervised by a sergeant and written up in a report detailing its actions.

Taped to the glass window of each classification booth, an illustrated "notice" informs the detainees of penal measures recently passed by the state assembly that may affect them:

> NOTICE: *If you are convicted as an adult of using a gun in a crime, no plea bargaining 10 years will be added to your sentence if you had a gun with you; 20 years will be added to*

your sentence if you fired a gun; 30 years will be added to your sentence if you injure someone with a gun.

At the "classification" stage, the detainee is invited to answer a series of questions listed on two sheets of paper also taped onto the clerk's window, the one in English and the other (at left) in Spanish, making it possible to determine his level of dangerousness and special needs:

1) Are you in a gang? Yes or No, if you answer Yes, name of gang
2) Have you ever escaped or walked away from custody or a halfway house? Yes or No, if you answer Yes, name of the jail/prison or gang [sic]
3) Are you currently on summary or formal probation: Yes or No
4) Are you currently on parole: Yes or No
5) Are you homosexual: Yes or No.

Under the "classification" questionnaire, another notice similarly posted directly onto the booth wall explains:

3) You will be in a medical clinic within 4–6 hours and will see a nurse; however, do you have an emergency medical or mental health condition that requires immediate *attention, right now? Y or N?*
4) Are you taking prescription medication that you seriously need within the next 6 hours?
5) Are you thinking of killing yourself?

If he responds "yes" to one of these questions, the "fish" is in principle rerouted to the "express lane" and sent straight away under the watch of a guard to the nurses' station for immediate examination. Deputy Eldridge estimates that five to twenty-five detainees "get expedited" through this procedure daily. The men being processed are horrified at the prospect of waiting another six or more hours, as they have generally spent over one half-day in detention already, in a police lock-up, being transported, and awaiting "booking," and they may be tempted to declare a false medical emergency. Bad move on their part, because the longest waiting lines are actually at the clinic, where one can be left to stew for 24 hours, sitting on a concrete bench, with only a sandwich and a bottle of fruit juice for victuals.

After registration and classification, the "fresh fish" is photographed and his completed file entered into the computer. He is undressed and showered (in "batches" of 70 men at peak hours). He trades his clothes in for the house's canvas uniform and rubber sandals. A 400-cubic-meter dressing-room equipped with nine gigantic elevated conveyer belts allows for the storage of as many as 35,000 bundles of personal effects. Then the new arrival goes through "medical triage" at the clinic of the reception center: a lung X-ray (for tuberculosis, which is making a big comeback in American prisons; women also undergo a pregnancy test), a four-minute video (in English and Spanish) on the most common and most contagious diseases, and an express check-up—one minute maximum—by a nurse's aide armed with a standardized questionnaire.* At the end of which he receives his "fish kit," a transparent plastic bag containing the necessary personal hygienic products: a tube of toothpaste and a small toothbrush, a mini-bar of soap, a black comb, a safety-head razor, four sachets of "Freshstart Deodorant Cream," four more of "Freshstart Conditioning and Shampoo" (similar to those one finds in the bathrooms of cheap hotels). Given that, in theory, an inmate showers every two days, this should suffice for the first week. The new resident then walks the inclined viaduct that takes him either to the "housing unit" he will occupy in an ultramodern "pod" in the Twin Towers, or to the other side of the street, to a cell in the dilapidated establishment of Men's Central Jail. There is a marked preference for the first option: "Twin Towers, it's the Hilton and, like, Men's Central Jail is Motel Six."**

Deputy Alexander asked a clinic staff to show me the video. I am alone; it is early and no "fresh fish" from the coming batch has yet made it through the long antechamber to the showers. There are a good forty detainees in the cells surrounding the triangular area, 150 feet long on each side, where the nurses bustle about, but they are waiting for their medical exam, some plopped down on the floor, others sleeping leaning against the concrete walls or upright with a dazed air. Wow, this "medical video" sure is (s)explicit! In a rapid, staccato rhythm, a gravelly voice exhorts the arrivals to inform the clinic staff if they suffer from "herpes, AIDS, gonorrhea, bad blood, chemical dependency," or if they have "wounds, a cast, lice, crabs, scabies, an artificial limb or any other prosthesis." The call is amplified, for each of these afflictions, by spectacular pictures of inmates suffering from acute cases that flash by in rush mode. "Anyone not able to pull back the skin of their penis . . ." Repulsive close-up. You would never expect anything like this displayed in public in a culture so puritanical and ashamed of the (undomesticated) body as American culture. But, obviously, this video is not for the consumption of your average American.

Another 600-foot long viaduct and several elevators (the complex has 24 in total) connect the reception center to the bus station nested in the building's

*In 1997, the LACJ clinic detected 800 HIV-positive inmates and 400 suffering from full-blown AIDS, 115 cases of tuberculosis, 317 cases of hepatitis C, and over 1,200 individuals suffering from syphilis. That same year, 29 residents died from illness at an average age of 40, including five from pulmonary embolism, six from AIDS, and three from infections or asthma. Another eight committed suicide. Between 1995 and 1997, the county disbursed $3 million in damages to settle lawsuits for grievous medical malpractice: one inmate who lost an eye after being injured in the woodworking shop of his institution received $150,000; a diabetic resident who had to suffer an amputation due to negligent care got $60,000, and the mother of a deceased asthmatic accepted $395,000.

**Motel Six is a chain of low-grade roadside hotels, whose name refers to the modest price of rooms when it first opened: six dollars per night.

entrails, where dozens of buses run nonstop, day and night, to pour out their cargo of "fish." The LACJ runs the largest carceral bus fleet in the United States, indispensable for conveying its tens of thousands of clients. An interminable maze of blind corridors with bare walls links the different parts of the complex. There are neither openings nor markings of any kind (save for four solid lines in different colors, each showing the pathway to follow to get to a different service), so that if an inmate ever manages to slip into one of these arteries, he would have no way of tracking an exit. Besides, all the movements, whether of inmates or personnel, are electronically controlled at every turn by means of fingerprints and bar codes.

The approximate cost of construction of this specimen was $400 million, a bonanza divided up among 59 companies. So much that the establishment remained splendidly deserted for 18 months after it was completed: the county had no money left to pay for the staff needed to run it.

III. PRIVILEGED TARGETS

In Europe the criminal is a luckless fellow who struggles to save his head from the authorities, whilst the population observes their struggle, as it were. In America, he is an enemy of the human race, and the whole of humankind is against him.

—ALEXIS DE TOCQUEVILLE, *De la démocratie en Amérique*, 1835*

*Alexis de Tocqueville, *Democracy in America*, ed. Richard Heffner (New York: Signet Classics, 2001), 70. My translation.

6

The Prison as Surrogate Ghetto: Encaging Black Subproletarians

It is impossible to describe, much less explain, the sudden "downsizing" of the social assistance sector of the state in America and the concurrent "upsizing" of its penal wing after the mid-1970s, leading, on the one side, to the shift from welfare to workfare and, on the other, to the grotesque growth of the carceral system and its supervisory extensions, without taking into full account the agency of that denegated form of ethnicity called "race." And to reckon fully with race, one must imperatively bring together the Marxian and the Durkheimian theoretical strands to grasp *together* the material and symbolic operations of punishment in relation to ethnoracial division. We noted earlier that the collective perception, fostered by protagonists in the journalistic and political fields after the ghetto uprisings of the 1960s, that the clientele of public aid and the customers of prisons were both primarily disruptive and unworthy lower-class *blacks* was the cognitive oil that greased the material machinery set in motion to craft the neoliberal state in the United States. But to fully elucidate the manifold routes wherethrough the deep and sharp ethnoracial cleavage that sets African Americans apart from all other categories in the social and symbolic space of the United States entered into the making of the new government of social insecurity requires a broader historical and institutional analysis than can be given here.[1]

This chapter is a compromise between the need to cover too much ground and the fear to say too little given the topical immensity and analytic complexity of the issue. It offers an abbreviated sketch of the role of the prison as organizational means for the capture and management of a population considered contemptible and expendable in the post–Civil Rights and post-welfare era. It focuses on *(sub)proletarian* blacks from the imploding (hyper)ghetto as the first of two target categories pursued with special diligence and severity by the penal state in the wake of the social and racial upheaval of the 1960s. The rabid hunt after the second-favored foil, sex offenders, and especially the roaming and isolated lower-class "pedophile," will be analyzed in depth in the next chapter. This pinpoint selectivity of the penal state is key to the sheer velocity and ferocity of its expansion and attests to the role of punishment as a device for (re)generating, marking, and enforcing symbolic boundaries, whose study must necessarily be paired with that of the material office of penality (as stipulated by the analytic principles laid out in the book's prologue).

The turn to the past of the *longue durée* is indispensable to illumine the intersection of race and imprisonment at the close of the Fordist-Keynesian age, insofar as it reveals that not one but several "peculiar institutions" have operated to define, confine, and control African Americans over the centuries in the history of the United States. The first is *chattel slavery* as the pivot of the plantation economy and inceptive matrix of ethnoracial division from the colonial era to the Civil War.* The second is the *Jim Crow system* of legally enforced discrimination and segregation from cradle to grave that anchored the predominantly agrarian society of the South from the close of Reconstruction to the Civil Rights revolution, which toppled it a full century after abolition.[2] America's third special device for containing the descendants of slaves in the Northern industrial metropolis is the *ghetto,* corresponding to the conjoint urbanization and proletarianization of African Americans from the Great Migration of 1914–30 to the 1960s, when it was rendered partially obsolete by the concurrent transformation of economy and state and by the mounting protest of blacks against continued caste exclusion, climaxing in the explosive urban riots chronicled by the Kerner Commission Report.[3] The fourth, I contend here, is the novel institutional complex formed by the *remnants of the imploding dark ghetto and the exploding carceral apparatus,* which have become joined by a relationship of structural symbiosis and functional surrogacy.

Viewed against the backdrop of the full historical trajectory of racial domination in the United States, the glaring and rapidly growing "disproportionality" in incarceration that has afflicted African Americans over the past three decades[4] can be understood as the result of the "extrapenological" functions that the prison system has come to shoul-

*At its origin around the time of the American revolution, the expression "peculiar institution" referred apologetically to slavery in the Southern society. See Kenneth M. Stampp, *The Peculiar Institution: Slavery in the Ante-Bellum South* (New York: Vintage, 1989 [1956]). The notion culminated with the positive civilizational defense of human bondage by the Virginia social thinker George Fitzhugh (1806–81), for whom slavery was morally and socially superior to free labor and democracy, in that it benefited slaves, masters, and society alike: it offered economic security, care, and protection to the laboring class; it dissolved conflicts over work and property; and it anchored a stable aristocratic order patterned after the patriarchal plantation. George M. Fredrickson, *The Black Image in the White Mind: The Debate on Afro-American Character and Destiny, 1817–1914* (Middletown, Conn.: Wesleyan University Press, 1987 [1971]), 59–60.

der in the wake of the crisis of the ghetto after the mid-1970s. Not crime, but the need to shore up an eroding caste cleavage, and to buttress the emergent regime of desocialized wage labor to which lower-class blacks are fated by virtue of their lack of marketable cultural capital, and which the most deprived among them resist by escaping into the illegal street economy, is the main impetus behind the stupendous expansion of America's penal state in the post-Keynesian age and its de facto policy of "carceral affirmative action" toward lower-class African Americans.[5]

"Racial Disproportionality" in Incarceration

Three brute facts stand out and give a measure of the grotesquely disproportionate impact of hyperincarceration upon African Americans. First, the ethnic composition of the inmate population of the United States has been virtually *inverted* in the past half-century, going from about 70 percent (Anglo) white in 1950 to less than 30 percent today. Contrary to common perception, the predominance of blacks behind bars is not a long-standing pattern but a novel and recent phenomenon, with 1988 as the turning point: it is the year when then–vice president George Bush (the father) ran his infamous "Willie Horton" advertisement during the presidential campaign, featuring sinister images of the black rapist of a white woman as emblematic of the contemporary "crime problem," as well as the year after which African-American men supply a majority of prison admissions for the country as a whole.[6]

Next, whereas the difference between arrest rates for whites and blacks has been stable, with the percentage for blacks oscillating between 29 and 33 percent of all arrestees for property crimes and between 44 and 47 percent for violent offenses between 1976 and 1992,[7] the white-black incarceration gap has grown rapidly in the past quarter-century, jumping from one for four in 1980 to about *one for eight today*. This trend is all the more striking for occurring during a period when significant numbers of African Americans entered into, and rose through, the ranks of the police, the courts, and the corrections administration and when the more overt forms of racial discrimination that were commonplace in these bureaucracies well into the 1970s have been greatly reduced, if not stamped out.[8]

Lastly, the lifelong cumulative probability of "doing time" in a state or federal penitentiary based on the imprisonment rates of the early 1990s is 4 percent for whites, 16 percent for Latinos and a staggering 29 percent for blacks.[9] Given the steep class gradient of incarceration documented in chapter 2, this figure suggests that *a majority of African Americans of (sub-)proletarian status serve a prison term* of one or several years (and in many cases several terms) at some point in their adult life. The prevalence of imprisonment among the black lower class

> entails a range of family, occupational, and legal disruptions, including the curtailment of social entitlements and civil rights and the temporary or permanent loss of the right to vote. As of 1997, nearly one black man in six nationwide was excluded from the ballot box due to a felony conviction and more than one-fifth of them were prohibited from casting a vote in Alabama, Connecticut, Florida, Iowa, Mississippi, New Mexico, Texas, Washington, and Wyoming.[10] A short thirty-five years after the Civil Rights movement finally gained African Americans effective access to the voting booth, a hundred years after the outlawing of slavery, this right is being taken back by the penal system via legal dispositions that are of dubious constitutional validity and violate in many cases (notably lifetime disenfranchisement) international conventions on human rights ratified by the United States.

Beyond the specifics of that recent phenomenon on the carceral front in the United States, there is much to be learned from a historical-cum-analytic comparison between ghetto and prison. For both belong to the same genus of organizations, namely, *institutions of forced confinement*: the ghetto is a manner of "social prison" while the prison functions as a "judicial ghetto." Both are entrusted with enclosing a stigmatized population so as to neutralize the material and/or symbolic threat that it poses for the broader society from which it has been extruded. And, for that reason, ghetto and prison tend to evolve relational patterns and cultural forms that display striking similarities and intriguing parallels deserving of systematic study in diverse national and historical settings.

Vehicles for Labor Extraction and Social Ostracization

America's first three "peculiar institutions"—slavery, Jim Crow, and the ghetto—have in common that they were all instruments for the conjoint *extraction of labor* and *social ostracization* of an outcast group deemed inassimilable by virtue of the indelible threefold stigma it carries. African Americans arrived under bondage in the land of freedom. Reduced to the level of chattel, they were deprived of the right to vote in the self-appointed cradle of democracy after the founding of the Republic (until 1965 for residents of the Southern states). And, for lack of a recognizable national affiliation, they were shorn of ethnic honor after abolition, which implies that, rather than simply standing at the bottom of the rank-ordering of group prestige in American society, they were barred from it *ab initio*, as Gunnar Myrdal reminds us:

> Among the groups commonly considered inassimilable, the Negro people is by far the largest. The Negroes do not, like the Japanese and the Chinese, have a politically organized nation and an accepted culture of their own outside of America to fall back upon. Unlike the Oriental, there attaches to the Negro an historical memory of slavery and inferiority. It is more difficult for them to answer prejudice with prejudice and, as the Orientals may do, to consider themselves and their history superior to the white Americans and their recent cultural achievements. The Negroes do not have these fortifications of self-respect. They are more helplessly *imprisoned* as a subordinate caste, a caste of people deemed to be lacking a cultural past and assumed to be incapable of a cultural future.[11]

Slavery is a highly malleable and versatile institution that can be harnessed to a variety of purposes, but in the Americas property-in-person was geared primarily to the provision and control of labor.[12] Its introduction in the Chesapeake, Middle Atlantic, and Low Country regions of the United States in the seventeenth century served to recruit and regulate the unfree workforce forcibly imported from Africa and the West Indies to cater to their tobacco, rice, and mixed-farming economy. (Indentured laborers from Europe and native Indians were not enslaved because of their greater capacity to resist and because their servitude would have impeded future immigration as well as rapidly exhausted a limited pool of labor.) By the close of the eighteenth century, slavery had become self-reproducing and expanded to the fertile crescent of the Southern interior, running from South Carolina to Louisiana, where it supplied a highly profitable organization of labor for cotton production and the basis for a plantation society distinctive for its feudal-like culture, politics, and psychology stamped by paternalism.[13]

An *unforeseen by-product* of the systematic enslavement and dehumanization of Africans and their descendants on North American soil was the creation of a racial caste line separating what would later become labeled "blacks" and "whites." As Barbara Fields has shown, the American ideology of "race," as putative biological division anchored by the inflexible application of the "one-drop rule," together with the principle of hypodescent, crystallized to resolve the blatant contradiction between human bondage and democracy around the time of the American revolution.[14] The religious and pseudo-scientific belief in racial difference reconciled the brute fact of unfree labor with the doctrine of liberty premised on natural rights by reducing the slave to live property—three-fifths of a man according to the sacred scriptures of the Constitution.

Racial division was a consequence, not a precondition, of US slavery, but once it was instituted, it became detached from its initial function and acquired a social potency of its own. Emancipation thus created a double dilemma for Southern white society: securing anew the labor of former slaves, without whom the region's economy would collapse, and sustaining the cardinal status distinction between whites and "persons of color," that is, the social and symbolic distance needed to prevent the odium of "amalgamation" with a population considered inferior, rootless, and vile. It is not by happenstance if the word *miscegenation*, a sulfurous neologism referring to the ghastly prospect of sexual mixing between so-called blacks and whites, leading to the soiling of "white blood" and hence to "race degeneracy," was introduced in American political discourse in 1864—in a journalistic hoax designed to tarnish abolitionists in the Republican administration of Abraham Lincoln by falsely suggesting that the latter favored racial interbreeding and equality. A common theme of public debate in the aftermath of the Civil War was that granting the right to vote to lustful Negro men was tantamount to inviting them into the bedrooms of white women.[15] After a protracted interregnum lasting into the 1890s, during which early white hysteria gave way to partial if inconsistent relaxation of ethnoracial strictures, when blacks were allowed to vote, hold public office, and even mix with whites to a degree in keeping with the intergroup intimacy fostered by slavery, the solution came in the form of the "Jim Crow" regime. It consisted of an ensemble of social and legal codes that prescribed the complete separation of the "races" and sharply circumscribed the life chances of African Americans while binding them to whites in a relation of suffusive submission and obligatory deference backed by legal coercion and terroristic violence.[16]

Imported from the North, where it had been experimented with in cities, this regime stipulated that blacks travel in separate trains, streetcars, and waiting rooms; that they reside in the "darktown" slums and be educated in separate schools (if at all); that they patronize separate service establishments and use their own bathrooms and water fountains; that they pray in separate churches, entertain themselves in separate clubs, and sit in separate "nigger galleries" in theaters; that they receive medical care in separate hospitals and exclusively from "colored" staff; and that they be incarcerated in separate cells and buried in separate cemeteries. Most crucial of all, laws joined mores in condemning the "unspeakable crime" of interracial marriage, cohabitation, or mere sexual congress so as to uphold the "supreme law of self-preservation" of the races and the myth of innate white superiority. Through continued white ownership of the land and the generalization of sharecropping and debt peonage, the plantation system remained virtually untouched as former slaves became a "dependent, propertyless peasantry, nominally free, but ensnared by poverty, ignorance, and the new servitude of tenantry."[17] While sharecropping tied African-American labor to the farm, a rigid etiquette ensured that whites and blacks never interacted on a plane of equality, not even on the track field or in a boxing ring—a Birmingham ordinance of 1930 made it unlawful for them to play checkers and dominoes with one another.* Whenever the "color line" was breached or even brushed, a torrent of violence was unleashed in the form of periodic pogroms, Ku Klux Klan and vigilante raids, public floggings, mob killings and lynchings, this ritual caste murder designed to keep "uppity niggers" in their appointed place. All this was made possible by the swift and near-complete disenfranchisement of blacks as well as by the enforcement of "Negro law" by courts which granted the latter fewer effective legal safeguards than slaves had enjoyed earlier by dint of being property as well as persons.

The sheer brutality of caste oppression in the South, the decline of cotton agriculture due to repeated floods and the boll weevil, and the pressing shortage of labor in Northern factories caused by the outbreak of the First World War created the impetus for African Americans to emigrate en masse to the booming industrial centers of the Midwest and Northeast (over 1.5 million left Dixie between 1910 and 1930, followed by another 3 million between 1940 and 1960). But as migrants from Mississippi to the Carolinas flocked to the Northern metropolis, what they discovered there was not the "promised land" of equality and full citizenship, as they had fervently hoped, but another system of ethnoracial enclosure, the ghetto, which, though it was less rigid and fearsome than the one they had escaped, was no less encompassing and constricting.

To be sure, greater freedom to come and go in public places and to consume in regular commercial establishments, the disappearance of the humiliating signs pointing to reserved facilities for "Colored" here and "White" there, renewed access to the ballot box and expanded protection from the courts, the possibility of limited economic advancement, release from personal subservience and from the dread of omni-

*The Mississippi legislature went so far as to outlaw the advocacy of social equality between blacks and whites in a law of 1920 that punished by a fine of $500 and six months of imprisonment anyone "found guilty of printing, publishing or circulating printed, typewritten or written matter urging or presenting for public acceptation or general information, arguments or suggestions in favor of social equality or of intermarriage." Neil R. McMillen, *Dark Journey: Black Mississippians in the Age of Jim Crow* (Urbana: University of Illinois Press, 1990), 8–9.

present white violence, all made life in the urban North incomparably preferable to continued peonage in the rural South: it was "better to be a lamppost in Chicago than President of Dixie," as migrants famously put it to Richard Wright.[18] But restrictive covenants forced African Americans to congregate in a "Black Belt" which quickly became overcrowded, underserved, and blighted by crime, disease, and dilapidation, while the "job ceiling" restricted them to the most hazardous, menial, and underpaid occupations in both industry and personal services. As for "social equality," understood as the possibility of "becoming members of white cliques, churches, and voluntary associations, or marrying into their families" and other intimate contact, it was firmly and definitively denied.[19]

Blacks had entered the Fordist industrial economy, to which they contributed a vital source of abundant and cheap labor willing to ride along its cycles of boom and bust. Yet they remained locked in a precarious position of structural economic marginality and consigned to a secluded and dependent microcosm, complete with its own internal division of labor, social stratification, and agencies of collective voice and symbolic representation: a "city within the city," moored in a complexus of black churches and press, businesses and professional practices, fraternal lodges and communal associations that provided both a "milieu for Negro Americans in which they [could] imbue their lives with meaning" and a bulwark "to 'protect' white America from 'social contact' with Negroes."[20] Continued caste hostility from without and renewed ethnic affinity from within converged to create the ghetto as the third vehicle to extract black labor while keeping black bodies at a safe distance, to the material and symbolic benefit of white society.

The era of the ghetto as the paramount mechanism of ethnoracial domination had opened with the urban riots of 1917–19 (in East St. Louis, Chicago, Longview, Houston, etc.), for overt white violence was indispensible to force blacks to accept it. It closed with a wave of clashes, looting, and burning that rocked hundreds of American cities from coast to coast, from the Watts uprising of 1965 to the riots of rage and grief triggered by the assassination of Martin Luther King in the summer of 1968.[21] Indeed, by the end of the sixties, the ghetto was well on its way to becoming functionally obsolete or, to be more precise, increasingly *unsuited* to accomplishing the twofold task historically entrusted to America's "peculiar institutions." On the side of *labor extraction*, the shift from an urban industrial economy to a suburban service economy and the accompanying dualization of the occupational structure, along with the upsurge of working-class immigration from Mexico, the Caribbean, and Asia, meant that large segments of the workforce contained within the "Black Belts" of the Northern metropolis were simply no longer needed. On the side of *ethnoracial closure,* the decades-long mobilization of African Americans against caste rule finally succeeded, in the propitious political conjuncture stemming from the Cold War, the Vietnam War, and assorted social unrest, in forcing the federal state to dismantle the legal machinery of caste exclusion. Having secured voting and civil rights, blacks were at long last full citizens who would no longer brook being shunted off into the separate and inferior world of the ghetto.

Such was the meaning of Martin Luther King's "Freedom Campaign" launched in Chicago in the summer of 1966: it sought to apply to the ghetto the techniques of collective mobilization and civil disobedience used with stunning success in the frontal attack on Jim Crow in the South to reveal and protest "the slow, stifling death of a kind of concentration camp life" to which blacks were condemned in the Northern metropolis.[22] However, the campaign to "make Chicago an open city" was swiftly crushed by a formidable combination of state repression (spearheaded by 4,000 National Guard troops), white mob violence, vitriolic media campaigns of denunciation by the *Chicago Tribune* and *Chicago Sun Times,* and furious resistance from City Hall, the real estate industry, and the courts, all with the knowing acquiescence of Congress and the White House.

The same liberal whites who had praised and supported King when he led marches and organized sit-ins against segregated facilities in the South "condemned his tactics as irresponsible and provocative" when he moved to confront the ghetto.[23] The shift of the civil rights campaign from the rural South to the urban North, the sudden rise of separatist Black Power groups spearheading militant demands for black self-determination, and the rising violence associated with public protests caused white backing for African-American demands to evaporate in a matter of months. And it triggered a virulent backlash that would grow over the next two decades to fuel the retrenchment of welfare, the abandonment of cities, and the aggressive expansion of the penal apparatus of the local and federal state.

While whites begrudgingly accepted "integration" in principle, in practice they strove to maintain an unbridgeable social and symbolic gulf with their compatriots of African descent. They abandoned public schools, shunned mixed public space, and fled to the suburbs by the millions to avoid mingling and ward off the specter of "social equality" in the city, thanks to federal government support for suburban development upholding the color line. As was noted in chapter 3, whites then turned against the welfare state and against those social programs targeted at the inner city upon which the collective advancement of blacks was most dependent. *A contrario*, they extended enthusiastic support for the "law-and-order" policies that vowed to firmly repress urban disorders connately perceived as racial threats.[24] Such policies pointed to yet another special institution capable of confining and controlling, not the entire African-American community, but its most disruptive, disreputable, and dangerous members: the prison.

An Ethnoracial Prison, a Judicial Ghetto

To grasp the deep kinship between ghetto and prison, which helps explain how the structural decline and functional redundancy of the one led to the unexpected ascent and astonishing growth of the other during the last quarter of the twentieth century, it is necessary first to accurately characterize the ghetto.* But here we come upon the troublesome fact that the social sciences have failed to develop a robust *analytic concept* of the ghetto; instead they have been content to borrow the *folk concept* current in political and popular discourse at each epoch. This has caused a good deal of confusion, as the ghetto has been successively conflated with—and mistaken for—a segregated district, an ethnic neighborhood, a territory of intense poverty, a zone of housing blight and even, with the rise of the policy myth of the "underclass" in the more recent period, a mere accumulation of urban pathologies and antisocial behaviors.[25]

A comparative and historical sociology of the reserved Jewish quarters in the cities of Renaissance Europe and of America's "Bronzeville" in the Fordist metropolis of the twentieth century reveals that a ghetto is essentially a sociospatial device that enables a dominant status group in an urban setting to simultaneously *ostracize and exploit* a subordinate group endowed with *negative symbolic capital*, that is, an incarnate property perceived to make contact with members of the cate-

*Remember that, as we noted in chapter 4, as of the mid-1970s, the carceral population of the United States had been steadily declining for nearly two decades to reach a low of about 360,000 inmates in 1973. The leading analysts of the penal question, from David Rothman to Michel Foucault to Alfred Blumstein, were then unanimous in predicting the imminent marginalization of the prison as an institution of social control or, in the worst-case scenario, the long-term stability of penal confinement at a historically moderate level. No one foresaw the impending quadrupling of the country's carceral population over the ensuing twenty years, which would lead it to cross the two million mark in 2000, even as the crime rate stagnated and then receded rapidly during that period.

gory degrading by virtue of what Max Weber calls a "negative social estimation of honor." Put differently, the ghetto is the materialization of a *relation* of ethnoracial control and closure built out of four elements: (i) stigma, (ii) constraint, (iii) territorial confinement, and (iv) institutional encasement. The resulting formation is a distinctive *space*, containing an ethnically homogeneous *population*, which finds itself forced to develop within it a set of interlinked *institutions* that duplicates the organizational framework of the broader society from which that group is banished and supplies the scaffoldings for the construction of its specific "style of life" and social strategies. This parallel institutional nexus affords the subordinate group a measure of protection, autonomy, and dignity, but at the cost of locking it in a relationship of structural subordination and dependency.

The ghetto, in short, operates as an *ethnoracial prison*: it encages a dishonored category and severely curtails the life chances of its members in support of the "monopolization of ideal and material goods or opportunities" by the dominant status group dwelling on its outskirts.[26] Recall that the ghettos of early modern Europe were typically delimited by high walls with one or more gates which were locked at night and within which Jews had to return before sunset after having dispatched their economic functions, on pain of severe punishment,[27] and that their perimeter was subjected to continuous monitoring by external authorities. Note next the structural and functional homologies with the prison conceptualized as a *judicial ghetto*: a jail or penitentiary is in effect a reserved *space* which serves to forcibly confine a legally denigrated *population* and wherein this latter evolves its distinctive *institutions*, culture, and sullied identity. It is thus formed of the same four fundamental constituents—stigma, coercion, physical enclosure, and organizational parallelism and insulation—that make up a ghetto, and for similar purposes.

Much as the ghetto protects the city's residents from the pollution of intercourse with the tainted but necessary bodies of an outcast group in the manner of an "urban condom," as Richard Sennett vividly put it in his depiction of the "fear of touching" in sixteenth-century Venice,[28] the prison cleanses the social body from the temporary blemish of those of its members who have committed crimes, that is, following Émile Durkheim, individuals who have violated the sociomoral integrity of the collectivity by infringing on "definite and strong states of the collective conscience."[29] Students of the "inmate society" from Donald Clemmer and Gresham Sykes to James Jacobs and John Irwin have noted time and again how the incarcerated develop their own argot roles, exchange systems, and normative standards, whether as an adaptive response to the "pains of imprisonment" or through selective importation of criminal and lower-class values from the outside, much like residents of the ghetto have elaborated or intensified a "separate sub-culture" to counter their sociosymbolic immurement.[30]

As for the secondary aim of the ghetto, to facilitate exploitation of the interned category, it was central to the "house of correction," which is the direct historical predecessor of the modern prison, and it has periodically played a major role in the evolution and operation of the latter. Describing the London Bridewell, the *Zuchthaus* of Amsterdam, and Paris's *Hôpital général*, Georg Rusche and Otto Kirschheimer write: "The essence of the house of correction was that it combined the principles of the poorhouse, workhouse and penal institution." Its main aim was "to make the labor power of the unwilling people socially useful" by forcing them to work under close supervision in the hope that, once released, "they would voluntarily swell the labor market."[31] Finally, both prison and ghetto are authority structures saddled with inherently dubious or problematic legitimacy whose maintenance is ensured by intermittent recourse to external force.[32]

By the end of the 1970s, then, as the racial and class backlash against the democratic advances won by the social movements of the preceding decade got into full swing, the prison abruptly returned to the forefront of American society and was offered as the universal and simplex solution to all manners of urgent social problems by politicians eager to reestablish state authority while rolling back state support for the poor. Chief among these problems was the "breakdown" of social order in the "inner city," which is a scholarly and policy euphemism for the patent incapacity of the dark ghetto to contain a dishonored and supernumerary population henceforth viewed not only as deviant and devious but as downright dangerous in light of the violent urban upheavals of the mid-sixties. As the walls of the ghetto shook and threatened to crumble, the walls of the prison were correspondingly extended, enlarged, and fortified, and "confinement of differentiation," aimed at keeping a specific category apart (the etymological meaning of *segregare*), gained primacy over "confinement of safety" and "confinement of authority"—to use the distinction proposed by French sociologist Claude Faugeron between three forms of penal custody.[33] Soon the black ghetto, converted into an instrument of naked exclusion by the concurrent retrenchment of wage labor and social protection, and further destabilized by the increasing penetration of the penal arm of the state, became bound to the jail and prison system by a triple relationship of functional equivalency, structural homology, and cultural syncretism, such that they now constitute a single *carceral continuum* which entraps a redundant population of younger black men (and increasingly women), who circulate in closed circuit between its two poles in a self-perpetuating cycle of social and legal marginality with devastating personal and social consequences.[34]

As the state pulls out the social safety net of welfare and urban subsidies to roll out the penal dragnet in and around the collapsing inner city, through the targeted policing and aggressive prosecution of street crime (especially low-level narcotics offenses), the institutional kinship between ghetto and prison moves from system to life-world—and from the plane of sociological possibility to that of everyday reality. It becomes actualized in the personal experience and collective trajectory of the unskilled African-American males trapped at the bottom of the class and caste order, for whom incarceration, like chronic joblessness and poverty, becomes a banal event and a modal pathway through adulthood. Estimates of the lifetime risks of being sentenced to prison for black and white men at different educational levels reveal that an astonishing 60 percent of African Americans born between 1965 and 1969 who did not complete high school had been convicted of a felony and had served time in a state penitentiary by 1999.[35] This nationwide rate suggests that the vast majority of black men from the core of the ghetto pass through the prison at the beginning of the twenty-first century.

Now, the carceral system had already functioned as an *ancillary* institution for caste preservation and labor control in the United States during one previous transition between regimes of racial domination, that between slavery and Jim Crow in the South. On the morrow of Emancipation, Southern prisons turned black overnight as "thousands of ex-slaves were being arrested, tried, and convicted for acts that in the past had been dealt with by the master alone"[36] as well as for refusing to behave as menials and follow the demeaning rules of racial etiquette in the presence of whites. Soon thereafter, the former Confederate states innovated "convict leasing" as a response to the moral panic of "Negro crime" that offered the double advantage of generating prodigious funds for the state coffers and furnishing abundant bound labor to till the fields, build the levees, lay down the railroads, clean the swamps, and dig the mines of the region under murderous conditions.*

*This is not a figure of speech: the annual mortality rate for convicts reached 16 percent in Mississippi in the 1880s, where "not a single leased convict ever lived long enough to serve a sentence of ten years or more." David M. Oshinsky, *Worse Than Slavery: Parchman Farm and the Ordeal of Jim Crow Justice* (New York: Free Press, 1996), 46. Hundreds of black children, many as young as six years old, were leased by

Indeed, penal labor, in the form of the convict-lease and its heir, the chain gang, played a major role in the economic advancement of the New South during the Progressive era, as it "reconciled modernization with the continuation of racial domination"[37] for several decades after the ending of bondage in that region of the United States.

What makes the racial intercession of the carceral system different today is that, unlike slavery, Jim Crow, and the ghetto of mid-century, it does not carry out a positive economic mission of recruitment and disciplining of an active workforce. The prison serves mainly to warehouse the precarious and deproletarianized fractions of the black working class in the dualizing city, be it that they cannot find employment owing to a combination of skills deficit, employer discrimination, and competition from immigrants, or that they refuse to submit to the indignity of substandard work in the peripheral sectors of the service economy—what ghetto residents, by a bitter historical twist, commonly label "slave jobs." But there is now mounting financial and ideological pressure, as well as renewed political interest, to relax restrictions on penal labor so as to (re)introduce mass unskilled work in private enterprises inside of American prisons: putting most inmates to work would help lower the country's escalating "carceral bill" as well as effectively extend to the inmate poor the workfare requirements now imposed upon the free poor as a requirement of citizenship.[38] The next decade will tell whether the prison remains an appendage to the crumbling dark ghetto or supersedes it to go it alone and become America's fourth "peculiar institution."

---

the state to the benefit of planters, businessmen, and bankers, to toil in conditions so brutal that even some patrician Southerners found it shameful and "a stain upon our manhood."

7

Moralism and Punitive Panopticism: Hunting Down Sex Offenders

> We have heard speakers at this conference use the term "zero tolerance" for sex offenders. I think we have accomplished that in Illinois. We have some great stories. We registered an eighty-six-year-old man in a nursing home, a quadriplegic, and an individual in the Federal Witness Protection program. We even registered a man currently in a coma, so I think our program has been pretty aggressive.—KIRK LONBOM, Assistant Director of Intelligence, Illinois State Police*

Sex offenders are, along with young black men from the neighborhoods of relegation in the big cities, the privileged target of the penal panopticism that has flourished on the ruins of America's charitable state over the past three decades. In the first two parts of this book, we traced how, in the wake of the political turmoil and ethnoracial backlash of the 1970s, the United States gradually converted the right to "welfare" into the obligation of "workfare" and supplemented the latter with a hyperactive police, judicial, and carceral state for which the criminalization of racialized poverty and the confinement of dispossessed and deviant categories have come to serve as a queer form of social policy toward the marginalized.

In this third part, we confirm that neither policy shift—the shrinking of the social safety net, the extension of the penal dragnet, and their meshing under the selfsame supervisory philosophy of moral behaviorism—has been rolled out indiscriminately. Rather, paternalistic assistance schemes and punitive criminal programs turn out to consistently converge onto *dangerous categories* in the double register of control and communication: "welfare mothers," believed to pose a moral threat to the ethic of work and sexual propriety in the domestic sphere (although most public aid recipients work off the books and are on the rolls for short stints), and "gang bangers" and assorted street criminals from the hyperghetto, perceived to represent a diffuse physical menace in public

*Kirk Lonbom quoted in *National Conference on Sex Offender Registries*, ed. Jan M. Chaiken, 72 (Washington, D.C.: Bureau of Justice Statistics, 1998).

space (even as they primarily jeopardize one another and their neighbors inside the isolated perimeter of the collapsing inner city).[1] A third figure has joined and embodied the sulfurous combination of physical and moral perils in the collective mind of America at century's close: the sex offender, and especially the roving, unattached pedophile.[2]

To be sure, those suspected or convicted of sexual offenses have long been the object of intense fears and severe sanctions, owing to the particularly virulent stigma that befalls them in a puritanical culture strangled in taboos that, until recently, made crimes of contraception, adultery, sex play (such as oral and anal intercourse) even between spouses, and of autoerotic practices as banal as masturbation and the perusal of pornographic materials, not to mention interracial marriage.* Thus the frenzied fright over sexual crimes that gripped the United States at the onset of the 1990s is not novel. It has at least two major historical precedents in the century, during the Progressive era, when sexual "perverts" were first identified and singled out for eugenic intervention, and in the period 1936–57, when hordes of "sex psychopaths" were believed to be roaming the country in search of innocent victims, ready to strike at every turn.[3]

"America's Shame"

The interwar panic solidified the notion, which had emerged in the early twentieth century, that sex-related lawbreakers are a distinctively menacing category of malefactors, and it triggered the wide diffusion of "sexual psychopath laws" across the country. Between 1937 and 1950, twelve states and the District of Columbia established a specific juridical status of "sex offender," authorizing their detention in mental hospitals for *preventive* purposes.[4] Between 1950 and 1972, another thirteen states added such statutes to their penal code. Even though these laws were eventually found to be in violation of the federal constitution

*As criminologist MacNamara noted in 1968, sex-related conduct in America is "rigidly circumscribed by law" and such strict legislation creates "a body of sexual offenders (perhaps exaggerated as to numbers and certainly exaggerated as to degree of social danger) who are differentially subjected to hysterical, almost sadistically punitive sanctions by public, police, courts, and corrections authorities." Donal E. J. MacNamara, "Sex Offenses and Sex Offenders," *Annals of the American Academy of Political and Social Science* 376 (March 1968): 148–55, citation at 148. Two illustrations: the last state law prohibiting black-white marriage was struck down in 1968; in the reputedly tolerant state of California, sodomy was a crime punishable by life imprisonment until 1975.

and were repealed, other legislation mandating reporting duties have enabled the authorities to keep former sex offenders on an especially tight judicial leash. In California, for instance, those convicted of sexual crimes have been required since 1947 to register with the police at their place of residence within five days of being released from jail or prison and to check in every year within five days of their birthday. And, since 1995, all sex offenders residing in the Golden State who do not fulfill this obligation are liable to 16 to 36 months of prison (and to an automatic life sentence if this qualifies as their third conviction under the state's severe "Three Strikes and You're Out" statute). They are also forbidden to hold an occupation or join an organization that would bring them into contact with minors, among many other restrictions. However, much like other ex-convicts, former sex offenders could until recently take advantage of their anonymity to start their lives over once their custodial sentence had been served. This is no longer the case since Congress passed "Megan's Law" in 1996, which requires the authorities to blacklist sex offenders and to deliver them over to the permanent scrutiny and open execration of the public. In addition, a dozen states have adopted statutes allowing for the "civil commitment" of certain categories of sex convicts after they have served their full sentence, in effect putting them into indefinite confinement for crimes they *might* commit.

Before we turn to an examination of the purpose, workings, and meaning of these penal innovations, we must note that the latest panic around sex criminals presents a number of striking similarities with its predecessors. First, like them, it has fastened on highly infrequent and particularly heinous acts while studiously overlooking ordinary forms of sexual assault, particularly those committed inside the family that make up the brunt of offenses. The notion of "sex offender" is an elastic and capacious term covering a wide gamut of behaviors from the consensual to the injurious, from the morally problematic to the physically violent, including exhibitionism and voyeurism, lewd acts with a minor and bestiality, possession of pornography and statutory rape, solicitation of or loitering for prostitution, incest, and sexual battery. In the recent public view, however, it has become virtually "indistinguishable from other highly damaging concepts such as molester, pedophile, and predator, that indicate the collectively persistent nature of the crime, a lack of response to any treatment or deterrence, and, above all, extreme dangerousness."[5]

Second, the current rash of public concern and legislation over sexual criminality is utterly disconnected from the statistical evolution of offenses: as before, clamors about an "epidemic" erupt just as the incidence of violations recedes. Thus the tally of rapes in the country recorded by the National Crime Victimization Survey reveals a stagnation at around 2.5 victims per 1,000 persons age twelve or older from 1973 till 1988, followed by a steady decline until 1995 (save for a single spike in 1991) to about 1 per thousand, just when the furor over sex-related crimes peaked. The trend in the volume of sexual offenses reported to the police shows a similar drop of 9 percent between 1991 and 1995, corresponding to a 12 percent reduction in terms of rate per capita. This is reflected by the steady decline in the incidence of arrests for sex crimes after 1990: by 1995, when Megan-type laws were spreading through the country like wildfire, the arrest rate for sexual offenses other than forcible rape was 30 percent below the figure for 1983. Meanwhile, the share of sexually motivated murders among all homicides had plummeted from 1.5 percent in 1976 to 0.7 percent in 1994.[6] If those data must be interpreted with caution, due to serious underreporting and other definitional and technical issues, they nonetheless consistently refute the notion that the country experienced a surge in sexual assaults over the past two decades.

Third, the public belief that sex offenders are treated leniently by the courts is also belied by judicial data showing that, while the incidence of sexual offenses sagged, the number of prisoners sentenced for sexual assault other than rape rose by an average of 15 percent per year between 1980 and 1995, twice the growth rate of the overall carceral population; and that time served increased significantly for all categories of sex convicts.[7] Fourth and relatedly, like the "sexual psychopath" craze of the 1940s, the "sex predator" campaign of the 1990s is very largely the result of the activism of the media and politicians. Sensational coverage by newspapers, television stations, and especially 24-hour news channels, and the growth of a veritable cultural industry specializing in the lurid portrayal of crime (with dedicated shows and cable channels, such as Court TV) have combined with the increased electoral exploitation of criminal violence to inflate the issue on the public stage out of all proportion.[8]

"Enough, Enough, Enough": Oprah Winfrey Rises Up against "the Definition of Evil"

In the Fall of 2003, surfing the surging wave of horror stories of crimes against children in the national media, the empress of talk shows Oprah Winfrey launched a personal campaign against sex offenders on television,[9] complete with the broadcast of a regularly updated list of "child predators" on the loose, programs on such topics as "Secret Lies: When the One You Love Is a Pedophile" and "Kidnapped by a Pedophile: The Shasta Groene Tragedy," and a lavish ransom from her personal purse to stimulate the capture of wanted sex convicts or suspects ("I plan to work with law enforcement officials, and if they tell me that one of you turned in one of these fugitives that we are exposing today, and that information leads to the capture and arrest of one of these men, I will personally give a $100,000 cash reward"). In the video segment advertising "Oprah's Child Predator List," the television superstar faces the viewer, dressed in a black top, set against a dark window, in a gloomy light. As the camera closes in on her stern visage, she intones somberly:

> Today I stand before you to say, in no uncertain terms—as a matter of fact in terms that I hope are *very certain*—that I have had enough. With every breath in my body, whatever it takes, and most importantly with *your support*, we are going to move heaven and earth to stop a *sickness, a darkness*, that I believe is the *de-fi-ni-tion of evil* that's been going on for far too long. The children of this nation, the United States of America, are being [slowly hammering each word] *stolen, raped, tortured*, and killed by *sexual predators*, who are walking right into your homes. How many times does it have to happen? And how many children have to be sacrificed? What price are we as a society willing to continue to pay before we rise up and take to the streets and say, [in a forceful hush] *e-nough*! *Enough! Enough!*

To help put an end to "America's shame," namely, the alleged penal laxness that allows an estimated 100,000 sex offenders to be on the lam on any given day, "Oprah's Child Predator Watch List" offers instructions on "Protecting Your Children," "Profiles of the Accused," and portraits of "Captured Fugitives." The web page cheerily reports: "We posted their pictures and viewers just like you turned them in. The tip, the big break, the capture . . . Get all the details! How you can claim the *next* $100,000 reward! Child molesters, we are coming after you!" And the rubric "Researching Sex Offenders in Your Community" walks the virtual visitor through an internet search, with step-by-step directives on how "to conduct your search online" to ferret and stamp out what is presented as new moral vermin threatening the very framework of American society.

Does this all mean that the latest hysteria is but a familiar repeat of cycles of public dread and demonization of sexual offenders, as historian Philip Jenkins suggests when he writes that "today's sex crime panic is as fierce as in the late 1940s, and it has given the predator a role in the national demonology that is quite as pronounced as that of his psychopathic predecessor"?[10] In this chapter, I will argue, to the contrary, that the current wave of public vituperation and penal castigation of sex lawbreakers is highly distinctive for its scope, intensity, and effects. Not only has it been greatly amplified by the new technologies available for the dissemination of information and surveillance of suspects and convicts for sexual mischief (in keeping with the explosive development of the means of the penal state surveyed in chapter 5). It has also focused on extending the judicial control of ex-offenders after their release from prison and beyond the expiration of their criminal sentence. And the technical voices of experts, such as psychiatrists and penologists, which played a lead role in previous campaigns, have been all but drowned out by the emotional drumbeat of journalists, elected officials, and especially crime victims and their families, who have emerged as major protagonists in the penal field since the late 1980s.[11]

Propelled by a vitriolic rhetoric that portrays the fight against crime as a moral battle to the death between good and evil—instead of an organizational matter of rights, responsibilities, and the rational allocation of penal and other means to prevent, mitigate, or suppress injurious deviance—the "sexual predator," typically portrayed in the colors of a "lowlife" social drifter, has acquired a central place in the country's expansive *public culture of vilification of criminals.* As the living embodiment of moral abjectness, he provides an urgent and perpetually refreshed motive for the full repudiation of the ideal of rehabilitation and the turn to fierce neutralization and vengeful retribution that has characterized US penal policy since the late 1970s. The virulence of the animus that now drives public action toward sex offenders then loops back and accelerates the expansion of the penal response to social problems at the bottom of the class and caste structure that has fed it in the first place.

The purpose of this chapter is not to provide a rounded explanation of the rise and role of vindictive sex-offender policies in the United States in the 1990s in their full complexity, their legal intricacies (which are tremendous), and their psychosexual bases (which are multilayered). Rather, it is to spotlight selected facets of this sector of changing state action that obey and thus help elucidate penalization as a generalized means for managing problem populations and sensitive symbolic boundaries. This is why, as with the analysis of the punitive tenor of "welfare reform" of 1996 sketched in the first part of this book, we limit our focus to the years of final incubation and initial implementation of Megan's Law as a moment of discursive crystallization and practical revelation of the deep logic of this innovation in penal control.

A methodological warning is in order here, as we are dealing with a highly sensitive topic liable to evoke strong emotions from readers, even reactions of dismay and disgust from some of them. Sexual crimes are without contest the most morally charged transgressions of the law in advanced societies, in which the sanctification of the person and her physical integrity have reached their civilizational peak.[12] When such violations strike the most vulnerable and "innocent" members of the collectivity, young children in particular, they are universally deemed odious beyond repair. Writing about religious fundamentalists amid a secular nation, anthropologist Susan Harding has noted the special difficulty posed by the "problem of the repugnant cultural other" when that other is seen as constitutively "aberrant" and looked down upon as the living negation of the modern rational subject.[13] She points out that, through circuitous routes, the discursive practices of scholars too often join with popular stereotypes and media images to (re)create an unbridgeable cultural chasm between the anàlyst (and her readers) and the abhorred object. We must beware of not locking ourselves with such a "chain of differentiating rhetorical moves" that safely seal the former from the latter and deepens as well as muddies the very abyss we are to probe.

Indeed, we shall see that the current portrayal of sex offenders as amoral and asocial beings, beastlike and subhuman, is a key constituent of the phenomenon to be dissected, in that it provides the symbolic oil that lubricates the wheels of the runaway train of penalization. It is therefore doubly imperative that we adopt a rigorously analytical attitude and avoid echoing the shrill rhetoric of the entrepreneurs in morality who have latched onto sexual lawbreakers as the heinous incarnation of criminal depravity. We must insist that the latter be treated like any other problem category handled by the penal arm of the state. This entails taking pains to recognize gradations in types of offenses and to describe sexual convicts who have served their sentence as *ex*–sex offenders (as one does with thieves, burglars, and murderers). For those who might feel uneasy about this *methodological stance*, it bears reaffirming here that the purpose of sociological analysis is never to indict or exculpate, but to explain and understand (which does not imply condoning or standing by morally unperturbed).[14] It is important also to remember that, as was emphasized in the book's prologue, the present analysis is not a study of crime and punishment but an investigation of the remaking of the state in its punitive capacities and activities. For this reason, we are not concerned in this chapter with digging deep into the "crime" side of the equation. The etiology, variety, and demography of sex offenders enter into our purview only insofar as they are relevant to the collective reactions they trigger in society and to the treatment they receive from official authorities.

Supervise and Stigmatize

With the resurgence of moralism in the political field and the rabid media projection of sexual crimes over the past decade, correlative of the relentless increase of journalistic coverage accorded to criminal violence, public attention has become focused like never before on sexual offenses against children.[15] As a result, not only has a consensus solidified in favor of giving such violations of the law the most severe penal response possible, with a dozen states implementing "two strikes" statutes that automatically send recidivist violent offenders to prison for life and a half-dozen allowing or requiring that repeat sex offenders be subjected to "chemical castration" through regular injections of Depo-Provera, a drug inhibiting the sex drive.[16] The punitive monitoring of this category of convict—and, through the halo effect of inclusive labeling, of nearly all former prisoners "sent down" on sexual charges, no matter how serious—has intensified and narrowed to the point where they are no longer considered disturbed persons susceptible to therapeutic action, but deemed incurable deviants posing an intolerable criminal threat *ad aeternitum*, regardless of their judicial status, social background, trajectory toward rehabilitation, and post-confinement behavior. This is why Megan's Laws, christened after Megan Kanka, a little girl from New Jersey who was raped and murdered by a paroled sexual offender who dwelled across the street from her parents without their knowledge, and whose 1994 murder unleashed an unstoppable national wave of legislation, requires city and county police in all fifty states not only to "register" (former) sex offenders but also to "notify the public" of their presence and (mis)deeds.[17]

The scope and means of these laws varies from one jurisdiction and location to the next.* In some states, notification is "passive": it must be initiated by the residents and often at their expense. In others, it is "active": it is the authorities who take the initiative and bear the cost of diffusing information among the local population. In some jurisdictions, it applies only to certain categories of sex offenders judged to be dangerous or especially prone to recidivism, those the law labels "sexual

*The measures collected under the generic label of "Megan's Law" for the sake of convenience pertain to a mesh of state laws patterned after Washington State's 1990 Community Protection Act as well as three batches of federal measures: the Jacob Wetterling Crimes Against Children and Sexually Violent Offender Registration Act of 1994 (named after a little boy from Minnesota kidnapped in October 1989 and missing since), which assigns to states the obligation to register convicts for pedophilia and acts of sexual violence; the federal version of "Megan's Law," passed in 1996, which requires them to notify the public of the presence of certain categories of sex offenders; and the Pam Lychner Sexual Offender Tracking and Identification Act (also voted in 1996 in reaction to the sexual assault suffered by a Houston real estate agent, Pam Lychner, while she was taking a client, who was a twice convicted ex-felon, on an apartment visit), which establishes a national computer databank on sex offenders under the aegis of the Federal Bureau of Investigation.

predators"; in others, it concerns all those convicted of sexual offenses, however minor.[18] Thus in Alabama a list of all those found guilty of rape, sodomy, sexual abuse, or incest is posted in city hall and in the police station nearest to the offenders' homes. In larger urban centers such as Birmingham, Mobile, and Huntsville, all residents within a 600-foot radius of a sex offender are personally alerted of his presence*—the perimeter of notification extends to 1,200 feet in towns and villages. In Louisiana, it is the (former) sex offender himself who is responsible for revealing his status in writing to his landlord, neighbors, and officials running the neighboring schools and public parks, on pain of one year imprisonment and a $1,000 fine. He must also, within 30 days, publish at his own cost in a local newspaper a note informing the "community" of his location. Beyond which the law authorizes "all forms of public notification," including the press, signs, flyers, and bumper stickers placed on the fenders of the sex offender's vehicle. The courts can even require ex-convicts for a sexual offense to don a distinctive garb indicating their judicial status—much like the star or the yellow linen caps worn by Jews in the princely cities of late medieval Europe.[19] The victim(s) of the sexual crime for which the convict was put under lock must also be informed in writing of the offender's release and place of residence, as must the witnesses called at his trial and anyone else the district prosecutor deems should be notified.[20] In North Carolina, the complete data files of all convicts for sexual assault and sex offenses against minors are sent to any organization dealing with children, the handicapped, or the elderly. In Florida, the information is broadcast via a toll-free number and a free internet site; in 1999, this site included, aside from the names, photos, and current addresses of 12,000 "sexual predators" convicted since 1993, the circumstances of their crimes and the age of their victims. And all sex offenders from other states must identify themselves to the local authorities within 48 hours of their arrival in the territory of the Sunshine State. In many states, the data broadcast to the public includes not only location information but the home and work telephone numbers, the car make, and the license plate number of the ex-offender.

The variant of "Megan's Law" passed by the Texas Assembly in 1997 (complementing the federal law) requires all ex-convicts of sexual offenses since 1970 to be registered in a computer databank that the correctional administration makes available to the public. "What this

*The masculine is apposite here since the overwhelming majority of sex offenders are male: 98.8 percent for rape and 92 percent for all other sexual offenses nationwide. Richard Tewksbury, "Experiences and Attitudes of Registered Female Sex Offenders," *Federal Probation* 68, no. 3 (2004): 30–33.

means to our citizens is easier access than ever before to information that can give an indication of the relative safety of a neighborhood in terms of potential sex crimes. It also can aid employers, schools and youth-oriented organizations in identifying sexual predators," explained Colonel Dudley Thomas, the Director of Public Safety, as he celebrated the development of "yet another high-tech tool that will help make Texas an even safer place to live." Individuals or organizations who wish to can purchase this database on CD-ROM for the modest sum of $35: "We want sex offenders in Texas to know that we know who you are," Thomas continued. "And now, more easily than ever before, the people of Texas can know where you are."[21]

In California, the municipal police make public the personal data (name, photograph, height, weight, and identifying marks), criminal records, and addresses of 64,600 convicts of sexual offenses categorized as "serious" or "high risk" (out of a total of 82,600) by means of flyers and small posters, press conferences, neighborhood and town-hall meetings, and door-to-door campaigns in their vicinity. As for the complete registry of sex offenders, in 1999 it could be consulted via a toll-free telephone number and on CD-ROMS made available at central police stations, municipal libraries, and at the annual county fairs. In the year after the statute came into effect, 213 "Megan's Law CD-ROMS" were distributed across the Golden State through 145 police departments. The latter diffused 6,500 flyers revealing the profiles of "high-risk" sex offenders (defined as those who had committed at least two offenses, including one with violence) and notified schools of the presence of 134 of them in their immediate vicinity. Within three months, over 24,000 people had consulted these CD-ROMS, for a positive response rate of 12 percent, while the "Sex Offender Identification Line" had received 7,845 calls (each requiring the payment of a $10 toll, billed automatically by the phone company), 421 of which resulted in the identification of an ex-convict for a sexual offense. Every year, the state adds around 3,000 new files to this computerized databank, which in 1998 already included one adult male Californian in 150.

In San Diego, shortly after passage of the law, the chief of police held a press conference to broadcast the identity of seven "high-risk" (former) sex offenders. For them, anonymity was no longer an option: the list of seven led the nightly television news and their names were carried by all the city's newspapers—although the *San Diego Tribune* coyly declined to print their photos on grounds that "they are dated and in some cases of low quality." In Los Angeles, the police alerted residents in the vicinity of schools by going house to house; in Santa Rosa, they also warned businesses and customers in shopping centers with leaflets. On the east side of the San Francisco Bay, the towns of Fremont and Hayward distributed maps to families with school-age children indicating the locations of sex offenders classified as "serious" and "high risk" residing within a one-mile radius of educational institutions: the incriminated streets (though not exact addresses) were designated by triangles so that concerned parents could advise their children to avoid them on their walk to school. In October 1998, in the rural county of Calaveras, the local daily, the *Ledger-Dispatch*, was the first newspaper in California to publish the complete list of the ex–sex offenders of the region, on the ground that the latter "pose a risk to the entire community."[22]

A New Attraction at the County Fair: "Outing" Former Sex Offenders

Since 1997, one of the most popular attractions at county fairs organized around summertime in California, along with horse races, pig contests, and churning or spitting contests, has been the "outing" of former sexual convicts. Between the doughnut stand, the shooting gallery, and the tent hawking regional delicacies, under an immense banner in screaming colors ("Free Access to Sex Offender Information—Check It Out"), the California Department of Justice set out six personal computers equipped with "Megan's Law" CD-ROMS, into which the fairgoer can type his home zip code and instantly see pop up on the screen photographs of the (former) sex offenders dwelling in her neighborhood.

To indulge in this cybernetic version of voyeurism that the "freak shows" common to America's fairgrounds up to the New Deal offered in an earlier era,[23] the enthusiastic rubberneckers who squash together in compact clusters around the stand must first present a driver's license as identity card, so that one can verify that they are not themselves on the sex offender registry—the authorities claim to fear that "perverts" will use the databank to find one another and form criminal rings. The experience promises strong emotions at a modest price: "Whoa! This guy lives across the street from us," cried Sergio Rubio, thirty-two, as the name and photo of an ordinary looking middle-aged man with a thick moustache flashed up on the screen in front of him. "His daughter goes to school with my six-year-old daughter! Just a week ago, I was getting a haircut and he sat down right next to me." Rubio announced that he was going to let all his neighbors know about this discovery as soon as he got back home from the fair. A few moments later, an elderly woman burst into tears upon discovering the picture of her longtime neighbor, who had been convicted of a sexual offense against a minor decades earlier. "What do I do? All our kids grew up together. It's really hard when you've known somebody for twenty-five years. He's a family man. It really just traumatized me seeing his picture there."[24] One mother had a panic attack upon discovering that her geographic sector contained no fewer than 63 sex offenders; another was greatly relieved to learn that hers harbored none.

California attorney general Dan Lundgren, who was refining there the dorsal theme of his upcoming reelection campaign,* made it a point of honor to inaugurate in person the "Megan stand" at the Los Angeles county fair, where it was one of the largest and most popular stands, judging by the crowd waiting in tightly packed ranks for a terminal to come free. He explained: "Most people don't know that [this information] is available and some are wary of walking into a police station. It occured to me, what better place is there than a fair?"[25] Lundgren was encouraged by the fact that, in less than a week, 4000 people consulted the Megan files between rides and flushed out 300 (former) sex offenders. The Attorney General then rushed to issue a press release commending the "law-abiding citizens" who thus found and denounced 16 ex–sex convicts who held jobs putting them in contact with minors: one of them was a sales clerk in a children's shoe store, another was a baseball coach, a third worked for his city's park district.

These data, which no one takes the trouble to verify, turned out to be erroneous in many cases. Indeed, in most districts more than half of the addresses in the registry of convicts of sexual offenses are incorrect (as those listed in it had died, moved, or been rearrested). Moreover, Megan's CD-ROM reports neither the dates of infractions—which can go all the way back to 1944—nor the fact that many of these infractions have long since stopped being punishable by law—this is the case with homosexual relations between consenting adults, which were decriminalized in California in 1976, but are still recorded under the same code as the sexual abuse of children. This led to thousands of elderly gay Californians finding themselves assimilated to "child molesters" and required to report annually to their local police station for a humiliating registration procedure submitting them to bottomless public opprobrium (until 1998, when the classification was discretely altered by a vote of the California Assembly at the behest of gay rights groups).

This rudimentary system of dissemination of criminal information was supplemented in 2004 by a web site run by the Office of the Attorney General. This site features the "California Sex Offender Locator Map," allowing surfers to search the registry by name, address, city, zip code, or by location of schools and parks (when the whimsical search engine cooperates, that is). The locator map is preceded by a full page of disclaimers that would seem to belie its utility, including warnings that the purpose of the site is "informational only," that "the California Department of Justice makes no representation, either express or implied, that

*In California, the attorney general, who heads the state's Department of Justice, is elected independently of the governor under whose authority he or she is placed, and he must therefore develop his own campaign agenda.

> the information on this site is complete or accurate," and that it "has not considered or assessed the specific risk that any convicted sex offender displayed on this web site will commit another offense."[26]

The incessant media racket around sexual crimes maintains a feverous anguish in the country such that the states that proved slow to disseminate the records of sex convicts were overtaken by counties and cities rushing to publish their own lists. In Michigan, senator David Jaye—who boasted of being the first elected official to put up his own "perv site"—took it upon himself to broadcast a map of sex offenders in his district on the web, in an effort to push the justice department of his state to speed up the electronic diffusion of Megan's list and put a "leash on rabid-dog sex predators."[27] In Alaska, in early 1998 an individual entrepreneur in morality opened an internet site called www.sexoffender.com, which promised direct access to 500,000 photos of convicts of sexual offenses in the fifty states of the Union as well as in Mexico, for a modest fee of $5 per inquiry.

In April of 2000, Stony Brook social worker Laura Ahearn launched Parents for Megan's Law to put the sex offender registry of New York State on the web (volunteers spent a year hand-copying names from judicial subdirectories into a master list) and operate a telephone hotline. The nonprofit organization, whose stated mission is "to promote zero tolerance for sex offenses committed against children," quickly received funding from Suffolk County and expanded its operation to run workshops, town-hall meetings, and its own web site (ParentsforMeganslaw.com). Through them, PFML promotes the "community approach to managing Megan's law," which entails systematic efforts by the citizenry to disseminate the information released by the authorities so that it seeps into every nook and cranny of the local society. Elected a New York State Senate Woman of Distinction for her activism, Mrs. Ahearn writes op-eds, appears regularly in the electronic media, and publishes a "report card" rating states on how well they implement Megan's Law. She also sells her book ("as seen on Fox, the John Walsh Show, Peter Jennings, CSPAN, ESPN and more"), *Megan's Law Nationwide and the Apple of My Eye Childhood Sexual Abuse Prevention Program*. The book purports to "shatter commonly held myths about Megan's Law and stranger danger while giving parents and caregivers real life answers on how to prevent children from being sexually abused," thanks to a list of "27 Tricks that predators use to access children, Red Flags to detect a predator in your midst, Ten Rules for Safety For Your Children and much more." The web site of the organization broadcasts this stern warning: "Sexual predators are smart, extremely cunning and are often the pillars of the community who we would least expect to molest our children. They will do anything to get access to children."

By the close of the decade, then, the hunt after ex–sex offenders had turned into a veritable cottage industry, mixing victims advocates, elected officials, the media, and self-professed experts engaged in a new and lucrative sector of symbolic entrepreneurship, feeding upon the personal experience, fear, or fantasy of sexual violence. The gruesome murders of Megan Kanka and Jacob Wetterling attained such iconic media status that their parents were able to set up charitable foundations devoted to campaigning for child safety on a national level (and to providing lifelong employment for the family).[28] They were soon joined by the Polly Klaas Foundation and by KlaasKids Foundation, rival outfits run by two branches of the family of Polly Klaas, a teenager from Petaluma, a small town in an affluent county north of San Francisco, whose kidnapping and murder by a twice-convicted violent offender on parole in the fall of 1993 propelled state politicians to vote the country's harshest "Three Strikes and You're Out" statute. The voice of these foundations and a host of similar organizations was amplified by major talk-show figures such as Oprah Winfrey, Geraldo Rivera, and John Walsh, another crime victim's father and host of the so-called reality show "America's Most Wanted" on Fox TV, and by the ability of their leaders to parlay familial tragedy into appointments on gubernatorial task forces, testimony before legislative commissions, and even keynote addresses at academic conferences.*

The Perverse Effects of Blacklisting "Perverts"

It did not take long to detect the fallout of the official dissemination of the identity and address of (former) sex offenders: the latter are regularly humiliated, frequently harassed and insulted, and increasingly forced to move owing to the hostility and threats of those around them. Many

*In her opening address to the National Conference on Sex Offender Registries, organized by the US Department of Justice in April 1998, "Mrs. Patty Wetterling, advocate for missing children and cofounder of the Jacob Wetterling Foundation" told "the details of her son's abduction and the emotional highs and lows that accompanied the aftermath" to a rapt audience of higher civil servants, lawyers, legislators, and statisticians. Patty Wetterling, "The Jacob Wetterling Story," in *National Conference on Sex Offender Registries*, ed. Chaiken, 3–7.

lose their homes and their jobs and find themselves suddenly subjected to virulent ostracism that pushes them down into marginality—driving them to suicide in some cases. Others see their reputations, their families, and their lives torn apart by the public revelation of a single, unrepeated infraction committed years or even decades before. Already one can sketch out the contours of a new phenomenon that may be labeled *Megan's flight*: the forced wandering of former sex offenders under the hateful pressure of local residents,* on the one hand, and ex-sexual convicts staying below the official radar or going into hiding in desperate hope of escaping public vilification, on the other. Not to mention the harm done to people wrongly accused of ignominious acts owing to the mistakes that abound in Megan registries or the malicious diffusion of false or duplicitous flyers. In 1999 alone, several hundred complaints were lodged against state correctional administrations on this basis.

From one end of the country to the other, incidents of vigilantism multiplied after Megan's Laws went into force. In June 1997, the residents of the El Caminito del Sur neighborhood in Monterey staged a virulent public demonstration in front of the apartment of an ex-convict for rape and attempted rape (committed in 1980 and 1983) and gathered several hundred signatures demanding his immediate expulsion after his past offenses had been made public by the police. One month later, a former sex offender working as a truck driver in Santa Rosa was verbally savaged by his neighbors, who launched a petition demanding that he be banished from the city—following which he was promptly dismissed by his employer and then arrested by the police on suspicion of having violated the terms of parole by talking to a neighborhood youth.** In July 1998, the dead body of Michael Alan Patton,

*This was the case of a notorious ex-rapist released after having served fourteen years behind bars who had to be relocated three times in less than four months by the California parole agency in reaction to furious protests by residents warned of his presence by the police due to the legal obligation of public notification. The quandary is such that the state correctional administration is considering creating a kind of "judicial reservation" in a desert zone of California where it would resettle sex parolees rejected by the population. "Doggy Door Rapist Out on Parole," "Rapist Moved from School Area: Residents Picketed Boarding House," and "Complaint Forces Rapist on Parole to Move Again," *San Francisco Chronicle*, 28 October, 11 November, and 9 December 1998, respectively.

**The California secretary of labor refused to intervene to reverse his dismissal, and he was later sent back to serve nine months in custody after the mother of the teenager to whom he had spoken traveled to the parole hearing to testify against him. "Monterey Dispute Tests Megan's Law: Residents Want Sex Offender to Move," "Publicized Child Molester Jailed on Parole Charge," and "Molester Sent to Jail for Violating Parole," *San Francisco Chronicle*, 20 June, 11 July, and 9 August 1997, respectively.

42 years old, was found hanging from a tree near the Santa Rosa exit on Route 10. He had committed suicide six days after the police had canvassed his neighborhood to distribute a flyer revealing his judicial background. A neighbor stated: "I see no problem with them giving out flyers, and I see no problem with that guy being dead. I saw his rap sheet."[29] The previous summer, a journalist at the *Paradise Post* in Butte, Montana, was fired after the newspaper discovered upon publishing the list of the state's former sex offenders that he appeared on it. In Oregon, a former sex-crime convict hastily left town after a burning cross was planted in his front yard at night. The car of an ex–sex offender was blown up by a bomb in Covina, a suburb of Los Angeles; another was stoned in Massachusetts. In Texas, the house of a former child rapist about to be paroled was destroyed in a criminal fire set on the eve of his release.

A survey conducted in 1996 in 30 of 39 counties in Washington State which applied a version of "Megan's Law" (it has been in force in that jurisdiction since 1990) among those most concerned with public education revealed 33 cases of "harassment" of former sex offenders following 942 public notifications, 327 of them involving "third-category" convicts (considered dangerous owing to their past behavior as "predators" or psychological problems). Among the incidents officially registered were a burned house, the "picketing" of an apartment, an assault on a minor, crowds demonstrating outside an ex–sex offender's residence, during which personal threats were made, and the illegal posting of notices of the neighborhood of an ex-convict.[30] These incidents were only the emerging tip of the iceberg of reactions against sex offenders, whose real dimensions no one knows: their targets are hardly inclined to go complain to the authorities since this brings them into intensified contact with law-enforcement agencies and eventually exposes them to seeing their parole status revoked.

In summer 1998, this time on the East Coast, five gunshots were fired in the middle of the night through the windows of the apartment of a man convicted of a sex crime in New Jersey by one of his neighbors who later confessed that he had "snapped" after learning that his younger sisters lived next to a (former) rapist. Frank P., age 56, had been convicted of sexual offenses against two teenagers in 1976 and, having served sixteen years in prison, lived in seclusion with his parents since his release. After police distributed flyers featuring his photo, address, and an abstract of his criminal file, the neighborhood children shouted after him ("child molester!"), the local people avoided him, teachers at the nearby school he had gone to fled from him, and he remained interred in the basement of his mother's house. "I can't move. I'm trapped. I can't work. I can't get a job. I have no money and no income. I can't live. Maybe I should go back to prison."[31]

The long unresolved pendulum swing of the state between the "medical model" and the "retributive model" for responding to sexual offenses has thus stopped onto retribution during the past decade.[32] And the "tension between the safety of the community and the civil liberties of sex offenders" was finally resolved by the *de facto abrogation of those liberties*.[33] The logic of punitive panopticism and segregative confinement that has informed the management of dispossessed, deviant, and dangerous categories in the United States following the denunciation of the Keynesian social contract is now applied to former sex offenders with all the more vigor as their misdeeds are more villainous and touch directly the foundations of the familial order at the very moment when the family has to compensate for the growing deficiencies of the protections offered by the state against the risks of wage-working life.[34]

This makes clear that Megan's Laws and related measures mark a rupture in the cyclical peregrinations of the penal state on this front. Whereas earlier waves of fear of sexual criminality had affirmed the medical model and bolstered the commitment to the philosophy of rehabilitation, the latest tide has eroded if not buried them—and this, with the full support of the courts, as we shall see shortly. The new policy toward sex offenders openly jettisons the priority on "correcting" conduct and reforming individuals predominant from the 1920s to the 1970s. Instead, it prioritizes the retribution, incapacitation, and stringent supervision of entire categories of convicts defined statistically through aggregate probabilities of deviant behavior. In this regard, Megan's Laws and kindred measures fuse the instrumentalism of the "new penology" of stochastic management and selective neutralization with the emotion-driven ferocity of punitive populism.[35] They decisively discard the therapeutic philosophy and make the sex offender an analogon to the market rejects of the crumbling ghetto on the civic front, a species of *moral trash to be disposed of* or incinerated, as it were, into the furnace of state punishment stoked by the broiling hostility of the citizenry. Thus the pervasiveness of an aversive idiom of revulsion, pollution, and fear of contagion in the public discourse on sex offenders, suggesting an intense desire to extirpate them physically as well as symbolically from the social body so as to maintain the latter's fictitious moral purity.[36]

This helps explain a second major difference between the fin-de-siècle hunt of sex offenders and its mid-century predecessor, namely the *short-circuiting of the expert* and the promotion of crime victims as authoritative bearers of folk wisdom and popular will on the question.* Whereas the panic over the "sexual psychopath" had affirmed and expanded the prerogatives of psychiatrists, the forms of social control fostered by the countrywide wave of Megan's Laws mandating the public notification of the whereabouts of former sex convicts and their indefinite detention on grounds of "mental abnormality" were frontally opposed by the official organizations of medical and mental health professionals. Thus the 1996 Report of the American Psychiatric Association Task Force on SVP (sexually violent predators) forcefully argued that such laws "misallocate psychiatric facilities and resources, and constitute an abuse of psychiatry."[37] But the collaboration of medical experts is no longer needed, since etiological and therapeutic considerations have virtually disappeared from the public debate on sexual delinquency. There is no longer any question of rehabilitating the 150,000-odd people who commit a serious sex crime every year; the aim now is only to "contain" them in order to "increase the security of the public and the protection of the victims."**

As with the castoffs from the market, the mentally ill, drug addicts, and the homeless, and prisoners released on parole,[38] *the penal government of poverty—sexual misery, in this case—tends to aggravate the very phenomenon it is supposed to fight* on the side of those who commit infractions as well as among the population that fears and rejects them. First of all, from the perspective of the public, the generalization of devices and programs for registering and notifying people of the presence and whereabouts of sex convicts, far from reassuring them, inflames the unreasoned fear of sexual assault, as can be seen from the open displays of hostility of which sex offenders have been the target, on the one hand, and from the mad rush on Megan's registries, on the other. The internet site of the state of Virginia, for example, welcomed 830,000 visitors in five months, who made over five million searches, when the state counts only 4,600 sex offenders on its official registry. In the two years after it went into service, the site of the Michigan Department of Justice received a daily average of 5,000 visits, equiva-

*It is revealing that the gubernatorial task force that recommended the passing of the first comprehensive civil commitment law of sex offenders on grounds of "mental abnormality" in Washington State in 1990 backgrounded psychiatrists and gave pride of place to crime victims. Roxanne Lieb, Vernon Quinsey, and Lucy Berliner, "Sexual Predators and Social Policy," *Crime and Justice* 23 (1998): 64–65.

**In 1997, some 234,000 sex offenders were under criminal justice supervision, about two-thirds of them released on parole. Yet there exists virtually no studies evaluating the (few) treatment programs to which they have access. Vernon L. Quinsey, "Treatment of Sex Offenders," *Handbook of Crime and Punishment*, ed. Michael Tonry, 403–28 (New York: Oxford University Press, 1998).

lent to the total number of individual files online every four days. At the county fairs of California, thousands of families with no particular reason to worry whether their neighbors had been convicted of sexual offenses find themselves caught in a kind of open-ended cybersafari for "perverts" that can only increase their anxiety—especially when the manhunt turns out to be successful. A report evaluating Washington State's notification program thus includes among the major *disadvantages* of this law the "*overreaction by the public*: communities can be unpredictable in their reactions towards sex offenders. Notification can cause public panic—'it's like hollering fire in a full theater'."[39]

A contrario, if Megan-type measures enhance the sense of security among the public, as their architects maintain, this feeling can be illusory and lead to a slackening of collective vigilance whose paradoxical consequence, everything else being equal, would be an increase of objective risk.* Indeed, apart from the fact that state registries of sexual offenders are riddled with errors (the Michigan correctional administration acknowledged in court that 20 to 40 percent of the names and addresses in its databank are incorrect), the vast majority of sex offenders are not known to the authorities, let alone under judicial supervision. According to the National Crime Victimization Survey, fewer than one in three sexual assaults in the country were reported to law enforcement in the 1990s, with the result that the 265,000 convicts for sexual crimes represented about 10 percent of all sex lawbreakers in the country.[40] Moreover, a large number of those among the small minority that are caught, tried, and convicted, persist in avoiding registration after their release from prison: in California, for instance, the "escape" rate from Megan's CD-ROM ranges from 35 to 70 percent depending on the year of the infraction, in spite of harsh penalties stipulated by the law. And this is without taking into account that nothing prevents a duly registered and correctly located (former) sex offender from committing a new offense *outside of his neighborhood*. Knowing that a "sexual predator" resides on the corner of such-and-such street does no more to reduce the chance of an offense than knowing that drunk drivers are more likely to be on the road at night decreases the chances of having a traffic accident in the afternoon. All in all, the "false sense of security"

*As Janet Howell, the Democratic senator who introduced the bill in the Virginia Senate, belatedly conceded: "This is the easy, feel-good, politically popular way of dealing with the problem, but it's only a small part of what could be done. I don't think that it does much to protect the public and I'm even afraid that it gives people a false sense of security." Cited by criminologist Susan Paisner in "Exposed: Online Registries of Sex Offenders Do More Harm than Good," *Washington Post*, 21 February 1999.

fostered by Megan's Law via its exclusive focus on vaguely defined and ill-circumscribed outsiders "may actually increase the risk to children to the degree that it lowers parental vigilance in monitoring the child's contacts with friends, relatives, and other trusted persons."[41]

Secondly, from the point of view of convicts for sexual crimes, Megan's Laws amount to instituting through legislative means a *second punishment of infamy*, whose term extends a decade or more beyond the prison term imposed by the courts—it stretches into perpetuity in the states leading the race to hyperincarceration*—which in effect abrogates their right to privacy. This "branding" is moreover applied *retroactively*, since, left to the whims of local legislators, the conviction date from which sex offenders come under the obligation of registration and public notification goes back years and sometimes decades before (the federal or state) Megan's Law was passed: the baseline date is 1992 in Louisiana, 1990 in Virginia, 1985 in Wyoming, 1970 in Texas, 1956 in Nevada, and 1947 in California. Despite this, in February 1998 the US Supreme Court refused to examine the law's constitutionality and let stand the decisions of several lower courts that it does not infringe on fundamental rights since, "notwithstanding the Legislature's subjective intent," the ostensive purpose of the law is not to "punish," but only to "regulate" with a view to ensuring "the protection of the public."**

But there is more: by threatening every sexual convict, including those who have mended their ways and are settled into a new life, with being "flushed out" and putting them in symbolic stocks before their families, friends, colleagues, and neighbors, these measures encourage ex–sex offenders to go underground and therefore live in illegality.[42] In cases of sexual abuse inside the family, the knowledge that the identity and

*The length of the obligation of registration and public notification runs to ten years in Arizona, Louisiana, Texas, and Illinois, and to fifteen years in Alaska, Michigan, and New Jersey (for former sex offenders who have no other conviction during this period and ask the state supreme court to have their name expunged from the register). It extends to the 90th birthday of the convict in Arizona and applies for life in fifteen states, including California, Texas, Florida, and Nevada. The files of sexual convicts remain in "Megan's registry" (available on the internet) *even after their death* in Florida, on the pretext that this can help the victims "achieve closure."

**In this argumentation, the "public" to be protected clearly does not include members of the family or household of the sex offender, considering that their right to privacy is automatically abrogated and that public notification has every chance of causing them new trauma (as in the case, for instance, of children who were the victims of incest). Robert Kwak in Ernie Allen and Nadine Strossen, "Megan's Law and the Protection of the Child in the On-Line Age (Panel Discussion)," *American Criminal Law Review* 35, no. 4 (winter 1998): 1319–41.

deeds of the offender will be made public is certain to dissuade some victims from going to the authorities, thus helping the perpetrators to go unnoticed. An in-depth study of 30 high-level sex convicts released in Wisconsin not only found that, in all cases, community notification "adversely affected their transition from prison to the outside world," with loss of employment, exclusion of residence, social isolation, and emotional distress creating added obstacles. It also revealed that the fraying of social ties essential to (re)integrating them into the local social structure extends to intimates around them: "One interviewee talked about his mother's 'broken heart', her anguish and depression following newspaper accounts stemming from notification. Another spoke of his son's decision to quit his high school freshmen football team because of ridicule from teammates, and a third related how his sister was shunned by her former friends. Still another stated that his wife threatened suicide because she could not handle the stress of constant media exposure." An incest perpetrator was especially distraught that his daughter was being taunted at her school by other children telling her that they knew "your daddy played sex with you."[43] This suggests that Megan's Law effects the *secondary penalization* of those who are or dare to step into the social circle of the ex-offender, subjecting them to attenuated variants of the mortification, torment, and ostracism that befalls the latter.[44]

In addition to creating abiding feelings of dejection, a sense of abject worthlessness (many wonder why they are alive at all), and a constant fear for their safety feeding paranoia, notification creates a corona of noxious notoriety under which all sex offenders are assimilated to the "worst of the worst" among them upon whom the media fixates. And it puts added bureaucratic pressure on parole agents to treat their "clients" harshly, increasing the chances that they will be returned to custody for minor administrative violations. The combination of psychological distress, exclusionary social pressure, bureaucratic intransigence, and pervasive labeling fostered by public notification cannot but have anti-therapeutic effects and boost relapse, as suggested bluntly by a Wisconsin ex–sex offender:

> If these people know that you're a sex offender and they keep saying—keep pointing at you and everything else, everything breaks under pressure, everything. No matter how strong he thinks he is. You taunt a dog long enough, no matter how calm and cool, . . . it might have been the most loving dog with children and everything else, it's going to bite. And that's exactly what this law does. It makes John Q. Public taunt the sex offenders. And sooner or later something is going to snap.[45]

All told, the main effect of the laws named after little Megan Kanka may paradoxically be to *amplify risk* and to *increase* the chances that convicts for sexual offenses will commit new crimes by condemning them to a manner of social exile without recourse or return and subjecting them to relentless pressure and intransigent surveillance.[46]

Finally, the political-journalistic onslaught around the measures of punitive surveillance established by Megan-type laws makes these measures self-perpetuating as it entrenches the public myth that sex offenders are incorrigible, and it saves the authorities from pursuing a realistic and sustained approach aimed at genuinely curbing their activities through a combination of prevention and treatment (relying on medication, psychotherapy, and techniques of behavior modification). It is at once cheaper financially in the short run and more profitable electorally to put up an internet site—or to offer as media sacrifice the castration of a few recidivists by way of hormonal injection or testicular removal, as practiced in Texas and Wisconsin—and to hurl colorful invectives against prisoners universally reviled as monsters than to set up a program of psychiatric treatment in correctional facilities and a network of therapy centers on the outside. And, for this purpose, it is more convenient to present sex offenders as an undifferentiated mass or in the guise of asocial and amoral psychopaths fated to reoffend than to establish categorical distinctions based on the seriousness and nature of their infraction, the risk they pose, and their varied needs and responsiveness to treatment.[47]

Of the nearly 300,000 prisoners released in 15 states studied by the Bureau of Justice Statistics researchers in 1994, two-thirds were rearrested within three years, one-half were convicted of a new crime, and one-fourth were sentenced to custody, but fully 52 percent of this cohort found themselves back behind bars as the combined result of new sentences and technical violations of parole stipulations.[48] Released prisoners with the highest rearrest rates—all new offenses tallied together—were those initially convicted of vehicle theft (79 percent), possession or sale of stolen property (77 percent), larceny (75 percent) and burglary (74 percent), followed by robbers (70 percent), drug offenders (67 percent), and drunken drivers (52 percent). Former inmates sentenced for rape (46 percent) and other sexual assaults (41 percent) sported the *lowest overall rearrest rate*, along with murderers (also at 41 percent).

Moreover, the vast majority of those 46 percent of ex-rapists recaptured by the police were charged not with violent crimes but mostly with offenses pertaining to public order (21 percent), property (15 percent), and drugs (11 percent). Only 18 percent were accused of a crime of violence, typically an assault (9 percent), and a mere 2.5 percent were rearrested on rape charges. Thus, if one considers the probability of rearrest for the same crime, *released rapists sport by far the lowest "specialist" reoffense rate of all prisoners,* along with murderers (1.2 percent), compared to 41 percent for drug offenders accused of a new narcotics violation within three years, 23 percent for ex-burglars embroiled again in burglary, 19 percent for those convicted of fraud, and 14 percent for robbers.

If the justification for the special surveillance of sex offenders is the seriousness of their recidivism, then one must note similarly that robbers, burglars, and car thieves, for instance, all have significantly higher rates of violent reoffending (30 percent, 27 percent, and 22 percent respectively) than do ex-rapists (18.6 percent). Finally, given that rapists are a tiny proportion of all inmates at release, their specialist recidivism produces far fewer rapes than the rapes perpetrated by other run-of-the-mill felons: of this cohort of 300,000, the 3,138 convicts for rape committed 78 new rapes within three years of release, whereas the 26,900 former robbers committed 322 rapes, the 88,516 drug convicts 265 rapes, and the 17,700 sentenced for assault 177. So, from the standpoint of preventing rape, the exclusive focus on sex offenders appears seriously misplaced.

The paradox here is that, of all the various kinds of offenders, convicts suffering from paraphiliac disorders (i.e., the deregulation of desire) are those who, when they are correctly diagnosed and receive the requisite care, sport *the lowest rate of recidivism*: less than 10 percent in the case of exhibitionists, pedophiles, and perpetrators of sexual assaults on women, and barely 3 percent in the case of pedophiles who complete the treatment program elaborated by the Sexual Disorders Clinic at Johns Hopkins University Medical School.[49] Despite this, they continue to be regarded as incorrigibly depraved, and in any case imprisonment in the United States no longer has for its object to "rehabilitate" anyone.[50] The result is that *barely 10 percent of convicts for sexual violence receive any treatment* in custody, and an even lower percentage are subject to therapeutic follow-up of any kind after release.*

A pioneer in this area, Washington State has since 1990 implemented one of the few sex offender notification programs that is attentive to

*In 1997, 95,700 inmates, corresponding to some 10 percent of the clients of state penitentiaries, were serving a sentence for rape (3.8 percent) and other forms of sexual violence (5.9 percent). Only 12,200 or 1.3 percent of the prisoners at these penitentiaries were following a treatment program for sex offenders. These figures are computed from Bureau of Justice Statistics, *Correctional Populations in the United States, 1995* (Washington, D.C.: Government Printing Office, 1997), 9, table 1.11; Camille Graham and George M. Camp, eds., *The Corrections Yearbook 1998* (Middletown, Conn.: Criminal Justice Institute, 1999), 114.

educating the public about this kind of offense. As part of their information campaign, the police take the trouble to distribute a series of notices explaining the workings of the 1990 Community Protection Act and warn against certain common misconceptions about sex offenders (for example, "you cannot identify a sex offender by looks, race, gender, occupation, or religion. A sex offender can be anyone, so precautions need to be taken at all times"). One of these notices is entitled "Punishing Sex Offenders: Who Pays?" Its goal is, quite prosaically, to remind the public that "*91% of imprisoned sex offenders* [in this state] *do not receive sex offender treatment.*" The evaluation report on the notification program notes in this regard: "Most people feel that when sex offenders go to prison, they are automatically sent to treatment. People are surprised to find that most sex offenders do not receive treatment. The additional cost of treatment helps people understand why treatment is not offered to every sex offender in prison."[51] Yet it did not come to the mind of the architects of the sex-offender notification program of Washington State to educate the population on the cost of this program, for instance by mentioning that it is a huge consumer of an already overworked personnel, since the law "is an unfunded mandate. It spreads resources thin, and is a very time-consuming task. Jurisdictions do not have the necessary manpower. 'Having one officer per 930 offenders is ludicrous'."[52] Or that their own studies show that the notification program has no impact on the recidivism rate of offenders thus placed under supervision.

Thus, whereas sex offenders in the United States enjoy medical and social care only by way of exception, they are now the object of an attentive police and penal supervision that ensures that an ever-growing number of them will be, not treated for their afflictions, but swiftly "neutralized" by means of confinement when they reoffend or fail to scrupulously fulfill registration requirements that periodically revivify the stigma and ostracism weighing upon this category of convicts.

From Blacklisting to Banishment

"Megan's Laws" are emblematic of legislative measures undergirding the expansion of the penal state and fostering the transition toward the punitive containment of poverty in the United States insofar as they effect a *triple diversion.* In the first place, they drain precious *resources,* in budget, personnel, and programs, from the social and medical wing to the police and judicial wing of the state. For example, while the psychiatric services of Michigan's correctional administration (and of its public hospitals) were screaming from famine, the state obtained and spent a federal subsidy of one-half million dollars to computerize its sex offender registry and put it on the web, while Virginia devoted more than $300,000 to its cybersurveillance site for sexual convicts in 1999. In New Jersey, where the courts are staggering under the weight of prosecutions being filed in connection with the "War on drugs" and probation services suffer, like everywhere else, from a severe dearth of funds, each of the 36 counties found itself forced, under the law of Megan passed by the state in 1994, to assign a full-time prosecutor to preside over hearings aimed at establishing the presumed dangerousness and thus the modalities of public notification for each sex offender awaiting parole release. These hearings alone already cost more in wages than all the trials for sex offenses put together.*

In June 1997, the US Attorney General announced the opening of the Center for Sex Offender Management, a national agency attached to the Center for Effective Public Policy at Silver Spring, Maryland, whose mission is to assist city, county, and state authorities to keep track of the roughly 145,000 sex offenders under community supervision across the land.[53] A pilot program endowed with $1.4 million was set up to train mixed teams composed of parole officers, polygraph technicians (handling the famous "lie detector"), and therapists. The mission of this "supervisory triangle": to detect the "deviant fantasies" of sex offenders on parole and anticipate their opportunities for access to potential victims in order to refine their surveillance and bolster the capacity to neutralize them. Yet there is no evidence that this will have an impact on their reoffense rate, let alone on the aggregate rate of sexual criminality.

Next, Megan's Laws redirect *tens of thousands of derelict bodies* from the social and medical sectors of the state to its penal sector, thereby bringing a supplement of "raw materials" to the ravenous growth of the carceral apparatus that contributes to turning imprisonment into an industrial-scale people-processing enterprise charged with "cleaning the social system by eliminating undesirable elements."[54] In this regard, the "sexual predator" craze of the close of the twentieth century marks a break with, indeed a reversal from, the "sexual psychopath" panic of the mid-century in that it weakens the welfare pole of the state and

*See the discussion by Strossen in Allen and Strossen, "Megan's Law and the Protection of the Child in the On-Line Age," 1340. In 1997 New Jersey spent $600,000 to try sex offenders and $700,000 just for the salaries of the lawyers appointed to serve at hearings required to categorize the risk posed by former sexual offenders. Elizabeth A. Pearson, "Status and Latest Developments in Sex Offender Registration and Notification Laws," in *National Conference on Sex Offender Registries*, ed. Chaiken, 45–49.

curtails the influence of experts (such as sexologists, psychiatrists, and criminologists) who had until then modulated and even limited the application of penal sanctions to this problem population.

In the third place, the new wave of sex-offender laws channel and amplify the diffuse current of animosity toward deviants and delinquents by giving it a legitimate, even officially encouraged, point of fixation and mode of expression. In so doing, it diverts *public attention* from the causes of sexual violence toward its symptoms, and it conceals the fact that such devices of post-prison marking and regimentation have, at best, no effect on the baseline incidence of crime and may even contribute to its aggravation.[55]

Like myriad other measures of high symbolic import adopted during the media-cum-political panics that have punctuated the irresistible ascent of the penal management of social insecurity (such as automatic life sentences for double recidivism, sanction enhancement for juvenile offenders, and mandatory minimum prison sentences for simple possession of small quantities of drugs), Megan's Laws were passed hurriedly in a highly overwrought climate, and in contravention of all penological sense[56]—the New Jersey bill was voted on before the parolee accused of Megan Kanka's rape and murder was even convicted. Thus, just when the members of the Union were eagerly vying to institute measures tending to judicially blacklist former sex offenders and pushing in unison for the federal government to do the same, there already existed an in-depth statistical study of five years of experimentation in Washington State concluding that public notification has *no detectible effect* on the recidivism rate of sex offenders.[57]

> This study compares the judicial trajectory of 125 "high-risk" sex offenders subject to public notification to that of a test-sample of convicts who remained anonymous during the period 1990–95. Aside from the absence of any statistically significant difference in their respective recidivism rate, it establishes that the sex offenders placed under registration and notification committed another sexual offense an average of two years after release, as against five years for their counterparts in the control group, but it cannot tell whether the greater "precocity of recidivism" of the former is due to the fact that they break the law more quickly (owing in particular to the more intense social isolation that results from the publicizing of their status) or to their being more liable to being detected and arrested by the authorities in case of a new infraction. The plausibility of the first hypothesis is strengthened by the fact that recidivists are generally less socially integrated than nonrecidivists: they are less often married, more likely to be ad-

dicted to drugs, and they are more numerous to commit a sexual offense against a stranger than a parent or affine.

The polarization of public debate around the solitary figure of the serial pedophile coming out of prison has the advantage of reinforcing the conventional idea that the criminal threat to children would emanate essentially from individuals deprived not only of morality but also of any social bond. And thus it *magically expels sexual violence outside of the family*,[58] even as all existing studies agree that the vast majority of offenses against children are committed by kin or other adults well-known to the victim, and that these offenses are closely correlated to violence against women. Between 1991 and 1996, only 14 percent of all targets of sexual assault were abused by strangers, with 27 percent of cases coming at the hands of family members and another 60 percent by acquaintances. For children under age 6, the proportion of strangers even drops to 3 percent and the share of parents booms to nearly one-half.[59]

The inverted representation that attributes sexual violence to a lone outsider unknown to the home is all the more attractive as the patriarchal family is subjected to stronger pressures emanating from the ongoing transformation of the relations between the sexes and the generations, on the one hand, and the erosion of the domestic sphere by deregulated wage labor, on the other (especially in the case of households where both parents are employed due to material necessity). The continual increase in the number of hours worked by Americans, the dispersion of the employment schedule across the week and year (with 40 percent of wage earners in the United States now working "non-traditional" hours), the growing competitiveness of the work environment and insecurity of jobs have combined with the diversification of domestic configurations to put extraordinary pressure on the family as a social container.[60] The escalating strains between mounting market forces and the established household form have been displaced into the political field with the *canonization* of the civic category of the "working family" (which now replaces the figure of the citizen during the electoral season) and into the penal realm with the *demonization* of the "sex predator." The hyperbolic execration of the stranger pedophile on the public stage thus serves to symbolically purify the family and reassert its established role as a haven against insecurity even as accelerating neoliberal trends in the culture and economy undermine it.

Finally, Megan's Laws throw the door wide open to the unlimited expansion of frameworks for the punitive surveillance and civic exclusion of categories that inspire fear and disgust. Within months of passage of the new legislation, politicians eager to secure the electoral dividends of seething hostility toward sex offenders rushed to promise, at public meetings with their indignant constituents, to pass still harsher laws.[61] (For instance, the California Assembly has repeatedly examined the possibility of using advanced techniques of biometric identification to submit ex–sex offenders to *daily* checks at a fixed location.) In June 1997, in a narrow five-to-four decision, *Kansas v. Hendricks*, 117, S. Ct. 2072, the United States Supreme Court upheld the constitutionality of the detention *for an indefinite period* in psychiatric hospitals of sex offenders deemed to present a danger due to "mental abnormality" *after they have served the entirety of their custodial sentence* and even when they did not receive any psychiatric care while in custody (as was the case with Leroy Hendricks during the ten years he spent in prison for molesting two 13-year-old boys). In January 1999, the California Supreme Court upheld one of the provisions of the 1996 Sexually Violent Predators Act authorizing the indefinite confinement of sex offenders in state asylums—which themselves have been discharging their patients onto the carceral system since the 1950s—on the mere *presumption* of dangerousness, until such time as a judge decides that they no longer present a risk of recidivism.

As of 2004, 17 states practiced some version of this internment for sociomental "abnormality," which is neither a civil commitment *stricto sensu*, which requires a *proof* and not a simple conjecture of dangerousness, nor a penal sanction, since the latter has *already* been served in full. On paper, the roughly 2,000 sex convicts who are ordered to be confined at the conclusion of their sentences are no longer criminals but "patients." In reality, they remain subject to the state correctional authority and live under severe penitentiary regimens. In Florida, for example, the treatment facility that accommodates them is a high-security, closed center to which they are led in chains, their heads shaved, and where they are immediately placed in isolation upon arrival. And the small but growing number of "sex offenders" whose custody is extended in this fashion (potentially for life) threatens to bankrupt the child and family welfare services, whose budget must cover their "care."[62] In California, Minnesota, and New Jersey, which sport the three largest populations of ex-convicts thus kept under indefinite preventative detention, the price for holding these special inmates comes to four times the average cost of incarceration per head. What is more, the therapeutic programs deployed in these warehouses for interned ex–sex offenders subordinate medical action to penal oversight: their application is erratic at best (the authorities lack the means to compel inmates to pursue them and lawyers frequently advise their charges not to participate in therapy sessions because of the absence of confidentiality). Their efficacy is unproven and the decision to release is largely disconnected from therapeutic success in any case.

If, as New York University law professor and ACLU president Nadine Strossen notes, the *Kansas v. Hendricks* decision is "deeply offensive to our idea of freedom, our idea of justice, our idea of the task of the mental health system, on the one hand, and our idea of the correctional system, on the other," it is on the contrary in full harmony with the new government of social insecurity. For the latter, precisely, revokes the traditional opposition between the medical and the correctional in order to subordinate the social to the penal response when it comes to the lower class and stigmatized (ethnic or judicial) categories. And Strossen is not wrong to see in this system "shades of the Soviet gulag: using psychiatric hospitals as places to put away people who are deemed to be undesirable or dangerous for various reasons,"[63] since we are indeed dealing here with a strategy of segregative confinement. Similarly, legal scholar Adam Falk is justified in arguing that such confinement is "a technique of social control fundamentally incompatible with our system of ordered liberty guaranteed by the constitution,"[64] except for the fact that convicts—like recipients of public aid and, more generally, the poor and the economically precarious—are no longer, under the blooming American regime of "liberal paternalism," citizens quite like the others. And it is clear that the possibility of extending these mechanisms of surveillance and "preventative" confinement to other categories of convicts will not go unexplored for long.* In February 1999, the state assembly of Virginia debated a bill aiming to put on free access via internet the complete list of *all those convicted of a criminal offense*, adults and minors, including minor driving violations and violations of licensing and registration statutes. Punitive panopticism has a bright future ahead in America.

To understand how and why the abhorrent figure of the socially disconnected sex offender has assumed a frontline position on America's penal scene at century's close, alongside the street "thug" from the

*Similarly, their extrajudicial consequences are continuing to reverberate. For example, public notification of the presence of ex–sex offenders directly affects the functioning of the real estate sector: the value of a house suddenly drops when a former sex convict resides in the neighborhood; posh condominiums seek to exclude individuals with a sexual crime sentence in order to preserve their moral probity and market value; apartment rental agencies are inclined to bar them so as not to risk seeing the other apartments sit vacant.

crumbling dark ghetto, it proved indispensable to break out of the narrow materialist register of the political economy of punishment, and to accord full attention to the expressive mission and political role of prisonfare that such an approach typically overlooks. Indeed, the accelerating train of measures designed to mark, track, and corral the lurking pedophile and his kind—henceforth treated as if they belonged to a distinct, inherently inferior and incorrigibly dangerous, human subspecies—are inexplicable from the strict standpoint of instrumental rationality, but they become readily comprehensible once control is construed expansively to encompass the communicative and generative dimensions. They operate primarily to accentuate sensitive social boundaries eroded by converging changes in gender relations, sexual practices, household forms, and economic location, as well as to trumpet the resurgent grit of the authorities to patrol the said boundaries. The explosive bouts of toxic collective effervescence these panoptic and segregative schemes periodically trigger at the intersection of the journalistic, political, and bureaucratic fields, and their practical reverberations inside the penal sector of the state, serve to signal and cement the moral unity of all those who implicitly define themselves through contraposition with heinous sorts of criminals.*

This symbolic logic of dichotomous demarcation explains why, by the 2000s, Megan's Laws rapidly metastatized into a ramifying web of state acts, county edicts, and city ordinances that are continually shrinking the physical and social lifespaces accessible to ex–sex offenders, by forbidding them to reside within a set perimeter (typically 2,000 feet) of schools, childcare centers, and parks and recreation grounds, as well as churches, libraries, swimming pools, gyms, bus stops, and bike trails. As the list of protected sites lengthens, former sex convicts find themselves effectively banned from the city, forced to abandon their homes or even leave homeless shelters to seek refuge in rural towns and under bridges, in parking lots and at isolated truck stops.[65] Spatial proscriptions intensify their material and emotional stress, entrench their social isolation, and heighten their judicial vulnerability, which in turn

*As Durkheim reminds us, on the sociosymbolic level, "the essential function of punishment is not to make the culprit expiate his fault by making him suffer, or to intimidate possible imitators by means of threats, but to reassure those consciences which the violation of the rule can and must necessarily disturb in their faith—even as they fail to realize it—and to show them that this faith continues to be justified." Émile Durkheim, *L'Éducation morale* (Paris: Presses Universitaires de France, 1963 [1902–3]), 140, my translation. Translated as *Moral Education: A Study in the Theory and Application of the Sociology of Education* (New York: Free Press, 1973 [1923]), 167.

makes them ideal targets in the pornographic politics of punishment. The same symbolic rationale accounts for the fact that frantic penal activity and special severity aimed at sexual criminals after release have burst forth during an extended phase of declining sexual violence, and points to another paradoxical feature of neoliberal penality: the state must actively sensationalize criminal deviancy—in the double sense of playing up its occurrence and stoking the shared emotions of indignation and aversion it evokes—precisely for the purpose of dramatizing its newfound commitment to reining it in, and thereby reaffirm both its capacity to act with zest and its resolve to sharpen the sociomoral boundaries constitutive of the civic community.

A drift from the medical to the penal management of sex offenders, fostered by the volatile combination of politicized moralism and punitive panopticism, is also discernible in Western Europe, albeit in a milder and more gradual form. As in the United States, sexual offenses have risen to the top of the public agenda throughout the continent over the past decade or so, even as their incidence decreased.[66] National authorities have focused in priority on the abuse of children and obsessed on the post-release oversight of sexual convicts; they have expanded registration schemes and they have dabbled in notification, as well as stressed the neutralization of specific subcategories of offenders.[67] Some of these developments have come through the imitation or invocation of American measures: Megan's Law has been exported into Britain, where Parliament adopted the Sex Offender Act in March 1997, mandating that former convicts who committed sexual crimes against children register with the police throughout the United Kingdom—and paving the way for the national campaign of "naming and shaming" waged by the country's major newspapers to press for the publication of these registries. This raises the question of the forces fostering the international diffusion of US-style penal theories and policies. The mechanisms and paths of the cross-border circulation of the mode of reasoning and action characteristic of neoliberal penality is the topic of the fourth and final part of this book.

IV. EUROPEAN DECLINATIONS

One of the things that most excited our curiosity when coming to America was to span the extreme limits of European civilization.

—ALEXIS DE TOCQUEVILLE, "Quinze jours au désert," 1831*

*Alexis de Tocqueville, "Fortnight in the Wilderness," in George Wilson Pierson, *Tocqueville in America* (Baltimore: The Johns Hopkins University Press, 1996), 231. My translation.

8

The Scholarly Myths of the New Law-and-Order Reason

The moral panic that has been raging throughout Europe in recent years about "street violence" and "delinquent youth," which are said to threaten the integrity of advanced societies and call for severe penal responses, has mutated, since the French presidential elections of 2002, into a veritable *law-and-order pornography*. In this heated symbolic climate, everyday incidents of "insecurity" are turned into a lurid media spectacle and a permanent theater of morality. The staging of "security" (*sécurité, Sicherheit, seguridad,* etc.), henceforth construed in its strictly criminal sense—after crime had itself been reduced to street delinquency alone, that is to say, in the final analysis, to the turpitudes of the lower class—has the primary function of enabling leaders in office (or competing for office) to reaffirm on the cheap the capacity of the state to act at the very moment when, embracing the dogmas of neoliberalism, they unanimously preach its impotence in economic and social matters.[1] The canonization of the "right to security" is the correlate of, and a fig leaf for, the dereliction of the right to work, a right inscribed in the French Constitution but flouted daily by the persistence of mass unemployment amid national prosperity, on the one side, and the growth of precarious wage labor that denies any life security to the growing numbers of those who are condemned to it, on the other.

At the beginning of 2002, as the presidential election campaign commenced, all the mainstream media and political parties in France chose to focus obsessively on the supposed ascent of "*l'insécurité*," in spite of the *decrease* in street crime officially recorded during that year. Driven by the logic of commercial and electoral competition, no one deemed it worthwhile to pay the slightest attention to the results of a series of solidly documented reports produced by INSEE (the National Institute for Statistics and Economic Studies) and other studies on the relentless rise of casual employment, the tenacious roots of mass joblessness in the urban periphery, and the correlative consolidation of a vast sector of the "working poor"—according to the new label freshly imported from America, along with the policies of industrial withdrawal and economic deregulation that fuel their ranks.*

Witness this hardly noticed study, soberly entitled "Sensitive Urban Areas: Rapid Increase in Unemployment between 1990 and 1999," published in March of 2002, just as the presidential campaign was heating up, which reveals that work instability and social insecurity became at once more prevalent and more concentrated during that decade, notwithstanding renewed economic growth and a drop in the official jobless figures at the national level.[2] Thus the share of precarious workers—those employed on short-term contracts, as temporary staff, in subsidized jobs, and in government-sponsored training programs—rose from one in eleven in 1990 (or 1.98 million people) to one in seven in 1999 (3.3 million). Among the 4.7 million residents of the 750 "sensitive urban areas" designated as such by the 1996 Urban Renewal Pact—amounting to one out of every thirteen French inhabitants—the proportion of those in precarious positions bordered on 20 percent.

So much to say that, for youths lacking recognized educational credentials living in France's neighborhoods of relegation, insecure wage work is no longer a deviant, fleeting, and atypical form of employment. Rather, it is the modal path of entry into a world of work now haunted by the specter of impermanence and unrestrained flexibility.[3] And this is for those "privileged" enough to get paid employment, since at the same time unemployment among 15–24 year-olds in these districts kept on climbing: between 1990 and 1999 the proportion of youths who looked in vain for a job rose from 19.9 percent to 25.6 percent nationwide; for their compatriots living in those urban areas coyly labeled "sensitive," the increase was much sharper, from 28.5 percent to nearly 40 percent. If one adds those holding precarious jobs to those out of work, it turns out that, whereas 42 percent of the youths in these dispossessed districts were economically marginalized in 1990, that figure had jumped to some 60 percent by 1999—before unemployment resumed its relentless forward march to push this rate higher still. And these figures do not include the growing ranks of those regularly employed at the lower end of the wage ladder, with earnings woefully insufficient to cover basic household needs.[4]

In light of these statistics, attesting to the silent normalization of social insecurity under an alleged Left government, one can better understand the pitiful

*INSEE, the main producer of official statistical data in France, introduced the category of "*travailleurs pauvres*" in its surveys and reports in 1996. It is borrowed directly from the US nomenclature of "working poor" (defined, incoherently, as any individual on the labor market during at least six months of the past year who lives in a household falling below the poverty line, thus confusing family, employment, and wage issues). In 1998, French parliament passed a Law to Fight Poverty and Exclusion, which entailed the creation of a permanent National Observatory on Poverty and Exclusion (suggesting that the fight will not be won anytime soon).

electoral score achieved among the working class by the Socialist Party candidate who boasted at his campaign meetings of having slain the dragon of unemployment and who, unaware of the spectacular deterioration of the (sub)proletarian condition during his term in office, was promising the return of "full employment" by the end of the next term—a truly obscene slogan for the residents of housing estates subjected for two generations to the rampant desocialization of wage work.[5] In the first round of the 2002 presidential contest which resulted in his stunning elimination, Jospin lost 2.5 million votes from his 1995 total. He captured only 14 percent and 19 percent respectively of the vote of manual workers and noncredentialed white-collar workers (compared to 23 percent and 20 percent for Le Pen), about half of what he had drawn five years earlier. Among those with less than a high-school education, Jospin's share plummeted from 25 percent to 16 percent in five years. Had the leader of the Socialist Party retained an additional three percentage points of the workers' vote, he would have garnered the 195,000 ballots needed to take second place and likely gone on to win the second round against a feeble Chirac (who had the lowest score of a sitting president in the history of the Fifth Republic in the first round).[6]

On the main television channels, the nightly news has mutated into a chronicle of run-of-the-mill crimes that suddenly seem to teem and threaten on every side—here a pedophile school teacher, there a murdered child, somewhere else a city bus stoned or an outer-city tobacconist insulted by a group of unruly youths. Special broadcasts multiply at peak listening times, such as this episode of the program "This Can Happen to You," which, under the rubric of "school violence," unwinds the tragic story of a child who committed suicide as a result of a racket on the playground of his primary school—a completely aberrant case, but one instantly converted into a paradigm for the sake of boosting audience ratings.* Magazines are full to bursting with features about "the true figures," the "hidden facts," and assorted "explosive reports" on delinquency in which sensationalism vies with moralism; they periodically draw up the frightful cartography of "no-go areas"; and they tender essential "practical advice" for dealing with dangers decreed omnipresent and multiform.[7]

On all sides one hears the obsessive lament about the idleness of the authorities, the ineptitude of the justice system, and the fearful or exasperated indignation of ordinary folks. At the beginning of 2002,

*On the television show "This Can Happen to You," devoted to "insecurity" and broadcast on TF1 (the country's leading network) in prime time on February 13, 2002, the anchor insisted after every ultraviolent report that the crimes obligingly reenacted threaten to strike everyone and everywhere.

the Plural Left government led by Lionel Jospin multiplied conspicuous measures for repressive show that even its most obtuse members could hardly fail to realize would have no traction on the problems these measures were supposed to treat. One example that verges on the caricatural: the ruinous purchase of a bullet-proof vest *for every single gendarme and police officer* in France when upward of 90 percent of them never encounter an armed villain in the course of their entire career and when the number of law-enforcement agents killed on duty has dropped by one-half in ten years. The right-wing opposition was not to be outdone on this front and promised to do exactly the same as the government on all counts—only faster, stronger, and tougher. With the exception of the nongovernmental Left and the Greens, all the candidates for elected office thus promoted "security" to the rank of absolute priority for public action and hurriedly proposed the same primitive and punitive solutions: to intensify police operations; to zero in on "youths" (meaning working-class and immigrant youths), "recidivists," and the so-called hard core of criminals encrusted in the defamed suburbs (which conveniently excludes white-collar crime and official corruption); to speed up judicial proceedings; to make sentences tougher; and to extend the use of custody, including for juveniles, even though it has been demonstrated time and again that incarceration is eminently criminogenic for them. And, to make it all possible, they demanded in unison an unlimited increase in the means devoted to the lawful enforcement of social order. The head of state Jacques Chirac, himself a multirecidivist offender responsible for the organized looting of hundreds of millions of euros in public funds while mayor of Paris for two decades, impervious to all sense of shame, dared to call for "zero impunity" for minor offenses perpetrated in the neighborhoods ringing the city, whose residents have taken to nicknaming him "*Supervoleur*" (Super-thief) in reference to the multiple scandals in which he has been directly implicated.[8]

But this new political-discursive figure of "security" that unites the most reactionary Right and the governmental Left in all the major countries of Europe does not merely reiterate the "old persistent and indestructible myth" of modern society, described by Jean-Claude Chesnais in his *History of Violence in Western Society from 1800 to Our Times*, according to which violence is a phenomenon resulting from a long-term evolution, yet always totally unprecedented, springing up suddenly and intrinsically urban.* Its originality resides in *drawing most of its force*

*According to Chesnais, the endlessly reactivated modern myth of violence is "an old, familiar monster with three heads: novelty, continuity, and urbanity. For violence,

of persuasion from these two contemporary symbolic powers that are science and America—and, better yet, from their cross-breeding, that is, American science applied to American reality.

Just as the neoliberal vision in economics rests on models of dynamic equilibrium constructed by an orthodox economic science "made in the USA," the country that holds a near-monopoly over Nobel prizes in that discipline, so the law-and-order vulgate of the turn of the century presents itself in the guise of a scholarly discourse purporting to put the most advanced "criminological theory" at the service of a resolutely "rational" policy, a policy deemed ideologically neutral and ultimately indisputable since it rests on pure considerations of effectiveness and efficiency. Like the doctrine of generalized subordination to the market, the new security *doxa* comes straight from the United States, which, since the abrupt collapse of the Soviet empire, has become the beacon country of all humanity, the sole society in history endowed with the material and symbolic means to convert its historical particularities into a transhistorical ideal and then to make that ideal come true by transforming reality everywhere in its image.[9] And so it was to New York that, over the past several years, French politicians (as well as their British, Italian, Spanish, and German colleagues) of the Left as well as the Right have traveled as one on a pilgrimage, to signify their newfound resolve to crush the scourge of street crime and, for this purpose, to initiate themselves into the concepts and measures adopted by the authorities in the United States.* Backed by the science and policy of "crime control" tested in America, the new one-track "security-think" that now rules in most of the countries of the First World, and many of the Second, presents itself in the form of a *concatenation of scholarly myths*, that is, according to Pierre Bourdieu, a web of statements that intermingle "two principles of coherence: a proclaimed coherence, of scientific appearance, which asserts itself by proliferating outward signs of scientificity, and a hidden coherence, mythic in its principle."[10]

---

at all times, has been said to be new, increasing, and urban." *Histoire de la violence en Occident de 1800 à nos jours* (Paris: Pluriel, 1981), 431.

*In summer 1998, the Association of French Mayors sent Gilles de Robien (UDF) and Jean-Marie Bockel (PS) on a mission to New York to observe there the virtues of "zero tolerance." To publicize his book *État de violence* (State of Violence), a rote compilation of all the ultrarepressive clichés of the moment, the *Nouvel Observateur* published on 8 November 2001 praised Socialist senator Julien Dray as "Jospin's ace" because he had fully assumed the law-and-order turn negotiated by the Socialist Party after 1997. The supposedly progressive weekly noted with approval: "Known as an 'agitator' of ideas, it is on the stomping ground of Giuliani, the highly repressive mayor of New York, that he went for lessons."

One can examine the texture and take apart the operant mechanisms of the scholarly myths behind the neoliberal law-and-order reason circling around the planet in four steps. The first considers the notion, spread by leading "security experts," that, as America pacified its "supercriminal" society, countries like France overtook the United States on the dangerousness ledger and would therefore benefit from the importation of US-style penal measures. The second scrutinizes the contention, ardently promoted by the Manhattan Institute and associated think tanks on both sides of the Atlantic, that it is the police that made crime melt away in the American metropolis in the 1990s. The third shows that, *if* the New York City police had an impact on the incidence of offenses (a proposition for which there is scant empirical support), it was not through the wholesome moralizing suasion postulated by the "broken-windows theory" of policing, but due to bureaucratic expansion and intensified surveillance that violate the neoliberal mantra of small government. Lastly, it turns out that the aggressive campaign of class-cleansing of the streets waged by the New York City authorities under Rudolph Giuliani was guided not by criminological theory but by a folk belief embedded in the occupational lore of the police called "breaking-balls theory."

"Supercriminal" America Pacified and Overtaken by France

According to the first media and political myth, until recently the United States was ravaged by astronomical levels of crime but, thanks to exacting innovations in policing and punishment, it has "solved" the crime equation after the manner of New York City. During the same period, owing to their laxity, the countries of old Europe have let themselves be caught in a lethal spiral of "urban violence" that has caused them to suffer an uncontrolled epidemic of crime on the American pattern. Thus, such a self-styled "expert" on the question as Alain Bauer, the chief executive officer of Alain Bauer Associates, a "security consulting" firm, who happens to be an influential adviser to French Socialist cabinet members and a grand master of the Grand Orient (the main French Masonic order), could announce with fanfare in a leading national newspaper that, following a "historic crossing over of the curves" depicting the crime statistics of the two countries in 2000, "France is more criminogenic than the US."*

*The title of the article in *Le Figaro*, 18 June 2001, deserves to be quoted in full: "The stunning results of a comparison between the criminal statistic of the [French]

This astonishing "revelation," instantly propagated by all the mainstream media (Agence France Presse, France-Info, the main commercial television channel TF1, etc.), demonstrates that, on the topic of "insecurity," one can say anything and everything and be taken seriously so long as one joins in the catastrophic and repressive refrain of the day. In reality, thanks to the International Crime Victimization Survey (ICVS),* it has been well established for a solid decade that the United States has entirely ordinary rates of crime when these are measured by the *prevalence of victimization*—rather than by the statistics of crimes reported to the authorities, which are not constructed and collated on the same basis across countries and which, as all "specialists" worthy of the name know, are a more reliable indicator of the activity of the police than of criminals. The US victimization rates have long been comparable to, and even generally lower than, those of a good many other advanced countries, with the notable and readily explicable exception of homicide.[11] Thus, among the eleven postindustrial nations covered by the ICVS in 1995, that is to say, before the full-scale implementation of "zero tolerance," the United States ranked second after England for car theft and robbery as well as for assaults and threats; tied third with France, and far behind Canada and England, on the burglary scale; came in seventh, trailing Switzerland, Austria, and Holland, among others, for sexual offenses; and right at the tail of the pack (ninth) for the incidence of personal theft, with a score half as high as that of the Netherlands (see table 15). In all, a combined index of victimization covering eleven types of offenses puts *the United States of 1995 in seventh position* (with 24.2 percent of its residents having suffered one or several crimes during the previous year), well below Holland (31.5 percent)

Ministry of the Interior and those of the FBI: France is more criminogenic than the United States." Stunning indeed since this comparison is devoid of validity—a fact that even Bauer implicitly acknowledges when he concedes that "the statistical design [used] is haphazard, relative, partial, fragmentary, and biased"! On the rise of these new consultants and advisers on security, fake researchers and genuine propagandists-salesmen, see Pierre Rimbert, "Les nouveaux managers de l'insécurité: production et circulation d'un discours sécuritaire," in *La Machine à punir*, ed. Gilles Sainatti and Laurent Bonelli, 161–202 (Paris: L'Esprit frappeur, 2001).

*The International Crime Victimization Survey (whose existence Alain Bauer, like the leading government experts on this matter, seems unaware of) is a questionnaire survey of households conducted about every four years since 1989 by criminologists at the University of Leiden under the aegis of the Dutch Ministry of Justice and the United Nations' Interregional Criminological Justice Research Institute (based in Rome). It measures and compares the prevalence, incidence, and evolution of rates of victimization in some fifteen advanced countries.

Table 15. Criminal victimization rates in eleven postindustrial countries in 1995*

	11 crimes (ranking)	car theft	theft (personal and property)	burglary & attempted burglary	robbery	assaults & threats	sexual inciden
Holland	31.5 (1)	0.4	6.8	5.9	0.6	4.0	3.6
England & Wales	30.9 (2)	2.5	5.0	6.4	1.4	5.9	2.0
Switzerland	26.7 (3)	0.1	5.7	2.0	0.9	3.1	4.6
Scotland	25.6 (4)	1.7	4.5	3.9	0.8	4.2	1.3
France	***25.3 (5)***	***1.6***	***4.0***	***4.5***	***1.0***	***3.9***	***3.9***
Canada	25.2 (6)	1.5	5.7	6.2	1.2	4.0	2.7
United States	***24.2 (7)***	***1.9***	***3.9***	***5.6***	***1.3***	***5.7***	***2.5***
Sweden	24.0 (8)	1.2	4.6	2.4	0.5	4.5	2.9
Austria	18.9 (9)	0.1	5.0	1.4	0.2	2.1	2.1
Finland	18.9 (9)	0.4	3.2	1.3	0.5	4.1	2.5
North Ireland	16.8 (11)	1.6	2.5	2.6	0.5	1.7	1.2

*Prevalence rate = percentage of persons victimized at least once during that year

SOURCE: Constructed from John van Kesteren, Pat Mayhew, and Paul Nieuwbeerta, *Criminal Victimization Seventeen Industrialized Countries: Key Findings from the 2000 International Crime Victims Survey* (The Hagu WODC, Ministry of Justice, 2000), 178–80.

and England (30.9 percent), but also behind Switzerland, Canada, and France (fifth with 25.3 percent).[12] The least "criminogenic" countries then were, and by a wide margin, Ireland (16.9 percent) and Austria (18.9 percent). Yet it is to New York City, and not Dublin or Vienna, that the politicians and the new experts in crime control rushed from across Europe in search of the holy grail of security.

Only its stupendous homicide rate distinguishes America from the countries of western Europe: with ten murders for every 100,000 inhabitants at the beginning of the past decade, and six per 100,000 in 2002, that level remains nearly five times higher than those of France, Germany, or England. It is for this reason that the legal scholars Franklin Zimring and Gordon Hawkins entitled their canonical work on the criminal question in the United States, *Crime Is Not the Problem: Lethal Violence in America*:[13] America has a highly specific problem of *deadly violence by firearms*, especially acute in its collapsing ghettos and linked, on the one hand, to the free possession and circulation of some 200 million guns and handguns (four million Americans carry one on a daily basis and one-half of all households have one at home) and, on the other, to the weakness of the social-welfare system, the cultural force of acquisitive individualism, rigid racial segregation, extreme poverty at the bottom of the class structure, and the deep rooting of the illegal street economy in the impoverished districts of its major cities.[14]

If America is not the "supercriminal" society it is commonly believed to be, neither does the trend-line in violent crime in France, and more generally in Europe, converge with that of the United States, dominated as it is by deadly violence. Indeed, the rate of homicides and attempted homicides (taken together) in France *fell* by one-fifth during the closing decade of the century, from 4.5 per 100,000 inhabitants in 1990 to 3.6 in 2000. It is true that cases of "*vols avec violence*" (corresponding roughly to robbery) increased noticeably during these years but, far from striking "everyone everywhere," as the media would have us believe, offenses against persons are rare (they befall about 2 percent of the population in any given year); they remain heavily concentrated among the young working-class population residing in the country's declining urban periphery; and they are in the main relatively benign: the "assaults" reported to the authorities are *exclusively verbal* in half of the cases, and they entail physical injury in only one incident in four (they lead to hospitalization or a work-leave in only one case in twenty). As for burglary and thefts from and of vehicles, which are vastly more common than offenses against people, since they represent about 70 percent of recorded crime, they have fallen steadily since 1993.[15]

These trends revealed by official French statistics are confirmed by the ICVS survey: between 1996 and 2000, that is, in the very period when the catastrophic discourse on the "explosion" of criminality swelled to the point of saturating France's political and journalistic fields, the cumulative incidence of victimization for ten categories of offense *fell* from 43 to 34 per 100,000, corresponding to a *decrease superior* by one-fifth to the decline in crime recorded by the United States (from 47 to 40 percent).* This drop occurred in all types of offenses except for assault and battery, which we already noted are typically much less serious than this designation suggests and are moreover relatively rare (the incidence of vehicle theft is six times that for robbery, which affects only 1.8 in every one hundred residents). Thus, with 34 offenses per 100 in the year 2000, France registered an overall victimization rate close to that of Denmark (35 percent) and Belgium (33 percent), placing it

*Incidence is measured by the total number of victimizations reported per 100,000 residents; it is superior to prevalence (the percentage of inhabitants who have suffered at least one offense), since the same person may have been the victim of several crimes in the course of the year. See John van Kesteren, Pat Mayhew, and Paul Nieuwbeerta, *Criminal Victimization in Seventeen Industrialized Countries: Key Findings from the 2000 International Crime Victims Survey* (The Hague: WODC, Ministry of Justice, 2000), table 2, 180–81.

behind the United States and Canada (39 percent), and far at the rear of Holland (48 percent) and England (54 percent).

So the assertion that America was "supercriminal" but is no longer so thanks to the coming of "zero tolerance," while France is infested by crime (understand: because it failed to import this policy as a matter of national emergency), does not pertain to criminological argumentation but to ideological claptrap.* This does not stop Alain Bauer, its author, from giving lessons in "methodology" to the French authorities who consult him with deference (as evidenced by his testimony before the senate Information Commission on Crime on March 28, 2000); or enjoying the reputation of being a rigorous "criminologist" (no joke intended) among supposedly trustworthy journalists;** or serving as president of the Steering Committee of the National Observatory on Crime inaugurated with great pomp by interior minister Nicolas Sarkozy in November 2003.

It Is the Police Who Make Crime Melt Away

A recent report by the Manhattan Institute—a major promoter of the "class cleansing" of the streets and nerve center of the worldwide campaign to penalize poverty†—asserts it with emphasis: the sustained

*Alain Bauer's proclamation—"We can confirm, without serious risk of being contradicted, that France has just overtaken the United States in its crime rate" ("La France plus criminogène que les États-Unis," *Le Figaro*, 18 June 2001)—would be risible if not for the fact that the law-and-order drivel of the country's premier private merchant in security services is regularly relayed by the media and mistaken for criminological truths by state decision-makers and local elected officials, bamboozled by the profusion of figures that lend a scholarly appearance to his delirious discourse. The heist is capstoned with his book (coauthored with Émile Perez, controller general of the national police and former secretary general of the police inspector's union), *L'Amérique, la violence, le crime. Les réalités et les mythes*, published in 2000 by Presses Universitaires de France in a series with the resounding title "International Criminality." Under the appearance of a scholarly tome, it delivers a mindless compilation of official data downloaded en masse across the Atlantic from the web sites of the US judicial authorities (such as the Bureau of Justice Statistics), crudely wrapped in the most overused clichés about America—on the Wild West, the wicked city, race riots, drugs, the police—seemingly issued straight out of Hollywood B movies.

**In his chronicle on the program "Mots croisés" (on the public television channel France 2), on which the CEO of the security firm had just appeared, Dominique Dhombres writes: "Alain Bauer, the criminologist [sic], was once again accurate and instructive in his deliberately dispassionate and statistical approach of the phenomenon." *Le Monde*, 23 October 2002.

†It is this neoconservative institute, founded by Anthony Fischer (Margaret

drop in the statistics of reported crime in the United States over the past decade is due to the energetic and innovative action of the law-enforcement forces, after they were finally freed from the ideological taboos and legal yokes that previously shackled them. The paradigmatic case for this is offered by the spectacular turnaround achieved in New York by the Republican mayor Rudolph Giuliani under the leadership of his master police chiefs William Bratton and William Safir.[16] But there is a catch: here again facts are more stubborn than ideology, and all scientific studies converge in concluding that the police did not play the key role that the advocates of the penal management of social insecurity assign to it as a matter of *petitio principii*—far from it.

The first proof is that the drop in reported criminal violence in New York began *three years before* Giuliani ascended to power at the end of 1993 and continued at exactly the same pace after he took over city hall. During the last two years in office of his predecessor, David Dinkins, the homicide rate had sagged by 4 percent and 7 percent respectively, but the vast majority of New Yorkers believed that it was on the rise due to increased media coverage of crime (exacerbated by the reverberations of two major racial clashes involving a black-led boycott of Korean stores in the Flatbush area of Brooklyn in 1990 and a murder-riot between blacks and Hasidic Jews in Crown Heights in 1991). Better still: the incidence of homicides committed without the use of firearms in the city had been falling slowly but steadily *since 1979*; only gun-related murders declined sharply after 1990, after having taken off between 1985 and 1990 due to the boom of the crack trade; and neither of these two curves displays any particular inflection under Rudolph Giuliani.[17] Digging further, one finds that, based on official data from the NYPD, the aggravated assault rate in the city started to drop in 1988, the robbery rate in 1980 (except for a moderate surge in 1987–90), burglary in 1980, and vehicle theft in 1990. The aggregate index for all property crimes, combining burglary, larceny-theft, and motor vehicle theft, fell for 14 consecutive years from 1988 to 2002 (or during 18 of 22 years since 1980).[18] So clearly crime has fallen precipitously in New York, but this fall started long before Giuliani and Bratton came on the scene.

The second proof is that the ebbing of criminal violence is just as marked *in cities that did not adopt* the New York policy of "zero tolerance," including those that opted for a diametrically opposed approach,

---

Thatcher's mentor), that canonized the "broken windows theory" and the policy of "zero tolerance," and then pushed for their export to Europe and Latin America, after having (successfully) campaigned for the dismantling of public aid during the 1980s. Loïc Wacquant, *Les Prisons de la misère* (Paris: Raisons d'agir, 1999), 14–22.

such as Boston, San Francisco, and San Diego—these cities applied variants of "problem-solving policing," which strives to establish ongoing relationships with residents aimed at preventing offenses, rather than dealing with them *ex post* by all-out penal sanction.[19] In San Francisco, a policy of systematic "diversion" of delinquent youth toward job-training programs, counseling, and social and medical treatment made it possible to deflate the number of jail admissions by more than one-half while reducing criminal violence by 33 percent between 1995 and 1999 (compared with a 26 percent drop in New York City, where the volume of jail entries swelled by one-third during the same period).

As third proof, from 1984 to 1987 New York mayor David Dinkins had already implemented an aggressive and assiduous law-enforcement policy similar to that deployed after 1993, under the code name "Operation Pressure Point." This campaign was accompanied by a sharp *increase* in criminal violence, and especially homicides, because during those years the street commerce in drugs was booming.[20] Whence it emerges that, contrary to the claims of the promoters and importers of the "Bratton model," the policing strategy adopted by New York during the 1990s is *neither necessary nor sufficient* to account for the crime drop observed in that metropolis.

The comparison with Canada, a neighboring country endowed with a similar economic, demographic, and political structure, and whose overall level of crime is practically identical (with the notable exception of the incidence of murders, which is three times lower than south of the border), confirms this conclusion. With a few rare exceptions, between 1991 and 2001 all the regions of Canada recorded a marked decline in homicides, armed robberies, and burglaries of the same magnitude as that observed in the United States, even as the strategies of the law-enforcement forces, judicial expenses, and resort to confinement remained unchanged there. Indeed, owing to fiscal constraints, the ratio of police supervision in Canada (given by the number of officers divided by the total population) *fell* by 9 percent, and the country's incarceration rate sagged by 7 percent, against increases of 10 percent and 47 percent respectively in the United States during that interval.

As criminologist Marc Ouimet notes, "such a similarity of trends for different kinds of crime, for different regions in the same country, and for two different countries, supports resorting to general explanations to account for the declines" and points toward two exogenous forces driving this remarkable parallelism between the United States and Canada: the one-fifth drop in the number of people in the 20- to 34-year-old age bracket on both sides of their common border and the marked drop in unemployment in both countries, which allowed unskilled lower-class youths to find work and thus encouraged them to withdraw from the criminal economy.[21]

In point of fact, six factors, *all of them independent of the activity of the police and the justice system*, have acted in combination to sharply curtail the incidence of violent offenses in the large cities of the United States in the 1990s.* First, *flourishing economic growth*, unparalleled in the country's history in its scale and duration, effectively provided jobs and supplied incomes to millions of young men hitherto doomed to idleness or illegal trades, including many in the ghettos and barrios where unemployment retreated noticeably.[22] But the boom did not for that dent the endemic poverty of the segregated neighborhoods of the American metropolis, because most of these new jobs remained casual and underpaid: even as the unemployment rate in New York was cut by nearly one-half between 1993 and 2000, the city's official poverty rate remained unchanged at 20 percent throughout the decade of the 1990s. In fact, it was above all young Latinos who directly benefited from the improvement in the state of the deskilled labor market, as they stand ahead of blacks in the "hiring queue" of urban low-wage employers.[23] For blacks, the euphoric economic climate acted indirectly by raising their hopes for future mobility and by encouraging a growing fraction of teenagers to pursue postsecondary schooling, which in turn greatly reduced their probability of being involved in violent street crime, either as victims or as perpetrators.[24] Notwithstanding the persistence of underemployment and the extremely low level of wages in the new service sectors, detailed statistical studies suggest that the direct and indirect impacts of the rapid decline in aggregate unemployment explain about 30 percent of the decrease in the national crime rate.[25]

The second factor is the *twofold transformation of the drug economy*. To begin with, the retail trade in crack in impoverished neighborhoods gained structure and stability, so that resort to violence as a means of

*We shall list here separately the various factors *other than policing strategy*, whose simple addition suffices to account for the crime drop in New York during the closing decade of the twentieth century, to discount the police as a *lead cause*. But, of course, these factors interacted dynamically with each other, as well as with the very condition they helped produce (a declining incidence of lawbreaking). The daunting conceptual and operational complexities involved in teasing out the workings of the two-way relationship between crime and penal policies (whether at the front end with policing or at the back end with incarceration) are laid out in William Spelman, "What Recent Studies Do (and Don't) Tell Us about Imprisonment and Crime," *Crime and Justice* 27 (2000): 419–94.

regulating competition between rival gangs receded abruptly.[26] At the end of the 1980s this trade experienced explosive growth and, given that barriers to entry were virtually nonexistent, new entrepreneurs, often young and independent, were constantly coming forward to engage in deadly territorial struggles: in 1991, 670 of the 2,161 homicides recorded in New York City were linked to narcotics trafficking. A decade later, demand had settled down and the sector had become "oligopolized," so that the number of dealers fell and relations between them were less conflictual. This translated into a precipitous plunge in the volume of drug-related homicides—it dropped below the one-hundred mark by 1998—since the greater part of that criminal street violence is violence *between criminals*.[27] Next, crack lost favor with consumers, who returned to other opiates and narcotics, such as marijuana (consumed in the form of a cigar called a "blunt"), heroin, and methamphetamines, the trade in which generates less brutality because it is dominated by sellers operating within networks of mutual acquaintance rather than through anonymous exchanges in public places.[28] It is difficult to quantify the overall impact of this twofold reorganization of the drug economy on violent crime in New York City, but it is sensible to think that it may be of the same order of magnitude as that of the expansion of the wage-labor economy.

Third, as noted earlier, the *number of young people* (especially those between 18 and 24) shrank, which translated almost mechanically into a decline in street crime, since these age categories are, always and everywhere, statistically the most inclined to violent law breaking. This demographic evolution alone accounts for at least one-tenth of the drop in offenses against persons during the period under consideration.[29] To which one must add, in the case of New York City, the ghoulish statistic of candidates for crime put out of commission by the AIDS pandemic among heroin users (19,000 deaths recorded between 1987 and 1997), those killed by drug overdoses (14,000), gangsters slain by their colleagues (4,150) and put behind bars or deported (5,250), making a total of some 43,000 "troublemakers" physically eliminated over a decade, equal to the number of convicts sent from the city every year to expiate their misdeeds in the penitentiaries that dot the upstate countryside.[30] The recessive effect of the decrease in the young and criminal population was moreover amplified by a strong *upsurge in immigration*, especially of predominantly feminine migration streams coming from countries such as the Dominican Republic, China, and Russia. Emigrants from these countries arriving in New York during the decade of the 1990s had access to "ethnic niches" that facilitated their entry into the local economy so that, thanks to their commercial activity and consumption, they revitalized declining districts on the edges of the large black ghettos, enabling their inhabitants to "reclaim public space and deter outdoor criminal activity."*

But economic and demographic causes are not the only ones operating here. One must include, among the forces that have cut crime in the United States, a *generational learning effect*, christened the "little brother syndrome" by criminologists, by virtue of which the new cohorts of youths born after 1975–80 drew away from hard drugs and the murderous lifestyle associated with them in a deliberate refusal to succumb to the macabre fate they had seen overtake their older brothers, cousins, and childhood friends fallen on the front line of the "street wars" of the end of the 1980s: uncontrolled drug addiction, imprisonment for life, violent and premature death.[31] Witness the "truces" and "peace treaties" signed by the gangs that controlled the ghettos of Los Angeles, Chicago, Detroit, and Boston in the early 1990s, which sharply reduced the number of homicides of poor young males. For their part, the organizations left or arising inside the zones of relegation of the US metropolis, such as churches, schools, the gamut of associations, neighborhood clubs, collectives of mothers of child victims of street killings (such as MAD, Mothers Against Drugs, in Chicago, and Mothers ROC, Mothers Reclaiming Our Children, in Los Angeles),[32] mobilized and exercised their capacity for informal social control wherever they still could. Their *awareness and prevention campaigns*, such as operation "Take Back Our Community" organized by the Grand Council of Guardians (the black police association of New York City), have accompanied and bolstered the spontaneous withdrawal of many youths from the predatory economy of the streets. One should underline here, with Benjamin Bowling, the fact that, like the improvement of the economy, these collective initiatives of the residents of poor neighborhoods have been totally blacked out in the dominant discourse on the fall in criminality in the US, and have even been virulently denigrated by Rudolph Giuliani and William Bratton.[33]

Finally, the levels of criminal violence recorded by the United States at the beginning of the 1990s were *abnormally high* by historical stan-

*"The largely unplanned social experiment in multiculturalism of bringing together people speaking 121 different languages seems to have worked out very well, in the sense that it put a break on spiraling crime rates and even helped turn the tide." Andrew Karmen, *New York Murder Mystery: The True Story behind the Crime Crash of the 1990s* (New York: New York University Press, 2000), 225. Few European politicians intent on establishing their law-and-order credentials would dare draw the logical policy implication of this empirical teaching of the great New York crime tale: that the state should increase immigration in order to depress urban violence.

dards and were therefore very likely to turn downward, in keeping with the statistical law of regression toward the mean. This was all the more likely as the factors that had stimulated them to jump outside the norm (such as the initial takeoff in the crack trade) could not persist. By placing it in the *longue durée* of the twentieth century, the historian Eric Monkkonnen has shown how the period 1975–90 was atypical of the basic trends in violent crime in New York City: between 1900 and 1960 the homicide rate in America's symbolic capital stood a notch below the national average; it left this bracket after the race riots of the 1960s to come to rest at three times the countrywide figure, due to the lightning development of a drug economy regulated by armed confrontation; the swift ebb of the decade of the 1990s simply brought it back to around the national average where it had been a quarter-century earlier.[34]

There remains one major factor to recount, or rather to discount: the incarceration boom. At the national level, the most sophisticated and comprehensive review of existing simulation and econometric studies concluded that, under the most favorable set of hypotheses, "between 79 percent and 96 percent of the violent-crime drop [of the 1990s] cannot be explained by prison expansion," and that this drop would have occurred even in the absence of the country's stupendous carceral buildup.* In New York City specifically, there is moreover a glaring disconnect between policing, prosecution, and imprisonment, in that both the indictment rate and the conviction rate for felony arrestees

*William Spelman, "The Limited Importance of Prison Expansion," in *The Crime Drop in America*, ed. Alfred Blumstein and Joel Wallman, 97–129 (New York: Cambridge University Press, 2000), citation at 108 and 125. Note, however, that two tacit assumptions make even these low figures significant *overestimates* of the role of carceral growth. First, the counterfactual posited throughout by Spelman (ibid., 105–7, 127) is that "the billions of dollars invested in prison beds over the past two decades" would not have been available for and invested in other social welfare and/or crime prevention measures. Second, all "62 combinations of possible assumptions" examined measure only the *crime-suppressive* effects of imprisonment (ibid., 111–13). The *crime-generative effects* of hyperincarceration are never factored into the analysis, despite mounting evidence that the massive lockup of young black men has profoundly deleterious impacts upon the social fabric of the lower-class neighborhoods wherefrom they come that cannot but stimulate and entrench illegalisms there. Loïc Wacquant, "Deadly Symbiosis: When Ghetto and Prison Meet and Mesh," *Punishment & Society* 3, no 1 (winter 2001): 95–133; Todd R. Clear, Dina R. Rose, Elin Waring, and Kristen Scully, "Coercive Mobility and Crime: A Preliminary Examination of Concentrated Incarceration and Social Disorganization," *Justice Quarterly* 20, no. 1 (spring 2003): 33–64; and Jeffrey Fagan, Jan Holland, and Valerie West, "Reciprocal Effects of Crime and Incarceration in New York City Neighborhoods," *Fordham Urban Law Journal* 30 (2003): 1551–1600.

dropped steadily after 1992.[35] This suggests that, under the CompStat regime, the city police did make vast numbers of arrests, but a growing share of these arrests were based on weak, vague, or false charges that could not be sustained in court. So that, contrary to public perception, police activism did not translate into a greater ability to produce guilty pleas and convictions of serious offenders. That the city penal machine was growing more inefficient as it was getting more voracious is confirmed by the data assembled in table 16 below (page 263), showing that the ratio of jail admissions over arrestees dropped from 39 percent in 1993 (107,000 divided by 273,000) to 34 percent in 1998 (130,000 divided by 376,000). This interpretation is further supported by the fact that the number of arrests for misdemeanors was nearly equal to the volume of jail entries at the beginning of the period but came up to nearly twice that figure at the end.

The conjunction of the six factors briefly reviewed above—the economic boom and the restructuring of the street drug trade, the shrinking share of young lower-class males, the generational learning effect and grassroots efforts at prevention, and the long-term cyclical evolution of the homicide rate—is amply sufficient to explain the crash in violent crime in the American metropolis over the past dozen years. But the long and slow pace of scientific analysis is not the rapid and spasmodic tempo of politics and the media. With the help of a new wave of think tanks led by the Manhattan Institute, Giuliani's propaganda machine pounced on the inevitable lag in criminological research to fill the explanatory gap with its prefabricated discourse on the efficacy of police repression, disinterred as the sole remedy for the congenital wantonness of the dangerous classes. This discourse was all the more seductive in that, being framed in the trope of "responsibility," it echoed the individualistic and utilitarian thematics carried by the neoliberal ideology, now hegemonic on both sides of the Atlantic. But let us admit, for the sake of argument, that the police have had a discernible impact on crime in New York City. The salient question would then remain to figure out *how* it could have produced this outcome.

Behind "Zero Tolerance," Bureaucratic Reorganization and Activism

According to the planetary mythology diffused by neoliberal policy institutes and their allies in the political and journalistic fields, the New York police laid low the hydra of crime by implementing a very specific policy, called "zero tolerance," which professes to pursue without fail or respite the most minor infractions committed in public space. Thus, after 1993, anyone caught panhandling or loitering in the city, playing their car stereo too loud, throwing away empty bottles or writing graffiti on the streets, or even violating a mere municipal ordinance, was supposed to be automatically arrested and immediately thrown behind bars: "No more D.A.T.s [desk appearance tickets, requiring one to report later to the local police station where charges may then be laid]. If you peed in the street, you were going to jail. We were going to fix the broken windows [i.e., punish the slightest external indicators of disorder] and prevent anyone from breaking them again." This strategy, claimed its mastermind William Bratton, "would work in any city in America" and it would work just as well "in any city in the world."*

In reality, this policing slogan of "zero tolerance"—which has made its way all around the globe when, paradoxically, it is scarcely used any longer as a law-enforcement strategy in the US, where even some conservative politicians deem it offensive—is what Kenneth Burke calls a "terministic screen" that conceals, by the very fact of amalgamating them, several concurrent but quite distinct transformations in day-to-day law enforcement.[36] The New York police department effectively underwent four sets of concurrent changes:

1. A sweeping bureaucratic restructuring, entailing the decentralization of services, the flattening out of hierarchical levels, the lowering of the age of its managers (through the firing of three out of every four top-ranking officers), and the devolution of direct responsibility to precinct captains, whose remuneration and promotion depend partly on the standardized crime "figures" they produce (which creates strong pressure to manipulate statistics, for example, by multiplying the number of false arrests to display activism).

2. A stupendous expansion of human and financial resources: the num-

*This statement is excerpted from *Turnaround,* the "autobiography" in which Bratton offers a paean to his own life and brief stint as NYPD head with the assistance of a journalist specialized in rose-tinted biographies of sporting and political stars. William W. Bratton and Peter Knobler, *Turnaround: How America's Top Cop Reversed the Crime Epidemic* (New York: Random House, 1998), 229, 309. After being summarily fired by Rudolph Giuliani (who deemed the popularity of his chief of police excessive relative to his own), Bratton reconverted as an international "consultant in urban security" to better sell his expertise in the four corners of the planet, where he was summoned by politicians anxious to demonstrate publicly their resolve to fight crime. In 2002, he was named chief of the Los Angeles Police Department but, curiously, "zero tolerance" has been invisible in his reorganization of policing there (in part because there he simply lacks the very high density of officers to population that he built up in New York).

ber of uniformed officers leaped from 27,000 in 1993 to 41,000 in 2001, amounting to half as many police as the whole of France for only eight million residents! This growth in personnel was only possible thanks to an increase in the police budget of 50 percent in five years, which allowed it to top 3 billion dollars in 2000,[37] despite reductions in local government spending (in the same period, funds for the city's social services were amputated by 30 percent). During his second term of office, for example, Rudolph Giuliani allocated $80 million to a program called "Operation Condor" that enabled city police to work a sixth day of overtime every week. Meanwhile, for contrast, the municipal libraries cut back their opening hours and services due to a budget shortfall of $40 million (amounting to one-sixth of their funding).

3. The deployment of new information technologies, including the famed CompStat program (a scientific-sounding abbreviation that tritely means "computer statistics"), an electronic data-gathering and data-sharing system making it possible to track and scan the evolution and distribution of criminal incidents in real time. This pooling of geographically coded police intelligence is then coupled with monthly meetings of police commanders to "brainstorm" over tactical moves and expeditiously reallocate staff and resources to "hot spots." (In 1996, CompStat won the "Innovations in American Government" prize given by the Ford Foundation and the Kennedy School of Government at Harvard University. It was soon elevated to the rank, not only of supreme tool for scientific policing, but of "paradigm" for public management generally.)[38]

4. Finally, a thoroughgoing review of the objectives and procedures of every service, according to schemas worked out by consultants in "corporate reengineering," and the implementation of targeted "action plans" focused on the possession of firearms, drug dealing in public places, domestic violence, traffic violations, etc.

All in all, the New York City police was a bureaucracy rightly reputed to be cowardly, puffing, and passive, as well as corrupt, and set in the habit of waiting for crime victims to come and file complaints, which it was content to merely record with a constant concern to make the least possible waves in the media and the courts. Under Giuliani, it was transmogrified into the veritable simile of a zealous "security firm," endowed with colossal human and material resources and an offensive outlook. This much one can grant without contest. But, if this bureaucratic mutation had a pronounced impact on crime—and no one has so far succeeded in conclusively documenting any*—this impact had

*Based on a painstaking statistical analysis of available official data, the John Jay College criminologist Karmen finds, for instance, that contrary to the claims of city

little to do with the *particular policing strategy* adopted by the forces of order at ground level. It was a byproduct of shifting from reactive to proactive policing, from desk jobs to street patrols, a shift which mechanically generates more activity, and thus more deterrence and neutralization. As for the role of CompStat in stimulating efficiency and spreading tactical innovations across the city's 76 police precincts thanks to the weekly meetings of their commanders it stipulates, it pertains to "problem-solving policing" and not to "zero tolerance," as one of the coinventors of the "broken windows theory" readily concedes.[39]

Paradoxically, if the crime control approach of Giuliani stands out in his bureaucratic overhaul of city hall, it is as a *violation* of neoliberal principles of small government and reduced public expenditures. Along with his counterparts in Baltimore, Philadelphia, and Cleveland, the Republican mayor of New York was an aggressive proponent of the so-called New Management Strategy, which purports to import business protocols into public administration. But he definitely did not apply the principles of debureaucratization, downsizing, and privatization to policing, on the contrary.[40] During his first five years in office, Giuliani boosted public safety funding by 20 percent in constant dollars and cut social services expenditures by 9 percent, despite mounting human needs (by contrast, Dinkins had held the public safety budget constant and increased that for social services by 19 percent between 1990 and 1993). This amounts to a transfer of nearly *one billion dollars from social services to public safety*, with the brunt of the monies going to pay for the increase in uniformed staff, whose average wages and long-term benefits are much higher than those of civilian employees. In short, the

alleged success of law enforcement in New York came, not by following the model of "the entrepreneurial city," publicly celebrated by Giuliani and his Manhattan Institute mouthpiece,[41] but thanks to a "big-government" strategy of increasing budget and personnel, expanding the scope of public service, and boosting the missions of a high-cost bureaucracy well beyond its usual perimeter.

---

authorities, the new police tactics implemented under Giuliani did not produce an increase in arrest for firearms possession, nor a rise in the rate of clearance of crime complaints, no more than they led to an improvement in indicators of the preventive or repressive efficacy of the police. Karmen, *New York Murder Mystery*, 263–64. Similarly, a full decade into the fad of CompStat, statisticians Langan and Durose had found no scientific evidence that it was related in any way to the drop in crime in New York. Patrick Langan and Matthew R. Durose, "The Remarkable Drop of Crime in New York City" (working paper presented at the International Conference on Crime, ISTAT, Rome, 18–19 December 2003).

Table 16. Trends in arrests, recorded crime, jail admissions, and complaints against police in New York City, 1993–98

	1993	1994	1995	1996	1997	1998
Total arrests	272,718	328,782	353,331	360,685	384,642	376,316
Evolution	*100*	*120*	*130*	*132*	*141*	*138*
Arrests for misdemeanors	133,446	175,128	202,545	205,277	228,070	227,574
Evolution	*100*	*131*	*153*	*154*	*171*	*171*
Crimes recorded by police	600,346	530,121	444,758	382,555	355,893	323,192
Evolution	*100*	*88*	*74*	*64*	*59*	*54*
Arrests per 1,000 crimes recorded	**454**	**609**	**793**	**942**	**1,081**	**1,164**
Admissions to city jail	106,868	110,410	125,959	127,683	133,300	129,998
Evolution	*100*	*103*	*118*	*120*	*124*	*122*
Complaints for police brutality	3,596	4,877	5,618	5,550	4,768	4,962
Evolution	*100*	*136*	*156*	*154*	*133*	*138*

SOURCE: Arrests from New York Police Department, *Statistical Report: Complaints and Arrests* (New York: NYPD Office of Management Analysis and Planning, 1993–98); jail admissions: *Sourcebook of Criminal Justice Statistics* (Washington, D.C.: Bureau of Justice Statistics, 1994–98); complaints from Civilian Complaint Review Board, 1994–98 (New York).

This excessive zeal can be readily detected in table 16 above which shows that, under Giuliani, the city police became a wildly hyperactive machine for mass arrests out of all proportion with public need. Between 1993 and 1998, the volume of arrests in New York ballooned by 41 percent, driven mainly by arrests for minor offenses (the number of misdemeanants caught boomed by 71 percent), even as the total number of offenses reported to the authorities plummeted by 46 percent. As a result, by the third year of Giuliani's first term, the city police were making *more arrests than there were offenses reported* to them, and the number of complaints for police brutality (including excessive use of force, abuse of authority, and offensive language) had jumped 50 percent. In 1998, the New York Police Department made 1,164 arrests per 1,000 recorded offenses, as against 454 five years earlier. This grotesque ballooning of police stops and bookings puts us on the path to the fourth scholarly myth of the new law-and-order *doxa*.

From "Broken Windows" to "Breaking Balls"

The last worldwide security myth come from America is no less droll. This is the notion that the policy of "zero tolerance," supposedly responsible for the policing triumph of New York City, rests on a *scien-*

tifically proven criminological theory, the celebrated "broken windows theory." The latter postulates that the immediate and stern repression of the slightest violations or nuisance on the streets stems the onset of major criminal offenses by (re)establishing a healthy climate of order—a queer illustration of the popular French adage "he who steals an egg steals an ox." Reasserting the norm dramatizes respect for the law and thereby stems deviance. Now, this so-called theory is of dubious scientific status, to say the least: it was formulated twenty years ago by the ultraconservative political scientist James Q. Wilson and his acolyte George Kelling (the former chief of police of Kansas City, since reconverted into a Senior Fellow at the Manhattan Institute) in the form of a short text of nine pages published, not in a criminological journal subject to peer review by competent researchers, but in the cultural magazine *The Atlantic Monthly*.* And it has never received even the beginnings of an empirical verification since then.

In support of the "broken windows theory," its advocates cite as if by rote the book *Disorder and Decline*, published in 1990 by the Chicago political scientist Wesley Skogan, which traces the causes of, and evaluates the remedies for, social and ecological dislocations in urban areas on the basis of a battery of surveys in 40 neighborhoods in 6 US cities. But, upon close reading, it turns out that this work shows that it is poverty and racial segregation, and not the climate of "urban disorder," that are the most potent determinants of crime rates in the metropolis. Moreover, its statistical conclusions have been invalidated due to an accumulation of measurement errors and missing data; and its author himself grants the illustrious "broken windows theory" the status of a mere "metaphor."[42] Indeed, no study designed to validate the ratchet (or scotch) effect postulated by this theory (according to which the suppression of minor offenses would limit the incidence of major ones), such as the survey carried out by Albert Reiss in Oakland, California, and that of Lawrence Sherman in the federal capital Washington, has succeeded in turning up evidence for it. The comparative analysis of systematic data collected in 196 districts of Chicago on the basis of interviews and daily video recordings has even conclusively shown that there exists no statistical relation between the visible indicators of "disorder" in a given area and its crime rates (with the possible and partial exception of burglary).[43]

*James Q. Wilson and George Kelling, "Broken Windows: The Police and Neighborhood Safety," *Atlantic Monthly* 249 (March 1982): 29–38. This did not prevent it from being published in French translation in 1999 in the official journal of the Institut des Hautes Études de la Sécurité Intérieure.

At the conclusion of a painstaking examination of the question, legal scholar Bernard Harcourt argues that if the New York police department contributed to the decline in crime, it was not by reestablishing civility and communicating a message of stern refusal of impunity, but by the simple fact of having massively increased the intensity of the surveillance it wields: in 1990 Giuliani's city had 38 police for every 100,000 inhabitants; ten years later it deployed twice that number, and their action was strongly targeted on dispossessed populations and districts.[44] In short, it is the *accentuation and concentration of police and penal repression*, and not the moral mechanism of the restoration of the norm postulated by the so-called theory of Wilson and Kelling, that would account for police effectiveness in the case—itself still hypothetical—where policing would have played a significant role in reducing crime.*

But there is a still more comical side to this tale: the adoption of permanent police harassment of the poor in public space by the city of New York had, *on the admission of its own inventors, no link whatsoever with any criminological theory*. The famous "broken windows theory" was in reality discovered and invoked by city officials only a posteriori, in order to dress up in rational garb measures that were popular with the (mostly white and bourgeois) electorate, but fundamentally discriminatory in both principle and implementation, and to give an innovative spin to what was nothing other than a reversion to an age-old police recipe, periodically put back to work and in fashion. Jack Maple, the "genius of the war against crime"[45] and Bratton's right-hand man, who was the initiator of "quality-of-life policing" in the subway before it was extended to the streets, says so explicitly in his autobiography published in 1999 under the cowboyish title *Crime Fighter*: "'Broken Windows' was merely an extension of what we used to call the 'Breaking Balls' theory," issued from conventional police wisdom. This folk notion stipulates that if the cops persistently go after a notorious bandit for peccadilloes, he will, for the sake of peace and quiet, end up leaving the neighborhood to go and commit his lawbreaking somewhere else. When he does the local rate of crime automatically diminishes. Maple's innovation consisted in "modernizing" this notion as "Breaking Balls

*One can only hope that the experts of the Institut des Hautes Études de la Sécurité Intérieure, who played a decisive role in spreading the scholarly myth of the "broken window" in France, will be eager to read and recommend (and, indeed, to publish in translation) Harcourt's meticulous critique of the theoretical corruptions and juridical perversions that underpin the doctrine and implementation of "zero tolerance" in the United States.

Plus" (to use his own expression), by linking identity checks to judicial databases so as to arrest the maximum number of villains sought for other offenses or already under judicial supervision via probation or parole.[46]

The architect of Giuliani's policing policy openly sneers at those who believe in the existence of "a mystical link between minor incidents of disorder and more serious crimes"—the core crime-inducing mechanism postulated by "broken windows." The idea that the police could reduce violent crime by cracking down on incivilities seems to him plainly "sad," and he gives a wealth of examples refuting this preposterous notion drawn from his professional experience in New York and New Orleans. He even compares a mayor who would adopt such a policing tactic to a doctor who "give[s] a face-lift to a cancer patient" or an underwater hunter who catches "dolphins instead of sharks." And, to avoid all ambiguity, Maple hammers the point home: "'Quality-of-Life Plus' is not 'zero tolerance'." Quite the opposite, it implies directing *police activity onto those social categories and territories presumed to be central crime vectors* to avoid wasting finite resources of time and personnel to enforce the law.[47]

This insider view confirms external observations suggesting that, in order to be applicable at ground level, the rhetoric of zero tolerance must mutate into its very opposite, selective intolerance and targeted enforcement, in definite places and times, of certain statutes chosen because of their high practical or political value*—such as those repressing the long string of lower-class "antisocial behaviors" appearing in Bratton's discriminating list of street nuisances.[48]

The Architect of "Zero Tolerance" Rejects the "Broken Windows Theory"

[Following] reports of a dramatic drop in violent crime [in New York], many people credited the "Broken Windows" notion that the crooks had suddenly taken to the

*In their approving review of the implementation of zero tolerance in New York in the 1990s, two noted police scholars remark: "Properly applied, assertive policing" devolves into "selective enforcement as part of overall strategies, targeted to specific problems, whether related to drugs, guns, youths or social clubs. . . . All are directed towards particular problems based on their geographical and temporal crime distributions that we know generally falls into clusters. . . . Thus *it is not only not viable but undesirable to practice zero tolerance everywhere all the time*." Eli B. Silverman and Jo-Ann Della-Giustina, "Urban Policing and the Fear of Crime," *Urban Studies* 38, nos. 5–6 (May 2001): 954. My emphasis.

> straight and narrow because they had picked up on the prevailing civility vibe. That's not how it works.
>
> Rapists and killers don't head for another town when they see that graffiti is disappearing from the subway. The average squeegee man doesn't start accepting contract murders whenever he detects a growing tolerance for squeegeeing. Panhandling doesn't turn a neighborhood into Murder Central. . . . Quality-of-life enforcement works to reduce crime because it allows the cops to catch crooks when the crooks are off-duty, like hitting the enemy planes while they're still on the ground.—JACK MAPLE, NYPD *Deputy Commissioner*[49]

Jack Maple would no doubt be astonished to read the following statement in "Memorandum No. 31," drafted by the "experts" of the Institut des Hautes Études de la Sécurité Intérieure, the pseudoresearch arm of the French Ministry of the Interior charged with conducting studies justifying the punitive turn of the Plural Left government, to guide mayors in elaborating "local security contracts" for their city:

> American studies have shown that the proliferation of incivilities is nothing but the early warning sign of a general rise in crime. The initial deviant behaviors, no matter how minor they seem, inasmuch as they become general, stigmatize a neighborhood, attract other forms of deviance into it, and herald the end of everyday social peace. The spiral of decline is set off, violence takes root, and with it every kind of crime: assaults, burglaries, drug trafficking, etc. (see J. Wilson and T. [*sic*] Kelling, "*The Broken Windows Theory*").
>
> It is on the basis of these research findings that the New York chief of police put in place a battle strategy called "zero tolerance" against the authors of incivilities, which seems to have been one of the causes of the very marked reduction of crime in that city.[50]

One finds it hard to curb a mounting *sentiment of incredulity* in the face of such an outpouring of falsehoods, not to say transatlantic tripe, and the gullibility to which they attest. For the tactic of permanent police persecution of the poor in the streets implemented in New York is nothing other than the systematic and deliberate application of folk "theories" based on the professional common sense of policemen. It pertains not to criminology but to "crookology," as Jack Maple would say (he was fond of defining himself as a "crookologist").* But, precisely, such common sense does not, in this instance, make much sense.

*France also has its academic "crookologists," the most active being political scientist Sébastien Roché (presented by his publisher as "one of the experts in matters of insecurity most frequently consulted by cities as well as national ministries"). With

A rigorous and thorough evaluation, by two of the country's best specialists, of the scientific inquiries conducted over the past twenty years in the United States with the aim of testing the effectiveness of the police in the fight against crime concludes, soberly, that neither the number of officers thrown into the battle, nor internal changes in the organization and culture of law-enforcement agencies (such as the introduction of community policing), nor the strategies that target places and groups with a strong criminal propensity (with the "possible and partial exception" of programs aimed at outdoors drug trafficking) have by themselves any impact on the evolution of offenses.* In a final twist of irony, among all the various police strategies reviewed, the authors spotlight "CompStat" and "zero tolerance" as "*the least plausible candidates* for contributing to the reduction of violent crime" in urban America in the 1990s, and they conclude: "There is one thing that is a myth: [that] the police have a substantial, broad, and *independent* impact on the nation's crime rate."[51]

Like Russian dolls, these four scholarly myths from across the Atlantic nest into each other so as to form a kind of logical chain, with the air of an implacable syllogism, making it possible to justify without resistance the adoption of an aggressive policy of "class cleansing" of the city streets. This policy is fundamentally discriminatory in that it rests on an equivalence between behaving outside the norm and being an outlaw, and it targets neighborhoods and populations suspected beforehand, if not held guilty on principle, of moral deficiencies, nay legal offenses. If it is true that US society, for so long "supercriminal," has been pacified by the action of the police just when other countries have been struck

---

figures aplenty, Roché applies himself with an energy that commands admiration to "extending" to France an American theory that has been invalidated in the United States, and the policies associated with it, even if he suggests using other channels to operationalize them—such as enrolling social workers in the machine to fight crime among the poor. See especially his book *Tolérance zéro? Incivilités et insécurité* (Paris: Odile Jacob, 2002), where, confusing correlation with causation, he maintains that "incivilities" lead to criminal offenses—as rain would invariably lead to fair weather—whose publication was rushed so as to fall right between the two rounds of the spring 2002 presidential election, with the effect of throwing a little scholarly fuel on the raging law-and-order fire.

*The two criminologists insist: "The most plausible hypothesis is that these police actions interacted with other criminal justice policies (such as imprisonment) and social forces (such as the aging of the population or the decline of outside retail drug markets). . . . Some form of interaction is more plausible than a claim that changes in policing were the sole or greatest contributor to the drop in violent crime." John E. Eck and Edward R. Maguire, "Have Changes in Policing Reduced Violent Crime?" in *The Crime Drop in America*, ed. Blumstein and Wallman, 245 and 248.

full force by an "explosion" of crime; that New York City, Mecca of the new American policing religion, has crushed criminal violence thanks to its policy of "zero tolerance"; and that this policy itself was articulated in conformity with a sound criminological theory ("broken windows"), then indeed how could one not rush to import these notions and instigate the measures for which they seemingly supply a rational foundation?

In reality, the four key propositions of the new "made-in-USA" security vulgate now being diffused throughout Western Europe are devoid of scientific validity, and their practical efficacy rests on a collective faith without foundation in reality. But, strung together, they function as a planetary launching pad for an intellectual hoax and an exercise in political legerdemain that effectively taps class fears and ethnic prejudice to justify the rolling out of the penal state. By giving a pseudo-academic warrant to sweeping police activism, these scholarly myths contribute powerfully to legitimating the shift toward the penal management of the social insecurity that is everywhere being generated by the social and economic disengagement of the state.

9

Carceral Aberration Comes to France

In March of 2003, the French Ministry of Justice launched a television advertising campaign aimed at furbishing the image of the country's correctional administration and thereby attract the 10,000-odd guards who needed to be hastily recruited to meet the programmed explosion of the country's carceral population. Three months later, the numbers under lock passed the 60,000 mark for 48,000 thousand beds, the highest figure posted since the end of German occupation during the second World War. Insalubrity, dilapidation, overcrowding pushed to the point of paroxysm, catastrophic hygiene, severe staff shortages and flagrant failings of job training and work programs debasing the goal of "reintegration" to the rank of a slogan as hollow as it is cruel, congestion of visiting rooms, multiplication of protest movements by convicts, and the relentless rise of serious incidents of violence and suicides (their rate doubled in twenty years to claim the European record) were the object of unanimous complaints by the guards and magistrates unions, the national bar association (Conseil national des Barreaux), human rights organizations, the families of inmates, and penal activists and researchers.[1] Without for that eliciting the slightest response on the part of the authorities, who even reduced the traditional presidential pardons on July 14 the better to display their firm will to fight what the head of state—who has rock-solid personal experience on this front*—called with theatrical ire "impunity."

At the end of January 2004, the European Committee for the Prevention of Torture published a scathing report on the "inhumane and degrading treatment" that is the common lot of French detainees stacked in conditions of quasi-feudal overcrowding, up to five in a twelve-square-meter cell in some jails, and whose elementary rights are thus flouted daily, starting with the right to an individual cell, established

*A constitutionally dubious claim to presidential immunity was the only hurdle that prevented Jacques Chirac from being indicted in 2000 for his personal involvement in a string of financial scandals at the City of Paris (of which he was mayor for two decades prior to acceding to the presidency). His surprise reelection in April 2002 extended the judicial shield for another five years.

by the law of June 15, 2000, on the presumption of innocence, whose application has been endlessly postponed in violation of the country's engagements before the Council of Europe. (This right, established in 1968 and confirmed in 1975, is supposed to allow for the individualization of penal sanctions, but it has never been respected by the correctional administration.) This report echoed those produced at the beginning of 2000 by three commissions of inquiry mandated by the National Assembly, the Senate, and the minister of justice, all of which denounced the drift of the French correctional system toward a "'skid row' prison" ("*une prison cour des miracles*") wherein "penal arbitrariness" and "the law of the stronger" reign—the senators went so far as to speak unanimously of a "humiliation for the Republic."[2] Yet one month later Justice Minister Perben smugly brushed aside the criticisms of the European jurists, asserting that France simply suffers from a delay in the construction of new penitentiaries, which it is working overtime to make up. And he promptly added that, with 98 inmates per 100,000 inhabitants, France has ample room for increase, since other European countries post incarceration rates at least a third higher.*

This is because the government of Jean-Pierre Raffarin has—after that of his left-wing predecessor Lionel Jospin—made policing zeal and penal severity into a major electoral theme, nay a political dogma. The result is that, in the two years following Chirac's reelection, the population behind bars rose by some 13,000 detainees and convicts to reach 64,813 in mid-2004. Increasing resources and intensifying actions by the forces of order in "sensitive zones"; putting bureaucratic and political pressure upon judges to stiffen sentences and speed up procedures (one-third of those committed to detention now come from summary proceedings involving no police inquiry and no possibility for bringing exculpatory witnesses and evidence called "*comparutions immédiates*," as against one-quarter a decade earlier); the general expansion of recourse to custody and upward translation of the scale of sanctions; the hardening of dispositions leading to remand detention, now

*The minister of justice cited in particular the rates of Spain and Portugal, which exceeded 130 per 100,000, while conveniently omitting countries that incarcerate less than France, among which figure Germany, Austria, Switzerland, the Scandinavian nations, Belgium, Ireland, Greece, and even Turkey. See Isabelle Mansuy, "Réponse au CPT: circulez y'a rien à voir!" *Dedans dehors* 42 (March 2004): 3–4. When France catches up with the European Union leader, Great Britain (which posted 143 prisoners per 100,000 inhabitants in April 2004 after a 55 percent increase in its carceral population in a decade), it will be time, according to this reasoning, to compare France with still more punitive countries, like Slovakia (165), then Romania (200) and Poland (224), and finally Ukraine (417) and Russia (584).

extended to youths between 13 and 16 for simple misdemeanors; the rolling back of intermediate sanctions and sentence relief measures; the decline of parole, probation, and placement in halfway houses: all these measures converge to swell the stock behind bars. If the country were to continue on this trend, it would double its carceral stock in less than five years, *twice as fast as the United States at the height of the carceral bulimia* of the 1980s that made it the world leader in penal confinement (with 710 detainees per 100,000 inhabitants in 2004).* Fascinated by the rapid deployment of novel digital technologies for crime control in the United States and the United Kingdom, France has also been moving at blinding speed in the compilation and use of a centralized data bank of genetic identification of crime convicts and suspects.[3]

The "national automated database for genetic fingerprints" (*fichier national automatisé des empreintes génétiques*, or FNAEG), created by the Guigou law of June 1998 in response to the arrest of a multirecidivist sexual killer identified thanks to DNA tracing, was initially reserved for sex offenders. But, only three years after its creation, the Vaillant law on "everyday security" of November 2001 surfed on the surging hysteria over terrorism to extend it to persons convicted of criminal violence and serious property crimes. In March of 2003, the Sarkozy law on "domestic security" not only further enlarged its scope to cover an array of run-of-the-mill offenses ranging from narcotics trafficking and pimping to fencing and minor acts of theft and vandalism (including "tagging" and the uprooting of genetically modified crops); it also authorized the storage of DNA profiles collected from mere suspects ("persons against which exists serious or converging indications making it plausible that they committed offenses"), and it stipulated that the refusal to submit a DNA sample to the authorities be punished by a fine of 7,500 euros and six months in jail. The Perben II law of 2004 capped this runaway extension by making the collection of genetic fingerprints mandatory for all inmates serving sentences in excess of ten years (but, remarkably, no financial and white-collar crime qualifies its convicts or suspects for DNA fingerprinting). As a result, the FNAEG has grown explosively, from 2,100 individuals in 2002 to 45,000 in 2004 to a whopping 283,000 by mid-2006. And there is plenty of room for growth since, on pretext of modernizing the technical and scientific means of

*Since such a stupendous growth would be unmanageable politically, materially, and financially, one can predict that the French government will continue to use the presidential "clemency right" as a queer safety valve and reduce sentences across the board yearly on Bastille Day (or similar measures) to limit through the backdoor the runaway expansion of the inmate population it is pursuing through the front door.

policing, the French authorities hope to catch up with Great Britain, which boasts a national criminal database covering three million individuals, fully 5 percent of the country's population.

Where the so-called Plural Left practiced a surreptitious and shameful penalization of poverty, the republican Right has fully assumed its choice to contain the social distress and disorders accumulating in the neighborhoods of relegation undermined by mass joblessness and flexible employment by deploying the police and justice apparatus with vigor and bombast. Indeed, making the fight against street delinquency into a moral spectacle enables the current political leaders (as it did their predecessors) to symbolically reaffirm the authority of the state at the very moment they declare its impotence on the economic and social front. The staging of this grim law-and-order spectacle also gives them the hope to attract a contingent of voters seduced by the authoritarian and xenophobic program of the National Front. And when the results at the polls turn out to be disappointing, as was the case for the Plural Left government in the 2001 municipal elections and for the new Right majority in the regional ballot of the winter of 2004, there is only one remedy: to further accentuate penal pressure and subordinate more closely the operations of the correctional administration to that of the justice system, and judicial policy to the unbridled activism of the police.

The Prison as Vacuum Cleaner of Social Detritus

But using the prison in the manner of a *social vacuum cleaner* to sweep up the human detritus from the ongoing economic transformations and to remove the dross of the market society from public space—occasional petty delinquents, the unemployed and the indigent, the homeless and undocumented immigrants, the drug addicts, handicapped, and mentally ill cast aside by the slackening of the health and social safety net, and youths from the (sub)proletariat consigned to a life of marginal jobs and hustling by the normalization of precarious wage labor—is an aberration in the strict sense of the term, defined by the 1835 *Dictionnaire de L'Académie française* as a "deviation of imagination" and an "error of judgment," political as well as penal.

It is an aberration, first of all, because the evolution of crime in France in no way justifies the stupendous boom of its carceral population after the moderate ebb of 1996–2001. In the preceding chapter we noted that burglary, auto theft, and theft from vehicles (which make up three-quarters of the offenses recorded by the authorities) have declined steadily since at least 1993. Homicide and manslaughter have likewise receded since 1995 according to police data, since 1984 according to figures from the National Institute for Health and Medical Research (Inserm). And, while "*vols avec violence*" (theft carried out by means of threats, corresponding roughly to robbery) that obsess the major media have indeed increased, this rise has been proceeding for twenty years at a steady rate, and these offenses are composed mainly of verbal "violence" (insults, threats).[4] There has been no sudden spike in crime that could mechanically explain the abrupt all-around interventionism of the state on this front.

Similarly, contrary to the overwhelming impression created by the recent fixation of the media on the question, the concern for security today is neither new nor exceptionally acute among the population. Surveys of "agorametry" show that fear of crime (as measured by agreement with the statement, "I do not feel safe") has remained relatively stable over the past two decades, aside from three modest peaks in 1978, 1983–85, and 1999–2001, and that, after increasing for three years, in 2001 it reached only the 1978 level.[5] Finally, we know that fear of crime is not related to its actual incidence, since the predominant image of anonymous violence that can strike anyone anywhere, but especially the most vulnerable people such as seniors, women, and ordinary passersby, is completely at odds with the social and spatial distribution of offenses. Thus one-half of French people who said they had been victim of an act of violence in 1996 (a tiny minority of 5 percent of the country's adults over 25) knew their aggressor; three percent of those questioned had been assaulted in the street as against 10 percent in their home and 13 percent at their workplace. Youths 25 to 29 were three times more likely to be victims of violence than those in their sixties, and men likelier than women (even controlling for their differential rate of presence in public space). Finally, the fear of crime at home was as common in rural areas as in cities (10 percent) and as pronounced in private residences as in large housing projects, whereas in both cases offenses are significantly more frequent in the latter.[6] In short, it is less crime that has changed in recent years than the gaze that politicians and journalists, as spokespersons for dominant interests, train on street delinquency and on the populations that are supposed to feed it—at the forefront of whom figure working-class youths issued from North-African immigration, fenced in the suburban housing projects eviscerated by three decades of economic deregulation and urban withdrawal by the state, so many gaping wounds that the administrative poultice of "urban policy" has failed to cauterize.

It is an aberration, next, because comparative criminology establishes beyond contest that there exists no robust correlation—in any country at any time—between the rate of imprisonment and the level of crime.[7] The United States is commonly invoked as an example of a nation that has rolled back offenses by reinforcing penal repression and committing to mass incarceration. But we saw in the previous chapter that the most rigorous studies on the question conclude, to the contrary, that the policing strategy of "zero tolerance" showcased in New York City and the fourfold increase in the population stock held behind bars over a quarter-century in the country played only a decorative role in a steep crime drop that resulted from an unusual conjunction of economic, demographic, and cultural factors. At any rate, in the scenario most favorable to repressive policies, prison only treats a tiny fraction of even violent crimes, owing to the cumulative evaporation that occurs at the different stages in the penal chain: in the United States, despite its grotesquely outsized police and carceral apparatus, the four million most serious offenses against persons identified in 1994 by studies of victimization (homicide, aggravated assault, robbery, and rape) produced fewer than two million complaints to the police. These triggered 780,000 arrests, which themselves ultimately led to only 117,000 admissions to prison—corresponding to 3 percent of the offenses committed, *leaving 97 percent of grievous criminal violence untouched*.[8] This means that, whether Right or Left, any policy claiming to treat even violent crime solely with the criminal justice apparatus is condemning itself to programmed inefficiency.

The same "funnel effect" can be observed in the functioning of penal justice in France, where fewer than 2 percent of complaints brought to prosecutors lead to a custodial sentence. The 5,461,024 complaints received by French prosecutors in 2002 produced 3,733,366 cases that could not be prosecuted (either because the offenses were incorrectly characterized or for failure to identify a culprit) and 1,350,393 that could be pursued by criminal justice. Of these, over a third (429,505 cases) led to an unconditional discharge (owing to a withdrawal of the complaint or the absence of the complainant, damages being too minimal, the deficient mental state of the culprit, the shared responsibility of the victim, etc.), while 289,483 triggered a procedure other than prosecution, for a remainder of 624,650 legal prosecutions (11.4 percent of the original total). Taking all jurisdictions together, these prosecutions led to 477,935 penal convictions, including 99,682 unsuspended prison sentences (in whole or in part) and 1,355 penalties of long-term reclusion—for a "carceral response" covering 1.8 percent of the complaints brought to prosecutors (101,037 divided by 5.4 million).[9] This is to say that, on both sides of the Atlantic, the prison is a grossly inefficient response to crime, fundamentally unfit for fighting petty and middling delinquency, and a fortiori "incivilities" that for the most part do not even pertain to the penal code (threatening looks, aggressive attitudes, insults, elbowing, gatherings and rowdiness in public places, minor deterioration, etc.). More evidence that penal repression is as ineffective in France as elsewhere, if any were needed: prison sentences for minors soared from 1,905 in 1994 to 4,542 in 2001, and the remand detention of adolescents practically doubled, shooting from 961 to 1,665, and yet juvenile delinquency increased continuously during this period, if official statements on the matter are to be believed. In short: France's recent penal record already proves that more youth incarceration does *not* produce a drop in youth delinquency, any more than carceral expansion reduces crime in general.

In the third place, the knee-jerk recourse to incarceration to stem urban disorders is a remedy that, in a good many cases, only aggravates the malady it is supposed to cure. As an institution predicated on brute force and operating at the margins of legality (despite the repeated recommendations of innumerable official commissions, French inmates are still deprived of a definite juridical status),[10] the prison is a crucible of violence and daily humiliations, a vector of family disaffiliation, civic distrust, and individual alienation. And, for many inmates marginally involved in unlawful activities, it is a school for training and even "professionalization" in criminal careers. For others, and this is hardly better, confinement is a bottomless pit, a hallucinogenic hell that extends the logic of social destruction they know on the outside by redoubling it with personal demolition.[11] The ordinary functioning of houses of detention is characterized by a complete disconnect between the punishment stipulated by judicial discourse and that effectively inflicted which generates a "radical skepticism reinforced by a deep feeling of injustice among the prisoners."* Penal history shows, moreover, that at no time and in no society has the prison been able to fulfill the task of rehabilitation and social reintegration which is supposed to be

*Gilles Chantraine, *Par-delà les murs. Expériences et trajectoires en maison d'arrêt* (Paris: Presses Universitaires de France, 2004), 249. From this angle, the chaos of carceral life only extends and intensifies the experience of judicial arbitrariness, as documented by the Cimade report, *Les Prétoires de la misère. Observation citoyenne du tribunal correctionnel de Montpellier* (Paris: Causes communes, special issue, January 2004), and the judicial chronicles of Dominique Simonnot, *Justice en France. Une loterie nationale* (Paris: Editions de La Martinière, 2003).

its mission from the point of view of reducing recidivism. As a French prison guard curtly noted, "reintegration, it's not something you do in prison. It's too late. You have to integrate people by giving them work, equal chances at the start, in school. You have to integrate. For us to 'do rehab' is fine, but it's too late."[12] Not to mention that everything, from the architecture of facilities to the organization of the daily chores of correctional officers to the indigence of institutional resources (for work, training, education, health), the deliberate drying up of parole release, and the absence of concrete programs of support upon exit, contradicts the supposed mission of "reforming" the convict. What is more, a growing segment of the carceral population is in need not of criminal correction but health care: according to various medical studies, 20 to 30 percent of inmates in France suffer from serious psychiatric disorders and should be urgently diverted into medical establishments.[13]

Finally, one must emphasize, in response to those who invoke the ideal of social justice to justify the intensification of penal repression in dispossessed neighborhoods, on the pretext that "security is a right; insecurity is a social inequality"[14] that affects primarily citizens at the bottom of the social ladder—as Lionel Jospin was fond of rehashing when he was prime minister*—that *carceral contention disproportionately strikes the most vulnerable social categories* on both the economic and cultural scales, and does so all the harder as they are more impoverished. Like their counterparts in other postindustrial countries, the inmates of France come overwhelmingly from the unstable fractions of the urban proletariat. Raised in large families (two-thirds have at least three siblings) which they left early (one in seven departed home before age 15), the majority lack educational credentials (three-quarters exited school before turning 18, as against 48 percent of adult males as a whole; one-third are estimated to be illiterate), which sentences them for life to the peripheral sectors of the employment sphere. One-half are sons of manual workers and uncredentialed white-collar staff, and one-half are themselves workers (as against 3 percent for the children of mid- to upper-level executives, who account for 13 percent of the economically active population). Four inmates in five have a father born abroad and 24 percent were themselves born on foreign soil.[15] What is more, incarceration only intensifies poverty and isolation: 60

*For his part, Jean-Pierre Chevênement, who as interior minister presided over the law-and-order conversion of the governmental Left, liked to emphasize the alleged "pedagogical virtues" of penal sanctions and even imprisonment. See his remarks in "La répression a aussi une vertu pédagogique," *Le Parisien*, 30 March 2000.

percent of those leaving the French prison system are jobless, compared to 50 percent of those entering it; 30 percent have no one supporting or waiting for them outside; more than one-quarter have no money (less than 15 euros) to meet the costs occasioned by their release; and one in eight has no place to live upon exit.[16] Even inside of penitentiaries, the trajectories and living conditions of inmates are stamped by deep class inequalities. From their initial admission and orientation to their transfers, access to internal resources, and sentence adjustments, every step in the carceral curriculum contributes to the cumulative impoverishment of the poorest inmates, owing to the absolute priority that day-to-day management places on the imperative of security.[17] In addition, the deleterious impact of incarceration is inflicted not only on the inmates but also, in a more insidious and unjust manner, upon their families, and especially their spouses: the deterioration of their financial situation, the waning of relations with friends and neighbors, the withering of emotional ties, educational problems among their children, and serious psychological disturbances connected to the feeling of being cast out aggravate the penal burden imposed upon the parents and partners of inmates.[18]

The reasoning—commonly invoked by the advocates of punitive policies—according to which carceral inflation necessarily translates into a mechanical reduction in crime by "neutralizing" convicts put out of commission between four walls, seems to make good sense, but it turns out to be specious upon examination. For, when it is applied to crimes of opportunity, indiscriminate confinement ends up "recruiting" new scofflaws through its *substitution effects*.[19] Thus a low-level drug peddler thrown behind bars is immediately replaced by another, so long as a solvent demand remains for his merchandise and the prospect of economic profit makes trafficking worthwhile. And, if his successor is a novice devoid of a local reputation, he will be more inclined to use violence to establish and secure his business, which will translate into an overall increase in illegalities. So the blanket extension of carceral sanctions as a means of criminal neutralization can turn out to generate more crime instead of less. As for "selective incapacitation," it is highly dependent on detecting and targetting high-frequency offenders but, by the time these offenders are identified as such by their accumulation of arrests and convictions, they are typically past their peak crime-committing years, so that throwing them behind bars is both superfluous and costly.[20] What is more, research on general deterrence has consistently shown that there exists no detectible correlation between actual and perceived levels of punishment, that active criminals are even *less likely* than the general population to have an accurate view of the certainty, celerity, and severity of the penal sanctions they risk incurring, and therefore that increasing the probability and the harshness of sentences cannot by itself reduce the incidence of crime (and might even increase it through its deviance-amplifying effects).[21]

The advocates of the penalization of urban disorders insist that the state must mete out swift and firm punishment for every act of deviance detected, even if this entails excessive police zeal, summary judicial treatment shading into the curtailment of basic rights, and erratic correctional administration. Blinded by a narrowly rationalist vision of law enforcement fixated on deterrence, they fail to realize that the citizenry complies with societal rules, not out of a cost-benefit analysis set by the probability and quantity of punishment they risk receiving relative to the gains they might reap through law-breaking, but essentially for expressive reasons of *legitimacy*. Tom Tyler has shown in his classic study *Why People Obey the Law* that citizens overwhelmingly accord primary consideration to the normative over the instrumental aspects of law enforcement. They abide by the law, and they collaborate with the agencies entrusted to uphold it, in effect policing themselves and others, to the degree that these agencies carry out their mission with "neutrality, lack of bias, honesty, efforts to be fair, politeness, and respect for citizens' rights."[22] It is the process and not the product of criminal control, what Tyler calls "procedural justice," that commands compliance with legal rules. And yet such procedural justice is grossly trampled over by policies of aggressive street policing, brutal judicial sanction, and systematic incarceration. In the United States, measures such as zero tolerance and the common use of disproportionate police force, mass arrests based on "racial profiling" and harsh prison sentences for minor narcotics violations, and three-strikes statutes have fed the collective perception that criminal justice is grossly inequitable, and it has sapped police-community relations in lower-class districts, with the result that law enforcement in them is ever more fractious and inefficient.[23] In France, the intensification of policing centered on deterrence through the multiplication of means, measures, and points of surveillance and repression, initiated by Jean-Pierre Chevênement and boosted later by Nicolas Sarkozy, has similarly eroded the legitimacy of the law and inflamed relations between the police and marginalized youths from the declining urban periphery. And they have everywhere swollen the national prison system well beyond its capacity to process and warehouse scofflaws.

Furthermore, the prison presents the peculiarity of being a sort of a two-way social pump: virtually all those who are "sucked" into it are eventually "flushed" back into the society. Even in the superpunitive

United States of today, 96 percent of convicts are ultimately released. But the prison is returning to society individuals who are more prone to offending due to the sociobiographic break effected by reclusion, the failings of rehabilitation and of "reentry" programs during and after captivity, and the string of prohibitions, disabilities, and assorted disadvantages connected to having a criminal record. A recent survey found that 52 percent of France's prisoners commit one (or more) offenses in the five years following their release and that the probability of recidivism varies strongly in *inverse* relation to the seriousness of their initial infraction: it runs from 23 percent for sexual offenses against children to 28 percent for homicide to 56 percent for drug sale and 59 percent for simple narcotics possession to 75 percent for nonviolent theft.* And yet nothing concrete is done to durably break the looping of the crime-prison-crime cycle, aside from stiffening penalties for recidivists even while the deterrent effect of incarceration is nearly nil for minor misdemeanors.

Finally, high-frequency imprisonment induces a process of *penal inoculation* among the populations it strikes with regularity, making them less and less susceptible to the preventive or retributive effects sought by the authorities.** By making judicial repression commonplace, the state dulls the aura that enshrouds it and blunts the stigma associated with it, so that it must continually increase the "doses" of punishment required to correct the behaviors of the unruly—a phenomenon that, from the standpoint of the fight against crime, could be summed up by a formula that would delight neoliberal economists: "Too much imprisonment kills imprisonment." Past a certain threshold of penal penetration, the negative symbolic charge of conviction is inverted and a sojourn at "the Graybar Hotel" becomes a badge of

*This figure is for general and not specific recidivism, that is, it includes all forms of reoffending—for example, a former murderer who steals in a store or passes a bad check after his release would qualify. Annie Kensey, Pierre-Victor Tournier, and Christelle Alméras, "La récidive des sortants de prison," *Les Cahiers de démographie pénitentiaire* 15 (April 2004): 1–4.

**This is a dilemma Durkheim warned about in his notations on "academic penality": "Every sanction, once applied, loses part of its efficacy by the very fact of its application. Because what gives it authority, what causes it to be feared, is not so much the pain it occasions than the moral shame implied in the blame it expresses. . . . Therefore punishment has this considerable inconvenient that it fetters one of the major spring of moral life and thus diminishes its own efficacy in the future. . . . Punishment should not be meted out in massive doses, as its effects are greater when it is more elaborately diluted." Émile Durkheim, *L'Éducation morale* (Paris: Presses Universitaires de France, 1963 [1902–3]), 166–67. My translation. Translated as *Moral Education* (New York: Dover, 2003), 199.

masculine honor and a valued mark of membership in a peer group devoted to the culture and economy of the street.[24] In the long run, by swallowing more and more individuals, the prison ends up feeding on its own products, in the manner of a malfunctioning social waste treatment center that throws back into the societal environment substances ever more noxious with each new cycle.[25]

How to Escape the Law-and-Order Snare

All of this to say that it is penally and politically aberrant to disconnect by fiat the politics and policy of criminal "insecurity" from the rise of social insecurity that feeds it in reality as well as in collective representations. It is just as absurd to deal with minor illegalities with an instrument as crude and inefficient as the prison. And it is urgent that we take full stock of the perverse judicial effects and social harm caused by the undifferentiated reinforcement of penal sanction and the uncontrolled expansion of an already overloaded carceral apparatus that, in its day-to-day functioning, discredits the very ideals of justice and equality it is supposed to uphold. To avoid getting locked in a penal escalation without end or exit, it is indispensable to reconnect the debate on crime with the paramount social question of the new century, which it now screens from view: the advent *of desocialized wage labor, vector of social insecurity,* and of increasing material, familial, educational, health, and even mental precariousness. For one can no longer order one's perception of the social world and conceive of the future when the present is obstructed and turns into a relentless struggle for day-to-day survival.*

It is not a matter of denying the reality of crime or the need to find a response or, rather, responses, *including penal ones* where they are appropriate. It is a matter of properly understanding its genesis, its changing physiognomy, and its ramifications by reembedding it in the complete system of social relations of force and meaning of which it is the expression, and which help explain its form and incidence as well as the hysterical reactions it provokes in the historical conjuncture of this

*As Pierre Bourdieu showed in the extreme case of Algerian subproletarians during the war of national liberation: "La hantise du chômage chez l'ouvrier algérien. Prolétariat et système colonial," *Sociologie du travail* 4, no. 4 (October 1962): 313–31. The relevance of this analysis for situations of urban marginality in contemporary societies is immediately apparent upon reading the portraits assembled by Vanessa Stettinger in *Funambules de la précarité. Vendeurs de journaux et mendiants du métro parisien* (Paris: Presses Universitaires de France, 2003).

century's turn. For this, it is necessary to stop gorging ourselves with apocalyptic discourses and to open a rational and informed debate on illegalities (plural), their springs and their imports. This debate should first of all clarify why it focuses on such particular manifestations of criminality—in the stairwells of public-housing projects rather than the corridors of city hall, on the snatching of handbags and cell phones rather than stock market swindles and infractions against labor laws and the tax code, etc. Let us recall here that the economic cost of white-collar and business crime in France (as in other advanced countries in Western Europe and America) is considerably higher than that of run-of-the-mill delinquency or even violent crime. In 1996, the monetary value of goods counterfeiting was estimated at 25 billion French francs, while employee benefits fraud reached 17 billion, as against 250 million for thefts from stores, 4 billion for automobile theft, and 11 billion for homicides. During that year, fiscal and customs fraud weighed in at 100 billion and the cost of traffic accidents exceeded 39 billion French francs.[26] From this point of view, the state's priority should be to enforce the tax and traffic codes. But attacking these two forms of *mass deviance* would entail recognizing that delinquency concerns most everyone and not a small, well-bounded, sulfurous subsector of society. And it would forbid targeting repressive action onto scapegoat categories, thereby sharply limiting the political profits gained by autonomizing and accentuating the symbolic functions of penal sanction.

A rational public debate on crime should differentiate among offenses and measure each of them with rigor and precision, rather than proceeding by way of amalgamation and approximation;[27] and it should avoid reasoning and reacting on the basis of extreme cases (e.g., the suicide of an elementary-school pupil due to "school violence" and the "mafia-style gangs" for drug trafficking centering on a stigmatized housing project). It should leave behind the short-term perspective and emotional cast of daily journalism to make a clear-cut differentiation between blips and groundswells, incidental variations from year to year and long-term trends, and not confuse the rising fear of crime, intolerance for crime, or concern over crime with an increase in crime itself. And it should factor in that spikes in the fear of or worry over crime are generally a response to orchestrated campaigns by the media and political crusades around the topic by city and state officials seeking gains or diversion from other, more discomforting issues.*

*Katherine Beckett demonstrated, in *Making Crime Pay: Law and Order in Contemporary American Politics* (New York: Oxford University Press, 1997), that the peaks and valleys of public worry over crime in the United States since the late 1960s follow

But above all, an intelligent policy on criminal insecurity must recognize that delinquent acts are the product, not of a singular and autonomous individual endowed with a warped will or vicious aims, but of a network of multiple causes and reasons entangled according to various logics (predation, exhibition, alienation, humiliation, transgression, confrontation with authority, etc.), and that they therefore call for remedies that are just as diverse and finely coordinated. These remedies will have to take full account of the congenitally low efficacy of the penal apparatus and transcend the shopworn alternative pointed by the complicit old couple of prevention and repression in order to put in place a *plurality of mechanisms of reduction and diversion*. This can be done by recognizing that police and penal treatments, which some nowadays dare present as a universal panacea, are generally of very limited application and prove in many circumstances to be worse than the harms they address if one takes even minimal account of their "collateral effects."[28]

Social science does not intervene here to "excuse" such and such behavior, as misinformed politicians like to bemoan, for the simple reason that it does not follow the logic of the trial, which aims to inculpate or exculpate. Its goal is to explain and to interpret, which is to say to supply the instruments of verifiable knowledge, which can also become tools for reasoned public action: "*Savoir pour prévoir, prévoir pour pouvoir*" ("Know in order to predict; predict in order to act"), said Auguste Comte, the forefather of modern sociology. Criminality is, in all societies, too serious a matter to be left to false experts and true ideologues, and even less so to the police and politicians eager to exploit the problem without accurately weighing or properly mastering it. Its contemporary transformations call not for a rejection but for a renewal of the sociological approach, which alone can free us from the *law-and-order pornography* that reduces the fight against delinquency to a ritualized spectacle that serves only to feed the fantasies of order of the citizenry and signify the virile authority of state decision-makers. No more than deregulated wage labor, which some strive to present as a kind of natural necessity (also coming from America) spawned by a "globalization" that is ineluctable if not always desirable,[29] enlarged

---

directly from the activism of politicians and the amplifying effects of the commercial media. For similar demonstrations in the case of France over the past decade, see Dominique Montjardet, "L'insécurité politique: police et sécurité dans l'arène électorale," *Sociologie du travail* 4 (October 2002): 543–55; Angélina Péralva and Eric Macé, ed., *Médias et "violences urbaines"* (Paris: La Documentation française, 2002); and Manuel Boucher, *Repolitiser l'insécurité. Sociographie d'une ville ouvrière en recomposition* (Paris: L'Harmattan, 2004).

recourse to the police and penitentiary arms of the state to stem the social and mental disorders engendered by the instability of work is not a fatality. Opposing the penalization of urban poverty and its correlates requires waging a triple battle.

First of all, at the level of *words and discourse*, one must fight to halt these seemingly harmless semantic drifts that shrink the space of the thinkable and hence the doable (for instance, by arbitrarily restricting the meaning of the word "security" to the criminal sphere, disconnected from employment security, income security, housing security, etc.) and contribute to banalizing the punitive treatment of tensions linked to the deepening of social inequalities (for instance, through the use of fuzzy and incoherent notions like "urban violence").* Here it is imperative to submit the importation of pseudotheories, concocted by heteronomous scholars and diffused by American think tanks and their European relay stations to justify the expansion of the penal state, to a severe customs control in the form of rigorous logical and empirical critique. This is what I tried to do in the preceding chapter for the "broken windows theory," which turns out to be little more than a police folk mythology, but one which has exerted very real and profoundly noxious effects on the reorganization of street-level law enforcement around the world.

Next, on the front of *judicial policies and practices*, it is necessary to block the multiplication of mechanisms that tend to "widen" the penal net and to propose, wherever possible, an economic, social, health, or educational alternative by showing how each, on its own level, helps to tackle the problem at its roots, whereas punitive containment most often only makes it worse, especially because by rendering its causes invisible it facilitates their germination. The predicament of poor persons suffering from severe psychological afflictions is a case in point: they have no business being held in penal establishments when the fundamental reason for their arrest and incarceration is the sheer lack of mental health care on the outside; the same is true for the homeless who find themselves thrown behind bars in increasing numbers due to the conjoint erosion of the low-wage and low-income housing markets, and the scandalous apathy of government in dealing with these

*For those who would be tempted to underestimate the importance of this struggle, or to see it as a preoccupation specific to intellectuals, Pierre Bourdieu reminds us that "the social world is the site of struggles about words that owe their gravity—and sometimes their violence—to the fact that words make things, in good part, and that to change words, and more generally representations, . . . is already to change things." Pierre Bourdieu, *In Other Words: Essays Toward a Reflexive Sociology* (Cambridge: Polity, 1990 [1987]), 69. My translation.

derelict populations. It is useful in this regard to stress unrelentingly the destructive conditions and effects of confinement, not only for the inmates, but also for their families and their neighborhoods. And to emphasize that the prison is not simply a shield against delinquency but a double-edged sword: an organism for coercion at once criminophagous and criminogenic which, when it develops to excess, as in the United States over the past quarter-century or in the Soviet Union during the Stalinist period, comes to mutate into an autonomous vector of pauperization and marginalization.[30]

Next, it is necessary to *defend the autonomy and dignity of the occupations making up the Left arm of the state,* social worker and psychologist, teacher and specialized educator, housing coordinator and child-care worker, nurse and doctor, at the risk of appearing to surrender to corporatist interests. These occupations must demand the budgetary and human resources needed to fulfill their mission and *nothing but their mission,** which is to say they must refuse to become an extension of the police and an annex of judicial administration under cover of better coordination between public services and bureaucratic efficiency. To be sure, synergies between public administrations are desirable in principle; the whole question is knowing which of them imposes its logic, language, criteria for action, temporal horizon, and objectives:[31] does coming together aim to increase the long-term "social security" of families and individuals facing hardships by affording them greater stability and capacity for managing their life, or to produce short-term "criminal security" (or, worse yet, its media staging) by forcing down the statistical indicators of recorded crime and making a show of paternalistic severity for electoral purposes? Which impulse of the state holds sway in this ongoing arm-wrestling contest between these two possible modalities of public action, the "Left hand," which nourishes and sustains, protects the dispossessed from the threats of life and reduces inequalities, or the "Right hand," charged with the enforcement of order, moral and economic as well as legal? On the side of the police and penal sector, too, the agents of the state must defend the dignity and integrity of their occupations and refuse to let themselves be roped into assuming degraded versions of social and health functions that do not properly fall to them (as when the psychiatric

*This imperative connects with the internal battles being waged by social workers across Europe over the objectives and modalities of their action in the era of mass unemployment and fragmented wage labor, as they confront the diversification of positions, the bureaucratization of their tasks, the rise of a managerialist approach, and the resurgence of voluntary work. See Jacques Ion, *Le Travail social au singulier* (Paris: Dunod, 1998).

clinic of a jail finds itself handling serious cases of mental illness which, because they were not treated by the hospital sector outside, have led to incarceration).

Finally, it is essential to *forge connections between activists and researchers on the penal and social fronts,* between members of unions and associations in the welfare, education, housing, and health sectors, on the one hand, and their counterparts mobilized around the police, justice, and correctional services, on the other. The double regulation of the poor through the conjoined assistantial and judicial wings of the state in the age of economic deregulation must be met by new alliances of analysts and militants taking account of the growing fusion between the Right hand and the Left hand of the state distinctive of the anatomy of the neoliberal state. Moreover, such civic and scientific synergy must be established not solely at the national level but also at the European level in order to optimize the intellectual and organizational resources that can be invested in the permanent struggle to redefine the perimeter and modalities of public action.[32] There exists a formidable pool of theoretical and practical knowledge to be exploited and shared across the continent to dissect and remake the organic link between social justice and criminal justice. For the true alternative to the drift toward the penalization of poverty, whether soft or hard, remains the construction of a European social state worthy of the name. Three and a half centuries after its birth, the most effective means for pushing back the prison still remains and will remain for the decades ahead to push social and economic rights forward.

Theoretical Coda: A Sketch of the Neoliberal State

Three analytic breaks have proven necessary to elaborate the diagnosis of the invention of a new government of social insecurity wedding restrictive "workfare" and expansive "prisonfare" presented in this book, and to account for the punitive policy turn taken by the United States and other advanced societies following its lead onto the path of economic deregulation and welfare retrenchment in the closing decades of the twentieth century.

The first consists in *breaking out of the crime-and-punishment poke*, which continues to straightjacket scholarly and policy debates on incarceration, even as the divorce of this familiar couple grows ever more barefaced. The runaway growth and fervent glorification of the penal apparatus in America after the mid-1970s—and its milder expansion and startling political rehabilitation in Western Europe with a two-decade lag—are inexplicable so long as one insists on deriving them from the incidence and composition of offenses. For the rolling out of the penal state after the peaking of the Civil Rights movement responds, not to rising *criminal insecurity*, but to the wave of *social insecurity* that has flooded the lower tier of the class structure owing to the fragmentation of wage labor and the destabilization of ethnoracial or ethnonational hierarchies (provoked by the implosion of the dark ghetto on the United States side and by the settlement of postcolonial migrants on the European side). Indeed, the obsessive focus on crime, backed by ordinary and scholarly common sense, has served well to hide from view the new politics and policy of poverty that is a core component in the forging of the neoliberal state.*

The second break requires *relinking social welfare and penal policies*, since these two strands of government action toward the poor have

*For instance, the excellent volume on *The Crime Drop in America* edited by Alfred Blumstein and Joel Wallman (New York: Oxford University Press, 2000), bringing together the foremost criminologists in the land to puzzle out the causes of the unexpected decline in offending, contains not one paragraph tackling the sea changes in welfare provision, public housing, foster care, health care, and related state policies that jointly set the life options of the populations most susceptible to street crime (as both perpetrators and victims).

come to be informed by the same behaviorist philosophy relying on deterrence, surveillance, stigma, and graduated sanctions to modify conduct. Welfare revamped as workfare and prison stripped of its rehabilitative pretension now form a single organizational mesh flung at the same clientele mired in the fissures and ditches of the dualizing metropolis. They work jointly to invisibilize problem populations—by forcing them off the public aid rolls, on the one side, and holding them under lock, on the other—and eventually push them into the peripheral sectors of the booming secondary labor market. Returning to their original historical mission at the birth of capitalism, poor relief and penal confinement collude to normalize, supervise, and/or neutralize the destitute and disruptive fractions of the postindustrial proletariat coalescing under the new economic conditions of capital hypermobility and labor degradation.

The third rupture involves *overcoming the customary opposition between materialist and symbolic approaches*, descended from the emblematic figures of Karl Marx and Émile Durkheim, so as to heed and hold together the instrumental and the expressive functions of the penal apparatus. Weaving together concerns for control and communication, the management of dispossessed categories and the affirmation of salient social boundaries, has enabled us to go beyond an analysis couched in the language of prohibition to trace how the expansion and redeployment of the prison and its institutional tentacles (probation, parole, criminal databases, swirling discourses about crime, and a virulent culture of public denigration of offenders) has reshaped the sociosymbolic landscape and remade the state itself. Tracking down the conjoint material and symbolic effects of punishment reveals that the penal state has become a potent cultural engine in its own right, which spawns categories, classifications, and images of wide import and use in broad sectors of government action and civic life.

Now, it is fruitful, to sharpen the analytic contours and clarify the theoretical implications of this inquiry into the punitive turn in public policy toward the poor taken in advanced society at century's dawn, to relate it to the works of Pierre Bourdieu on the state, Frances Fox Piven and Richard Cloward on welfare, Michel Foucault and David Garland on punishment, and David Harvey on neoliberalism. This leads us, by way of theoretical coda, to draw a sociological sketch of that wooly and ominous configuration extending beyond its usual economic characterization.

When Workfare Joins Prisonfare: Theoretical (Re)Percussions

In *The Weight of the World* and related essays, Pierre Bourdieu has proposed that we construe the state, not as a monolithic and coordinated ensemble, but as a splintered space of forces vying over the definition and distribution of public goods, which he calls the "bureaucratic field."[1] The constitution of this space is the end-result of a long-term process of concentration of the various species of capital operative in a given social formation, and especially of "juridical capital as the objectified and codified form of symbolic capital" which enables the state to monopolize the official definition of identities and the administration of justice.[2] In the contemporary period, the bureaucratic field is traversed by two internecine struggles. The first pits the "higher state nobility" of policy-makers intent on promoting market-oriented reforms and the "lower state nobility" of executants attached to the traditional missions of government. The second opposes what Bourdieu calls the "Left hand" and the "Right hand" of the state. The Left hand, the feminine side of Leviathan, is materialized by the "spendthrift" ministries in charge of "social functions"—public education, health, housing, welfare, and labor law—which offer protection and succor to the social categories shorn of economic and cultural capital. The Right hand, the masculine side, is charged with enforcing the new economic discipline via budget cuts, fiscal incentives, and economic deregulation.

By inviting us to grasp in a single conceptual framework the various sectors of the state that administer the life conditions and chances of the lower class, and to view these sectors as enmeshed in relations of antagonistic cooperation as they vie for preeminence inside the bureaucratic field, this conception has helped us map the ongoing shift from the social to the penal treatment of urban marginality.[3] The present investigation fills in a gap in Bourdieu's model by inserting the police, the courts, and *the prison as core constituents of the "Right hand"* of the state, alongside the ministries of the economy and the budget. It suggests that we need to bring penal policies from the periphery to the center of our analysis of the redesign and deployment of government programs aimed at coping with the entrenched poverty and deepening disparities spawned in the polarizing city by the discarding of the Fordist-Keynesian social compact. The new government of social insecurity put in place in the United States and offered as model to other advanced countries entails both a shift from the social to the penal wing of the state (detectible in the reallocation of public budgets, personnel, and discursive precedence) and the colonization of the welfare sector by the panoptic and punitive logic characteristic of the postrehabilitation penal bureaucracy (examined in chapters 2 and 3). The slanting of state activity from the social to the penal arm and the incipient penalization of welfare, in turn, partake of the *remasculinization of the state*, in reaction to the wide-ranging changes provoked in the political field by the women's movement and by the institutionalization of social rights antinomic to commodification. The new priority given to duties over rights, sanction over support, the stern rhetoric of the "obligations of citizenship," and the martial reaffirmation of the capacity of the state to lock the troublemaking poor (welfare recipients and criminals) "in a subordinate relation of dependence and obedience" toward state managers portrayed as virile protectors of the society against its wayward members:* all these policy planks pronounce and promote the transition from the kindly "nanny state" of the Fordist-Keynesian era to the strict "daddy state" of neoliberalism.

In their classic study *Regulating the Poor*, Frances Fox Piven and Richard Cloward forged a germinal model of the management of poverty in industrial capitalism. According to this model, the state expands or contracts its relief programs cyclically to respond to the ups and downs of the economy, the corresponding slackening and tightening of the labor market, and the bouts of social disruption that increased unemployment and destitution trigger periodically among the lower class. Phases of welfare expansion serve to "mute civil disorders" that threaten established hierarchies, while phases of restriction aim to "enforce works norms" by pushing recipients back onto the labor market.[4] The present book contends that, while this model worked well for the Fordist-Keynesian age and accounts for the two major welfare explosions witnessed in the United States during the Great Depression and the affluent but turbulent 1960s, it has been rendered obsolete by the neoliberal remaking of the state over the past quarter-century. In the era of fragmented labor, hypermobile capital, and sharpening social inequalities and anxieties, "the central role of relief agencies in the regulation of marginal labor and in the maintenance of social order"[5] is displaced and duly supplemented by the vigorous deployment of the police, the courts, and the prison in the nether regions of social space. To the single oversight of the poor by the Left hand of the state succeeds the *double regulation of poverty by the joint action of punitive*

*Iris Marion Young, "The Logic of Masculinist Protection: Reflections on the Current Security State," in *Women and Citizenship*, ed. Marilyn Friedman (New York: Oxford University Press, 2005), 16. Young's argument about the "security state" on the foreign front after 9/11 can be transposed and applied to the domestic front in the state's two-pronged "war" on dependent poverty and street crime.

welfare-turned-workfare and a diligent and belligerent penal bureaucracy. The cyclical alternation of contraction and expansion of public aid is replaced by the continual contraction of welfare and the runaway expansion of prisonfare.

This organizational coupling of the Left hand and Right hand of the state under the aegis of the same disciplinary philosophy of behaviorism and moralism is an unprecedented institutional innovation which overturns the accepted categories of social theory, empirical research, and public policy—starting with the safe separation between those who manage or study "welfare" and those who track "crime." It can be understood, first, by recalling the shared historical origins of poor relief and penal confinement in the chaotic passage from feudalism to capitalism. Both policies were devised in the sixteenth century to "absorb and regulate the masses of discontented people uprooted" by this epochal transition.* Similarly, both policies were overhauled in the last two decades of the twentieth century in response to the socio-economic dislocations provoked by neoliberalism: in the 1980s alone, in addition to reducing public assistance, California voted nearly one thousand laws expanding the use of prison sentences; at the federal level, the 1996 reform that "ended welfare as we know it" was complemented by the sweeping Crime Omnibus Act of 1993 and bolstered by the No Frills Prison Act of 1995.

The institutional pairing of public aid and incarceration as tools for managing the unruly poor can also be understood by paying attention to the structural, functional, and cultural similarities between workfare and prisonfare as "people-processing institutions" targeted on kindred problem populations.[6] It has been facilitated by the transformation of welfare in a punitive direction and the activation of the penal system to handle more of the traditional clientele of assistance to the destitute—the incipient "penalization" of welfare matching the degraded "welfarization" of the prison. Their concurrent reform over the past thirty years has helped cement their organizational convergence, even as they have obeyed inverse principles. The gradual erosion of public aid and its revamping into workfare in 1996 have entailed restricting entry into the system, shortening "stays" on the rolls, and speeding up exit, resulting

*Frances Fox Piven and Richard A. Cloward, *Regulating the Poor: The Functions of Public Welfare*, new expanded ed. (New York: Vintage, 1993 [1971]), 21. Penal expansion and activism in the sixteenth century is acknowledged in passing by Piven and Cloward: "The relief system was by no means the only solution. This was an era of brutal repression; indeed in no other domestic matters was Parliament so active as in the elaboration of the criminal code." Ibid., 20, n. 32.

in a spectacular reduction of the stock of beneficiaries (it plummeted from nearly five million households in 1992 to under two million a decade later). Trends in penal policy have followed the exact opposite tack: admission into jail and prison has been greatly facilitated, sojourns behind bars lengthened, and releases curtailed, which has yielded a spectacular ballooning of the population under lock (it jumped by over one million in the 1990s). The operant purpose of welfare has shifted from passive "people processing" to active "people changing" after 1988 and especially after the abolition of AFDC in 1996, while the prison has traveled in the other direction, from aiming to reform inmates (under the philosophy of rehabilitation, hegemonic from the 1920s to the mid-1970s) to merely warehousing them (as the function of punishment was downgraded to retribution and neutralization). The sudden deflation of the welfare rolls has been touted as evidence of the success of the new welfare policy, while the grotesque inflation of the country's carceral stock has been hailed as positive proof that criminal policy is working. Poverty has not receded, but the social visibility and civic standing of the troublemaking poor have been reduced.

The shared historical roots, organizational isomorphism, and operational convergence of the assistantial and penitential poles of the bureaucratic field in the United States are further fortified by the fact that, as revealed in chapters 2 and 3, the social profiles of their beneficiaries are virtually identical. AFDC recipients and jail inmates both live near or below 50 percent of the federal poverty line (for one-half and two-thirds of them, respectively); both are disproportionately black and Hispanic (37 percent and 18 percent versus 41 percent and 19 percent). The majority did not finish high school and are saddled with serious physical and mental disabilities interfering with their participation in the workforce (44 percent of AFDC mothers as against 37 percent of jail inmates). And they are closely bound to one another by extensive kin, marital, and social ties, reside overwhelmingly in the same impoverished households and barren neighborhoods, and face the same bleak life horizon at the bottom of the class and ethnic structure.

Punishing the Poor avers, not only that the United States has shifted from the single (welfare) to the double (social-cum-penal) regulation of the poor, but also that "the stunted development of American social policy" skillfully dissected by Piven and Cloward[7] stands in close causal and functional relation to America's uniquely overgrown and hyperactive penal policy. *The misery of American welfare and the grandeur of American prisonfare at century's turn are the two sides of the same political coin.* The generosity of the latter is in direct proportion to the stinginess of the former, and it expands to the degree that both are driven by moral behaviorism. The same structural features of the American state (underscored in chapter 2) that have facilitated the organized atrophy of welfare in reaction to the racial crisis of the 1960s and the economic turmoil of the 1970s have also fostered the uncontrolled hypertrophy of punishment aimed at the same precarious population. Moreover, we stressed in chapter 6 that the "tortured impact of slavery and institutionalized racism on the construction of the American polity" has been felt, not only on the "underdevelopment" of public aid and the "decentralized and fragmented government and party system" that distributes it to a select segment of the dispossessed,[8] but also on the overdevelopment and stupendous severity of its penal wing. The social potency of the denegated form of ethnicity called race and the activation of the stigma of blackness are key to explaining the initial atrophy and accelerating decay of the American social state in the post–Civil Rights era, on the one hand, and the astonishing ease and celerity with which the penal state arose on its ruins, on the other.[9]

To track the fate of the poor in the polarizing class structure of neoliberal capitalism, then, it will not suffice to supplement the traditional analysis of welfare with the study of workfare. For the residualization of public assistance as protective buffer against the sanction of the deregulated labor market has been prolonged by the gargantuan growth of prisonfare, which now shares in the task of encasing the social relations and consequences of normalized social insecurity in the lower reaches of urban space. In *Workfare States,* his provocative analysis of the deployment of workfare as "a reactive reform strategy and as a would-be successor regime to the welfare state," Jamie Peck draws an *analogy* between supervisory workfare and the criminal justice system. He points out their common symbolic function of moral exemplification and corresponding capacity to exercise disciplining effects well beyond their official clientele:

> Just like workhouses and prisons, workfare regimes are intended to throw a long shadow, shaping the norms, values, and behaviors of the wider populations, and *maintaining a form of order.* Sticking with the penal analogy, what matters in these situations is not just the activities and immediate fate of the inmates, nor the particularities of prison architecture, but the broader social, political and economic effects of the criminal justice system.*

*Jamie Peck, *Workfare States* (New York: Guilford, 2001), 23, emphasis in the original. Later, Peck elaborates: "Workfare maintains order in the labor market in an *analogous fashion* to the way in which prisons contribute to the maintenance of the social

This argument is insightful, but it vastly underestimates the operative connections between these two sectors of the bureaucratic field and the practical overlap between their respective activities. For workfare and prisonfare are linked, not by a mere analogy, but through organizational *homology* and functional complementarity. Rather than operating in kindred fashion, they *run jointly* at ground level, by applying the same principles of deterrence, diversion, individualized supervision, and sanction to the same population according to a gendered division of labor of submission to the dictate of flexible work as de facto norm of citizenship at the foot of the class structure. Peck overlooks the fact that, much like workfare is "the logical social-policy complement to flexible labor-market policies,"[10] expansive and aggressive prisonfare is the logical justice-policy complement to both workfare and the normalization of contingent jobs. Similarly, in her book *Flat Broke with Children*, Sharon Hays misjudges the active entwining of the social and penal treatments of poverty when she warns about a future negative interaction between new-style public aid and the criminal justice system and other institutions entrusted with the custody of social derelicts, should workfare not be amended.* She does not realize that these two planks of poverty policy are already working in tandem, and that Malthusian welfare and penal Keynesianism, far from being at loggerheads, form a complementary institutional duo.

Reversing the historical bifurcation of the labor and crime questions achieved in the late nineteenth century, *punitive containment* as a government technique for managing deepening urban marginality has effectively rejoined social and penal policy at the close of the twentieth century. It taps the diffuse social anxiety coursing through the middle and lower regions of social space in reaction to the splintering of wage work and the resurgence of inequality, and converts it into popular animus toward welfare recipients and street criminals cast as the twin detached and defamed categories which sap the social order by their dissolute morality and dissipated behavior, and must therefore be placed under severe tutelage.** The new government of poverty invented by

---

order: as well as disciplining the individuals directly concerned, they symbolize the price that has to be paid for breaking the rules." Ibid., 349, my emphasis.

*"If nothing changes and welfare reform isn't itself reformed, by the close of the first decade of the twenty-first century we will see the beginnings of the measurable impacts on prison populations, mental health facilities, domestic violence shelters, children's protective services, and the foster care system." Sharon Hays, *Flat Broke with Children: Women in the Age of Welfare Reform* (New York: Oxford University Press, 2003), 229.

**This animus is noted with glee by the ideologues of state paternalism: "The politi-

the United States to enforce the normalization of social insecurity thus gives a whole new meaning to the notion of "poor relief": punitive containment offers relief not *to* the poor but *from* the poor, by forcibly "disappearing" the most disruptive of them, from the shrinking welfare rolls on the one hand and into the swelling dungeons of the carceral castle on the other. With the shift from the one-handed maternalist to the two-handed paternalist modality of poverty policy, the bright line between the deserving and the undeserving poor, the wholesome "working families" and the corrupt and fearsome "underclass," is drawn in concert by workfare and prisonfare. And incarceration takes its place at the center of the spectrum of state programs trained on the precarious fractions of the postindustrial proletariat.

Michel Foucault has advanced the single most influential analysis of the rise and role of the prison in capitalist modernity, and it is useful to set my thesis against the rich tapestry of analyses he has stretched and stimulated. As indicated earlier, I concur with the author of *Discipline and Punish* that penality is a protean force that is eminently fertile and must be given pride of place in the study of contemporary power.[11] While its originary medium resides in the application of legal coercion to enforce the core strictures of the sociomoral order, punishment must be viewed not through the narrow and technical prism of repression—as most critics of the contemporary punitive upsurge continue to do on both sides of the Atlantic—but by recourse to the notion of production. We have seen in this book how the assertive rolling out of the penal state has engendered new categories and discourses, novel administrative bodies and government policies, fresh social types and associated forms of knowledge across the criminal and social welfare domains. In sum, the penalization of poverty has proved to be a prolific vector for the construction of social reality and for the reengineering of the state geared toward the *ordering of social insecurity* in the age of deregulated capitalism. But, from here, my argument diverges sharply

cal basis for supporting policies to restore order is broader today than it was a century ago. Then the leaders of social control were mostly local notables offended by the immoralities of urban life, often linked to prostitution and drink. They wanted to clean up cities by outlawing vice and saloons, but the public was more tolerant. Today, however, crime and drugs dominate some urban areas. Among the needy, female-headed families on welfare are much commoner and steady employment much rarer than during the era of social reform. Basic order and functioning, not only morals, are now at risk. Accordingly tougher crime, welfare, and education policies enjoy strong support, which helps explain the attractiveness of paternalism." Lawrence M. Mead, ed., *The New Paternalism: Supervisory Approaches to Poverty* (Washington, D.C.: Brookings Institution, 1997), 15–17.

from Foucault's view of the emergence and functioning of the punitive society in at least four ways.*

To start with, Foucault erred in spotting the retreat of the penitentiary. Disciplines may have diversified and metastasized to thrust sinewy webs of control across the society, but the prison has not for that receded from the historical stage and "lost its raison d'être."** On the contrary, penal confinement has made a stunning comeback and reaffirmed itself among the central missions of Leviathan just as Foucault and his followers were forecasting its demise. After the founding burst of the 1600s and the consolidation of the 1800s, the turn of the present century ranks as the third "age of confinement" that penologist Thomas Mathiesen forewarned about in 1990.[12] Next, whatever their uses in the eighteenth century, disciplinary technologies have *not* been deployed inside the overgrown and voracious carceral system of our *fin de siècle*. Hierarchical classification, elaborate time schedules, nonidleness, close-up examination and the regimentation of the body: these techniques of penal "normalization" have been rendered impracticable by the demographic chaos spawned by overpopulation, bureaucratic rigidity, resource depletion, and the studious indifference if not hostility of penal authorities toward rehabilitation (documented in chapters 4 and 5). In lieu of the *dressage* ("training" or "taming") intended to fashion "docile and productive bodies" postulated by Foucault, the contemporary prison is geared toward brute neutralization, rote retribution, and simple warehousing—by default if not by design. If there are "engineers of consciousness" and "orthopedists of individuality" at work in the mesh of disciplinary powers today, they surely are not employed by departments of corrections.[13]

In the third place, "devices for normalization" anchored in the car-

*It is not possible to offer here the nuanced discussion that Foucault's analyses of penality merit. Suffice it to note that there are at least two Foucaults dialoguing in his writings on the topic. The first portrays punishment as "a regular function, coextensive with the society" (Michel Foucault, *Surveiller et punir. Naissance de la prison* [Paris: Gallimard, 1975], translated as *Discipline and Punish: The Birth of the Prison* [New York: Vintage, 1977], 92/90) that exemplifies a new form of pastoral "power-knowledge" geared toward producing subjectivities distinctive of the modern era. The second insists on the political and economic profitability of penal sanction, its role in reproducing "an opposition between the classes," and the link between the restructuring of "the economy of illegalisms" and the requirements of capitalist production. Ibid., 89/87.

**"A subtle carceral net, graduated, with compact institutions but also parcellary and diffused procedures, has taken over the task of the arbitrary, massive, ill-integrated confinement of the classical age. . . . As for the carceral archipelago, it transports this technique of the penal institution to the entire social body." Ibid., 304–5/297–98.

ceral institution have *not* spread throughout the society, in the manner of capillaries irrigating the entire body social. Rather, the widening of the penal dragnet under neoliberalism has been remarkably discriminating: in spite of conspicuous bursts of corporate crime (epitomized by the Savings and Loans scandal of the late 1980s and the folding of Enron a decade later), it has affected essentially the denizens of the lower regions of social and physical space. Indeed, the fact that the class and ethnoracial selectivity of the prison has been maintained, nay reinforced, as it vastly enlarged its intake demonstrates that penalization is not an all-encompassing master logic that blindly traverses the social order to bend and bind its various constituents. On the contrary: it is a skewed technique proceeding along sharp gradients of class, ethnicity, and place, and it operates to divide populations and to differentiate categories according to established conceptions of moral worth (as demonstrated *per absurdum* by the hysterical treatment of sex offenders leading to social excommunication examined in chapter 7).[14] At the dawn of the twenty-first century, America's urban (sub)proletariat lives in a "punitive society," but its middle and upper classes certainly do not. Similarly, efforts to import and adapt US-style slogans and methods of law-enforcement—such as zero tolerance policing, mandatory minimum sentencing, or boot camps for juveniles—in Europe have been trained on lower-class and immigrant offenders relegated in the defamed neighborhoods at the center of the panic over "ghettoization" that has swept across the continent over the past decade.

Lastly, the crystallization of *law-and-order pornography*, that is, the accelerating inflection and inflation of penal activity conceived, represented, and implemented for the primary purpose of being displayed in ritualized form by the authorities—the paradigm for which is the half-aborted reintroduction of chain gangs in striped uniforms—suggests that news of the death of the "spectacle of the scaffold" has been greatly exaggerated. The "redistribution" of "the whole economy of punishment"[15] in the post-Fordist period has entailed, not its disappearance from public view as proposed by Foucault, but its institutional relocation, symbolic elaboration, and social proliferation beyond anything anyone envisioned when *Discipline and Punish* was published. In the past quarter-century, a whole galaxy of novel cultural and social forms, indeed a veritable industry trading on representations of offenders and law-enforcement, has sprung forth and spread. The theatricalization of penality has migrated from the state to the commercial media and the political field in toto, and it has extended from the final ceremony of sanction to encompass the full penal chain, with a privileged place accorded to police operations in low-income districts and courtroom confrontations around celebrity defendants. The Place de Grève, where the regicide Damiens was famously quartered, has thus been supplanted not by the Panopticon but by Court TV and the profusion of crime-and-punishment "reality shows" that have inundated television (*Cops, 911, America's Most Wanted, American Detective, Bounty Hunters, Inside Cell Block F,* etc.), not to mention the use of criminal justice as fodder for the daily news and dramatic series.* So much to say that the prison did not "replace" the "social game of the signs of punishment and the garrulous feast that put them in motion."[16] Rather, it now serves as its institutional canopy.

One might even argue that the mutation of penality at century's turn has inverted the historical schema postulated by Michel Foucault as characteristic of Western modernity: "the right to punish has" not "been displaced from the vengeance of the sovereign to the defence of society."[17] Instead, punishment has returned as society's revenge against the social misfits onto whom displaced societal anxiety fastens and as the defense of the sovereign weakened by the self-professed impotence of state managers on the economic and social fronts. Everywhere the law-and-order *guignol* has become a core civic theater onto whose stage elected officials prance to dramatize moral norms and display their professed capacity for decisive action, thereby reaffirming the political relevance of Leviathan at the very moment when they organize its powerlessness with respect to the market.

This brings us to the question of the political proceeds of penalization, a theme central to David Garland's book *The Culture of Control,* the most sweeping and stimulative account of the nexus of crime and social order put forth since Foucault. According to Garland, "the distinctive social, economic, and cultural arrangements of late modernity" have fashioned a "new collective experience of crime and insecurity," to which the authorities have given a reactionary interpretation and a bifurcated response combining practical adaptation via "preventative

*In the United States, law-enforcement drama is "the single most popular form of television entertainment." So much so that "in a given week of prime-time viewing, the typical audience member will watch 30 police officers, 7 lawyers and 3 judges but only 1 scientist or engineer and only a small number of blue-collar workers." Katherine Beckett and Theodore Sasson, *The Politics of Injustice* (Thousand Oaks, CA: Pine Forge Press, 2000), 104. Crime-centered "reality shows" have proliferated in other advanced societies in the 1990s (e.g., *Crimewatch UK* in Great Britain, *Aktenzeichen XY . . . Ungelöst* in Germany, *Témoin Numéro Un* in France, *Oposporing Verzocht* in the Netherlands), which have also been flooded by programs from the United States. Indeed, the refurbished law-and-order imaginary of America has gone global via the planetary diffusion of television series such as *CSI, Law and Order, Miami Vice, NYPD Blue,* and *Prison Break.*

partnerships" and hysterical denial through "punitive segregation."[18] The ensuing reconfiguration of crime control bespeaks the inability of rulers to regiment individuals and normalize contemporary society, and its very disjointedness has made glaring to all the "limits of the sovereign state."* For Garland, the "culture of control" coalescing around the "new criminological predicament" pairing high crime rates with the acknowledged limitations of criminal justice both marks and masks a political failing. On the contrary, *Punishing the Poor* asserts that punitive containment has proved to be a remarkably successful political strategy: far from "eroding one of the foundational myths of modern society" which holds that "the sovereign state is capable of delivering law and order,"[19] it has revitalized it.

By elevating criminal safety (*sécurité, Sicherheit, sicurezza,* etc.) to the frontline of government priorities, state officials have condensed the diffuse class anxiety and simmering ethnic resentment generated by the unraveling of the Fordist-Keynesian compact and channeled them toward the (dark-skinned) street criminal, designated as guilty of sowing social and moral disorder in the city, alongside the profligate welfare recipient. Rolling out the penal state and coupling it with workfare has given the high state nobility an effective tool to both foster labor deregulation and contain the disorders that economic deregulation provokes in the lower rungs of the sociospatial hierarchy. Most importantly, it has allowed politicians to make up for the deficit of legitimacy which besets them whenever they curtail the economic support and social protections traditionally granted by Leviathan. Contra Garland, then, I find that the penalization of urban poverty has served well as a vehicle for the *ritual reassertion of the sovereignty of the state* in the narrow, theatricalized domain of law enforcement that it has prioritized *for that very purpose,* just when the same state is effectively conceding its incapacity to control flows of capital, bodies, and signs across its borders. This divergence of diagnosis, in turn, points to three major differences between our respective dissections of the punitive drift in First-World countries.

First, the fast and furious bend toward penalization observed at the *fin de siècle* is not a response to *criminal* insecurity but to *social* in-

*"The denials and expressive gestures that have marked recent penal policy cannot disguise the fact that the state is seriously limited in its capacity to provide security for its citizens and deliver adequate levels of social control. . . . In the complex, differentiated world of late modernity, effective, legitimate government must devolve power and share the work of social control with local organizations and communities." David Garland, *The Culture of Control: Crime and Social Order in Contemporary Society* (Chicago: University of Chicago Press, 2001), 205.

security.[20] To be more precise, the currents of social anxiety that roil advanced society are rooted in *objective* social insecurity among the postindustrial working class, whose material conditions have deteriorated with the diffusion of unstable and underpaid wage labor shorn of the usual social "benefits," and *subjective* insecurity among the middle classes, whose prospects for smooth reproduction or upward mobility have dimmed as competition for valued social positions has intensified and the state has reduced its provision of public goods. Garland's notion that "high rates of crime have become a normal social fact—a routine part of modern consciousness, an everyday risk to be assessed and managed" by "the population at large," and especially by the middle class, is belied by both official crime statistics and victimization studies. We saw in chapter 4 that law breaking in the United States declined or stagnated for twenty years after the mid-1970s before falling precipitously in the 1990s, while exposure to violent offenses varied widely by location in social and physical space.* We also noted in chapter 8 that European countries sport crime rates similar to or higher than America (except for the two specific categories of assault and homicide, which compose but a tiny fraction of all offenses), and yet have responded quite differently to criminal activity, with rates of incarceration one-fifth to one-tenth the American rate even as they have risen. In any case, parsing out trends in offending does nothing to resolve the conundrum of why the United States became five times more punitive in the closing quarter of the century, holding crime constant.

This takes us to the second difference: for Garland, the reaction of the state to the predicament of high crime and low justice efficiency has been disjointed and even schizoid, whereas I have stressed its overall coherence. But this coherence becomes visible only when the analytic compass is fully extended *beyond the crime-and-punishment box and across policy realms*, to link penal trends to the socioeconomic restructuring of the urban order, on the one side, and to join workfare and prisonfare, on the other. What Garland characterizes as "the structured

*Between 1975 and 1995, the homicide rate for whites remained consistently stuck at one-sixth that for blacks (stable at about 5 per 100,000 versus 28 to 39 per 100,000). In 1995, the incidence of robberies in the suburbs was one-third that in cities; the rate for suburban white females stood at 2.0 per 1,000 compared to 24.6 for black men in urban centers. US Department of Justice, *Sourcebook of Criminal Justice Statistics 2000* (Washington, D.C.: Government Printing Office, 2001). Victimization studies in the United States and Western Europe likewise converge to refute the idea that "the middle classes [have] found themselves becoming regular victims of crime." Garland, *The Culture of Control*, 153.

ambivalence of the state's response" is not so much ambivalence as a predictable organizational division in the labor of management of the disruptive poor. Bourdieu's theory of the state is helpful here in enabling us to discern that the "adaptive strategies" recognizing the state's limited capacity to stem crime by stressing prevention and devolution are pursued in the penal sector of the *bureaucratic* field, while what Garland calls the "nonadaptive strategies" of "denial and acting out" to reassert that very capacity operate in the *political* field, especially in its relation to the journalistic field.[21] These strategic tacks are the two complementary components of the same state response of penalization—"adaptation" at the administrative level and "acting out" at the political level—which has trumped the alternatives of socialization and medicalization, and it has proved well suited to governing the new social insecurity.

Garland does report similarities in the recent evolution and aims of social and penal policies. But, like Joel Handler and Jamie Peck coming from the welfare side, he reduces these to simple analogies or to parallel by-products of broad external factors undeserving of an extended analysis.* This is all the more surprising since, in his earlier work on the historical transition from late Victorian penality to the modern "penal-welfare complex" in England a century ago, Garland had fruitfully connected social and criminal policies by tracing how the "techniques, images, and principles" of poor relief, social insurance, moral education, and social work were extended to punishment so that "the institutions of penality came to support and extend those of the social realm."[22] And so, even as he skillfully connects crime control to a vast array of social forces and cultural sentiments, he continues to isolate its analysis from that of the spectrum of state programs which set the life parameters and chances of the (sub)proletariat, whereas *Punishing the Poor* insists on the necessity to bring poverty and justice policies into a single analytic framework. As noted in chapter 1, Garland views changes

*"The institutional and cultural changes that have occurred in the crime control field are *analogous* to those that have occurred in the welfare state more generally." *The Culture of Control*, 174, emphasis added. And, again, in the closing pages of the book: "The themes that dominate crime policy . . . have come to organize the politics of poverty as well. The same premises and purposes that transformed criminal justice are evident in the programmes of 'welfare reform' that have been adopted" in both the United States and the United Kingdom, such that "*the parallels* with the new field of crime control are impossible to miss." Ibid., 196 and 197. But Garland devotes a mere two pages to analyzing these parallels, when workfare would deserve to be placed at the policy epicenter of his "culture of control."

in penality over the past thirty years as primarily cultural, precisely because he overlooks the structural and functional linkages established between astringent welfare and munificent prisonfare, leading to the creation of a novel disciplinary apparatus to supervise the troublemaking poor and submit them to the rule of deregulated wage labor. For him, "the correctionalist apparatus associated with penal-welfarism is, for the most part, still in place." It has been greatly enlarged; it has lost its professional autonomy; and it has been supplemented by a "third sector" of crime control composed of public-private partnerships. But morphological changes in crime management pale before changes in the "cognitive assumptions, normative commitments, and emotional sensibilities" that make up the crystallizing culture of control.[23] By contrast, I argue that the gargantuan growth of America's penal state has de facto altered its architecture and purpose, sapping the design of "corrections" from within, and that it has been supplemented, not just by "the organized activities of communities and commercial organizations" outside the bureaucratic field but, more crucially, by the restrictive revamping of welfare into workfare inside of it under the aegis of the same paternalist philosophy of moral behaviorism.

Thirdly, like other leading analysts of contemporary punishment such as Jock Young, Franklin Zimring, and Michael Tonry, Garland sees the punitive turn as the reactionary progeny of right-wing politicians.[24] But this book has demonstrated, first, that the penalization of poverty is not a simple return to a past state of affairs but a genuine institutional innovation and, second, that it is by no means the exclusive creature of neoconservative politics. If politicians of the Right invented the formula, it was employed and refined by their centrist and even "progressive" rivals. Indeed, the president who oversaw by far the biggest increase in incarceration in American history (in absolute numbers and growth rate of the inmate population as well as in budgets and personnel) is not Ronald Reagan but William Jefferson Clinton.* Across the Atlantic, it is the Left of Blair in England, Schröder in Germany, Jospin in France, d'Alema in Italy, and Gonzalez in Spain that negotiated the shift to proactive penalization, not their conservative predecessors. This is because the root cause of the punitive turn is *not late modernity but neoliberal-*

*Under Reagan, the prison population of the United States jumped from 320,000 to 608,000, adding 288,000 convicts, compared to a rise from 851,000 to 1,316,000 for a gain of 465,000 convicts on Clinton's watch. Total direct correctional expenditures grew by $8 billion (from $4.2 billion to $12.4 billion) under Reagan, but ballooned by nearly $15 billion (from $18.7 billion to $33 billion) under Clinton. Bureau of Justice Statistics, *Sourcebook of Criminal Justice Statistics* (Washington, D.C.: Government Printing Office, 2006), tables 6.1 and 1.9.

ism, a project that can be indifferently embraced by politicians of the Right or the Left.

The jumble of trends that Garland gathers under the umbrella term of late modernity—the "modernizing dynamic of capitalist production and market exchange," shifts in household composition and kinship ties, changes in urban ecology and demography, the disenchanting impact of the electronic media, the "democratization of social life and culture" (including unbridled individualism and the proliferation of plural identities and "communities of choice")—are not only exceedingly vague and loosely correlated. They are either not peculiar to the closing decades of the twentieth century, specific to the United States, or show up in their most pronounced form in the social-democratic countries of Northern Europe, which have *not* been submerged by the international wave of penalization.* Moreover, the onset of late modernity has been gradual and evolutionary, whereas the recent permutations of penality have been abrupt and revolutionary.

Punishing the Poor contends that it is not the generic "risks and anxieties" of "the open, porous, mobile society of strangers that is late modernity"[25] that have fostered retaliation against lower-class categories perceived as undeserving and deviant types seen as irrecuperable, but the specific *social* insecurity generated by the fragmentation of wage labor, the hardening of class divisions, and the erosion of the established ethnoracial hierarchy guaranteeing an effective monopoly over collective honor to whites in the United States (and to nationals in the European Union). The sudden expansion and consensual exaltation of the penal state after the mid-1970s is not a culturally reactionary reading of "late modernity," but a ruling-class response aiming to redefine the perimeter and missions of Leviathan, so as to establish a new economic regime based on capital hypermobility and labor flexibility and to curb the social turmoil generated at the foot of the urban order by the public policies of market deregulation and social welfare retrenchment that are core building blocks of neoliberalism.

*Ibid., 77–89. By most measures, Scandinavian countries are the most "late modern" nations, yet they have best resisted the drift toward the punitive containment of urban marginality. In 2004, Norway sported an incarceration rate of 65 inmates for 100,000 residents, Finland 66, Denmark 70, and Sweden 85, in spite of crime rates very similar to those of the United States (aside from lethal violence). The total number of inmates of these four countries (17,715) was inferior to the number of jail detainees in the sole city of Los Angeles (18,512).

A Sociological Specification of Neoliberalism

The invention of the double regulation of the insecure fractions of the postindustrial proletariat via the wedding of social and penal policy at the bottom of the polarized class structure is a major *structural innovation* that takes us beyond the model of the welfare-poverty nexus elaborated by Piven and Cloward just as the Fordist-Keynesian regime was coming unglued. The birth of this institutional contraption is also not captured by Michel Foucault's vision of the "disciplinary society" or by David Garland's notion of the "culture of control," neither of which can account for the unforeseen timing, socioethnic selectivity, and peculiar organizational path of the abrupt turnaround in penal trends in the closing decades of the twentieth century. For the punitive containment of urban marginality through the simultaneous rolling back of the social safety net and the rolling out of the police-and-prison dragnet and their knitting together into a carceral-assistantial lattice is not the spawn of some broad societal trend—whether it be the ascent of "biopower" or the advent of "late modernity"—but, at bottom, an exercise in *state crafting*. It partakes of the correlative revamping of the perimeter, missions, and capacities of public authority on the economic, social welfare, and penal fronts. This revamping has been uniquely swift, broad, and deep in the United States, but it is in progress—or in question—in all advanced societies submitted to the relentless pressure to conform to the American pattern.

Yet Michel Foucault was right to advise us to "take penal practices less as a consequence of juridical theories than as a chapter in political anatomy."[26] Accordingly, the present book has been intended, not as a variation on the well-rehearsed score of the political economy of imprisonment, so much as a contribution to the political sociology of the transformation of the field of power in the era of triumphant neoliberalism. For tracking the roots and modalities of America's stupendous drive to hyperincarceration opens a unique route into the sanctum of the neoliberal Leviathan. It leads us to articulate two major theoretical claims. The first is that *the penal apparatus is a core organ of the state*, expressive of its sovereignty and instrumental in imposing categories, upholding material and symbolic divisions, and molding relations and behaviors through the selective penetration of social and physical space. The police, the courts, and the prison are not mere technical appendages for the enforcement of lawful order, but vehicles for the political production of reality and for the oversight of deprived and defamed social categories and their reserved territories. Students of American politics, stratification, poverty, race, and civic culture who neglect them do so at huge analytic and policy costs. The second thesis is that the ongoing capitalist "revolution from above" commonly called *neoliberalism entails the enlargement and exaltation of the penal sector* of the bureaucratic field, so that the state may check the social reverberations caused by the diffusion of social insecurity in the lower rungs of the class and ethnic hierarchy as well as assuage popular discontent over the dereliction of its traditional economic and social duties.

Neoliberalism readily resolves what for Garland's "culture of control" remains an enigmatic paradox of late modernity, namely, the fact that "control is now being re-emphasized in every area of social life—*with the singular and startling exception of the economy*, from whose deregulated domain most of today's major risks routinely emerge."[27] The neoliberal remaking of the state also explains the steep class, ethnoracial, and spatial bias stamping the simultaneous retraction of its social bosom and expansion of its penal fist: the populations most directly and adversely impacted by the convergent revamping of the labor market and public aid turn out also to be the privileged "beneficiaries" of the penal largesse of the authorities. Finally, neoliberalism correlates closely with the international diffusion of punitive policies in both the welfare and the criminal domains. It is not by accident that the advanced countries that have imported, first workfare measures designed to buttress the discipline of desocialized wage work and then variants of US-style criminal justice measures, are the Commonwealth nations which also pursued aggressive policies of economic deregulation inspired by the "free market" nostrums come from America, whereas the countries which remained committed to a strong regulatory state curbing social insecurity have best resisted the sirens of "zero tolerance" policing and "prison works." Similarly, societies of the Second World such as Brazil, South Africa, and Turkey, which adopted superpunitive penal planks inspired by American developments in the 1990s and saw their prison population soar as a result, did so not because they had at long last reached the stage of "late modernity," but because they had taken the route of market deregulation and state retrenchment.* But

*Loïc Wacquant, *Les Prisons de la misère* (Paris: Raisons d'agir Éditions, 1999), translated as *Prisons of Poverty* (Minneapolis: University of Minnesota Press, 2009); and L. Wacquant, "Towards a Dictatorship over the Poor? Notes on the Penalization of Poverty in Brazil," *Punishment & Society* 5, no. 2 (April 2003): 197–205. British developments provide a pellucid illustration of this process of sequential policy transfer from the economic to the social welfare to the penal realm. The Thatcher and Major governments first deregulated the labor market and subsequently introduced US-style welfare-to-work measures, as recounted by David P. Dolowitz, *Learning from America: Policy Transfer and the Development of the British Workfare State* (Eastbourne: Sussex

to discern these multilevel connections between the upsurge of the punitive Leviathan and the spread of neoliberalism, it is necessary to develop a precise and broad conception of the latter. Instead of discarding neoliberalism, as Garland does, on account of it being "rather too specific" a phenomenon to account for penal escalation,[28] we must expand our conception of it and move from an economic to a fully sociological understanding.

Neoliberalism is an elusive and contested notion, a hybrid term awkwardly suspended between the lay idiom of political debate and the technical terminology of social science, which moreover is often invoked without clear referent. For some, it designates a hard-wired reality to which one cannot but accommodate (often equated with "globalization"), while others view it as a doctrine that has yet to be realized and ought to be resisted. It is alternately depicted as a tight, fixed, and monolithic set of principles and programs that tend to homogenize societies, or as a loose, mobile, and plastic constellation of concepts and institutions adaptable to variegated strands of capitalism. Whether singular or polymorphous, evolutionary or revolutionary, the prevalent conception of neoliberalism is essentially economic: it stresses an array of market-friendly policies such as labor deregulation, capital mobility, privatization, a monetarist agenda of deflation and financial autonomy, trade liberalization, interplace competition, and the reduction of taxation and public expenditures.[29] But this conception is thin and incomplete, as well as too closely bound up with the sermonizing discourse of the advocates of neoliberalism. We need to reach beyond this economic nucleus and elaborate a thicker notion that identifies the institutional machinery and symbolic frames through which neoliberal tenets are being actualized.

A minimalist sociological characterization can now be essayed as follows. Neoliberalism is a *transnational political project* aiming to remake the nexus of market, state, and citizenship from above. This project is carried by a new global ruling class in the making, composed of the heads and senior executives of transnational firms, high-ranking politicians, state managers and top officials of multinational organizations (the OECD, WTO, IMF, World Bank, and the European Union),

---

Academic Press, 1998). Then Anthony Blair expanded workfare and complemented it by overhauling the criminal justice system through the slavish imitation of American penal remedies, with the result that England now sports "the highest imprisonment rate, the most crowded prisons, the severest sentencing practices, the most hyperbolic anti-crime rhetoric, and the worst racial disparities in Europe." Michael H. Tonry, *Punishment and Politics: Evidence and Emulation in the Making of English Crime Control Policy* (London: Willan, 2004), 168.

and cultural-technical experts in their employ (chief among them economists, lawyers, and communications professionals with germane training and mental categories in the different countries).[30] It entails, not simply the reassertion of the prerogatives of capital and the promotion of the marketplace, but the articulation of four institutional logics:

1. *economic deregulation*, that is, reregulation aimed at promoting "the market" or market-like mechanisms as the optimal device, not only for guiding corporate strategies and economic transactions (under the aegis of the shareholder-value conception of the firm), but for organizing the gamut of human activities, including the private provision of core public goods, on putative grounds of efficiency (implying deliberate disregard for distributive issues of justice and equality).

2. *welfare state devolution, retraction, and recomposition* designed to facilitate the expansion and support the intensification of commodification, and in particular to submit reticent individuals to the discipline of desocialized wage labor via variants of "workfare" establishing a quasi-contractual relationship between the state and lower-class recipients treated not as citizens but as clients or subjects (stipulating their behavioral obligations as condition for continued public assistance).

3. the *cultural trope of individual responsibility*, which invades all spheres of life to provide a "vocabulary of motive"—as C.-Wright Mills would say—for the construction of the self (on the model of the entrepreneur), the spread of markets, and legitimation for the widened competition it subtends, the counterpart of which is the evasion of corporate liability and the proclamation of state irresponsibility (or sharply reduced accountability in matters social and economic).

4. *an expansive, intrusive, and proactive penal apparatus* which penetrates the nether regions of social and physical space to contain the disorders and disarray generated by diffusing social insecurity and deepening inequality, to unfurl disciplinary supervision over the precarious fractions of the postindustrial proletariat, and to reassert the authority of Leviathan so as to bolster the evaporating legitimacy of elected officials.

A central *ideological* tenet of neoliberalism is that it entails the coming of "small government": the shrinking of the allegedly flaccid and overgrown Keynesian welfare state and its makeover into a lean and nimble workfare state, which "invests" in human capital and "activates" communal springs and individual appetites for work and civic participation through "partnerships" stressing self-reliance, commitment to paid work, and managerialism. The present book demonstrates that the neoliberal state turns out to be quite different *in actuality*:

while it embraces laissez-faire at the top, releasing restraints on capital and expanding the life chances of the holders of economic and cultural capital, it is anything but laissez-faire at the bottom. Indeed, when it comes to handling the social turbulence generated by deregulation and to impressing the discipline of precarious labor, the new Leviathan reveals itself to be fiercely interventionist, bossy, and pricey. The soft touch of libertarian proclivities favoring the upper class gives way to the hard edge of authoritarian oversight, as it endeavors to direct, nay dictate, the behavior of the lower class. "Small government" in the economic register thus begets "big government" on the twofold frontage of workfare and criminal justice. The results of America's grand experiment in creating the first society of advanced insecurity in history are in: *the invasive, expansive, and expensive penal state is not a deviation from neoliberalism but one of its constituent ingredients.*

Remarkably, this is a side of neoliberalism that has been obfuscated or overlooked by its apologists and detractors alike. This blind spot is glaring in Anthony Giddens's celebrated reformulation of neoliberal imperatives into the platform of New Labour. In his manifesto for the *The Third Way*, Giddens highlights high rates of crime in deteriorating working-class districts as an indicator of "civic decline" and curiously blames the Keynesian welfare state for it (not deindustrialization and social retrenchment): "The egalitarianism of the old left was noble in intent, but as its rightist critics say has sometimes led to perverse consequences—visible, for instance, in the social engineering that has left a legacy of decaying, crime-ridden housing estates." He makes "preventing crime, and reducing fear of crime" through state-locality partnerships central to "community regeneration," and he embraces the law-and-order mythology of "broken windows": "One of the most significant innovations in criminology in recent years has been the discovery [sic] that the decay of day-to-day civility relates directly to criminality. . . . Disorderly behavior unchecked signals to citizens that the area is unsafe."* But Giddens studiously omits the punishment side of the equation: *The Third Way* contains not a single mention of the prison and glosses over the judicial hardening and carceral boom

*Anthony Giddens, *The Third Way: The Renewal of Social Democracy* (Cambridge: Polity Press, 1999), 16, 78–79, and 87–88. In support of order-maintenance policing, Giddens repeatedly cites George Kelling and Catherine Coles's *Fixing Broken Windows*, the "how-to-cut-crime handbook" sponsored by the Manhattan Institute which "demonstrate[s] that the broken windows thesis is 100 percent correct," according to the fervent back cover endorsement of John DiIulio (apostle of mass incarceration and founding director of the White House Office of Faith-Based and Community Initiatives under George W. Bush).

that have everywhere accompanied the kind of economic deregulation and welfare devolution it promotes. This omission is particularly startling in the case of Britain, since the incarceration rate of England and Wales jumped from 88 inmates per 100,000 residents in 1992 to 142 per 100,000 in 2004, even as crime was receding, with Anthony Blair presiding over the single largest increase of the convict population in the country's history (matching the feat of Clinton, his cosponsor of the "Third Way" on the other side of the Atlantic).

A similar oversight of the centrality of the penal institution to the new government of social insecurity is found in the works of eminent critics of neoliberalism. David Harvey's extended characterization of "the neoliberal state" in his *Brief History of Neoliberalism* is a case in point, which appositely spotlights the obdurate limitations of the traditional political economy of punishment which the present book has sought to overcome. For Harvey, neoliberalism aims at maximizing the reach of market transactions via "deregulation, privatization, and withdrawal of the state from many areas of social provision." As in previous eras of capitalism, the task of Leviathan is "to facilitate conditions for profitable capital accumulation on the part of both domestic and foreign capital," but now this translates into penal expansion:

> The neoliberal state will resort to coercive legislation and policing tactics (anti-picketing rules, for instance) to disperse or repress collective forms of opposition to corporate power. Forms of surveillance and policing multiply: in the US, incarceration became a key state strategy to deal with problems arising among the discarded workers and marginalized populations. *The coercive arm of the state is augmented to protect corporate interests* and, if necessary, to *repress dissent*. None of this seems consistent with neoliberal theory.[31]

With barely a few passing mentions of the prison and not a line on workfare, Harvey's account of the rise of neoliberalism is woefully incomplete. His conception of the neoliberal state turns out to be surprisingly restricted, first, because he remains wedded to the repressive conception of power, instead of construing the manifold missions of penality through the expansive category of production. Subsuming penal institutions under the rubric of coercion leads him to ignore the expressive function and ramifying material effects of the law and its enforcement, which are to generate controlling images and public categories, to stoke collective emotions and accentuate salient social boundaries, as well as to activate state bureaucracies so as to mold social ties and strategies. Next, Harvey portrays this repression as aimed at political opponents to corporate rule and dissident movements that challenge the hegemony of private property and profit, whereas this book shows that the primary targets of penalization in the post-Fordist era have been the precarious fractions of the proletariat concentrated in the tainted districts of dereliction of the dualizing metropolis who, being squeezed by the urgent press of day-to-day subsistence, have little capacity or care to contest corporate rule.*

Third, for the author of *Social Justice and the City* the state "intervenes" through coercion only when the neoliberal order breaks down, to repair economic transactions, ward off challenges to capital, and resolve social crises. By contrast, *Punishing the Poor* argues that the present penal activism of the state—translating into carceral bulimia in the United States and policing frenzy throughout Western Europe—is an ongoing, routine feature of neoliberalism. Indeed, it is not economic failure but economic success that requires the aggressive deployment of the police, court, and prison in the nether sectors of social and physical space. And the rapid turnings of the law-and-order merry-go-round are an index of the reassertion of state sovereignty, not a sign of its weakness. Harvey does note that the retrenchment of the welfare state "leaves larger and larger segments of the population exposed to impoverishment" and that "the social safety net is reduced to a bare minimum in favor of a system that emphasizes individual responsibility and the victim is all too often blamed."[32] But he does not recognize that it is precisely these normal disorders, inflicted by economic deregulation and welfare retrenchment, that are managed by the enlarged penal apparatus in conjunction with supervisory workfare. Instead, Harvey invokes the bogeyman of the "prison-industrial complex," suggesting that incarceration is a major plank of capitalist profit-seeking and accumulation when it is a disciplinary device entailing a gross drain on the public coffers and a tremendous drag on the economy.**

*Harvey lists as the main targets of state repression radical Islam and China on the foreign front and "dissident internal movements" such as the Branch Davidians at Waco, the participants in the Los Angeles riots of April 1991 (triggered by the acquittal of the policemen involved in the videotaped beating of motorist Rodney King), and the antiglobalization activists that rocked the G-8 meeting in Seattle in 1999. David Harvey, *A Brief History of Neoliberalism* (New York: Oxford University Press, 2005), 83. But squashing episodic and feeble mobilizations against corporate power and state injustice hardly requires throwing millions behind bars.

**"The rise of surveillance and policing and, in the case of the US, incarceration of recalcitrant elements in the population indicates a more sinister turn toward intense social control. The prison-industrial complex is a thriving sector (alongside personal security services) in the US economy." Ibid., 165. We saw in chapter 5 that the growth of private incarceration stopped cold with the stock market crash of 2000, that it is

Fourth and last, Harvey views the neoconservative stress on coercion and order restoration as a temporary fix for the chronic instability and functional failings of neoliberalism, whereas I construe authoritarian moralism as an *integral constituent of the neoliberal state* when it turns its sights on the lower rungs of the polarizing class structure. Like Garland, Harvey must artificially dichotomize "neoliberalism" and "neoconservatism" to account for the reassertion of the supervisory authority of the state over the poor because his narrow economistic definition of neoliberalism replicates its ideology and truncates its sociology.* To elucidate the paternalist transformation of penality at century's turn, then, we must imperatively escape the "crime-and-punishment" box, but also exorcise once and for all the ghost of Louis Althusser, whose instrumentalist conception of Leviathan and crude duality of ideological and repressive apparatuses gravely hamstring the historical anthropology of the state in the neoliberal age. Following Bourdieu, we must fully attend to the internal complexity and dynamic recomposition of the bureaucratic field, as well as to the constitutive power of the symbolic structures of penality to trace the intricate meshing of market and moral discipline across the economic, welfare, and criminal justice realms.[33]

For the spread of economic deregulation and the about-turn in social policy observed in nearly all advanced societies, away from broad-based entitlements and automatic benefits toward a selective approach promoting private operators, contractual incentives, and targeted support conditional on certain behaviors aimed at closing the exit option from the labor market, have been accompanied everywhere by the enlargement and reinforcement of the facilities, activities, and reach of penal bureaucracies effectively pointed at the lower end of the class, ethnic, and spatial spectrum. The so-called *enabling state* that dominates policy making at the top on both sides of the Atlantic at century's

---

a phenomenon derivative of the expansion of the penal state, and that the weight of corrections in the national economy is negligible in any case.

*For Harvey, neoconservatism is a rival political formation which "veers away from the principles of pure neoliberalism" in "its concern for order as an answer to the chaos of individual interests" and "for an overweening morality." It might replace the neoliberal state, as the latter is "inherently unstable." Ibid., 81–82. Garland adopts a similar tack to resolve the empirical contradiction between the libertarian ethos of late modernity and the authoritarian tendencies of neoliberalism: "While the neoliberal agenda of privatization, market competition and spending restraints that shaped much of the administrative reform that government imposed on criminal justice agencies behind the scenes, it was the very different neo-conservative agenda that dictated the public face of penal policy." Garland, *The Culture of Control*, 131.

dawn[34] turns out to be a *disabling state* for those at the bottom who are adversely affected by the conjoint restructuring of the economy and polity, in that it acts toward them in ways that systematically curtail social opportunities and cut off social ligatures—to recall the two components of "life chances" according to Ralf Dahrendorf.[35]

In his meticulous comparison of eugenic measures in the 1920s, compulsory work camps in the 1930s, and workfare schemes in the 1990s in England and America, Desmond King has shown that "illiberal social policies" which seek to direct citizens' conduct coercively are "intrinsic to liberal democratic politics" and reflective of their internal contradictions.[36] Even as they contravene standards of equality and personal liberty, such programs are periodically pursued because they are ideally suited to highlighting and enforcing the boundaries of membership in times of turmoil; they are fleet vehicles for broadcasting the newfound resolve of state elites to tackle offensive conditions and assuage popular resentment toward derelict or deviant categories; and they diffuse conceptions of otherness that materialize the symbolic oppositions anchoring the social order. With the advent of the neoliberal government of social insecurity mating restrictive workfare and expansive prisonfare, however, it is not just the policies of the state that are illiberal, but *its very architecture*. Tracking the coming and workings of America's punitive politics of poverty after the dissolution of the Fordist-Keynesian order and the implosion of the black ghetto reveals that neoliberalism brings about, not the shrinking of government, but the erection of a *centaur state*, liberal at the top and paternalistic at the bottom, which presents radically different faces at the two ends of the social hierarchy: a comely and caring visage toward the middle and upper classes, and a fearsome and frowning mug toward the lower class.

It bears stressing here that the building of a Janus-faced Leviathan practicing liberal paternalism has not proceeded according to some master-scheme concocted by omniscient rulers. To reiterate the warnings sounded in the book's prologue: the overall fitness of punitive containment to regulate urban marginality at century's dawn is a rough *post-hoc functionality* born of a mix of initial policy intent, sequential bureaucratic adjustment, and political trial-and-error and electoral profit-seeking at the point of confluence of three relatively autonomous streams of public measures concerning the low-skill employment market, public aid, and criminal justice. The complementarity and interlocking of state programs in these three realms is partly designed and partly an emergent property, fostered by the practical need to handle correlated contingencies, their common framing through the lens of moral behaviorism, and the shared ethnoracial bias stamping their routine operations—with (sub)proletarian blacks from the hyperghetto figuring at the point of maximum impact where market deregulation, welfare retrenchment, and penal penetration meet. The coalescing government of social insecurity is neither a preordained historical development, propelled by an irresistible systemic logic, nor an organizational constellation free of contradictions, incongruities, and gaps. Indeed, both workfare and the penitentiary as we know them at the outset of the twenty-first century are riven by deep irrationalities, glaring insufficiencies, and built-in imbalances,[37] and their coupling is doubly so. The refusal of "the functionalism of the worst" is inseparably a rebuff of the conspiratorial view of class rule and a rejection of the flawed logic of structural hyperdeterminism which transmutes the *historically conditioned outcome of struggles*, waged over and inside the bureaucratic field to shape its perimeter, capacities, and missions, into a necessary and ineluctable fact.

Whatever the modalities of their advent, it is indisputable that the linked stinginess of the welfare wing and munificence of the penal wing under the guidance of moralism have altered the makeup of the bureaucratic field in ways that are profoundly injurious to democratic ideals.[38] As their sights converge onto the same marginal populations and territories, deterrent workfare and the neutralizing prison foster vastly different profiles and experiences of citizenship across the class and ethnic spectrum. They not only contravene the fundamental principle of equality of treatment by the state and routinely abridge the individual freedoms of the dispossessed. They also undermine the consent of the governed through the aggressive deployment of involuntary programs stipulating personal responsibilities just as the state is withdrawing the institutional supports necessary to shoulder these and shirking its own social and economic charges. And they stamp the precarious fractions of the proletariat from which public aid recipients and convicts issue with the indelible seal of unworthiness. In short, the penalization of poverty splinters citizenship along class lines, saps civic trust at the bottom, and sows the degradation of republican tenets. The establishment of the new government of social insecurity discloses, *in fine*, that *neoliberalism is constitutively corrosive of democracy*.

***

In 1831, Alexis de Tocqueville and his friend Gustave de Beaumont were dispatched to the United States by King Louis-Philippe to gather evidence on the workings of the American prison system and make recommendations for its application in France. Much as with zero-tolerance policing in the 1990s, the US penitentiary had then captured the imagination of policy-makers in Western Europe who wished to learn from it how to stem the brewing disorders associated with the massing of the emerging proletariat in and around the industrializing cities.[39] It is in the course of that journey of penal exploration that Tocqueville gathered the materials for his celebrated tome on *Democracy in America*. In it, the master-thinker of liberalism marveled at the fluidity and vibrancy of a society stamped by the "prevalence of the bourgeois classes" driven by the love of commerce, industry, and consumption, which illumined the future of modernity in the glow of capitalist optimism. In a darker corner of his writings from that trip, Tocqueville also extolled the American prison as an efficient and benevolent variant of despotism, capable, by the sheer press of the social isolation and anxiety it puts on inmates, of stripping criminal dispositions and inculcating in their stead wholesome habits of labor, thrift, and submission to conventional morality among the recalcitrant poor. He was positively struck that, whereas "society in the United States gives the example of the most extended liberty, the prisons of the same country offer the spectacle of the most complete despotism."[40] Some one-hundred and seventy years on, America's relapse into what Tocqueville christened the "monomania of the penitentiary" has combined with the shift to punitive workfare to effectively extend the formula of despotic control from the prison to the neoliberal regulation of social marginality.

Acknowledgments

The present book draws upon investigations of urban marginality, penality, and welfare carried out across a decade (1996–2006). This long stretch of research, extending deep into domains initially foreign to me, was made possible by the support of a MacArthur Foundation Fellowship, a Mellon Fellowship from the Center for Social Theory and Comparative History at UCLA, Russell Sage Foundation backing for an interdisciplinary conference called "Probing the Penal State" (organized in collaboration with Bruce Western, then at Princeton University), and small grants from the Committee on Research and the Center for European Studies at the University of California, Berkeley. Special thanks are due to Robert Brenner and Iván Szelényi for facilitating the 1998 sojourn in Los Angeles during which I carried out the pilot fieldwork on big-city jails and to the New School for Social Research for a similar stint in New York City the following year.

Punishing the Poor is the second volume in a sort of trilogy seeking to unravel the tangled triangular connections between class restructuring, ethnoracial division, and state crafting in the era of neoliberal ascendancy. The first book, *Urban Outcasts: A Comparative Sociology of Advanced Marginality* (Cambridge: Polity Press, 2008), centers on the class/race nexus in the postindustrial city. In it, I trace the sudden implosion of the black American ghetto after the acme of the civil rights movement to turns in public policies and contrast it to the slow decomposition of European working-class territories. I refute the thesis of the transatlantic convergence of neighborhoods of relegation on the pattern of the dark ghetto; and I diagnose the emergence of a new regime of urban marginality abetted by the fragmentation of wage labor, the retrenchment of the social state, and territorial stigmatization. The sequel, *Punishing the Poor,* takes up the class/state nexus on both the social and penal fronts. It charts how public officials responded to this emerging marginality (which their own economic and social policies have spawned) through punitive containment. It shows that the new politics and policy of poverty wedding restrictive workfare and expansive prisonfare, invented in America over the past two decades, partake of the neoliberal project, properly reconceptualized. The third volume, *Deadly Symbiosis: Race and the Rise of the Penal State* (Cambridge: Polity Press, 2010), examines how ethnoracial partition lubricates and intensifies penalization, and how rolling out the penal state in turn remakes race. It starts with a historical and theoretical model of the mutual interpenetration of the collapsing hyperghetto and the overgrown prison in the United States, moves to encompass the overincarceration of postcolonial migrants in the European Union, and ends with plumbing the militarization of marginality in the Brazilian metropolis as revelator of the deep logic of penalization. Readers wishing to track down the full antecedents and ramifications of the arguments offered in the present tome are advised to work through the three volumes in succession; but each book is self-standing and can be ascertained in its own terms (provided that the overall economy of the research project in which they arise is understood).

The template for *Punishing the Poor* was laid out in a presentation entitled "La montée de l'État pénal en Amérique" to Pierre Bourdieu's Workshop on the Sociology of the State at the Ecole des hautes études en sciences sociales, Paris, in May 1997, and in the thematic issue of *Actes de la recherche en sciences sociales* (124, September 1998) on the transition "From Social State to Penal State." This issue initiated two lines of research. The first explores the modalities and mechanisms of the international diffusion of "made in the USA" techniques of law enforcement (incarnated by "zero tolerance" policing) and led to the publication of *Prisons of Poverty* (Raisons d'agir Editions, 1999, which has since appeared in 18 languages; in English with University of Minnesota Press, 2009). The second tackles the implications of punitive workfare for the urban (sub)proletariat and the coupling of the Right and Left hand of the state elaborated in *Punishing the Poor*, which revises and supersedes my earlier analyses of the nexus of penality and neoliberalism. (A truncated French version of this work was released illegally in book form in 2004 by a rogue publisher in France; the present volume, revised in Fall 2006–Winter 2007, is the correct and complete statement of my investigations into the topic.) A earlier version of Chapter 6 appeared in the special issue of *Theoretical Criminology* on "New Social Studies of the Prison" edited by Mary Bosworth and Richard Sparks (vol. 4, no. 3, 2000, pp. 395–407).

Punishing the Poor owes much to the intellectual stimuli and personal support received throughout its long gestation from colleagues and friends in Paris, New York, Berkeley, Keele, Bologna, Rotterdam, and Rio de Janeiro, too numerous to be mentioned here individually. Special mention must be made of the constant and judicious counsel of Pierre Bourdieu; the generosity of Nilo Batista and Vera Malaguti at the

Instituto Carioca de Criminologia; the enthusiasm of Lucas Rubinich and Horacio Verbitsky in Buenos Aires; the hearty encouragements of David Garland and Franklin Zimring to trespass and forage on their turf; and the analytic and editorial perspicuity of Megan Comfort, Franck Poupeau, and Gretchen Purser. Anthony Chen, Eric Klinenberg, Josh Guetzkow and Joshua Page supplied first-rate research assistance at various stages. James Ingram provided decisive assistance by producing an early working draft of a shorter French version of this book.

I benefited from the oral comments and written exchanges triggered by presentations on the themes of this book at a variety of venues, including the annual meetings of the American Society for Criminology, the American Anthropological Association, the American Sociological Association, the International Sociological Association, the Society of the Advancement of Socioeconomics, and the International Labor Organization, as well as to keynote addresses to the German, French, Portuguese, and Norwegian Sociological Associations, the Annual York Lecture, the Westergard Lecture at Claremont College, and the Oxford Amnesty Lecture. Public debates organized outside of academe by activist groups, unions, and professional organizations ranging from correctional officers and teachers to criminal lawyers, social workers, and inmates in a half-dozen countries were instrumental in keeping me honest, motivated, and alert to the practical bearing of my analyses across borders. Finding an intellectual abode in the "Politics, History, and Culture" series at Duke University Press stimulated me to bring out the Bourdieusian grounding of my model left implicit in earlier publications on the topic and to better explicate the inseparably material and symbolic mode of analysis it entails. For this I am grateful to Julia Adams, George Steinmetz, and Reynolds Smith.

Notes

Prologue

1. Linda Williams, *Hard Core: Power, Pleasure, and the "Frenzy of the Visible"* (Berkeley: University of California Press, 1989), and Michael S. Kimmel, *Men Confront Pornography* (New York: Crown, 1990).

2. Max Weber, *Economy and Society*, ed. Guenther Roth and Claus Wittich (Berkeley: University of California Press, 1978 [1918–20]), 2:905.

3. Frédéric Ocqueteau, ed., *Community Policing et Zero Tolerance à New York et Chicago. En finir avec les mythes*, La sécurité aujourd'hui (Paris: La Documentation française, 2003), back-cover text.

4. An extended analysis of this double process of state retrenchment and "polarization from below" in the metropolis of the First World is Loïc Wacquant, *Urban Outcasts: A Comparative Sociology of Urban Marginality* (Cambridge: Polity Press, 2008).

5. For the materialist lineage, see in particular, Karl Marx and Friedrich Engels, "Marx and Engels on Crime and Punishment" (a selection of texts), in *Crime and Capitalism: Readings in Marxist Criminology*, ed. David Greenberg, 45–56 (Palo Alto, Calif.: Mayfield, 1981); Ian R. Taylor, Paul Walton, and Jock Young, *The New Criminology: For a Social Theory of Deviance* (London: Routledge, 1988); and Stanley Cohen and Thomas Blomberg, eds., *Punishment and Social Control* (New York: Aldine de Gruyter, 2003). On the symbolic side, see Émile Durkheim, *The Division of Labor in Society* (New York: Free Press, 1994 [1893]), bk. 1; Stephen Lukes and Andrew Scull, eds., *Durkheim and the Law* (Stanford, Calif.: Stanford University Press, 1995); Kai Erikson, *Wayward Puritans: A Study in the Sociology of Deviance* (New York: Wiley, 1966); and Pierre Bourdieu, "Rethinking the State: On the Genesis and Structure of the Bureaucratic Field," *Sociological Theory* 12, no. 1 (March 1994 [1993]): 1–19 (reprinted in abridged form in *Practical Reasons* [Cambridge: Polity, 1998 (1994)], 35–63).

6. W. E. B. Du Bois, *The Philadelphia Negro: A Social Study* (Philadelphia: University of Pennsylvania Press, 1996 [1899]), 235.

7. Georg Rusche and Otto Kirschheimer, *Punishment and Social Structure* (New Brunswick, N.J.: Transaction Press, 2003 [1939]); on the recent rebirth of studies of criminal policy inspired by this book in Europe and North America, read the excellent preface to this new edition by Dario Melossi.

8. Pierre Bourdieu, *Language and Symbolic Power* (Cambridge: Polity Press, 1990 [1985]), 229–33 and 248–51.

9. For a provocative discussion of the contradictory impulses in early US carceral history, read David Rothman, *Conscience and Convenience: The Asylum and its Alternatives in Progressive America* (New York: Aldine, 1980, new

ed. 2002); for a rich historical illustration of the concrete workings of multiple paradigms of welfare policy-making at different levels of the same bureaucratic field, see George Steinmetz, *Regulating the Social: The Welfare State and Local Politics in Imperial Germany* (Princeton, N.J.: Princeton University Press, 1993).

10. A warning against "identifying a policy regime with a single determining principle" is effectively sounded by Julia Adams and Tasleem Padamsee, "Signs and Regimes: Reading Feminist Work on Welfare States," *Social Politics* 8, no. 1 (Spring 2001): 1–23.

11. See, for example, among many interchangeable sources, "Critical Resistance to the Prison-Industrial Complex," ed. Rose Braz et al., special issue, *Social Justice* 27, no. 3 (2000); Angela Y. Davis and Cassandra Shaylor, "Race, Gender, and the Prison Industrial Complex: California and Beyond," *Meridians: Feminism, Race, Transnationalism* 2, no. 1 (Spring 2001): 1–26; and David Lapido, "The Rise of America's Prison-Industrial Complex," *New Left Review* 7 (January 2001), 109–23.

12. For a different approach that distinguishes between five "idioms of poverty" determining as many possible treatments by the state, Godfried Engbersen et al., *De effecten van armoede* (Amsterdam: Amsterdam University Press, 1998), 13–26.

13. Leonard C. Feldman, *Citizens without Shelter: Homelessness, Democracy, and Political Exclusion* (Ithaca, N.Y.: Cornell University Press, 2004).

1. Social Insecurity and the Punitive Upsurge

1. For an overview of the penal scene in the main countries of the First World, see John Pratt et al., eds., *The New Punitiveness: Trends, Theories, and Perspectives* (London: Willan Publishing, 2004); Iñaki Rivera Beiras, *Recorrídos y posibles formas de la penalidad* (Barcelona: Anthropos Editorial, 2004); Laurent Mucchielli and Philippe Robert, eds., *Crime et sécurité. L'état des savoirs* (Paris: La Découverte, 2002); Alessandro Dal Lago, *Giovani, stranieri e criminali* (Rome: Manifestolibri, 2001); and Wolfgang Ludwig-Mayerhofer, ed., *Soziale Ungleichheit, Kriminalität und Kriminalisierung* (Opladen: Leske & Budrich, 2000).

2. The emergence of this discursive nebula is described in detail in the French case by Annie Collovald, "Des désordres sociaux à la violence urbaine," *Actes de la recherche en sciences sociales* 136–37 (March 2001): 104–14.

3. See in particular, on these points, Serge Paugam, *Le Salarié de la précarité* (Paris: Presses Universitaires de France, 2000); Göran Therborn, *Between Sex and Power: Family in the World 1900–2000* (London: Routledge, 2004); Loïc Wacquant, *Urban Outcasts: A Comparative Sociology of Advanced Marginality* (Cambridge: Polity Press, 2008); Hartmut Häußermann, Martin Kronauer, and Walter Siebel, eds., *An den Rändern der Städte: Armut und Ausgrenzung* (Frankfurt-am-Main: Suhrkamp, 2004); and Stéphane Beaud, *80% au bac et après? Les enfants de la démocratisation scolaire* (Paris: La Découverte, 2002).

4. On the punitive turn of Blair's New Labour, the product of a servile imitation of US policies, and its disastrous results by the twofold yardstick of criminal and social justice, read Michael Tonry, *Punishment and Politics: Evi-*

dence and Emulation in the Making of English Crime Control Policy (London: Willan Publishing, 2004); the *aggiornamento* of the Italian Left in penal matters is described by Salvatore Verde, *Massima sicurezza. Dal carcere speciale allo stato penale* (Rome: Odradek, 2002); the law-and-order conversion of the neosocialists under Jospin's leadership in France is retraced in Loïc Wacquant, *Les Prisons de la misère* (Paris: Raisons d'agir Éditions, 1999).

5. Loïc Wacquant, "The Rise of Advanced Marginality," *Acta sociologica* 39, no. 2 (1996): 121–39, and Ian Taylor and Ruth Jamieson, "Fear of Crime and Fear of Falling: English Anxieties Approaching the Millennium," *European Journal of Sociology* 39, no. 1 (Spring 1998): 149–75.

6. Norwegian criminologist Thomas Mathiesen detected and denounced it as early as 1990 on the carceral front; see Thomas Mathiesen, *Prison on Trial: A Critical Assessment* (London: Sage, 1990), 11–14.

7. For a detailed case study of these struggles in the exemplary case of Mexico, read Sarah L. Babb, *Managing Mexico: Economists from Nationalism to Neoliberalism* (Princeton, N.J.: Princeton University Press, 2001); see also Marion Fourcade-Gourinchas and Sarah L. Babb, "The Rebirth of the Liberal Creed: Paths to Neoliberalism in Four Countries," *American Journal of Sociology* 108 (November 2002): 533–79, and the double issue of *Actes de la recherche en sciences sociales* coordinated by Yves Dezalay on the "Sociology of Globalization" (nos. 151–52, February 2004).

8. Jamie Peck, *Workfare States* (New York: Guilford, 2001), and Catherine Lévy, *Vivre au minimum. Enquête dans l'Europe de la précarité* (Paris: Editions La Dispute, 2003), chap. 4.

9. Mike Hawkins, *Social Darwinism in European and American Thought, 1860–1945: Nature as Model and Nature as Threat* (Cambridge: Cambridge University Press, 1997).

10. Pierre Bourdieu et al., *La Misère du monde* (Paris: Seuil, 1993), 219–28, translated as *The Weight of the World* (Cambridge: Polity Press, 1999), and P. Bourdieu, *Contre-feux* (Paris: Raisons d'agir Editions, 1997), 9–15, translated as *Acts of Resistance: Against the Tyranny of the Market* (Cambridge: Polity Press, 1999).

11. Ann Chih Lin, "The Troubled Success of Crime Policy," in *The Social Divide: Political Parties and the Future of Activist Government*, ed. Margaret Weir, 312–57 (Washington, D.C.: Brookings Institution and Russell Sage Foundation, 1998).

12. "M. Jospin contre la pense unique internationale. Un entretien avec le Premier Ministre," *Le Monde*, 7 January 1999. My emphasis.

13. "Le gouvernement veut allier prévention et répression contre la délinquance," *Le Monde*, 20 March 1999. My emphases. We recognize here in passing the trope of "perversity," dear to reactionary thought. Albert O. Hirschman, *The Rhetoric of Reaction: Perversity, Futility, Jeopardy* (Cambridge, Mass.: Belknap Press, 1991).

14. Ronald Reagan, "Remarks at the Conservative Political Action Conference Dinner," 18 February 1983.

15. Transcript from the National Assembly debate on the orientation and programming bill for domestic security (nos. 36 and 53), first session of Tuesday 16 July 2002, presided by Jean-Louis Debré; available online at www.assemblee-nat.fr. My emphases.

16. Ibid. Later in the debate, Maurice Leroy thanks Julien Dray on behalf of the UDF (center-right) parliamentary group for his intervention and his hearty "spirit of responsibility."

17. Michel Foucault, "Du gouvernement des vivants," in *Résumé des cours, 1970–1982* (Paris: Juillard, 1989), 123. For a historiographic illustration of this notion, read Giovanna Procacci, *Gouverner la misère. La question sociale en France, 1789–1848* (Paris: Seuil, 1993); for a conceptual reconsideration and elaboration, Nikolas Rose and Mariana Valverde, "Governed by Law?" *Social & Legal Studies* 7, no. 4 (December 1998): 541–52.

18. Michael K. Brown, *Race, Money, and the American Welfare State* (Ithaca, N.Y.: Cornell University Press, 1999), 323–53.

19. Loïc Wacquant, "Deadly Symbiosis: When Ghetto and Prison Meet and Mesh," *Punishment & Society* 3, no. 1 (winter 2001): 95–133.

20. Michel Pialoux and Florence Weber, "La gauche et les classes populaires. Réflexions sur un divorce," *Mouvements* 23 (September–October 2002): 10–21.

21. Frances Fox Piven and Richard A. Cloward, *Regulating the Poor: The Functions of Public Welfare*, new expanded ed. (New York: Vintage, 1993 [1971]), xvii.

22. The organic connections between race and welfare in America are disentangled by Jill Quadagno, *The Color of Welfare: How Racism Undermined the War on Poverty* (New York: Oxford University Press, 1994), and Kenneth Neubeck and Noel A. Cazenave, *Welfare Racism: Playing the Race Card against America's Poor* (New York: Routledge, 2001). I endeavor to untie the Gordian knot of racial division and penality in my book *Deadly Symbiosis: Race and the Rise of the Penal State* (Cambridge: Polity Press, 2009).

23. Piven and Cloward, *Regulating the Poor*, 381–87, 395–97.

24. Similarities in the culture and organization of the supervision of single mothers who received public aid and convicts behind bars or released on parole are immediately apparent upon the parallel reading of Sharon Hays, *Flat Broke with Children: Women in the Age of Welfare Reform* (New York: Oxford University Press, 2003), and John Irwin, *The Warehouse Prison* (Los Angeles: Roxbury, 2004).

25. See Ann Orloff, "Gender in the Welfare State," *Annual Review of Sociology* 22 (1996): 51–78, and the influential essay by Julia Adams and Tasleem Padamsee, "Signs and Regimes: Reading Feminist Research on Welfare States," *Social Politics* 8, no. 1 (Spring 2001): 1–23, as well as the literature they review and cite.

26. Dorothy Roberts, "Welfare and the Problem of Black Citizenship," *Yale Law Journal* 105, no. 6 (April 1996): 1563–1602.

27. Piven and Cloward, *Regulating the Poor*, 407.

28. Ibid., 10, 13, and 128 for prison; 20 and 317–18 for jail.

29. Ibid., 367.

30. David J. Rothman, *The Discovery of the Asylum: Social Order and Disorder in the New Republic* (New York: Aldine de Gruyter, 2002 [1971]), and Thomas L. Dumm, *Democracy and Punishment: Disciplinary Origins of the United States* (Madison: University of Wisconsin Press, 1987).

31. Joel F. Handler and Yeshekel Hasenfeld, *We the Poor People: Work, Poverty, and Welfare* (New Haven, Conn.: Yale University Press, 1997).

32. Edwin Amenta, Chris Bonastia, and Neal Caren, "U.S. Social Policy in Comparative and Historical Perspective: Concepts, Images, Arguments, and Research Strategies," *Annual Review of Sociology* 27 (2001): 213–34; Alice O'Connor, "Poverty Research and Policy in the Post-Welfare Era," *Annual Review of Sociology* 26 (2000): 547–62; Paul Pierson, "Three Worlds of Welfare State Research," *Comparative Political Studies* 33, nos. 6/7 (September 2000): 791–821.

33. See, among an endless roster of similar volumes, Edward J. Latessa et al., eds., *Correctional Contexts: Contemporary and Classical Readings* (Los Angeles: Roxbury Publishing, 2001).

34. Michael Tonry, *Malign Neglect: Race, Crime, and Punishment in America* (New York: Oxford University Press, 1995), 7 and 10.

35. David Garland, *The Culture of Control: Crime and Social Order in Contemporary Society* (Chicago: University of Chicago Press, 2001), 174 and viii.

36. Ibid., 174 and 175. Original emphasis.

37. Ibid., 205.

38. I have sketched the implications of the punitive containment of marginality in Brazil in "Towards a Dictatorship over the Poor? Notes on the Penalization of Poverty in Brazil," *Punishment & Society* 5, no. 2 (April 2003): 197–205.

39. Loïc Wacquant, "The Penalisation of Poverty and the Rise of Neoliberalism," *European Journal of Criminal Policy and Research*, Special issue on "Criminal Justice and Social Policy," 9, no. 4 (winter 2001): 401–12. On the accelerating international circulation of crime-fighting discourses and policies in recent years, and the preponderant influence of American products in these exchanges, see the studies collected by Tim Newburn and Richard Sparks, eds., *Criminal Justice and Political Cultures: National and International Dimensions of Crime Control* (London: Willan Publishing, 2004).

40. Vivien Stern, "Mass Incarceration: 'A Sin Against the Future'?" *European Journal of Criminal Policy and Research* 3 (October 1996): 14.

41. Jerome G. Miller, *Search and Destroy: African-American Males in the Criminal Justice System* (Cambridge: Cambridge University Press, 1996), 102–3. In 1989, the federal government reportedly spent an astonishing $89 million in payment to "snitches" as part of the national War on drugs. Dan Baum, *Smoke and Mirrors: The War on Drugs and the Politics of Failure* (Boston: Little, Brown, 1996), 307.

42. Bernard Brunet, "Le traitement en temps réel: la justice confrontée à l'urgence comme moyen habituel de résolution de la crise sociale," *Droit et société* 38 (1998): 91–107; Gilles Sainatti, "Le souverainisme policier, nouvelle doctrine pénale," *Justice* 161 (July 1999): 12–18; and Laurent Bonelli, "Evolutions et régulations des illégalismes populaires en France depuis le début des années 1980," *Cultures et conflits* 51 (fall 2003): 9–42.

43. "La préfecture de Nîmes fiche secrètement 179 jeunes," *Libération*, 10 January 2000. Thanks to Aline Cahoreau and Jean Launay, from the Nîmes branch of the Syndicat de la Magistrature, for sending me the various pieces of this file.

44. David Downes and René van Swaaningen, "The Road to Dystopia? Changes in the Penal Climate of the Netherlands," in *Crime and Justice in the Netherlands*, ed. Michael Tonry and Catrien Bijleveld, 31–72 (Chicago: University of Chicago Press, 2006).

45. For two different, but in this regard converging, assessments of the evolution of (post)national prerogatives in Western Europe, see Yasemin Nuhoğlu Soysal, *Limits of Citizenship: Migrants and Postnational Membership in Europe* (Chicago: University of Chicago Press, 1994), and Christian Joppke, *Immigration and the Nation-State: The United States, Germany, and Great Britain* (Oxford: Oxford University Press, 1999).

46. Patrick Bruneteaux and Corinne Lanzarini, *Les Nouvelles figures du sous-prolétariat* (Paris: L'Harmattan, 2000); for a more complex and nuanced picture, Sébastien Schehr, *La Vie quotidienne des jeunes chomeurs* (Paris: Presses Universitaires de France, 1999).

47. Gøsta Esping-Andersen, ed., *Welfare States in Transition: National Adaptations in Global Economies* (London: Sage, 1996).

48. On this point, see the account of Abdel Mabrouki and Thomas Lebègue, *Génération précaire* (Paris: Le Cherche-Midi, 2004), and the practical recommendations of Attac, *Travailleurs précaires, unissez-vous* (Paris: Mille et une nuits, 2003); on the other side of the Atlantic, Dan Clawson, *The Next Upsurge: Labor and New Social Movements* (Ithaca, N.Y.: Cornell University Press, 2003), and the scenarios discussed in Rick Fantasia and Kim Voss, *Hard Work: Remaking the American Labor Movement* (Berkeley: University of California Press, 2004), chap. 5.

49. David Lyon, *The Electronic Eye: The Rise of the Surveillance Society* (Minneapolis: University of Minnesota Press, 1994), and William G. Staples, *Everyday Surveillance: Vigilance and Visibility in Postmodern Life* (Lanham, Md.: Rowman & Littlefield, 2000).

50. On the notion of the "infrastructural power" of the state, as against its "despotic power," see Michael Mann, "The Autonomous Power of the State: Its Origins, Mechanisms and Results," *Archives européennes de sociologie* 25, no. 2 (summer 1984): 185–213.

51. The nightmarish functioning of this "digital poorhouse" in a remote region of the Appalachian mountains is described in painstaking detail from the inside by John Gilliom, *Overseers of the Poor: Surveillance, Resistance, and the Limits of Privacy* (Chicago: University of Chicago Press, 2001); the proximate social control of recipients of public aid in Europe is discussed by Lévy, *Vivre au minimum*, 69–89.

52. Michel Foucault, "Two Lectures," (1976), in *Power/Knowledge: Selected Interviews and Other Writings, 1972–1977*, ed. Colin Gordon (New York: Pantheon, 1980), 97. Elsewhere Foucault elaborates: "What makes power hold good" is that "it traverses and produces things, it induces pleasure, forms of knowledge, and produces discourse. It needs to be considered as a productive network which runs through the whole social body, much more than as a negative instance whose function is repression." Michel Foucault, "Vérité et pouvoir," *L'Arc* 70 (1977), reprinted in *Power/Knowledge*, 119. My translation.

53. Karl Marx, *Theories of Surplus Value*, cited in Tom Bottomore and Maximilien Rubel, eds., *Karl Marx: Selected Writings in Society and Social Philosophy* (New York: McGraw-Hill, 1958), 159.

54. The scholarly and policy collaboration involved in the invention of the administrative notion of "sensitive neighborhood" in France is dissected by Sylvie Tissot, "Identifier ou décrire les 'quartiers sensibles'? Le recours aux

indicateurs statistiques dans la politique de la ville," *Genèses* 54 (spring 2004): 90–111.

55. On the invention of this category by the Renseignements généraux (the division of the French police entrusted with "domestic spying"), see Laurent Bonelli, "Renseignements Généraux et violences urbaines," *Actes de la recherche en sciences sociales* 136–37 (March 2001): 95–103; also Laurent Mucchielli, "L'expertise policière de la 'violence urbaine': sa construction intellectuelle et ses usages dans le débat public français," *Déviance et société* 24, no. 4 (December 2000): 351–75.

56. The "power-knowledge" constellation that subtends the genesis and success of the biological theory of crime (then and now) is explored by David Horn in *The Criminal Body: Lombroso and the Anatomy of Deviance* (New York: Routledge, 2003).

57. To recall the savory expression of one of the prophets of law-and-order catastrophe, former police commissioner Richard Bousquet, author of *Insécurité: nouveaux risques. Les quartiers de tous les dangers* (Paris: L'Harmattan, 1998), with a preface by the unshakeable "urban security" entrepreneur Alain Bauer. The properties and social bases of the success of these new experts are dissected by Pierre Rimbert, "Les nouveaux managers de l'insécurité: production et circulation d'un discours sécuritaire," in *La Machine à punir*, eds. Gilles Sainati and Laurent Bonelli, 203–34 (Paris: Dagorno, 2001).

58. Most of the commonplaces conveyed in a "technicized" form by the IHESI can be found in the veritable compendium of idiocies of the "one-way security-think" published by the Socialist leader and former minister of the interior Daniel Vaillant, *La Sécurité, priorité à gauche* (Paris: Omnibus, 2003).

59. See Laurent Mucchielli, *Violences et insécurités. Fantasmes et réalités dans le débat français* (Paris: La Découverte, 2001), 34–37, and the file "Christian de Bongain, alias Xavier Raufer," assembled by Réseau Voltaire (www.reseauvoltaire.net).

60. From the department's introductory brochure, available online at www.drmcc.org (dated January 2004).

61. Eric Debardieux, "Insécurité et clivages sociaux: l'exemple des violences scolaires," *Les Annales de la recherche urbaine* 75 (June 1997): 43–50, and Franck Poupeau, *Contestations scolaires et ordre social. Les enseignants de Seine-Saint-Denis en grève* (Paris: Syllepse, 2004).

62. On this topic, one can turn to Austin Sarat, *The Killing State: Capital Punishment in Law, Politics, and Culture* (New York: Oxford University Press, 1998); and Franklin E. Zimring, *The Contradictions of American Capital Punishment* (New York: Oxford University Press, 2003). For a stimulating critique of the thesis of "American exceptionalism" on this front, read David Garland, "Capital Punishment and American Culture," *Punishment & Society* 7, no. 4 (October 2005): 347–76.

63. Antoine Garapon and Ioannis Papadopoulos, *Juger en Amérique et en France. Culture juridique française et common law* (Paris: Odile Jacob, 2003), 277.

2. The Criminalization of Poverty in the Post–Civil Rights Era

1. Robert Castel, "La 'guerre à la pauvreté' et le statut de la misère dans une société d'abondance," *Actes de la recherche en sciences sociales* 19 (January 1978): 47–60; Michael Katz, *Poverty and American Policy* (New York: Academic Press, 1983); and Walter I. Trattner, *From Poor Law to Welfare State: A Social History of Welfare in America*, 6th ed. (New York: Free Press, 1998).

2. John Irwin and James Austin, *It's About Time: America's Imprisonment Binge*, 2nd ed. (Belmont, Calif.: Wadsworth, 1997).

3. Peter Dreier and John Atlas, "US Housing Policy at the Crossroads," *Journal of Urban Affairs* 18, no. 4 (October 1997): 341–70.

4. The notion of bureaucratic field is elaborated by Pierre Bourdieu, "Rethinking the State: On the Genesis and Structure of the Bureaucratic Field," *Sociological Theory* 12, no. 1 (March 1994 [1993]): 1–19.

5. Alan Wolfe, *The Limits of Legitimacy: Political Contradictions of Contemporary Capitalism* (New York: Free Press, 1977).

6. Theda Skocpol, "A Society without a 'State'? Political Organization, Social Conflict, and Welfare Provision in the United States," *Journal of Public Policy* 7, no. 3 (December 1988): 349–71, and T. Skocpol, "Formation de l'État et politiques sociales en Amérique," *Actes de la recherche en sciences sociales*, 96/97 (March 1993), 21–38.

7. New York Times, *The Downsizing of America* (New York: Times Books, 1996), 56–57.

8. Michael J. Lipsky, *Street-Level Bureaucracy: Dilemmas of the Individual in Public Services* (New York: Russell Sage Foundation, 1980).

9. Donald T. Critchlow and Ellis W. Hawley, eds., *Federal Social Policy: The Historical Dimension* (University Park: Pennsylvania State University Press, 1988).

10. Jacob S. Hacker, *The Divided Welfare State: The Battle over Public and Private Social Benefits in the United States* (New York: Cambridge University Press, 2002), 3.

11. Theda Skocpol, *Social Policy in the United States* (Cambridge, Mass.: Harvard University Press, 1995), esp. 209–27; and Hacker, *The Divided Welfare State*, chaps. 6 and 7.

12. For a pointed analysis of the ignominious vocabulary and disgraced images attached to welfare, see Sanford F. Schram, *Words of Welfare: The Poverty of Social Science and the Social Science of Poverty* (Minneapolis: University of Minnesota Press, 1995).

13. Robert Havemann, *Poverty Policy and Poverty Research: The Great Society and the Social Sciences* (Madison: University of Wisconsin Press, 1987).

14. According to the typology put forth by Richard Titmuss in his *Essays on the Welfare State* (Boston: Beacon, 1969).

15. On the troubled and troubling history of public assistance to single mothers, read the masterful study by Linda Gordon, *Pitied but Not Entitled: Single Mothers and the History of Welfare* (New York: Free Press, 1994).

16. Frances Fox Piven and Richard A. Cloward, *Regulating the Poor: The Functions of Public Welfare*, exp. ed. (New York: Vintage, 1994 [1971]); and Margaret Weir, *Politics and Jobs: The Boundaries of Employment Policy in the United States* (Princeton, N.J.: Princeton University Press, 1992).

17. Michael Goldfield, *The Color of Politics: Race and the Mainsprings of American Politics* (New York: New Press, 1997), and the vast body of work surveyed by Vincent L. Hutchings and Nicholas A. Valentino, "The Centrality of Race in American Politics," *Annual Review of Political Science* 7 (2004): 383–408.

18. David Roediger, *The Wages of Whiteness: Race and the Making of the American Working Class* (New York: Verso, 1991).

19. On the articulation between racial schism and the structure and functioning of the state during these three historical periods, see, respectively, Robert Lieberman, *Shifting the Color Line: Race and the American Welfare State* (Cambridge, Mass.: Harvard University Press, 1998); Jill Quadagno, *The Color of Welfare: How Racism Undermined the War on Poverty* (New York: Oxford University Press, 1994); and Martin Gilens, *Why Americans Hate Welfare: Race, Media, and the Politics of Anti-Poverty Policy* (Chicago: University of Chicago Press, 2000).

20. Sheldon Danziger and Peter Gottschalk, *America Unequal* (Cambridge, Mass.: Harvard University Press, 1995); Laurence Mishel, Jared Bernstein, and John Schmidt, *The State of Working America, 1996–1997* (New York: M. E. Sharpe, 1997); and John W. Sloan, "The Reagan Presidency, Growing Inequality, and the American Dream," *The Policy Studies Journal* 25, no. 3 (fall 1997): 371–86.

21. Herbert Gans, *The War against the Poor: The Underclass and Antipoverty Policy* (New York: Basic Books, 1995).

22. Gary Oldfield and Carole Askinaze, *Closing the Door: Conservative Policy and Black Opportunity* (Chicago: University of Chicago Press, 1991), and Thomas Byrne Edsall and Mary D. Edsall, *Chain Reaction: The Impact of Race, Rights, and Taxes on American Politics* (New York: W. W. Norton, 1991).

23. Piven and Cloward, *Regulating the Poor*, 375–76.

24. This is asserted with the utmost seriousness by political scientist Lawrence Mead in *The New Politics of Poverty: The Nonworking Poor in America* (New York: Basic Books, 1992), 237.

25. Lyke Thompson, "The Death of General Assistance in Michigan," in *The Politics of Welfare Reform*, ed. Donald F. Morris and Lyke Thompson, 79–108 (Thousand Oaks, Calif.: Sage, 1995).

26. Fayyaz Hussain, *Social Welfare Reform in Michigan: Intent and Implications for the Poor*, Research Report 17 (Lansing, Mich.: Julian Samora Research Institute, 1996).

27. Geoffrey deVerteuil, Woobae Lee, and Jennifer Wolch, "New Spaces for the Local Welfare State? The Case of General Relief in Los Angeles County," *Social & Cultural Geography* 3, no. 3 (September 2002): 229–46.

28. Committee on Ways and Means, U.S. House of Representatives, *1996 Green Book* (Washington, D.C.: US Government Printing Office, 1996), 329, 332, and 341.

29. *1996 Green Book*, 920–21.

30. *1996 Green Book*, 932 and 933; and Demetrios Caraley, "Dismantling the Federal Safety Net: Fictions versus Realities," *Political Science Quarterly* 111, no. 2 (summer 1996): 225–58, esp. 243–45.

31. Robert Mohl, "Shifting Patterns of American Urban Policy since 1900," in *Urban Policy in Twentieth-Century America*, ed. Arnold R. Hirsch and Ray-

mond A. Mohl, 1–45 (New Brunswick, N.J.: Rutgers University Press, 1993); and R. Allen Hays, *The Federal Government and Urban Housing: Ideology and Change in Public Policy*, 2nd ed. (Stony Brook: State University of New York Press, 1995).

32. Loïc Wacquant, "The New Urban Color Line: The State and Fate of the Ghetto in Postfordist America," in *Social Theory and the Politics of Identity*, ed. Craig J. Calhoun, 231–276 (Cambridge, Mass.: Basil Blackwell, 1994).

33. Katherine McFate, *Poverty, Inequality, and the Crisis of Social Policy: Summary of Findings* (Washington, D.C.: Joint Center for Political and Economic Studies, 1991), 1–2. These international disparities are consistent across measures: the United States sports the highest poverty rate of all postindustrial nations whether one uses as threshold the official US Census definition of the "poverty line," 40 percent of median national income, or 50 percent of the same, and whether these formulas are applied to the national population or to children only. Timothy M. Smeeding, Lee Rainwater, and Gary Burtless, *United States Poverty in Cross-National Context*, LIS Working Paper 244 (Luxembourg, Luxembourg Income Study, 2001).

34. Valerie Polakow, *Lives on the Edge: Single Mothers and Their Children in the Other America* (Chicago: University of Chicago Press, 1993).

35. Arne L. Kalleberg, Barbara F. Reskin, and Ken Hudson, "Bad Jobs in America: Standard and Nonstandard Employment Relations and Job Quality in the United States," *American Sociological Review* 65, no. 2 (April 2000): 256–78; and Margaret M. Blair and Thomas Kochan, eds., *The New Relationship: Human Capital in the American Corporation* (Washington, D.C.: Brookings Institution, 2000).

36. Robert E. Parker, *Flesh Peddlers and Warm Bodies: The Temporary Help Industry and Its Workers* (New Brunswick, N.J.: Rutgers University Press, 1994). For additional data and analyses, see Lewis M. Segal and Daniel G. Sullivan, "The Growth of Temporary Services Work," *Journal of Economic Perspectives* 11, no. 2 (spring 1997): 117–36; and Steven Hipple, "Contingent Work in the Late 1990s," *Monthly Labor Review* 124, no. 3 (March 2001): 3–27.

37. For instance, in 1998, the share of "contingent workers" exceeded 5 percent of employment in 7 of 20 industrial sectors, ranging from construction to social services to automotive repair services. Hipple, "Contingent Work in the Late-1990s," table 3, p. 7.

38. On this point, see Chris Tilly, *Half a Job: Bad and Good Part-Time Jobs in a Changing Labor Market* (Philadelphia: Temple University Press, 1996); Lonnie Golden, "The Expansion of Temporary Help Employment in the US, 1982 to 1992: A Test of Alternative Economic Explanations," *Applied Economics* 28, no. 9 (September 1996): 1127–41; and Beth A. Rubin, "Flexible Accumulation, the Decline of Contract, and Social Transformation," *Research in Social Stratification and Mobility* 14 (1995): 297–323.

39. David M. Gordon, *Fat and Mean: The Corporate Squeeze of Working Americans and the Myth of Managerial "Downsizing"* (New York: Free Press, 1996).

40. The active antiunionization campaign waged by American employers during this period is described in detail in Richard Freeman, ed., *Working Under Different Rules* (New York: Russell Sage Foundation, 1995), and Rick

Fantasia and Kim Voss, *Hard Work: Remaking the American Labor Movement* (Berkeley: University of California Press, 2004), chap. 2.

41. Peter Capelli et al., *Change at Work* (New York: Oxford University Press, 1997), and Art Budros, "The New Capitalism and Organizational Rationality: The Adoption of Downsizing Programs, 1979–1994," *Social Forces* 76, no. 1 (September 1997): 229–49.

42. New York Times, *The Downsizing of America*, and the data culled by Paul Osterman, *Securing Prosperity: The American Labor Market. How It Has Changed and What to Do about It* (Princeton, N.J.: Princeton University Press, 1999).

43. See Stephen Steinberg, *Turning Back: The Retreat from Racial Justice in American Thought and Policy* (Boston: Beacon, 1995). It should, however, be noted that women are much more favorably disposed toward such measures, as they are for most matters of social policy.

44. Ruth Horowitz, *Teen Mothers: Citizens or Dependents?* (Chicago: University of Chicago Press, 1995).

45. Gary Burtless, "The Effect of Reform on Employment, Earnings, and Income," in *Welfare Policy for the 1990s*, ed. David T. Ellwood and Phoebe H. Cottingham (Cambridge, Mass.: Harvard University Press, 1989); and Kathryn Edin and Laura Lein, *Making Ends Meet: How Single Mothers Survive Welfare and Low-Wage Work* (New York: Russell Sage Foundation, 1997).

46. Piven and Cloward, *Regulating the Poor*, 396.

47. Michael Tonry, *Malign Neglect: Race, Class, and Punishment in America* (New York: Oxford University Press, 1995).

48. William M. Adler, *Land of Opportunity: One Family's Quest for the American Dream in the Age of Crack* (New York: Atlantic Monthly Press, 1995); John M. Hagedorn, *People and Folks: Gangs, Crime and the Underclass in a Rustbelt City* (Chicago: Lakeview Press, 1988); and Wacquant, "The New Urban Color Line," 246–54 and 258–64.

49. William Julius Wilson, *The Truly Disadvantaged: The Underclass, the Inner City, and Public Policy* (Chicago: University of Chicago Press, 1987), and Christopher Jencks and Paul Peterson, eds., *The Urban Underclass* (Washington, D.C.: Brookings Institution, 1991).

50. All figures in this paragraph are from Tonry, *Malign Neglect*, 110–11 and 112, whose probing analysis of racial disparity in the War on drugs deserves close reading.

51. Jerome G. Miller, *Hobbling a Generation: Young African-American Males in the Criminal Justice System of America's Cities* (Alexandria, Va.: National Center on Institutions and Alternatives, 1992).

52. Troy Duster, "The New Crisis of Legitimacy in Controls, Prisons, and Legal Structures," *American Sociologist* 26, no. 1 (spring 1995): 20–27.

53. Charles Logan, *Private Prisons: Pros and Cons* (New York: Oxford University Press, 1990); J. Robert Lilly and Mathieu Deflem, "Profit and Penality: An Analysis of the Corrections-Industrial Complex," *Crime & Delinquency* 42, no. 1 (January 1996): 3–20; and, from a sea of interchangeable journalistic reports, this typical article: "For Privately Run Prisons, New Evidence of Success," *New York Times*, 19 August 1995, A6.

54. For a discussion of the "deliberately confrontational and destabilizing

intention" that makes California's version of Three Strikes "stand apart," see Franklin Zimring, Gordon Hawkins, and Sam Kamin, *Punishment and Democracy: Three Strikes and You're Out in California* (New York: Oxford University Press, 2001), 4–6 and 17–24.

55. Cf. Bernard Harcourt, *Illusions of Order: The False Promise of Broken Windows Policing* (Cambridge, Mass.: Harvard University Press, 2001), 46–55.

56. William Ruefle and Kenneth Mike Reynolds, "Curfews and Delinquency in Major American Cities," *Crime and Delinquency* 41, no. 3 (1995): 361.

57. See David McDowall, Colin Loftin, and Brian Wiersema, "The Impact of Youth Curfew Laws on Juvenile Crime Rates," *Crime & Delinquency* 46, no. 1 (January 2000): 76–91, and Kenneth Adams, "The Effectiveness of Juvenile Curfews at Crime Prevention," *Annals of the American Academy of Political and Social Science* 587 (May 2003): 136–59.

58. Howard Snyder, "Juvenile Arrests, 1999," *Juvenile Justice Bulletin*, US Department of Justice (December 2000): 10.

59. Malcolm Feeley and Jonathan Simon, "The New Penology: Notes on the Emerging Strategy of Corrections and Its Implications," *Criminology* 30, no. 4 (November 1992): 466.

60. Alfred Blumstein and Joel Wallman, eds., *The Crime Drop in America* (New York: Cambridge University Press, 2000).

61. Brenda C. Coughlin and Sudhir Alladi Venkatesh, "The Urban Street Gang after 1970," *Annual Review of Sociology* 29 (2003): 45–46. Life course studies have consistently shown that persistence in criminal activity is strongly tied to lack of economic options and paucity of social ties to the "legit world." John H. Laub and Robert J. Sampson, *Shared Beginnings, Divergent Lives: Delinquent Boys to Age 70* (Cambridge, Mass.: Harvard University Press, 2003).

62. John F. Bauman, *Public Housing, Race, and Renewal: Urban Planning in Philadelphia, 1920–1974* (Philadelphia: Temple University Press, 1987); Adam Bickford and Douglas S. Massey, "Segregation in the Second Ghetto: Racial and Ethnic Segregation in American Public Housing, 1977," *Social Forces* 69, no. 4. (June 1991): 1011–36; and William H. Carter, Michael H. Schill, and Susan M. Wachter, "Polarisation, Public Housing and Racial Minorities in US Cities," *Urban Studies* 35, no. 10 (October 1998): 1889–1911.

63. Conservative estimates by experts cited in the findings section of the Prison Rape Elimination Act of 2003 give a prevalence rate of 13 percent. A multisite study of men's prisons in the Midwest found that 21 percent of convicts had experienced at least one episode of forced sexual contact. Cindy Struckman-Johnson and David Struckman-Johnson, "Sexual Coercion Rates in Seven Midwestern Prison Facilities for Men," *Prison Journal* 80, no. 4 (December 2000): 379–90. See Gerald G. Gaes and Andrew L. Golberg, *Prison Rape: A Critical Review of the Literature* (Washington, D.C.: National Institute of Justice, 2004), for a broader survey and cautions on data sensitivity and reliability among this peculiarly pressured population.

64. J. P. May, M. G. Ferguson, R. Ferguson, and K. Cronin, "Prior Nonfatal Firearm Injuries in Detainees of a Large Urban Jail," *Journal of Health Care for the Poor and Underserved* 6, no. 2 (1995): 162–76.

65. J. P. May, D. Hemenway, R. Oen, and K. Pitts, "When Criminals Are Shot: A Survey of Washington, DC, Jail Detainees," *MedGenMed* 2, no. 2 (28 June 2000): E1.

66. The estimates come from Theodore M. Hammett, Mary Patricia Harmon, and William Rhodes, "The Burden of Infectious Disease among Inmates of and Releasees from US Correctional Facilities, 1997," *American Journal of Public Health* 92, no. 11 (November 2002): 1789–94; for a broader discussion, Megan Comfort and Olga Grinstead, "The Carceral Limb of the Public Body: Jail Detainees, Prisoners, and Infectious Disease," *Journal of the International Association of Physicians in AIDS Care* 3, no. 2 (April–June 2004): 45–48.

67. H. Richard Lamb and Linda E. Weinberger, "Persons with Severe Mental Illness in Jails and Prisons: A Review," *Psychiatric Services* 49 (April 1998): 483–92.

68. Stephen K. Smith and Carol J. De Frances, *Indigent Defense* (Washington, D.C.: Bureau of Justice Statistics, 1996).

69. Steven Donziger, *The Real War on Crime* (New York: Harper Perennial, 1996), 188–89. On the indigence of legal assistance to the indigent, which translates into the massive and systematic violation of their basic constitutional rights, see David Cole, *No Equal Justice: Race and Class in the American Criminal Justice System* (New York: New Press, 1999).

70. Robert L. Spangenberg and Marea L. Beeman, "Indigent Defense Systems in the United States," *Law and Contemporary Problems* 58, no. 1 (winter 1995): 31–49, citation p. 48.

71. John Irwin, *The Jail: Managing the Underclass* (Berkeley: University of California Press, 1985), 39–40, 111, 118.

72. For a stimulating discussion of the analytic dangers of "declassifying" crime, read John Hagan, "The Poverty of a Classless Criminology," *Criminology* 30, no. 1 (February 1992): 1–19.

3. Welfare "Reform" as Poor Discipline and Statecraft

1. See "Edelman Decries President's Betrayal of Promise 'Not to Hurt Children,'" *New York Times*, 31 July 1996.

2. Daniel Patrick Moynihan and Paul Simon, editorials published in the *Houston Chronicle*, 2 August 1996 (two among many of the same ilk).

3. "Welfare Hysteria," *New York Times*, 5 August 1996, A11.

4. R. Kent Weaver, *Ending Welfare As We Know It* (Washington, D.C.: Brookings Institution, 2000), 336–38.

5. "Consensus over Welfare," *Washington Post*, 20 August 1996.

6. For a standard efficiency-driven argument drawing "seven lessons" for European policy-makers, which focuses on (dis)incentives to work and typically overlooks the moral(istic) and civic dimensions of the establishment of workfare, see Rebecca Blank, "U.S. Welfare Reform: What's Relevant for Europe?" *Economic Studies* 49, no. 1 (January 2003): 49–74. It stresses this important teaching: that "significant behavioral revolutions [sic] are possible" among the poor (66).

7. Michael Katz, *In the Shadow of the Poorhouse: A Social History of Welfare in America* (New York: Basic Books, 1996).

8. There is already an immense (as well as immensely uneven and mostly technical) literature on this question, despite the lack of historical distance. The most thorough single source to start from is Weaver, *Ending Welfare As*

We Know It, along with Joel Handler's brief but punchy *The Poverty of Welfare Reform* (New Haven, Conn.: Yale University Press, 1995), which shrewdly anticipated many twists and turns of this policy saga.

9. Ruth Sidel, *Keeping Women and Children Last: America's War on the Poor* (New York: Viking, 1996); for the transatlantic comparison, see Ulrike Liebert and Nancy J. Hirschmann, eds., *Women and Welfare: Theory and Practice in the United States and Europe* (New Brunswick, N.J.: Rutgers University Press, 2001), esp. chap. 1; and Jonah D. Levy, "Vice into Virtue? Progressive Politics and Welfare Reform in Continental Europe," *Politics & Society* 27, no. 2 (1999): 239–74.

10. Nancy Folbre and the Center for Popular Economics, *The New Field Guide to Economic Life in America* (New York: New Press, 1996), 68.

11. Martha L. Fineman, "Images of Mothers in Poverty Discourses," *Duke Law Journal* 2 (April 1991): 274–95, and Molly Ladd-Taylor and Lauri Umansky, eds., *"Bad" Mothers: The Politics of Blame in Twentieth-Century America* (New York: New York University Press, 1997), for the broader backdrop.

12. Linda Gordon, *Heroes of Their Own Life: The Politics and History of Family Violence* (New York: Penguin, 1988), 86.

13. Valerie Polakow, *Lives on the Edge: Single Mothers and Their Children in the Other America* (Chicago: University of Chicago Press, 1993).

14. Sanford F. Schram, Joe Soss, and Richard C. Fording, eds., *Race and the Politics of Welfare Reform* (Ann Arbor: University of Michigan Press, 2003).

15. For typical uses of this inchoate notion in the debate on "welfare dependency," see, among others, Lawrence Mead, *The New Politics of Poverty: The Non-Working Poor in America* (New York: Basic Books, 1992); William Kelso, *Poverty and the Underclass: Changing Perceptions of the Poor in America* (New York: New York University Press, 1993); and the caricatural, but for that very reason instructive, essay by Myron Magnet, a member of the editorial board of *Fortune* and "Fellow" at the Manhattan Institute, *The Dream and the Nightmare: The Sixties' Legacy to the Underclass* (New York: William Morrow, 1993).

16. Michael Harrington, *The Other America: Poverty in the United States* (New York: Macmillan, 1962).

17. Martin Gilens, "How the Poor Became Black: The Racialization of American Poverty in the Mass Media," in Schram, Soss, and Fording, eds., *Race and the Politics of Welfare Reform*, 101–30.

18. Evelyn Z. Brodkin, "The Making of an Enemy: How Welfare Policies Construct the Poor," *Law and Social Inquiry* 18, no. 4 (fall 1993): 647–70; also Karen Seccombe, Delores James, and Kimberly Battle Walters, "'They Think You Ain't Much of Nothing': The Social Construction of the Welfare Mother," *Journal of Marriage and the Family* 60, no. 4 (November 1998): 849–65.

19. Loïc Wacquant, "The Great Penal Leap Backward: Incarceration in America from Nixon to Clinton," in *The New Punitiveness: Trends, Theories, Perspectives*, ed. John Pratt et al., 3–26 (London: Willan Publishing, 2004).

20. James I. Patterson, *America's Struggle against Poverty, 1900–1985* (Cambridge, Mass.: Harvard University Press, 1986). For Handler, this notion has been recurring for "560 years," since the Statute of Labourers enacted in England in 1349 sought to compel "valiant beggars" to seek work by restricting the giving of alms. *The Poverty of Welfare Reform*, 5.

21. A compact depiction of these social types and analysis of their import for public debate is Holloway Sparks, "Queens, Teens, and Model Mothers: Race, Gender, and the Discourse of Welfare Reform," in Schram, Soss, and Fording, eds., *Race and the Politics of Welfare Reform*, 171–95. For a fuller examination, read Ange-Marie Hancock, *The Politics of Disgust: The Public Identity of the Welfare Queen* (New York: New York University Press, 2004).

22. Kathleen Mullan Harris, "Work and Welfare among Single Mothers in Poverty," *American Journal of Sociology* 99, no. 2. (September 1993): 317–52; and Kathryn Edin, *There Is a Lot of Month at the End of the Money: How AFDC Recipients Make Ends Meet in Chicago* (New York: Garland, 1993).

23. Kathryn Edin and Laura Stein, *Making Ends Meet: How Single Mothers Survive Welfare and Low-Wage Work* (New York: Russell Sage Foundation, 1997), 43–45.

24. Mark Robert Rank, *Living on the Edge: The Realities of Welfare in America* (New York: Columbia University Press, 1994), 168–73, and Handler, *The Poverty of Welfare Reform*, 50–51.

25. Chad Broughton, "Reforming Poor Women: The Cultural Politics and Practices of Welfare Reform," *Qualitative Sociology* 26, no. 1 (March 2003): 35–51, citation p. 42.

26. Randy Albelda, "Fallacies of Welfare-to-Work Policies," *The Annals of the American Academy of Political and Social Science* 577, no. 1 (January 2001): 66–78.

27. Rank, *Living on the Edge*, 128–44.

28. Harry J. Holzer, *What Employers Want: Job Prospects for Less-Educated Workers* (New York: Russell Sage Foundation, 1996).

29. On this point, see also Phil Moss and Chris Tilly, *Why Black Men Are Doing Worse in the Labor Market: A Review of Supply-Side and Demand-Side Explanations* (New York: Social Science Research Council, 1991).

30. David A. Long and Tammy Ouellette, *Private Employers and TANF Recipients: Final Report Prepared for the Office of the Assistant Secretary for Planning and Evaluation, U.S. Department of Health and Human Services* (Cambridge, Mass.: Abt Associates Inc., 2004), 4–5.

31. National Research Council, *Losing Generations: Adolescents at Risk* (Washington, D.C.: National Academy Press, 1993).

32. See Handler, *The Poverty of Welfare Reform*, 28, on welfare; and Margo Schlanger, "Inmate Litigation," *Harvard Law Review* 116, no. 6 (April 2003): 1555–706, esp. 1627–64, on the "sea change" provoked by the PLRA of 1996 on the side of convicts.

33. Mark Greenberg, *Contract with Disaster: The Impact on States of the Personal Responsibility Act* (Washington, D.C.: Center for Law and Policy, 1994).

34. Martha Burt, *Over the Edge: The Growth of Homelessness in the 1980s* (New York: Russell Sage Foundation, 1992), 57.

35. Cited in "Asylums behind Bars: Prisons Replace Hospitals for the Nation's Mentally Ill," *New York Times*, 5 March 1998. The aggregate transfer of the mentally ill from the hospital system to the carceral system is confirmed by an in-depth statistical analysis of national data by George Palermo, Maurice Smith, and Frank Liska, "Jails versus Mental Hospitals: A Social Dilemma," *International Journal of Offender Therapy and Comparative Criminology* 35, no. 2 (summer 1992): 97–106.

36. The figures for public hospital patients are taken from Andrew Rouse, *Substance Abuse and Mental Health Statistics* (Washington, D.C.: Department of Health and Human Services, 1998). For an overview of this mental health policy and its impacts, see David Mechanic and David A. Rochefort, "Deinstitutionalization: An Appraisal of Reform," *Annual Review of Sociology* 16 (1990): 301–27.

37. Loïc Wacquant, "Les rebuts de la société de marché: toxicomanes, psychopathes et sans-abri dans les prisons de l'Amérique," *Amnis* 3 (fall 2003): 229–44.

38. Margaret Weir, "The Politics of Racial Isolation in Europe and America," in *Classifying by Race*, ed. Paul E. Peterson, 217–42 (Princeton, N.J.: Princeton University Press, 1995).

39. Michael Lipsky, "Bureaucratic Disentitlement in Social Welfare Programs," *Social Service Review* 58 (1984): 2–27.

40. Neil Smith, "Giuliani Time: The Revanchist 1990s," *Social Text* 57, no. 4 (winter 1998): 1–20.

41. This point is argued effectively by Theodor Marmor, Jerry Mashaw, and Philip Harvey, *America's Misunderstood Welfare State: Persistent Myths, Enduring Realities* (New York: Basic Books, 1990).

42. Lee Rainwater and Timothy M. Smeeding, *Doing Poorly: The Real Income of American Children in Comparative Perspective*, Luxemburg Income Study Working Paper 127 (Syracuse, N.Y.: Maxwell School of Citizenship and Public Affairs, 1995); see also Greg J. Duncan and Jeanne Brooks-Gunn, "Urban Poverty, Welfare Reform, and Child Development," in *Locked in the Poorhouse: Cities, Race, and Poverty in the United States*, ed. Fred R. Harris and Lynn A. Curtis, 21–32 (Lanham, Md.: Rowman and Littlefield, 1998).

43. Elaine McCrate, "Welfare and Women's Earnings," *Politics & Society* 25, no. 4 (December 1997): 417–42.

44. A synthesis of the main perspectives and disputes can be found in two review articles typical of the radical and positivist approaches, respectively: Sandra Morgen and Jeff Maskovsky, "The Anthropology of Welfare 'Reform'," *Annual Review of Anthropology* 32 (2003): 315–38; and Daniel T. Lichter and Jayakody R. Rukamalie, "Welfare Reform: How Do We Measure Success?" *Annual Review of Sociology* 28 (2002): 117–41.

45. Martha Coven, *An Introduction to TANF* (Washington, D.C.: Center of Budget and Policy Priorities, 2003).

46. Mike Hout had identified the EITC as the mechanism that would likely deflect the harshest consequences of PRWOA in "Inequality at the Margins: The Effects of Welfare, the Minimum Wage, and Tax Credits on Low-Wage Labor," *Politics & Society* 25, no. 4 (December 1996): 513–24.

47. Coven, *An Introduction to TANF*, 2.

48. Robert A. Moffit, *Welfare Reform: What the Evidence Shows*, Policy Brief no. 13 (Washington, D.C.: Brookings Institution, 2002), and Sharon Hays, *Flat Broke with Children: Women in the Age of Welfare Reform* (New York: Oxford University Press, 2003), 111–12.

49. Heather Boushey and Jeff Wenger, *When Work Just Isn't Enough: Measuring Hardships Faced by Families After Moving from Welfare to Work* (Washington, D.C.: Economic Policy Institute, 2003), 9.

50. Ibid., 15.

51. Pamela Loprest, "Fewer Welfare Leavers Employed in Weak Economy," Snapshots of America's Families 3, n. 5, Urban Institute (August 2003), 2.

52. Pamela Loprest, "Use of Government Benefits Increases among Families Leaving Welfare," Snapshots of America's Families 3, n. 6, Urban Institute (September 2003).

53. Pamela Loprest, "Disconnected Welfare Leavers Face Serious Risks, Use of Government Benefits Increases among Families Leaving Welfare," Snapshots of America's Families 3, n. 6, Urban Institute (September 2003).

54. U.S. Census Bureau, *Historical Poverty Tables, 1970 to 2002* (Washington, D.C.: Government Printing Office, 2003), table 5, accessible online at www.census.gov/hhes/poverty/histpov.

55. Center on Budget and Policy Priorities, *Poverty Increases and Median Income Declines for Second Consecutive Year* (Washington, D.C.: CBPP, September 2003).

56. Coven, *An Introduction to TANF*, 1. "Inflation calculator" available on the web page of the US Department of Labor: www.stats.bls.gov/.

57. US Bureau of Census, *Historical Poverty Tables, 1970 to 2002*, table 18. On the lasting presence and no less tenacious sociopolitical invisibility of impoverished wage earners in America, read David Shipler, *The Working Poor* (New York: Knopf, 2004).

58. Dorothy Roberts, "Welfare and the Problem of Black Citizenship," *Yale Law Journal* 105, no. 6 (April 1996): 1563–602.

59. The AFDC characteristics are for first-time recipients, taken from *Green Book*, 507, and Hays, *Flat Broke with Children*, 254 and 165 (for exposure to violence and health data); the properties of jail detainees are detailed *supra*, 70–74.

60. Sharon Dolovich, "Recent Legislation: Welfare Reform—Punishment of Drug Offenders—Congress Denies Cash Assistance and Food Stamps to Drug Felons," *Harvard Law Review* 110, no. 4 (February 1997): 983–88.

61. This is a specific instance of a more general policy process spotlighted by Anne Schneider and Helen Ingram, "Social Construction of Target Populations: Implications for Politics and Policy," *American Political Science Review* 87, no. 2 (June 1993): 334–47.

62. Handler, *The Poverty of Welfare Reform*, 29; and Wacquant, "The Great Penal Leap Backward," 23.

63. Nancy Fraser and Linda Gordon, "A Genealogy of 'Dependency': Tracing a Keyword of the US Welfare State," *Signs: Journal of Women in Culture and Society* 19, no. 2 (winter 1994): 309–36.

64. The strategies whereby welfare staff reconstruct their new mission as a benefit to clients, in the face of excessive caseloads, unrealistic bureaucratic expectations, and conflicting mandates, are explored by Sandra Morgen, "The Agency of Welfare Workers: Negotiating Devolution, Privatization, and the Meaning of Self-Sufficiency," *American Anthropologist* 103, no. 3 (fall 2001): 747–61.

65. Hays, *Flat Broke with Children*, 10 and 221.

66. On the dynamics of moral rearmament, read Erving Goffman, *Asylums: Essays on the Social Situation of Mental Patients and Other Inmates* (Garden

City, N.Y.: Doubleday, 1961), esp. chap. 2; on the drilling of mental categories, Pierre Bourdieu, *The State Nobility: Elite Schools in the Field of Power* (Cambridge: Polity Press, 1996 [1989]), esp. 73–101.

67. The classic discussion of these carceral techniques of correction, or "correct training," in the early days of the prison, including "hierarchical surveillance," "normalizing sanction," and "examination," which "surrounded by all its documentary techniques, makes each individual a 'case'," is Michel Foucault, *Discipline and Punish: Birth of the Prison* (New York: Pantheon, 1978 [1975]), 170–94.

68. Hays, *Flat Broke with Children*, 26.

69. Ibid., 38–42, and 60; and Michael Tonry, "Intermediate Sanctions," in *The Handbook of Crime and Punishment*, ed. Michael Tonry, 683–711 (New York: Oxford University Press, 1998), esp. 690–92.

70. Katz, *In the Shadow of the Poorhouse.*

71. Lester M. Salamon, "The Marketization of Welfare: Changing Non-Profit and For-Profit Roles in the American Welfare State," *Social Service Review* 67, no. 1 (1993): 11–28.

72. Henry Brady and Barbara West Snow, *Data Systems and Statistical Requirements for the Personal Responsibility and Work Opportunity Act of 1996* (Berkeley: University of California, 1996), a mimeographed document prepared for the Committee on National Statistics of the National Research Council, National Academy of Science.

73. Government Accounting Office, *Welfare Reform: Interim Report on Potential Ways to Strengthen Federal Oversight of State and Local Contracting* (Washington, D.C.: Government Printing Office, 2002), and S. F. Liebschutz, ed., *Managing Welfare Reform in Five States* (Albany, N.Y.: Rockefeller Institute Press, 2000).

74. Sheila B. Kamerman and Alfred J. Kahn, eds., *Privatization and the Welfare State* (Princeton, N.J.: Princeton University Press, 1989).

75. Mary Bryna Sanger, *The Welfare Marketplace: Privatization and Welfare Reform* (Washington, D.C.: Brookings Institution, 2004), 96. A cautionary note on the built-in limitations of contracting in the US bureaucratic field is sounded by David M. Van Slyke, "The Mythology of Privatization in Contracting for Social Services," *Public Administration Review* 63, no. 3 (May 2003): 296–315.

76. Demetra Smith Nightingale and Nancy M. Pindus, *Privatization of Public Social Services: A Background Paper* (Washington, D.C.: Urban League, 1997).

77. "Giant Companies Entering Race to Run State Welfare Programs," *New York Times*, 15 September 1996, A1 and A14; Barbara Ehrenreich, "Spinning the Poor into Gold: How Corporations Seek to Profit from Welfare Reform," *Harper's Magazine* 295 (fall 1997): 44–52; and Adam Field, "Corporate Caseworkers," *In These Times*, 16 June 1997, 14–16.

78. William P. Ryan, "The New Landscape for Nonprofits," *Harvard Business Review* 77, no. 1 (January 1999): 127–37, and Nicole P. Marwell, "Privatizing the Welfare State: Non-Profit Community-Based Organizations as Political Actors," *American Sociological Review* 69, no. 2 (April 2004): 265–91. The early impact of the marketization of workfare delivery appears to be particularly negative upon nonprofit organizations serving the residents of poor black neighborhoods, according to James Jennings, "Welfare Reform and Neighbor-

hoods: Race and Civic Participation," *Annals of the American Academy of Political and Social Science* 577, no. 1 (January 2001): 94–106; and Michael Reisch and David Sommerfeld, "Race, Welfare Reform, and Nonprofit Organizations," *Journal of Sociology and Social Welfare* 29 (2002): 155–77.

79. J. Robert Lilly and Paul Knepper, "The Corrections Commercial Complex," *Crime and Delinquency* 39, no. 2 (1993): 150–66. I return to the controversial question of the links between private enterprise and incarceration in chapter 5.

80. Handler, *The Poverty of Welfare Reform*, 137.

81. Lawrence Mead, "Welfare Policy: The Administrative Frontier," *Journal of Policy Analysis and Management* 15, no. 3 (summer 1996): 587–600, at 587.

82. It is he, in particular, who pushed for the principle of time limits on benefits inside the Democratic administration. David Ellwood recapitulates his hopes and disappointments in this debate in "Welfare Reform As I Knew It," *The American Prospect* 26 (May–June 1996): 22–29. On the objective and subjective collaboration of "liberal" scholars to the punitive turn of American social policy, read Mimi Abramovitz and Ann Withorn, "Playing by the Rules: Welfare Reform and the New Authoritarian State," in *Without Justice for All: The New Liberalism and Our Retreat from Racial Equality*, ed. Adolph Reed Jr., 151–73 (Boulder, Colo.: Westview, 1999); and Weaver, *Ending Welfare As We Know It*, chaps. 6 and 9.

83. Jamie Peck, *Workfare States* (New York: Guilford, 2001), 341.

84. Frances Fox Piven and Richard A. Cloward, *Regulating the Poor: The Functions of Public Welfare*, expanded ed. (New York: Vintage, 1993 [1971]), and David Rothman, *The Discovery of the Asylum: Social Order and Disorder in the New Republic* (Boston: Little, Brown, 1971).

85. Émile Durkheim, *Moral Education* (New York: Free Press, 1973 [1923]), twelfth lecture on "Academic Penality."

86. Loïc Wacquant, "La généralisation de l'insécurité salariale en Amérique: restructuration d'entreprises et crise de reproduction sociale," *Actes de la recherche en sciences sociales* 115 (November 1996): 65–79; and John E. Schwartz, *Illusions of Poverty: The American Dream in Question* (New York: W. W. Norton, 1998).

87. Mead, "Welfare Policy: The Administrative Frontier," 588.

4. The Great Confinement of the Fin de Siècle

1. On this prison revolt and the orgy of state violence it unleashed, read the still-gripping account of Tom Wicker, *A Time to Die: The Attica Prison Revolt* (New York: Quadrangle Books, 1975).

2. On the (periodic re-) discovery of a hard core of incorrigible criminals, see Sheldon L. Messinger and Richard A. Berk, "Dangerous People," *Criminology* 25, no. 3 (August 1987): 767–81; on the judicial activism that opened the era of the mobilization for prisoners' rights, David F. Greenberg and Fay Stender, "The Prison as a Lawless Agency," *Buffalo Law Review* 21, no. 3 (October 1972): 799–838; on the movement pushing for the civic and legal claims of inmates, James B. Jacob, "The Prisoner's Rights Movement and Its Impacts, 1960–1980," in *Crime and Justice*, ed. Norval Morris and Michael Tonry, 215–43 (Chicago:

University of Chicago Press, 1980); and William L. Selke, *Prisons in Crisis* (Bloomington: Indiana University Press, 1993), 28–36.

3. The hypothesis of a stable incarceration rate is discussed by Franklin E. Zimring and Gordon Hawkins, *The Scale of Imprisonment* (Chicago: University of Chicago Press, 1991), 14–37; on the revisionist history of the prison, see the classic works of David Rothman, *The Discovery of the Asylum: Social Order and Disorder in the New Republic* (Boston: Little, Brown and Co., 1971), and Michel Foucault, *Discipline and Punish: The Birth of the Prison* (New York: Vintage, 1977 [1975]).

4. One finds a conventional overview of the evolution of American carceral institutions and policies in the typical handbook of "penology" by Joycelyn M. Pollack, ed., *Prisons: Today and Tomorrow* (Gaithersburg, Md.: Aspen Publishers, 1997), and a photographic portrait in Michael Jacobson-Hardy, *Behind the Razor Wire: Portrait of a Contemporary American Prison System* (New York: New York University Press, 1999).

5. Norval Morris, "The Contemporary Prison," in *The Oxford History of the Prison: The Practice of Punishment in Western Society*, eds. Norval Morris and David Rothman (New York: Oxford University Press, 1995), 227. Read especially the detailed description of the daily schedule and activities of an inmate at Stateville penitentiary (Illinois), 226–36, and the autobiographical account by Victor Hassine, an educated "lifer" in a high-security prison in Pennsylvania, *Life without Parole: Living in Prison Today* (Los Angeles: Roxbury Publishing, 1996).

6. Alfred Blumstein, "Prisons," in *Crime*, ed. James Q. Wilson and Joan Petersilia, 387–88 (San Francisco: Jossey-Bass, 1995).

7. Christopher Mumola and Allen Back, *Prisoners in 1996* (Washington, D.C.: Bureau of Justice Statistics, 1997), 4–6.

8. David Greenberg and Valerie West, "State Prisons and their Growth, 1971–1991," *Criminology* 39, no. 3 (August 2001): 615–54.

9. Camille Graham and George M. Camp, eds., *The Corrections Yearbook 1998* (Middletown, Conn.: Criminal Justice Institute, 1999), 24 and 85. The critical impact of the courts on correctional functioning during this period and its determinants are dissected by Malcolm Feeley and Edward L. Rubin, *Judicial Policy Making and the Modern State: How the Courts Reformed America's Prisons* (New York: Oxford University Press, 1998).

10. Darell K. Gilliard, *Prison and Jail Inmates at Midyear 1998* (Washington, D.C.: Bureau of Justice Statistics, 1999), 8.

11. "Agency Blocks Use of Automated Bail System in Santa Clara County," *Los Angeles Times*, 27 November 1998.

12. Brian A. Reaves and Timothy C. Hart, *Felony Defendants in Large Urban Counties, 1996* (Washington, D.C.: Bureau of Justice Statistics, 1999), 6.

13. Figures in this paragraph are taken from Bureau of Justice Statistics, *Criminal Victimization in the United States, 1975–1995* (Washington, D.C.: US Government Printing Office, 1997). For a more detailed examination, see Loïc Wacquant, "The Great Penal Leap Backward: Incarceration in America from Nixon to Clinton," in *The New Punitiveness: Trends, Theories, Perspectives*, ed. John Pratt et al., 3–26 (London: Willan Publishing, 2005); and Alfred Blumstein, "The US Criminal Justice Conundrum: Rising Prison Populations and Stable Crime Rates," *Crime and Delinquency* 44, no. 1 (January 1998): 127–35.

14. Patrick Langan, "America's Soaring Prison Population," *Science* 251 (1991): 1568–73. According to the head statistician of the Bureau of Justice Statistics, half of the rise of state prison populations in the period 1974 to 1983 came from an increase in court convictions, one-fifth from demographic changes (through the swelling of younger cohorts), and one-tenth from inflation of arrests for drug offenses. But the period covered by his study ends at the moment the "War on drugs" started.

15. The view that bourgeois criminals benefit from "class advantage" is expounded in the classic essay by Edwin H. Sutherland, "White-Collar Criminality," *American Sociological Review* 5, no. 1 (February 1940): 1–12; the notion that corporate offences are inherently difficult to prosecute and punish due to their collective nature and social complexity is elaborated by Susan P. Shapiro, "Collaring the Crime, Not the Criminal: Reconsidering the Concept of White-Collar Crime," *American Sociological Review* 55, no. 3 (June 1990): 346–65.

16. Jeffrey Reiman, *And the Poor Get Prison: Economic Bias in American Criminal Justice* (Boston: Allyn and Bacon, 1996), 114.

17. Kitty Calavita, Robert Tillman, and H. N. Pontell, "The Savings and Loan Debacle, Financial Crime, and the State," *Annual Review of Sociology* 23 (1997): 19–38.

18. Susan P. Shapiro, "The Road Not Taken: The Elusive Path to Criminal Prosecution for White-Collar Offenders," *Law and Society Review* 19, no. 2 (1985): 261–87.

19. Kitty Calavita, Henry N. Pontell, and Robert Tillman, *Big Money Crime: Fraud and Politics in the Savings and Loan Crisis* (Berkeley: University of California Press, 1997), 226.

20. Kathleen Day, *S & L Hell: The People and the Politics behind the Savings and Loan Scandal* (New York: W. W. Norton, 1993). For details on the convictions of the main culprits in the Savings and Loan debacle, see Reiman, *And the Poor Get Prison*, 115–24; Fenton Bailey, *Fall from Grace: The Untold Story of Michael Milken* (New York: Carol Publishing Co., 1992); and "The Reincarnation of Michael Milken," *Business Week*, 10 May 1999, cover story.

21. Dario Melossi, "Gazette of Morality and Social Whip: Punishment, Hegemony, and the Case of the USA, 1970–92," *Social and Legal Studies* 2, no. 3 (September 1993), 259–80.

22. On the historical origins of the prison, see Georg Rusche and Otto Kirschheimer, *Punishment and Social Structure* (New Brunswick, N.J.: Transaction Books, 2003 [1939]), and Scott Christianson, *With Liberty for Some: Five Hundred Years of Imprisonment in America* (Boston: Northeastern University Press, 1998).

23. Paula Ditton and Doris James Wilson, *Truth in Sentencing in State Prisons* (Washington, D.C.: Bureau of Justice Statistics, 1999), 7; Mumola and Beck, *Prisoners in 1996*, 11.

24. Hilde Tubex and Sonja Snacken, "L'évolution des longues peines de prison: sélectivité et dualisation," in *Approches de la prison*, ed. Claude Ferguson, Antoinette Chauvenet, and Philippe Combessie, 221–44 (Brussels: De-Boeck University, 1997); Vincenzo Ruggiero, Mick Ryan, and Joe Sim, eds., *Western European Penal Systems: A Critical Anatomy* (London: Sage, 1995). The figures on admissions to jail and prison are for 1983 and 1993 for Greece, 1985 and 1996 for Spain, and 1984 and 1996 for Holland; they are taken from

Conseil de l'Europe, *Statistique pénale annuelle de Conseil de l'Europe. Enquête 1997* (Strasbourg: Conseil de l'Europe, 1999).

25. John Irwin and John Austin, *It's About Time: America's Imprisonment Binge* (Belmont, Calif.: Wadsworth, 1994), 23.

26. Bureau of Justice Statistics, *Prisoners in 1996*, 10 and 11.

27. Irwin and Austin, *It's About Time*, 32–57, citation at 33.

28. Ibid., 54–55.

29. US Department of Justice, *Nation's Probation and Parole Population Reached New High Last Year* (Washington, D.C.: Bureau of Justice Statistics, 1998). All figures in the following paragraph are taken from this publication.

30. On these notions and the kindred concept of "transcarceration," see Barbara Hudson, "Social Control," in *The Oxford Handbook of Criminology* (Oxford: Clarendon, 1997), 451–72; and the classic work of Stanley Cohen, *Visions of Social Control* (Cambridge: Polity, 1985).

31. Diana Gordon, *The Justice Juggernaut: Fighting Street Crime* (New Brunswick, N.J.: Rutgers University Press, 1991).

32. US Department of Justice, *Survey of State Criminal History Information Systems, 1997* (Washington, D.C.: Bureau of Justice Statistics, 1999), and Steven Donziger, *The Real War on Crime* (New York: Harper Perennial, 1996), 36.

33. US Department of Justice, *Survey of State Criminal History Information Systems, 1997*, passim.

34. Gary T. Marx, *Undercover: Police Surveillance in America* (Berkeley: University of California Press, 1988), and Cyrille Fijnaut and Gary T. Marx, eds., *Police Surveillance in Comparative Perspective* (The Hague: Kluwer, 1995). The latitude given to law-enforcement agencies to carry out covert activities expanded exponentially under cover of fighting terrorism after the attacks of September 11.

35. Jerome Miller, *Search and Destroy: African-American Males in the Criminal Justice System* (Cambridge: Cambridge University Press, 1997), 109–10.

36. Telephone interview with the author, 12 April 1998.

37. Shauna Briggs et al., *Private Providers of Criminal History Records: Do You Get What You Pay For?* Economics Department Working Paper (College Park: University of Maryland, 2004).

38. Harry Holzer, *What Employers Want: Job Prospects for Less-Educated Workers* (New York: Russell Sage Foundation, 1996), 45–62.

39. Shelley Albright and Furjen Deng, "Employer Attitudes toward Hiring Ex-Offenders," *Prison Journal* 76, no. 2 (June 1996): 118–37.

40. Holzer, *What Employers Want*, 61–62. See also Devah Pager, "The Mark of a Criminal Record," *American Journal of Sociology* 108, no. 5 (March 2003): 937–75; Harry J. Holzer, Stephen Raphael, and Michael A. Stoll, "Will Employers Hire Former Offenders? Employer Preferences, Background Checks, and their Determinants," in *Imprisoning America: The Social Effects of Mass Incarceration*, ed. Mary Pattillo, David F. Weiman, and Bruce Western, 205–43 (New York: Russell Sage Foundation, 2004); and Shawn Bushway, "Labor Market Effects of Permitting Employer Access to Criminal History Records," *Journal of Contemporary Criminal Justice* 20, no. 3 (August 2004): 276–91.

41. Bruce Western, Katherine Beckett, and David Harding, "Système penal et marché du travail aux Etats-Unis," *Actes de la recherche en sciences sociales*

124 (September 1998): 27–35, and Bruce Western and Becky Pettit, "Incarceration and Racial Inequality in Men's Employment," *Industrial and Labor Relations Review* 54 (2000): 3–16. See also Joel Waldfogel, "Does Conviction have a Persistent Effect on Income and Employment?" *International Review of Law and Economics* 14, no. 1 (March 1994): 103–19; Jeffrey Grogger, "The Effects of Arrests on the Employment and Earnings of Young Men," *Quarterly Journal of Economics* 110 (1995): 51–71; Karen E. Needels, "Go Directly to Jail and Do Not Collect? A Long-Term Study of Recidivism, Employment, and Earnings Patterns among Prison Releasees," *Journal of Research in Crime and Delinquency* 33, no. 4 (November 1996): 471–86; Jeffrey R. Kling, "The Effect of Prison Sentence Length on the Subsequent Employment and Earnings of Criminal Defendants," Working Papers 156 (Princeton University, Woodrow Wilson School of Public and International Affairs, 1999); Jeffrey Fagan and Richard B. Freeman, "Crime and Work," *Crime and Justice: A Review of Research* 25 (1999): 113–78.

42. "Governor Praises Welfare Crackdown," *New York Daily News*, 18 November 1996.

43. "DNA Database to Be Used to Fight Crime," *Los Angeles Times*, 13 October 1998.

44. On the fascination with technological solutions in the fight against crime, Gene Stephens, "Drugs and Crime in the Twenty-First Century," *Futurist* 26, no. 3 (May–June 1992): 19–22.

45. "Get DNA from All Arrested—Safir" and "Dems Rip Safir's DNA Plan: Politicians See 'Police State' Tactic," *New York Daily News*, 2 and 16 December 1998. According to a survey conducted by the National Association of Police Chiefs at the beginning of 1999, 80 percent of the country's police chiefs are in favor of generalized genetic fingerprinting. "NACOP Releases Survey of U.S. Police Chiefs," *U.S. Newswire*, 31 March 1999.

46. On the uncontrolled, metastatic expansion of surveillance entailed in the escalating expansion of the use of DNA technology and mandatory genetic databases by government authorities, and the lack of a corresponding reflection on the civic risks and sociolegal implications of this spread, read Dorothy Nelkin and Lori Andrews, "DNA Identification and Surveillance Creep," *Sociology of Health and Illness* 21, no. 5 (September 1999): 689–706.

47. Joan Petersilia, "Parole and Prisoner Reentry in the United States," in *Prisons*, ed. Michael Tonry and Joan Petersilia, 413–514 (Chicago: University of Chicago Press, 1999).

48. Jonathan Simon, *Poor Discipline: Parole and the Social Control of the Underclass, 1890–1990* (Chicago: University of Chicago Press, 1993); L. Phillips, "The Political Economy of Drug Enforcement in California," *Contemporary Policy Issues* 10, no. 1 (January 1992), 91–100. On the practical obstacles to, and limitations of, the "new penology" at ground level, read Mona Lynch, "Waste Managers? The New Penology, Crime Fighting, and Parole Agent Identity," *Law and Society Review* 32, no. 4 (December 1998), 839–69.

49. Norman Holt, "The Current State of Parole in America," in *Community Corrections: Probation, Parole, and Intermediate Sanctions*, ed. Joan Petersilia, 28–41 (New York: Oxford University Press, 1997). Richard McClork and John P. Crank warn against the temptation to exaggerate the social dimension

of parole supervision in the Fordist-Keynesian period in "Meet the New Boss: Institutional Change and Loose Coupling in Parole and Probation," *American Journal of Criminal Justice* 21, no. 1 (1996): 1–25.

50. Joan Petersilia, "Parole and Prisoner Reentry in the United States," 421.

51. "Stay Clean, or Stay in Jail: Probationers in Maryland Must Pass Drug Tests or Face Swift Punishment Beginning This Fall" and "Maryland's New 'Break the Cycle' Drug Program Is Launched in Howard," *Baltimore Sun*, 25 April and 1 July 1998.

52. Irwin and Austin, *It's About Time*, 133.

53. Los Angeles County Sheriff's Department, *Fifth Semiannual Report by Special Counsel Merrick J. Bobb and Staff* (February 1996), 14.

54. Darryl Fears, "'Like Living in Hell'," *Los Angeles Times*, 27 March 1998.

5. The Coming of Carceral "Big Government"

1. Dan Baum, *Smoke and Mirrors: The War on Drugs and the Politics of Failure* (Boston: Little, Brown and Co., 1996), and Craig Reinarman and Harry Gene Levine, eds., *Crack in America: Demon Drugs and Social Justice* (Berkeley: University of California Press, 1997).

2. Barry Bluestone and Bennett Houston, *The Great U-Turn* (New York: Basic Books, 1990); Richard Freeman, ed., *Working under Different Rules* (New York: Russell Sage Foundation, 1994); and William Julius Wilson, *When Work Disappears: The World of New Urban Poor* (New York: Knopf, 1996).

3. Stuart A. Scheingold, "Politics, Public Policy, and Street Crime," *Annals of the American Academy of Political and Social Science* 539 (May 1995): 155–68, and Elliott Currie, *Crime and Punishment in America* (New York: Henry Holt and Co., 1998).

4. Randy Adelba and Nancy Folbre, *The War on the Poor: A Defense Manual* (New York: New Press, 1996), 6.

5. William Jefferson Clinton, 1996 State of the Union address, available online at various government web sites.

6. Bureau of the Census, *Government Finances* (Washington, D.C.: US Government Printing Office, 1992), 28.

7. Franklin E. Zimring and Gordon Hawkins, "The Growth of Imprisonment in California," special issue, *British Journal of Criminology* 34 (1994): 83–96.

8. California Department of Corrections, *1995–2000 Five-Year Facilities Master Plan* (Sacramento: CDC, 1995). These forecasts were later adjusted downward, with the 200,000-mark to be reached only in 2005.

9. Vincent Shiraldi, *The Undue Influence of California's Guards' Union* (San Francisco: Center for Juvenile and Criminal Justice, 1994), 2.

10. John Hurst, "The Big House That Don Novey Built," *Los Angeles Times Magazine*, 6 February 1994, 16–22.

11. Robert E. Parker, *Flesh Peddlers and Warm Bodies: The Temporary Help Industry and Its Workers* (New Brunswick, N.J.: Rutgers University Press, 1994). See also *supra*, chapter 3.

12. Steve Gold, *Trends in State Spending* (Albany, N.Y.: Center for the Study of the States, Rockefeller Institute of Government, 1991), and Steve Donziger, *The Real War on Crime* (New York: Harper Perennial, 1996), 47–54.

13. Beth A. Rubin, James D. Wright, and Joel A. Devine, "Unhousing the Poor: The Reagan Legacy," *Journal of Sociology and Social Welfare* 19, no. 1 (March 1992): 111–47.

14. For a devastating critique of the crude statistical fallacies committed by the researchers of the US Department of Justice in their effort to justify the policy of penal escalation, see Franklin E. Zimring and Gordon Hawkins, "The New Mathematics of Imprisonment," *Crime & Delinquency* 34, no. 4 (October 1988): 425–36.

15. Kristin Luker, *Dubious Conceptions: The Politics of Teen Pregnancy* (Cambridge, Mass.: Harvard University Press, 1996).

16. Cited in "County Panel Makes a Hard Choice: Charity Over Prisons," *Los Angeles Times*, 13 September 1996.

17. Center for Juvenile and Criminal Justice, *Trading Books for Bars: The Lopsided Funding Battle between Universities and Prisons* (San Francisco: CJCJ, 1994).

18. Joe Domanick, "Who's Guarding the Guards?" *LA Weekly*, 2–8 September 1994, 20–26.

19. Tara-Jen Ambrosio and Vincent Schiraldi, *Trading Classrooms for Cell Blocks: Destructive Policies Eroding D.C. Communities* (Washington, D.C.: The Justice Policy Institute, 1997), 7.

20. Jerome G. Miller, *Hobbling a Generation: Young African-American Males in Washington D.C.'s Criminal Justice System* (Alexandria, Va.: Center on Institutions and Alternatives, 1992).

21. Statement cited by Jason Ziedenberg, "D.C. Dumping Ground: The Private Prison Planned for Anacostia," *Washington Post*, 18 October 1998, C8.

22. Cited by Ambrosio and Schiraldi, *Trading Classrooms for Cell Blocks*, 1.

23. Jonathan Kozol, *Savage Inequalities* (New York: Crown Books, 1991), 182–84.

24. In his book *Crime and Punishment in America*, Elliott Currie effectively dismantles these three fictions, to which certain criminology strives to give credit.

25. Donziger, *The Real War on Crime*, 21ff.

26. Camille Graham and George M. Camp, eds., *The Corrections Yearbook 1998* (Middletown, Conn.: Criminal Justice Institute, 1999), 87.

27. Cynthia Seymour, "Children with Parents in Prison: Child Welfare Policy, Program, and Practice Issues," *Child Welfare* 77, no. 5 (September 1998): 469–93.

28. Joan Moore, "Bearing the Burden: How Incarceration Policies Weaken Inner City Communities," in *The Unintended Consequences of Incarceration*, 67–90 (New York: Vera Institute of Justice, 1996); Lori Kepford, "The Familial Effects of Incarceration," *International Journal of Sociology and Social Policy* 14, no. 3 (1994): 54–90; Bruce Western and Sarah McLanahan, "Fathers Behind Bars: The Impact of Incarceration on Family Formation," *Families, Crime, and Criminal Justice* 2 (2000): 309–24; Megan L. Comfort, "'Papa's House': The Prison as Domestic and Social Satellite," *Ethnography* 3, no. 4 (Winter 2002): 467–99; H. Watts and D. S. Nightingale, "Adding It Up: The Economic Impact of Incarceration on Individuals, Families, and Communities," *Journal of the Oklahoma Justice Research Consortium* 3 (1996): 55–62; Jerome Miller, *Search and Destroy: African-American Males in the Criminal Justice System* (Cam-

bridge: Cambridge University Press, 1997), chap. 4; Susan Phillips and Barbara Bloom, "In Whose Best Interest? The Impact of Changing Public Policy on Relatives Caring for Children with Incarcerated Parents," *Child Welfare* 77 (1998): 531–41; John Hagan and Ronit Dinovitzer, "Collateral Consequences of Imprisonment for Children, Communities, and Prisoners," *Crime and Justice* 26 (1999):121–62; Loïc Wacquant, "Deadly Symbiosis: When Ghetto and Prison Meet and Mesh," *Punishment & Society* 3, no. 1 (Winter 2001): 95–133; Todd R. Clear, Dina R. Rose, and Judith A. Ryder, "Incarceration and Community: The Problem of Removing and Returning Offenders," *Crime & Delinquency* 47, no. 3 (July 2001): 335–51; Marc Mauer and Meda Chesney-Lind, eds., *Invisible Punishment: The Collateral Consequences of Mass Imprisonment* (New York: New Press, 2002); Mary Pattillo, David F. Weiman, and Bruce Western, eds., *Imprisoning America: The Social Effects of Mass Incarceration* (New York: Russell Sage Foundation, 2004); Jeremy Travis and Michelle Waul, *Prisoners Once Removed: The Impact of Incarceration and Reentry on Children, Families, and Communities* (Washington, D.C.: Urban Institute Press, 2004).

29. Jerome Skolnick, "'Three Strikes, You're Out' and Other Bad Calls on Crime," *The American Prospect* 17 (Spring 1994): 30–37; Robert J. Sampson and John H. Laub, *Crime in the Making: Pathways and Turning Points Through Life* (Cambridge, Mass.: Harvard University Press, 1993).

30. Laura Maruschak and Allen Beck, *Medical Problems of Inmates, 1997* (Washington, D.C.: Bureau of Justice Statistics, 2001), 2–4, and Laura Maruschak and Allen Beck, *Mental Health Treatment in State Prisons* (Washington, D.C.: Bureau of Justice Statistics, 2001), 9.

31. Douglas C. McDonald, "Medical Care in Prisons," in *Prisons*, ed. Michael Tonry and Joan Petersilia, 437–78 (Chicago: University of Chicago Press, 1999); Ronald Braithwaite, Theodore M. Hammett, and Robert M. Mayberry, *Prisons and AIDS: A Public Health Challenge* (San Francisco: Jossey-Bass, 1996); and Megan Comfort, Olga Grinstead, Bonnie Faigeles, and Barry Zack, "Reducing HIV Risk among Women Visiting Their Incarcerated Male Partners," *Criminal Justice and Behavior* 27, no. 1 (January 2000): 57–71.

32. Graham and Camp, *The Corrections Yearbook 1998*, 114.

33. According to a Rand Corporation estimate cited by Donziger, *The Real War on Crime*, 34.

34. For a historical overview of private imprisonment in the United States, see Alexis M. Durham, "Origins and Interest in the Privatization of Punishment: The Nineteenth and Twentieth Century American Experience," *Criminology* 71, no. 1 (January 1989): 107–39.

35. Joel Dana, *A Guide to Prison Privatization* (Washington, D.C.: Heritage Foundation Backgrounder, 1988).

36. Charles Logan and Sharla Rausch, "Punish and Profit: The Emergence of Private Enterprise Prisons," *Justice Quarterly* 2, no. 3 (September 1985): 303–18, and Charles Logan, "Well Kept: Comparing Quality of Confinement in Private and Public Prisons," *Journal of Criminal Law and Criminology* 83, no. 3 (fall 1992): 577–613.

37. Charles W. Thomas, Dianne Bolinger, and John L. Badlamenti, *Private Adult Correctional Facility Census*, 10th ed. (Gainesville: Center for Studies in Criminology and Law, University of Florida, 1997). Mimeograph, 56 pages.

38. Graham and Camp, *The Corrections Yearbook 1998*, 172.

39. Alex Lichtenstein, *Twice the Work of Free Labor: The Political Economy of Convict Labor in the New South* (New York: Verso, 1996).

40. Cited in "New Role for U.S. Prisons: Rent Collector," *Los Angeles Times*, 6 August 1997, 17.

41. Susan Sturm, "The Legacy and Future of Corrections Litigation," *University of Pennsylvania Law Review* 142 (1993): 693–738.

42. Jessica Portner, "Jailed Youth Shortchanged on Education," *Education Week* 16, no. 5 (October 1996): 12–23.

43. For a description of the extreme conditions—bordering on torture—to which the residents of high-security prisons are routinely subjected, read Michael Olivero, "Marion Federal Penitentiary and the 22-Month Lockdown: The Crisis Continues," *Crime & Social Justice* 27–28 (1987): 234–55, and Human Rights Watch, *Cold Storage: Super-Maximum Security Confinement in Indiana* (New York: HRW, 1997).

44. Wendy Imatani Peloso, "Les Misérables: Chain Gangs and the Cruel and Unusual Punishments Clause," *Southern California Law Review* 70 (1997): 1459–1512.

45. *Corrections Digest*, November 1997, 12; and K. Bland, "Parenting Programs Few at Arizona Prisons," *Arizona Republic*, 15 November 1998.

46. Gresham Sykes, *The Society of Captives* (Princeton, N.J.: Princeton University Press, 1971 [1958]).

47. "The Bleak House," *Atlanta Journal and Constitution*, 19 November 1995.

48. "Acting Tough: Stock, Pillories Next?" *Charleston Gazette*, 21 September 1996, 4A.

49. Mark Curriden, "Hard Times," *American Bar Association Journal* 81 (July 1995): 72, and Richard Lacayo, "The Real Hard Cell," *Time Magazine*, 4 September 1995.

50. Wesley Johnson, Katherine Bennett, and Timothy J. Flanagan, "Getting Tough on Prisoners: Results from the National Corrections Executive Survey, 1995," *Crime & Delinquency* 43, no. 1 (January 1997): 25–26.

51. Curriden, "Hard Times," 73.

52. Johnson, Bennett, and Flanagan, "Getting Tough on Prisoners," 24–41.

53. Frances Cullen et al., "The Correctional Orientation of Prison Wardens: Is the Rehabilitative Ideal Supported?" *Criminology* 31 (1993): 69–92.

54. Press release by the Texas Governors' Office, Austin, Texas, March 23, 1996.

55. "State Prison Inmates Join Battle against Floods"; "Update: More Inmate Crews Join Flood Fighting Effort"; and "State Prison Inmates Join Battle against Fires," *Corrections: Public Safety, Public Service*, California Department of Corrections press releases, January 2 and September 29, 1997.

56. "California Inmates Donating Their Hair to Sick Children Who Need Wigs," *Corrections: Public Safety, Public Service*, California Department of Corrections press release, February 18, 1998.

57. "Folsom State Prison to Deliver Halloween Baskets to Child Protective Services," *Corrections: Public Safety, Public Service*, California Department of Corrections press release, October 28, 1996.

58. "State Corrections Official Formally Dedicate Salinas Valley State Prison," *Corrections: Public Safety, Public Service*, California Department of Corrections press release, October 22, 1996.

59. "Corrections Victim Contributions Top $10 Million," *Corrections: Public Safety, Public Service*, California Department of Corrections press release, December 16, 1996.

60. Description of conditions of detention supplied by the Texas Department of Public Safety on its web site.

61. Senator Phil Gramm (Texas), Senate debate, August 25, 1994, *Congressional Record*, Washington, D.C., accessible on the US Senate web site.

62. Cynthia Young, "Punishing Labor: Why Labor Should Oppose the Prison Industrial Complex," *New Labor Forum* 7 (fall–winter 2000): 41–53. One can find a summation of this myth of the economic exploitation of prisoners in the United States that is typical to the point of caricature in Joel Dyer, *The Perpetual Prisoner Machine: How America Profits from Crime* (Boulder, Colo.: Westview, 2001).

63. Rod Miller, Mary Shelton, and Tom Petersik (Subcommittee on Correctional Industries), *Inmate Labor in America's Correctional Facilities* (Chicago: American Bar Association, 1998), 11.

64. Ibid.

65. William G. Staples, "In the Interest of the State: Production Politics in the Nineteenth-Century Prison," *Sociological Perspectives* 33, no. 3 (fall 1990): 375–95, and Scott Christianson, *With Liberty for Some: Five Hundred Years of Imprisonment in America* (Boston: Northeastern University Press, 1998).

66. For a sample of this brewing debate, consult Charles H. Logan, *Private Prisons: Cons and Pros* (New York: Oxford University Press, 1990); Rod Miller, George E. Sexton, and Victor J. Jacobsen, *Making Jails Productive* (Washington, D.C.: National Institute of Justice, 1991); Gary W. Bowman, Simon Hakim, and Paul Seidenstat, eds., *Privatizing Correctional Institutions* (New Brunswick, N.J.: Transaction, 1993); T. J. Flanagan and K. McGuire, "A Full-Employment Policy for Prisons in the United States: Some Arguments, Estimates, and Implications," *Journal of Criminal Justice* 21, no. 2 (summer 1993): 117–30; Morgan O. Reynolds, *Using the Private Sector to Deter Crime*, Policy Report 181 (Dallas: National Center for Policy Analysis, 1994); Greg Wees, "Prison Industries 1997: Outside Federal System, Inmate-Employees Remain an Elite Group," *Corrections Compendium* (June 1997): 1–4 and 10–11; Subcommittee on Correctional Industries, *Inmate Labor in America's Correctional Facilities*; and Brian Hauck, "Prison Labor," *Harvard Journal on Legislation* 113, no. 3 (January 2000): 279–97.

67. George Goldman, Bruce McWilliams, and Vijay Pradhan, *The Economic Impact of Production in California's Prison Industries* (Berkeley: University of California, Department of Agricultural and Resource Economics, 1998), mimeograph, 19 pages.

68. Jamie Peck and Nik Theodore, "Work First: Workfare and the Regulation of Contingent Labour Markets," *Cambridge Journal of Economics*, 24, no. 2 (April 2000): 119–38, and Beth Shulman, *The Betrayal of Work: How Low-Wage Jobs Fail 30 Million Americans* (New York: New Press, 2003).

69. For an extended discussion of the role of penality as cultural engine see

David Garland, "Punishment and Culture: The Symbolic Dimension of Criminal Justice," *Studies in Law, Politics and Society* 11 (1991): 191–222.

70. On this principle, see Georg Rusche and Otto Kirschheimer, *Punishment and Social Structure* (New Brunswick, N.J.: Transaction, 2003 [1939]); on its effects on the relations between the social and penal sectors of the modern state, read David Garland, *Punishment and Welfare: A History of Penal Strategies* (Aldershot: Gower, 1985).

71. Olveen Carrsquillo et al., "Trends in Health Insurance Coverage, 1989–1997," *International Journal of Health Services* 29, no. 3 (1999): 467–84; Marion Nestle, "Hunger in America: A Matter of Policy," *Social Research* 66, no. 1 (spring 1999): 257–79; and James Wright, Beth Rubin, and Joel Devine, *Beside the Golden Door: Policy, Politics, and the Homeless* (New York: Aldine de Gruyter, 1998).

72. "Incarceration Takes Its Toll: Prisons and Jails Passing Along Costs to the Inmates," *Boston Globe*, 15 October 1998; Lacayo, "The Real Hard Cell"; see also "On the Job: Sheriff with a Vengeance Joe Arpaio Believes His Job Is to Make Prisoners Long to Be Elsewhere," *People Magazine*, 7 October 1996, 131–33.

73. Mary Pattillo, David F. Weiman, and Bruce Western, eds., *Imprisoning America: The Social Effects of Mass Incarceration* (New York: Russell Sage Foundation, 2004); Christopher Mele and Teresa Miller, eds., *Civil Penalties, Social Consequences* (New York: Routledge, 2004).

6. The Prison as Surrogate Ghetto

1. A full-blown analysis is proposed in Loïc Wacquant, *Deadly Symbiosis: Race and the Rise of the Penal State* (Cambridge: Polity Press, 2010).

2. On the Jim Crow regime, see C. Vann Woodward, *The Strange Career of Jim Crow*, 3rd rev. ed. (New York: Oxford University Press, 1989 [1957]); Leon F. Litwack, *Trouble in Mind: Black Southerners in the Age of Jim Crow* (New York: Knopf, 1998); and William Chaffe et al., eds., *Remembering Jim Crow* (New York: New Press, 2001).

3. The rise and crisis of the ghetto as an instrument of ethnoracial control and containment are chronicled in Allan H. Spear, *Black Chicago: The Making of a Negro Ghetto, 1890–1920* (Chicago: University of Chicago Press, 1968); Gilbert Osofsky, *Harlem: The Making of a Ghetto—Negro New York, 1890–1930*, 2nd ed. (New York: Harper, 1971); and Kerner Commission, *The Kerner Report: The 1968 Report of the National Advisory Commission on Civil Disorders* (New York: Pantheon, 1988 [1968]).

4. Michael Tonry provides a systematic analysis of the increasing enmeshment of African Americans in the criminal justice system over the past two decades in his master book, *Malign Neglect: Race, Class, and Punishment in America* (New York: Oxford University Press, 1995).

5. Loïc Wacquant, "Crime et châtiment en Amérique de Nixon à Clinton," *Archives de politique criminelle* 20 (spring 1998): 123–38, and *Les Prisons de la misère* (Paris: Raisons d'agir Éditions, 1999), translated as *Prisons of Poverty* (Minneapolis: University of Minnesota Press, 2009), 71–94.

6. David C. Anderson, *Crime and the Politics of Hysteria: How the Willie Horton Story Changed American Justice* (New York: Times Books, 1995).

7. Tonry, *Malign Neglect*, 64.

8. Alfred Blumstein, "Racial Disproportionality of U.S. Prison Revisited," *University of Colorado Law Review* 64, no. 3 (1993): 743–60; but see the powerful counterargument, offered by David Cole in *No Equal Justice: Race and Class in the American Criminal Justice System* (New York: New Press, 1999), that the functioning of the US criminal justice system "affirmatively depends on inequality" and is riddled with racial double standards.

9. Thomas Bonczar and Allen Beck, "Lifetime Likelihood of Going to State or Federal Prison," *Bureau of Justice Statistics Special Report* (Washington, D.C.: Bureau of Justice Statistics, 1997), 1; for a state-by-state analysis, see Marc Maurer, "Racial Disparities in Prison Getting Worse in the 1990s," *Overcrowded Times* 8, no. 1 (February 1997): 9–13.

10. John Hagan and Ronit Dinowitzer, "Collateral Consequences of Imprisonment for Children, Communities, and Prisoners," in *Prisons*, ed. Michael Tonry and Joan Petersilia, 121–62 (Chicago: University of Chicago Press, 1999); Jamie Fellner and Marc Mauer, *Losing the Vote: The Impact of Felony Disenfranchisement in the United States* (Washington, D.C.: Sentencing Project and Human Rights Watch, 1998); for an extended analysis of the ethnoracial bases and import of the extensive measures of civic exclusion striking convicts in post-Fordist America, see Loïc Wacquant, "Race as Civic Felony," *International Social Science Journal* 181 (spring 2005): 127–42.

11. Gunnar Myrdal, *An American Dilemma: The Negro Problem and Modern Democracy* (New York: Harper Torchbook, 1962 [1944]), 54. My emphasis.

12. The remarkable functional, structural, and cultural flexibility of slavery is amply documented in Seymour Drescher and Stanley L. Engerman, *A Historical Guide to World Slavery* (New York: Oxford University Press, 1998).

13. See, for example, Gavin Wright, *The Political Economy of the Cotton South* (New York: W. W. Norton, 1978), and Peter Kolchin, *American Slavery: 1619–1877* (New York: Hill and Wang, 1993). For a dissenting view which portrays Southern slavery as a regional variation on US capitalism, read James Oakes, *The Ruling Race: A History of American Slaveholders* (New York: W. W. Norton, 1982).

14. Barbara Jeanne Fields, "Slavery, Race, and Ideology in the United States of America," *New Left Review* 181 (May–June 1990): 95–118.

15. Martha Hodes, *White Women, Black Men: Illicit Sex in the Nineteenth-Century South* (New Haven, Conn.: Yale University Press, 1997): 145–46, and Elise Virginia Lemire, *"Miscegenation": Making Race in America* (Philadelphia: University of Pennsylvania Press, 2002), on the prevalence of the representation of interracial desire and sex as a nightmarish monstrosity leading to the dissolution of American civilization in the northeastern United States between the Revolution and the Civil War.

16. C. Vann Woodward, *The Strange Career of Jim Crow*; and, for a highly original approach that gets to the core of the question of group (dis)honor, Hodes, *White Women, Black Men*, esp. chaps. 7 and 8.

17. Neil R. McMillen, *Dark Journey: Black Mississippians in the Age of Jim Crow* (Urbana: University of Illinois Press, 1990), 126.

18. Richard Wright, *Twelve Million Black Voices* (New York: Thundermouth's Press, 1988 [1941]), 88.

19. St. Clair Drake and Horace Cayton, *Black Metropolis: A Study of Negro Life in a Northern City* (New York: Harper and Row, 1962 [1945]), 1:112–28.

20. Ibid., 2:xiv.

21. William M. Tuttle, Jr., *Race Riot: Chicago in the Red Summer of 1919* (Urbana: University of Illinois Press, 1993 [1970]); Arthur Waskow, *From Race Riot to Sit In, 1919 to the 1960s* (Garden City, N.Y.: Doubleday, 1966); Robert E. Conot, *Rivers of Blood, Years of Darkness: The Unforgettable Classic Account of the Watts Riot* (New York: William Morrow, 1967); and Kerner Commission, *The Kerner Report.*

22. M. L. King Jr., cited by Stephen B. Oates, *Let the Trumpet Sound: The Life of Martin Luther King* (New York: New American Libra, 1982), 373.

23. Adam Fairclough, *Better Day Coming: Blacks and Equality, 1890–2000* (New York: Penguin Books, 2001), 201.

24. Thomas Byrne Edsall and Mary D. Edsall, *Chain Reaction: The Impact of Race, Rights, and Taxes on American Politics* (New York: W. W. Norton, 1991); Jill Quadagno, *The Color of Welfare: How Racism Undermined the War on Poverty* (Oxford: Oxford University Press, 1994); Martin Gilens, *Why Americans Hate Welfare* (Chicago: University of Chicago Press, 1999); and Katherine Beckett and Theodore Sasson, *The Politics of Injustice* (Thousand Oaks, Calif.: Pine Forge Press, 2000), 49–74.

25. For a historical recapitulation of the meanings of "ghetto" in American society and social science, leading to a diagnosis of the curious expurgation of race from a concept expressly forged to denote a mechanism of ethnoracial domination, which ties it to the changing concerns of state elites over the nexus of poverty and ethnicity in the metropolis, read Loïc Wacquant, "Gutting the Ghetto: Political Censorship and Conceptual Retrenchment in the American Debate on Urban Destitution," in *Globalization and the New City*, ed. Malcolm Cross and Robert Moore, 32–49 (Basingstoke: Macmillan, 2001).

26. Max Weber, *Economy and Society*, ed. Guenter Roth and Claus Wittich (Berkeley: University of California Press, 1978 [1918–20]), 935.

27. Louis Wirth, *The Ghetto* (Chicago: University of Chicago Press, 1928), 32.

28. Richard Sennett, *Flesh and Stone: The Body and the City in Western Civilization* (New York: W. W. Norton, 1994), 237.

29. Émile Durkheim, *The Division of Labor in Society* (New York: Routledge, 1984 [1893]), 73.

30. Drake and Cayton, *Black Metropolis*, 2:xiii. For a recapitulation of the "prisonization" versus "importation" debate in the study of the inmate society, both of which views concur to find that the prison population exhibits a distinctive set of social and cultural patterns, see Richard Sparks, Anthony E. Bottoms, and Will Hay, *Prisons and the Problem of Order* (Oxford: Clarendon, 1996), 58–62.

31. Georg Rusche and Otto Kirscheimer, *Punishment and Social Structure* (New York: Columbia University Press, 1939), 42. On this point, see also Dario Melossi and Massimo Pavarini, *The Prison and the Factory: Origins of the Penitentiary System* (London: Macmillan, 1981), and Pieter Spierenburg, *The*

Prison Experience: Disciplinary Institutions and Their Inmates in Early Modern Europe (New Brunswick, N.J.: Rutgers University Press, 1991).

32. The chronically problematic nature of the internal legitimacy of the prison as an organization is explored at length by Sparks et al., *Prisons and the Problem of Order.*

33. Claude Faugeron, "La dérive pénale," *Esprit* 215 (October 1995): 132–44; see also her "Prison: Between the Law and Social Action," in *The New European Criminology: Crime and Social Order in Europe*, ed. Vincenzo Ruggiero, Nigel South, and Ian Taylor, 104–18 (London: Routledge, 1998).

34. A fuller treatment of this fateful coupling of hyperghetto and prison in the post–Civil Rights era and its role in the remaking of race in America at the close of the twentieth century is in Wacquant, *Deadly Symbiosis*, chaps. 3 and 4.

35. Becky Pettit and Bruce Western, "Mass Imprisonment and the Life Course: Race and Class Inequality in US Incarceration," *American Sociological Review* 69, no. 2 (April 2004): 151–69.

36. David M. Oshinsky, *Worse Than Slavery: Parchman Farm and the Ordeal of Jim Crow Justice* (New York: Free Press, 1996), 32.

37. Alex Lichtenstein, *Twice the Work of Free Labor: The Political Economy of Convict Labor in the New South* (New York: Verso, 1996), 195.

38. Expert testimony presented to the Committees on the Judiciary and Crime of the US House of Representatives during discussion of the "Prison Industries Reform Act of 1998" explicitly linked welfare reform and the need to expand private prison labor.

7. Moralism and Punitive Panopticism

1. See, respectively, Ange-Marie Hancock, *The Politics of Disgust: The Public Identity of the Welfare Queen* (New York: New York University Press, 2004), and Elijah Anderson, *Streetwise: Race, Class, and Change in an Urban Community* (Chicago: University of Chicago Press, 1992).

2. The sociopolitical production of the "dangerous offender" as a central fixture for the collective anxiety of the citizens of rationalized Western societies is analyzed in Mark Brown and John Pratt, eds., *Dangerous Offenders: Punishment and Social Order* (London: Routledge, 2000).

3. Estelle B. Freedman, "'Uncontrolled Desires': The Response to the Sexual Psychopath, 1920–1960," *Journal of American History* 74, no. 1 (January 1987): 83–106, and Philip Jenkins, *Moral Panic: Changing Concepts of the Child Molester in Modern America* (New Haven, Conn.: Yale University Press, 1998). To place these episodes of panic within the broader social evolution of sexualities in the country, see John D'Emilio and Estelle B. Freedman, *Intimate Matters: A History of Sexuality in America*, 2nd ed. (Chicago: University of Chicago Press, 1998).

4. This process is dissected in the classic article by Edwin H. Sutherland, "The Diffusion of Sexual Psychopath Laws," *American Journal of Sociology* 56, no. 2 (September 1950): 142–48. A compressed account of the fate of these laws is in Roxanne Lieb, Vernon Quinsey, and Lucy Berliner, "Sexual Predators and Social Policy," *Crime and Justice* 23 (1998): esp. 55–65.

5. Philip Jenkins, "How Europe Discovered its Sex-Offender Crisis," in *How Claims Spread: Cross-National Diffusion of Social Problems*, ed. Joel Best (New York: Aldine de Gruyter, 2001), 147–68, citation at 148.

6. See, respectively, Michael R. Rand, James P. Lynch, and David Cantor, *Criminal Victimization, 1973–1995* (Washington, D.C.: Bureau of Justice Statistics, 1997), 3; Federal Bureau of Investigation, *Uniform Crime Reports: Crime in the United States, 1995* (Washington, D.C.), 21, available online at the Federal Bureau of Investigation web site; and Lieb et al., "Sexual Predators and Social Policy," 51–53.

7. Lawrence A. Greenfeld, *Sex Offenses and Offenders: An Analysis of Data on Rape and Sexual Assault* (Washington, D.C.: Bureau of Justice Statistics, 1997).

8. Jeremy H. Lipschultz and Michael L. Hilt, *Crime and Local Television News: Dramatic, Breaking, and Live from the Scene* (Washington, D.C.: LEA Books, 2001); William J. Chambliss, *Power, Politics, and Crime* (Boulder, Colo.: Westview Press, 1999), chaps. 1 and 2.

9. To situate Oprah Winfrey and her television show, based on the tropes of suffering and self-help, on the moral landscape of American commercial and (a)political culture, read Eva Illouz, *Oprah Winfrey and the Glamour of Misery: An Essay on Popular Culture* (New York: Columbia University Press, 2003). "Oprah's Child Predator Watch List" was found at: http://www.oprah.com/presents/2005/predator/predator_main.jhtml, visited August 2006.

10. Jenkins, *Moral Panic*, 312.

11. Frank J. Weed, *Certainty of Justice: Reform in the Crime Victim Movement* (New York: Aldine de Gruyter, 1995).

12. Julian V. Roberts, Loretta J. Stalans, David Indermaur, and Mike Hough, *Penal Populism and Public Opinion: Lessons from Five Countries* (New York: Oxford University Press, 2002), 129–42.

13. Susan Harding, "Representing Fundamentalism: The Problem of the Repugnant Cultural Other," *Social Research* 58, no. 2 (summer 1991): 373–93.

14. Pierre Bourdieu, "Understanding," *Theory, Culture, & Society* 13, no. 2 (May 1996 [1993]): 13–37.

15. On the explosive expansion of media interest in crime, see Steven Donziger, ed., *The Real War on Crime* (New York: Basic Books, 1996), 63–73, and Stevan Chermak, *Victims in the News: Crime and the American New Media* (Boulder, Colo.: Westview Press, 1995); on the waves of collective hysteria over the (largely imaginary) threats to children that the United States experiences periodically, read Joel Best, *Threatened Children: Rhetoric and Concern about Child-Victims* (Chicago: University of Chicago Press, 1990), and, for a longer historical perspective, Paula Fass, *Kidnapped: Child Abduction in America* (New York: Oxford University Press, 1997).

16. Ronald M. Holmes and Stephen T. Holmes, *Current Perspectives on Sex Crimes* (Thousand Oaks, Calif.: Sage Publications, 2002).

17. Robert J. Martin, "Pursuing Public Protection through Mandatory Community Notification of Convicted Sex Offenders: The Trials and Tribulations of Megan's Law," *Boston Public Interest Law Journal* 29, no. 6 (fall 1996): 29–35; Nadine Strossen, ed., "Critical Perspectives on Megan's Law: Protection vs. Privacy," *New York Law School Journal of Human Rights Annual* 13, no. 2 (1996): 2–178; and Lieb et al., "Sexual Predators and Social Policy."

18. One finds two examples illustrating the functioning of these two types of mechanisms in the cases of Florida and Michigan, respectively, in Donna M. Uzzell, "The Florida Sex Offender Registration and Notification System," in *National Conference on Sex Offender Registries*, ed. Jan M. Chaiken, 68–71 (Washington, D.C.: Bureau of Justice Statistics, 1998); and Mike Welter, "Development of the Illinois Sex Offender Registration and Community Notification Program," ibid., 72–77.

19. Kenneth Stow, *Alienated Minority: The Jews of Medieval Latin Europe* (Cambridge, Mass.: Harvard University Press, 1992).

20. Scott A. Cooper, "Community Notification and Verification Practices in Three States," in *National Conference on Sex Offender Registries*, ed. Chaiken, 103–6.

21. Texas Department of Public Safety, press release, 13 January 1999, available on the web site of the Texas correctional administration (www.txdps.state.tx.us). By May 1999, fifteen states had put their registry of sex convicts on the internet.

22. "Sheriff Releases Names, Photos of Sex Offenders," *San Diego Union-Tribune*, 19 March 1998; "South Gate Police Maps Sex Offenders," *Los Angeles Times*, 6 April 1999; "Megan's Law Notices Given Out: Santa Rosa Cops Go Door to Door to Warn about Sex Offenders" and "Parents to Get Maps Locating Sex Offenders: Warnings near Schools in Alameda County," *San Francisco Chronicle*, 2 July 1998 and 30 October 1997; "Calaveras Newspaper Prints Offender List," *San Francisco Chronicle*, 2 October 1998.

23. Roger Bodgan, "Le commerce des monstres," *Actes de la recherche en sciences sociales* 104 (September 1994): 34–46; and R. Bodgan, *Freak Show: Presenting Human Oddities for Amusement and Profit* (Chicago: University of Chicago Press, 1988).

24. "At the Los Angeles County Fair, 'Outing' Sex Offenders," *Washington Post*, 20 September 1997.

25. "County Fair Opens with New Exhibit: Safety—Access to Megan's Law Database Offered," *Los Angeles Times*, 12 September 1997.

26. See web site of the office of the attorney general, California Department of Justice: http://meganslaw.ca.gov/disclaimer.htm.

27. Statement by David Jaye, cited in "It Takes a Perv to Catch a Perv," *Toronto Star*, 25 December 1998.

28. Ray Surette, "Predator Criminals as Media Icons," in *Media, Process, and the Social Construction of Crime*, ed. Gregg Barak, 131–58 (New York: Garland, 1994).

29. "Death of Sex Offender Is Tied to Megan's Law," *New York Times*, 9 July 1998; "Last Days of a Sex Offender: Santa Rosa Neighbors Said He Looked Depressed," *San Francisco Chronicle*, 8 July 1998.

30. Scott Matson and Roxanne Lieb, *Community Notification in Washington State: 1996 Survey of Law Enforcement* (Seattle: Washington State Institute for Public Policy, 1996), 8 and 15.

31. "Neighbor Admits Firing Gun into Home of Paroled Rapist" and "Paroled Rapist Says He's the Victim Now: Target of Gunman Contends 'Megan's Law' Has Stolen His Freedom," *New York Times*, 10 and 14 November 1998.

32. M. E. Wolfgang, "The Medical Model versus the Just Deserts Model,"

Bulletin of the American Academy of Psychiatry and the Law 16 (1988): 111–21; Dayle Karyn Jones, "The Media and Megan's Law: Is Community Notification the Answer?" *Journal of Humanistic Counseling, Education and Development* 38, no. 2 (December 1999): 80–88.

33. Vernon. L. Quinsey, "Treatment of Sex Offenders," in *Handbook of Crime and Punishment*, ed. Michael Tonry, 403–28 (New York: Oxford University Press, 1998); Anne-Marie McAlinden, "Sex-Offender Registration: Some Observations on 'Megan's Law' and the Sex Offenders Act 1997," *Crime Prevention and Community Safety: An International Journal* 1, no. 1 (1999): 41–54. The pope of "communitarianism," Amitai Etzioni, sees in the "belated development" of the so-called Megan's Laws the symptom of the excessive weight placed until recently on the right to privacy (of ex-offenders) to the detriment of the "common good" (of the "community"). Amitai Etzioni, *The Limits of Privacy* (New York: Basic Books, 1999).

34. Frances Fox Piven, "Welfare and Work," *Social Justice* 25, no. 1 (1998): 67–81, and Robert Castel, "The Roads to Disaffiliation: Insecure Work and Vulnerable Relationships," *International Journal of Urban and Regional Research* 24, no. 3 (September 2000): 519–35.

35. Jonathan Simon, "Managing the Monstrous: Sex Offenders and the New Penology," *Psychology, Public Policy, and Law* 4, no. 1 (January 1998): 452–67.

36. Mona Lynch, "Pedophiles and Cyber-Predators as Contaminating Forces: The Language of Disgust, Pollution, and Boundary Invasion in Federal Debates on Sex Offender Legislation," *Law and Social Inquiry* 27, no. 3 (2002): 529–67.

37. Cited in Robert A. Prentky, Eric S. Janus, and Michael C. Seto, eds., *Sexually Coercive Behavior: Understanding and Management* (New York: Annals of the New York Academy of Sciences, 2003), 26. See also Robert M. Wettstein, "A Psychiatrist's Perspective on Washington's Sexually Violent Predators Statute," *University of Puget Sound Law Review* 15 (1992): 597–634, and the discussion in Lieb et al., "Sexual Predators and Social Policy," 68–69.

38. Terry Kupers, *Prison Madness* (San Francisco: Jossey-Bass, 1999), and Joan Petersilia, "Parole and Prisoner Reentry in the United States," in *Prisons*, ed. Michael Tonry and Joan Petersilia, 479–529 (Chicago: University of Chicago Press, 1999).

39. Matson and Lieb, *Community Notification in Washington State*, 16.

40. Greenfeld, *Sex Offenses and Offenders*, 43.

41. James F. Quinn, Craig J. Forsyth, and Carla Mullen-Quinn, "Societal Reaction to Sex Offenders: A Review of the Origins and Results of the Myths Surrounding Their Crimes and Treatment Amenability," *Deviant Behavior* 25, no. 3 (May 2004): 215–32, citation at 216.

42. Jenny A. Montana, "An Ineffective Weapon in the Fight Against Child Sexual Abuse: New Jersey's Megan's Law," *Journal of Law and Policy* 3, no. 2 (June 1995): 569–604.

43. Richard G. Zevitz and Mary Ann Farkas, "Sex Offender Community Notification: Managing High Risk Criminals or Exacting Further Vengeance?" *Behavioral Sciences and the Law* 18, nos. 2–3 (June 2000): 375–91, citation at 383–84.

44. This argument is adapted from Comfort's concept of "secondary prisoni-

zation." See Megan L. Comfort, "In the Tube at San Quentin: The 'Secondary Prisonization' of Women Visiting Inmates," *Journal of Contemporary Ethnography* 32, no. 1 (January 2003): 77–107.

45. Zevitz and Farkas, "Sex Offender Community Notification," 388. The perception that notification is unfair and abusive can also have antitherapeutic effects according to B. J. Winick, "Sex Offender Law in the 1990s: A Therapeutic Jurisprudence Analysis," *Psychology, Public Policy, and Law* 4, nos. 1/2 (January 1998): 505–70.

46. Lyn Hinds and Kathleen Daly, "The War on Sex Offenders: Community Notification in Perspective," *The Australian and New Zealand Journal of Criminology* 34, no. 3 (December 2001): 256–76; see also M. V. Rajeev Gowda, "Integrating Politics with the Social Amplification of Risk Framework: Insights from an Exploration in the Criminal Justice Context," in *The Social Amplification of Risk*, ed. Nick Pidgeon, Roger E. Kasperson, and Paul Slovic, 305–25 (Cambridge: Cambridge University Press, 2003).

47. Quinsey, "Treatment of Sex Offenders," 416–20.

48. Patrick A. Langan and David J. Levin, *Recidivism of Prisoners Released in 1994* (Washington, D.C.: Bureau of Justice Statistics, 2002). All the figures in this section are computed from the tables in this report.

49. L. Furby, M. R. Weinrott, and L. Blackshaw, "Sex Offender Recidivism: A Review," *Psychological Bulletin* 105 (1989): 3–30; Fred S. Berlin et al., "A Five-Year Follow-Up Survey of Criminal Recidivism within a Treated Cohort of 406 Pedophiles, 111 Exhibitionists, and 109 Sexual Aggressives: Issues and Outcomes," *American Journal of Forensic Psychiatry* 12, no. 3 (1991): 5–28; and Earl F. Martin and Marsha Kline Pruett, "The Juvenile Sex Offender and the Juvenile Justice System," *American Criminal Law Review* 35, no. 2 (winter 1998): 279–332. Many studies report that prison-based programs are effective if they are well designed and administered, for example, Danielle M. Polizzi, Doris Layton MacKenzie, and Laura J. Hickman, "What Works in Adult Sex Offender Treatment? A Review of Prison- and Non-Prison-Based Treatment Programs," *International Journal of Offender Therapy and Comparative Criminology* 43, no. 3 (June 1999): 357–74. Cognitive-behavioral and hormonal treatments have been found to be significantly more effective than behavioral treatments but not different from each other, according to Mario J. Scalora and Calvin Garbin, "A Multivariate Analysis of Sex Offender Recidivism," *International Journal of Offender Therapy and Comparative Criminology* 47, no. 3 (June 2003): 309–23; and C. G. Hall, "Sexual Offender Recidivism Revisited: A Meta-analysis of Recent Treatment Studies," *Journal of Consulting and Clinical Psychology* 63, no. 5 (October 1995): 802–9. This sprawling domain of biomedical and psychiatric research is obsessed with issues of technical propriety, intricacies of measurement, and standards of methodological rigor, when it would benefit most from an infusion of sociological thinking allowing it to embed offenders in their milieu and place its findings in their broader cultural and political context.

50. Loïc Wacquant, "La prison est une institution hors-la-loi," *R de réel* 3 (May–June 2000): 33–38; see also the penetrating characterization of the "crisis of penal modernism" in David Garland, *The Culture of Control* (Oxford: Oxford University Press, 2001), chap. 3.

51. Matson and Lieb, *Community Notification in Washington State*, 12.

52. Ibid., 16.

53. "Sex and Justice: Justice Department to Open Center for Sex Offender Management," *U.S. News and World Report* 122, no. 22 (June 9, 1997): 24–25; Office of Justice Programs, *Comprehensive Approaches to Sex Offender Management Grant Program* (Washington, D.C.: U.S. Department of Justice, 1999).

54. Nils Christie, *Crime Control as Industry: Towards Gulags, Western Style* (London: Routledge, 1994), 13.

55. Stuart A. Scheingold, Toska Olson, and Jana Pershing, "Sexual Violence, Victim Advocacy, and Republican Criminology: Washington State's Community Protection Act," *Law and Society Review* 28, no. 4 (October 1994): 729–63; "Symposium: Throwing Away the Key: Social and Legal Response to Child Molesters," *Northwestern University Law Review* 92, no. 4 (summer 1998), 1247–77; and, in the case of the United Kingdom, McAlinden, "Sex-Offender Registration."

56. Michael Tonry, "Rethinking Unthinkable Punishment Policies in the United States," *UCLA Law Review* 46, no. 1 (1999): 1–38, and Franklin E. Zimring, "The New Politics of Criminal Justice: Of 'Three Strikes,' Truth-in-Sentencing, and Megan's Laws," *Perspectives in Crime and Justice: 1999–2000 Lecture Series* 4 (2001): 1–22.

57. Donna Schram and Cheryl Darling Millroy, *Community Notification: A Study of Offender Characteristics and Recidivism* (Seattle: Urban Policy Institute, 1995), 14–17.

58. Neil Websdale, "Predators: The Social Construction of 'Stranger-Danger' in Washington State as a Form of Patriarchal Ideology," *Women and Criminal Justice* 7, no. 2 (1996): 43–68; Carol L. Kunz, "Toward Dispassionate, Effective Control of Sexual Offenders," *American University* 47 (December 1997): 453–62. Jenny Kitzinger emphasizes the same process in the British case in "The Ultimate Neighbour from Hell? Stranger Danger and the Media Framing of Paedophiles," in *Social Policy, the Media and Misrepresentation*, ed. Bob Franklin, 207–21 (London: Routledge, 1999).

59. Howard N. Snyder, *Sexual Assault of Young Children as Reported to Law Enforcement: Victim, Incident, and Offender Characteristics* (Washington, D.C.: Bureau of Justice Statistics, 2000), 10–11.

60. The increasing cultural and structural diversification of domestic forms is mapped out by Judith Stacey, *Brave New Families: Stories of Domestic Upheaval in Late-Twentieth-Century America* (New York: Basic Books, 1990), and Stephanie Coontz, with Maya Parson and Gabrielle Raley, eds., *American Families: A Multicultural Reader* (New York: Routledge, 1999). The growing functional and temporal mismatch between the press of the US economic system and the needs of families is explored in Phyllis Moen, ed., *It's About Time: Couples and Careers* (Ithaca, N.Y.: Cornell University Press, 2003), and Jerry A. Jacobs and Kathleen Gerson, *The Time Divide: Work, Family, and Gender Inequality* (Cambridge, Mass.: Harvard University Press, 2004).

61. Among many accounts in the press echoing this escalating demand for severity, see, for example, "Watching 'Megan's Law' in Practice," *New York Times*, 4 January 1998.

62. "Sexual Predators Treatment Examined," *Tampa Tribune*, 16 February 1999.

63. Strossen in Allen and Strossen, "Megan's Law and the Protection of the Child in the On-Line Age," 1336.

64. Adam J. Falk, "Sex Offenders, Mental Illness and Criminal Responsibility: The Constitutional Boundaries of Civil Commitment after *Kansas vs Hendricks*," *American Journal of Law and Medicine* 25 (1999): 117–54.

65. Jill S. Levenson, "The Impact of Sex Offender Residence Restrictions: 1,000 Feet From Danger or One Step From Absurd?" *International Journal of Offender Therapy and Comparative Criminology* 49, no. 2 (2005): 168–78.

66. Jenkins, "How Europe Discovered its Sex-Offender Crisis," 147–50.

67. Roxanne Lieb, "Social Policy and Sexual Offenders: Contrasting United States' and European Policies," *European Journal on Criminal Policy and Research* 8, no. 4 (December 2000): 423–40.

8. The Scholarly Myths of the New Law-and-Order Reason

1. Loïc Wacquant, "The Penalization of Poverty and the Rise of Neoliberalism," in "Criminal Justice and Social Policy," special issue, *European Journal of Criminal Policy and Research* 9, no. 4 (winter 2001): 401–12, and "Urban Disorders: Sociological Perspectives," special issue, *Déviance et société* 24, no. 4 (December 2000).

2. Jean-Luc Le Toqueux and Jacques Moreau, "Les zones urbaines sensibles. Forte progression du chômage entre 1990 et 1999," *INSEE Première* 334 (October 2000); see also Cyprien Avenel, *Sociologie des "quartiers sensibles"* (Paris: Armand Colin, 2004), and the data assembled in Jean Rigaudiat, "À propos d'un fait social majeur: la montée des précarités et des insécurités sociales et économiques," *Droit social* 3 (March 2004): 243–61.

3. For a gripping account of the conditions of routine superexploitation of the "floating" labor force, read Daniel Martinez, *Carnets d'un intérimaire* (Marseille: Agone, 2003); on the repression by employers of the attempts at mobilization of this deskilled, young workforce often issued of recent North African immigration, see Abdel Mabrouki and Thomas Lebègue, *Génération précaire* (Paris: Le Cherche-Midi, 2004). A ground-level portrait of how a lower-class immigrant family manages social insecurity day-to-day is drawn by Catherine Delcroix, *Ombres et lumières de la famille Nour. Comment certains résistent face à la précarité* (Paris: Payot, 2001).

4. Margaret Maruani, *Les Mécomptes du chômage* (Paris: Bayard, 2002), esp. 106–16.

5. On the social and political bases of the growing split between the governmental Left and the working-class electorate, read Olivier Masclet, *La Gauche et les cités. Enquête sur un rendez-vous manqué* (Paris: La Dispute, 2003).

6. These figures are taken from the exit polls carried out by France's main polling firm, SOFRES, on the day of the first-round ballot.

7. Annie Collovald, *Violence et délinquance dans la presse. Politisation d'un malaise social et technicisation de son traitement* (Paris: Editions de la DIV, 2000), and Serge Halimi, "L''insécurité' des media," in *La Machine à punir*, ed. Gilles Sainatti and Laurent Bonelli, 203–34 (Paris: L'Esprit frappeur, 2001).

8. "*Supervoleur*" is a derivation of "*Supermenteur*" (Superliar), the television character decked out in cape and mask featuring Chirac as an inveterate liar on the political muppet show *Les Guignols de l'Info* (broadcast daily just before the nightly news on the cable channel Canal Plus).

9. See the two issues of *Actes de la recherche en sciences sociales* devoted to "L'exception américaine," 138 and 139 (June and September 2001).

10. Pierre Bourdieu, "La rhétorique de la scientificité: contribution à une analyse de l'effet Montesquieu," in *Ce que parler veut dire. L'économie des échanges linguistiques* (Paris: Fayard, 1982), 227–39, citation at 228. Regrettably, this essay was omitted from the expanded and modified English language edition of that book, *Language and Symbolic Power* (Cambridge: Polity Press, 1990).

11. This point is underlined by Leena Kurki, "International Crime Survey: American Rates About Average," *Overcrowded Times* 8, no. 5 (1997): 4–7, and Michael Tonry and Richard S. Frase, eds., *Sentencing and Sanctions in Western Countries* (New York: Oxford University Press, 2001), 12–14.

12. John van Kesteren, Pat Mayhew, and Paul Nieuwbeerta, *Criminal Victimization in Seventeen Industrialized Countries: Key Findings from the 2000 International Crime Victims Survey* (The Hague: WODC, Ministry of Justice, 2000).

13. Franklin E. Zimring and Gordon Hawkins, *Crime Is Not the Problem: Lethal Violence in America* (New York: Oxford University Press, 1997).

14. Douglas Massey, "Getting Away with Murder: Segregation and Violent Crime in Urban America," *University of Pennsylvania Law Review* 143, no. 5 (May 1995): 1203–32; Lauren Krivo and Ruth D. Peterson, "Extremely Disadvantaged Neighborhoods and Urban Crime," *Social Forces* 75, no. 2 (December 1996): 619–48; and Garen Wintemute, "Guns and Gun Violence," in *The Crime Drop in America*, ed. Alfred Blumstein and Joel Wallman, 45–96 (New York: Cambridge University Press, 2000). For a complementary perspective that stresses the role of class and neighborhood-level social dislocations from opposite methodological perspectives, see Philippe Bourgois, *In Search of Respect: Selling Crack in El Barrio* (New York: Cambridge University Press, 1995), and James F. Short, *Poverty, Ethnicity, and Violent Crime* (Boulder, Colo.: Westview, 1997).

15. Laurent Mucchielli, *Violences et insécurité. Fantasmes et réalités dans le débat français* (Paris: La Découverte, 2001), 67 and 61.

16. George L. Kelling and William H. Sousa, *Does Police Matter? An Analysis of the Impact of NYC's Police Reforms*, Civic Report no. 22 (New York: Manhattan Institute, December 2001).

17. Jeffrey Fagan, Franklin Zimring, and June Kim, "Declining Homicide in New York City: A Tale of Two Trends," and Alfred Blumstein and Richard Rosenfeld, "Explaining Recent Trends in U.S. Homicide Rates," both in *Journal of Criminal Law and Criminology* 88, no. 4 (summer 1998): 1277–1324 and 1175–1216 respectively.

18. See Patrick Langan and Matthew R. Durose, "The Remarkable Drop of Crime in New York City" (working paper presented at the International Conference on Crime, ISTAT, Rome, December 2003), 2–6. Langan and Durose find that these trends are corroborated by independent data obtained from victimization studies and the US census.

19. Judith A. Greene, "Zero Tolerance: A Case Study of Police Policies and Practices in New York City," *Crime and Delinquency* 45, no. 2 (April 1999): 171–87; Khaled Taqi-Eddin and Dan Macallair, *Shattering "Broken Windows": An Analysis of San Francisco's Liberal Crime Policies* (Washington: Justice Policy

Institute, 1999); and Loïc Wacquant, "Mister Bratton Goes to Buenos Aires: Prefacio à la edición para América latina," in *Las Cárceles de la miseria*, 11–17 (Buenos Aires: Ediciones Manantial, 2000).

20. Benjamin Bowling, "The Rise and Fall of New York Murder: Zero Tolerance or Crack's Decline?" *British Journal of Criminology* 39, no. 4 (autumn 1999): 531–54; Robert Panzarella, "Bratton Reinvents 'Harassment Model' of Policing," *Law Enforcement News*, 15–30 June 1998.

21. Marc Ouimet, "Oh, Canada! La baisse de la criminalité au Canada et aux États-Unis entre 1991 et 2002," *Champ pénal* 1, no. 1 (January 2004): 33–49. Available at web site of *Champ pénal*: http://champpenal.revues.org.

22. Richard B. Freeman, "Does the Booming Economy Help Explain the Drop in Crime?" in *Perspectives on Crime and Justice: 1999–2000 Lectures Series* (Washington: US Department of Justice, 2000).

23. Philip Moss and Chris Tilly, *Stories Employers Tell: Race, Skill, and Hiring in America* (New York: Russell Sage Foundation, 2001), and Roger Waldinger and Michael I. Lichter, *How the Other Half Works: Immigration and the Social Organization of Labor* (Berkeley: University of California Press, 2003), chap. 8.

24. Andrew Karmen, *New York Murder Mystery: The True Story behind the Crime Crash of the 1990s* (New York: New York University Press, 2000), 209–13.

25. Jared Bernstein and Ellen Houston, *Crime and Work: What We Can Learn from the Low-Wage Labor Market* (Washington: EPI Books, 2000).

26. One will find a gripping insider description of the day-to-day operation of the crack trade in East Harlem in Bourgois, *In Search of Respect*, and, from the viewpoint of the police, in Robert Jackall, *Wild Cowboys: Urban Marauders and the Forces of Order* (Cambridge, Mass.: Harvard University Press, 1997).

27. Bruce A. Jacobs, *Robbing Drug Dealers: Violence beyond the Law* (New York: Aldine de Gruyter, 2000).

28. Daniel Cork, "Examining Space-Time Interaction in City-Level Homicide Data: Crack Markets and the Diffusion of Guns among Youth," *Journal of Quantitative Criminology* 15, no. 4 (1999): 379–406; Bowling, "The Rise and Fall of New York Murder"; and Bruce D. Johnson, Andrew Golub, and Eloise Dunlap, "The Rise and Decline of Hard Drugs, Drug Markets, and Violence in Inner-City New York," in Blumstein and Wallman, *The Crime Drop in America*, 164–206.

29. James Alan Fox, "Demographics and U.S. Homicide," in Blumstein and Wallman, *The Crime Drop in America*, 288–317.

30. Karmen, *New York Murder Mystery*, 242–43.

31. Richard Curtis, "The Improbable Transformation of Inner-City Neighborhoods: Crime, Violence, Drugs, and Youth in the 1990s," *Journal of Criminal Law and Criminology* 88, no. 4 (summer 1998): 1233–76, and Johnson, Golub, and Dunlap, "The Rise and Decline of Hard Drugs, Drug Markets, and Violence in Inner-City New York." Narrative illustrations of this generational effect can be found in Reymundo Sanchez: *Once a King, Always a King: The Unmaking of a Latin King* (Chicago: Chicago Review Press, 2003).

32. Mary Pattillo, "Sweet Mothers and Gangbangers: Managing Crime in a Black Middle-Class Neighborhood," *Social Forces* 76, no. 3 (March 1998): 747–74, and Ruth Wilson Gilmore, "You Have Dislodged a Boulder: Mothers

and Prisoners in the Post-Keynesian California Landscape," *Transforming Anthropology* 8, nos. 1–2 (1999): 12–38.

33. Bowling, "The Rise and Fall of New York Murder."

34. Eric Monkkonen, *Murder in New York City* (Berkeley: University of California Press, 2001).

35. Karmen, *New York Murder Mystery*, 153–56.

36. Eli B. Silverman and P. E. O'Connell, "Organizational Change and Decision Making in the New York City Police Department," *International Journal of Public Administration* 22, no. 2 (1998): 217–59, and Karmen, *New York Murder Mystery*, chap. 3.

37. Citizens Budget Commission, *New York City and New York State Finances, Fiscal Year 1999–2000*, Five-Year Pocket Summary (New York: CBC, 2000).

38. See Phyllis P. McDonald, *Managing Police Operations: Implementing the NYPD Crime Control Model Using CompStat* (Belmont, Calif.: Wadsworth, 2001), and Vincent E. Henry, *The Compstat Paradigm: Management Accountability in Policing, Business and the Public Sector* (New York: Looseleaf Law Publications, 2002). In a Manhattan Institute Report, George Kelling effusively calls CompStat "perhaps the single most important organizational/administrative innovation during the latter half of the twentieth century." Kelling and Sousa, *Does Police Matter?* 2.

39. Ibid., 12.

40. Lynn A. Weikart, "The Giuliani Administration and the New Public Management in New York City," *Urban Affairs Review* 36, no. 3 (January 2001): 359–81.

41. Address by Rudolph W. Giuliani on "The Entrepreneurial City," The Manhattan Institute, Wednesday, 3 December 1997. See also *The Entrepreneurial City: A How-To Handbook for Urban Innovators* (New York: Manhattan Institute, 2000), in which Giuliani introduces the section devoted to "Crime: Making Citizens Safer."

42. Loïc Wacquant, "Désordre dans la ville," review essay of *Disorder and Decline*, by Wesley Skogan, *Actes de la recherche en sciences sociales* 99 (September 1993): 79–82; Bernard E. Harcourt, "Reflecting on the Subject: A Critique of the Social Influence Conception of Deterrence, the Broken Windows Theory, and Order-Maintenance Policing New-York Style," *Michigan Law Review* 97, no. 2 (November 1998): 291–389; Wesley G. Skogan, review of *Fixing Broken Windows: Restoring Order and Reducing Crime in Our Communities*, by George Kelling and Catherine M. Coles, *American Journal of Sociology* 103, no. 2 (September 1997): 510–12.

43. Albert J. Reiss Jr., *Policing a City's Central District: The Oakland Story* (Washington, D.C.: National Institute of Justice Research Report, April 1985); Lawrence Sherman, "Police Crackdowns: Initial and Residual Deterrence," *Crime and Justice: A Review of Research* 12 (1990): 1–48; Robert J. Sampson and Stephen W. Raudenbush, "Systematic Social Observation of Public Spaces: A New Look at Disorder in Urban Neighborhoods," *American Journal of Sociology* 105, no. 3 (November 1999): 603–51.

44. Bernard Harcourt, *Illusions of Order: The False Promise of Broken Windows Policing* (Cambridge, Mass.: Harvard University Press, 2001).

45. According to the title conferred by Rudolph Giuliani at the official funeral

given by the city to Jack Maple: "Master Crime Fighter Given Eulogy to Match His Success," *New York Times*, 10 August 2001.

46. Jack Maple and Chris Mitchell, *The Crime Fighter: How You Can Make Your Community Crime-Free* (New York: Broadway Books, 1999), 152–53.

47. "The units enforcing quality-of-life laws must be sent where the maps [distributing the statistics of recorded offenses] show concentrations of crimes and criminals, and the rules governing the stops have to be designed to catch the sharks and not the dolphins." Ibid., 154–55.

48. Rudolph Giuliani and William Bratton, *Police Strategy No. 5: Reclaiming the Public Spaces of New York* (New York: City of New York Office of the Mayor, 1994).

49. Jack Maple, quoted in Maple and Mitchell, *Crime Fighter*, 154–55.

50. Institut des Hautes Études de la Sécurité Intérieure, *Guide pratique pour les contrats locaux de sécurité* (Paris: La documentation française, 1998), 133–34. "Local security contracts" are compacts passed by a city with the central government to activate and coordinate crime prevention and repression strategies in targeted domains and neighborhoods.

51. John E. Eck and Edward R. Maguire, "Have Changes in Policing Reduced Violent Crime?" in Blumstein and Wallman, *The Crime Drop in America*, 249. My emphasis.

9. Carceral Aberration Comes to France

1. One finds a detailed and dispiriting portrait of the current state of French jails and prisons in Observatoire international des prisons, *Les Conditions de détention en France: Rapport 2003* (Paris: La Découverte, 2003). For a panorama of salient issues in the recent period, see Xavier Lameyre and Denis Salas, eds., "Prisons: Permanence d'un débat," *Problèmes politiques et sociaux* 902 (July 2004).

2. Report by Mr. Guy Canivet, submitted to Ms. Guigou, minister of justice, 6 March 2000; report by Mr. Jacques Floch, no. 2521, submitted to the National Assembly, 28 June 2000; report by Mr. Guy-Pierre Cabanel, no. 449, submitted to the Senate, 28 June 2000.

3. D. Saint Dizier, "Fichier national automatisé des empreintes génétiques FNAEG," *Médecine et Droit* 53 (March 2002): 1–5; and Fabien Jobard and Niklas Schultze-Icking, *Preuves hybrides. L'administration de la preuve pénale sous l'influence des techniques* (Paris: CESDIP, 2004).

4. For a more disaggregated analysis, consult the chapters corresponding to these offenses in Laurent Mucchielli and Philippe Robert, eds., *Crime et sécurité. L'état des savoirs* (Paris: La Découverte, 2002).

5. Philippe Robert and Marie-Lys Pottier, "'On ne se sent plus en sécurité': délinquance et insécurité, une enquête sur deux décennies," *Revue française de science politique* 47, no. 6 (December 1997): 707–40; and Philippe Robert, *L'Insécurité en France* (Paris: Repères, 2002), 13–16, for the 1995–2001 period.

6. Emmanuelle Crenner, "Insécurité et sentiment d'insécurité," *INSEE Première* 501 (December 1996): 1–4.

7. Nils Christie, *Crime Control as Industry: Towards Gulags, Western Style*, 3rd ed. (London: Taylor and Francis, 2000), and Robert Weiss, *Comparing*

Prison Systems: Toward a Comparative and International Penology (New York: Gordon and Breach, 1998).

8. Michael Rand, *Criminal Victimization in the United States, 1994* (Washington, D.C.: Bureau of Justice Statistics, 1997); Federal Bureau of Investigation, *Uniform Crime Report 1995* (Washington, D.C.: Government Printing Office, 1997); and Jodi M. Brown and Patrick A. Langan, *State Court Sentencing of Convicted Felons, 1994* (Washington, D.C.: Bureau of Justice Statistics, 1998).

9. See Statistiques du Ministère de la justice, *Activité des parquets en 2002*, available from the web site of the French Ministry of Justice: http://www.justice.gouv.fr/.

10. On the weakness and incoherence of French carceral law, despite significant progress made over the past decade, see Martine Herzog-Evans, *La Gestion du comportement du détenu. Essai de droit pénitentiaire* (Paris: L'Harmattan, 1998).

11. Jean-Marc Rouillan, "Chroniques carcérales," in *Lettres à Jules* (Marseille: Agone, 2004), 75–143; Claude Lucas, *Suerte. La réclusion volontaire* (Paris: Plon, 1995); and K. C. Carceral, *Behind A Convict's Eyes: Doing Time in a Modern Prison* (Belmont, Calif.: Wadsworth, 2003).

12. Cited by Antoinette Chauvenet, Françoise Orlic, and Georges Benguigui, *Le Monde des surveillants de prison* (Paris: Presses Universitaires de France, 1994), 38.

13. Jean-Marc Antoine, "Maladie mentale et sanction pénale, la double peine," *Vie sociale et traitement* 75, no. 3 (September 2002): 43–44. Similar or higher rates are found in other European countries. S. Fazel and J. Danesh, "Serious Mental Disorder in 23,000 Prisoners: A Systematic Review of 62 Surveys," *The Lancet* 359 (2002): 545–50. In England and Wales, for instance, it was estimated that at least 12,000 of the 74,000 under lock in 2004 should be diverted to psychiatric establishments instead of being confined in jails and prisons.

14. "Sécurité: Le gouvernement souhaite étendre la politique de proximité," *Le Monde*, 8 December 1999.

15. These figures are taken from a survey of 1,719 inmates in 23 jails and 5 prisons, conducted jointly by the National Institute for Statistics and Economic Studies (INSEE) and the correctional administration as a component of a larger study of family histories. See Francine Cassan and Laurent Toulemont, "L'histoire familiale des hommes détenus," *INSEE Première* 706 (April 2000): 1–4.

16. Maud Guillonneau, Annie Kensey, and Philippe Mazuet, "Les ressources des sortants de prison," *Les Cahiers de démographie pénitentiaire* 5 (February 1998), 1–4.

17. Anne-Marie Marchetti, "Carceral Impoverishment: Class Inequality in the French Penitentiary," *Ethnography* 3, no. 4 (December 2002): 416–34.

18. Patrick Dubéchot, Anne Fronteau, and Pierre Le Quéau, "La prison bouleverse la vie des familles de détenus," *CRÉDOC—Consommation et modes de vie* 143 (May 2000), and Megan Comfort, "'Papa's House': The Prison as Domestic and Social Satellite," *Ethnography* 3, no. 4 (December 2002): 467–99.

19. On the grey zones, perverse effects, and other counterintuitive consequences of the "neutralization" philosophy of imprisonment, one can read with considerable profit Franklin E. Zimring and Gordon Hawkins, *Incapacitation:*

Penal Confinement and the Restraint of Crime (New York: Oxford University Press, 1995).

20. William Spelman, *Criminal Incapacitation* (New York: Plenum, 1994).

21. Daniel S. Nagin, "Criminal Deterrence Research at the Outset of the Twentieth Century," *Crime and Justice: A Review of Research* 23 (1998): 1–42, and Gary Kleck, "Constricted Rationality and the Limits of General Deterrence," in *Punishment and Social Control*, ed. Stanley Cohen and Thomas Blomberg, 291–310 (New York: Walter de Gruyter, 2003), esp. 304–8.

22. Tom Tyler, *Why People Obey the Law* (Princeton, N.J.: Princeton University Press, 1990), 6–7.

23. Tom R. Tyler and Yen J. Huo, *Trust in the Law: Encouraging Public Cooperation with the Police and Courts* (New York: Russell Sage Foundation, 2002), and Bernard Harcourt, "Rethinking Racial Profiling," *University of Chicago Law Review* 71, no. 4 (2004): 1275–1381.

24. For examples, see Gilles Chantraine, *Par-delà les murs. Expériences et trajectoires en maison d'arrêt* (Paris: Presses Universitaires de France, 2004), 85–103, for France, and David Simon and Edward Burns, *The Corner: A Year in the Life of an Inner-City Neighborhood* (New York: Broadway Books, 1997), for the United States.

25. The growing weight of endogenous factors in carceral hyperinflation in the United States is highlighted by Theodore Caplow and Jonathan Simon, "Understanding Prison Policy and Population Trends," in *Prisons*, ed. Michael Tonry and Joan Petersilia, 63–120 (Chicago: University of Chicago Press, 1999).

26. Christophe Palle and Thierry Godefroy, *Coûts du crime. Une estimation monétaire des infactions en 1996* (Guyancourt: CESDIP, 1999); I have used the high estimates for each category of crime.

27. The blatant shortcomings of current instruments of measurement of crime in the French case are emphasized by Lorraine Tournyol du Clos, "Les statistiques incertaines de la délinquance," *Futuribles* 274 (April 2002): 25–34. One has serious reasons to doubt that the National Observatory on Delinquency, inaugurated with bombast in November 2003 by interior minister Nicolas Sarkozy, will be able to rectify these deficiencies, considering that the 27 members of its steering committee include not a single criminologist or recognized researcher (the only "academic" is Frédéric Ocqueteau, director of the in-house journal of the IHESI, the state's main propaganda organ for punitive security measures, see chapter 2), and that it is placed under the presidency of the country's leading merchant of "urban security," Alain Bauer, whose statistical incompetence is amply documented (see chapter 8, 248–52).

28. For a selective yet instructive panorama, see Mary Pattillo, David Weiman, and Bruce Western, eds., *Imprisoning America: The Social Effects of Mass Incarceration* (New York: Russell Sage Foundation, 2004), and Loïc Wacquant, "From Slavery to Mass Incarceration: Rethinking the 'Race Question' in the United States," *New Left Review*, 2nd series, 13 (February 2002): 40–61.

29. A bracing empirical and theoretical critique of this core belief of the reigning economic neo-Darwinism is Gøsta Esping-Andersen and Marino Regini, eds., *Why Deregulate Labour Markets?* (Oxford: Oxford University Press, 2000).

30. For a detailed demonstration focusing on the punitive containment of

residents of the remnants of the black American ghetto at the close of the twentieth century, read Loïc Wacquant, *Deadly Symbiosis: Race and the Rise of the Penal State* (Cambridge: Polity Press, 2009), chap. 3.

31. A concrete case of this struggle between justice and social work as concerns child protective services is studied by Delphine Serre, "La judiciarisation en actes: le signalement d'"enfants en danger'," *Actes de la recherche en sciences sociales* 136–37 (March 2001): 70–82.

32. Antonio Pedro, ed., *Prisões na Europa. Um debate que apenas começa* (Oeiras: Celta Editora, 2003).

Theoretical Coda

1. Pierre Bourdieu, "Rethinking the State: On the Genesis and Structure of the Bureaucratic Field," *Sociological Theory* 12, no. 1 (March 1994 [1993]): 1–19, and P. Bourdieu, "The Abdication of the State," in *The Weight of the World*, Pierre Bourdieu et al., 181–88 (Cambridge: Polity Press, [1993] 1999).

2. Bourdieu, "Rethinking the State," 4 and 9. For a further analysis of the distinctive role of the law in the field of power, see Pierre Bourdieu, "La force du droit. Eléments pour une sociologie du champ juridique," *Actes de la recherche en sciences sociales* 64 (September 1986): 3–19. Translated as "The Force of Law: Toward A Sociology of the Juridical Field," *The Hastings Law Journal* 38 (2001): 814–53.

3. See the issue of *Actes de la recherche en sciences sociales* devoted to the transition "From Social State to Penal State," no. 124, September 1998 (with contributions from David Garland, Bruce Western, Katherine Beckett, David Harding, Richard B. Freeman, Nils Christie, Dario Melossi, and Loïc Wacquant).

4. Frances Fox Piven and Richard A. Cloward, *Regulating the Poor: The Functions of Public Welfare*, new expanded ed. (New York: Vintage, 1993 [1971]), xvi and passim.

5. Ibid., xviii.

6. Yeheskel Hasenfeld, "People Processing Organizations: An Exchange Approach," *American Sociological Review* 37, no. 3 (June 1972): 256–63.

7. Piven and Cloward, *Regulating the Poor*, 409.

8. Ibid., 424–25.

9. The catalytic role of ethnoracial division in the remaking of the state after the junking of the Fordist-Keynesian social compact and the collapse of the dark ghetto is the topic of another book which complements this study of the nexus of class and state restructuring. See Loïc Wacquant, *Deadly Symbiosis: Race and the Rise of the Penal State* (Cambridge: Polity Press, 2010).

10. Jamie Peck, *Workfare States* (New York: Guilford, 2001), 342.

11. Michel Foucault, *Surveiller et punir. Naissance de la prison* (Paris: Gallimard, 1975), translated as *Discipline and Punish: The Birth of the Prison* (New York: Vintage, 1977); a cogent elaboration of this view of Foucault is David Garland, *Punishment and Modern Society* (Chicago: University of Chicago Press, 1990), esp. 151–55. All translations of Foucault in this discussion are mine.

12. Thomas Mathiesen, *Prison on Trial: A Critical Assessment* (London: Sage, 1990), 14.

13. Foucault, *Discipline and Punish*, 301/294; see the meticulous critique of C. Fred Alford, "What Would It Matter If Everything Foucault Said about Prison Were Wrong? *Discipline and Punish* after 20 Years," *Theory & Society* 29, no. 1 (February 2000), 125–46, based on extensive field observation in a Maryland penitentiary.

14. Rising incarceration has also been increasingly selective by class and ethnonational origins in Western Europe; see Loïc Wacquant, "Penalization, Depoliticization, and Racialization: On the Overincarceration of Immigrants in the European Union," in *Perspectives on Punishment: The Contours of Control*, ed. Sarah Armstrong and Lesley McAra, 83–100 (Oxford: Clarendon Press, 2006).

15. Foucault, *Discipline and Punish*, 13/7.

16. Ibid., 134/131.

17. Ibid., 93/90.

18. David Garland, *The Culture of Control: Crime and Social Order in Contemporary Society* (Chicago: University of Chicago Press, 2001), 139–47 and passim.

19. Ibid., 109. For an earlier, more compact statement, read David Garland, "The Limits of the Sovereign State: Strategies of Crime Control in Contemporary Society," *British Journal of Criminology* 36, no. 4 (autumn 1997): 445–71.

20. A useful discussion of the merits and limits of theories of social change stressing the displacement of collective angst is Alan Hunt, "Anxiety and Social Explanation: Some Anxieties about Anxiety," *Journal of Social History* 32, no. 3 (spring 1999): 509–28.

21. On the analytic and historical differentiation of the political from the bureaucratic field, and their respective location inside the field of power, see Loïc Wacquant, ed., *The Mystery of Ministry: Pierre Bourdieu and Democratic Politics* (Cambridge: Polity Press, 2005), esp. 6–7, 14–17, and 142–46.

22. David Garland, *Punishment and Welfare: A History of Penal Strategies* (Aldershot, UK: Gower, 1985), 233–34.

23. Garland, *The Culture of Control*, 168–74 and 175–90 for these two arguments (citations at 169 and 175 respectively).

24. Jock Young, *The Exclusive Society: Social Exclusion, Crime and Difference in Late Modernity* (London: Sage, 1999); Franklin Zimring, Gordon Hawkins, and Sam Kamin, *Punishment and Democracy: Three Strikes and You're Out in California* (New York: Oxford University Press, 2001); Michael Tonry, *Thinking about Crime: Sense and Sensibility in American Penal Culture* (New York: Oxford University Press, 2004).

25. Garland, *The Culture of Control*, 165.

26. Foucault, *Discipline and Punish*, 33/28. My translation.

27. Garland, *The Culture of Control*, 165. My emphasis.

28. Ibid., 77.

29. From among a vast (and uneven) literature across the disciplines, see the pointed analyses of Neil Fligstein, *The Architecture of Markets* (Princeton, N.J.: Princeton University Press, 2001); John Campbell and Ove Pedersen, eds., *The Rise of Neoliberalism and Institutional Analysis* (Princeton, N.J.: Princeton University Press, 2001); Jean Comaroff and John L. Comaroff, *Millennial Capitalism and the Culture of Neoliberalism* (Durham, N.C.: Duke University Press, 2001); Neil Brenner and Nik Theodore, eds., *Spaces of Neoliberalism: Urban Re-*

structuring in North America and Western Europe (New York: Wiley/Blackwell, 2002); and Gérard Duménil and Dominique Lévy, *Capital Resurgent: Roots of the Neoliberal Revolution* (Cambridge, Mass.: Harvard University Press, 2004).

30. On the rise of a corporate class shorn of attachment to locality or nationality, read Leslie Sklair, *The Transnational Capitalist Class* (Oxford: Basil Blackwell, 2001). The long-standing cosmopolitan orientation of the high bourgeoisie is stressed by Michel Pinçon and Monique Pinçon-Charlot, *Sociologie de la bourgeoisie* (Paris: La Découverte, 2000). The respective roles of economists and lawyers in the incubation, elaboration, and diffusion of the neoliberal project across borders is probed by Sarah L. Babb, *Managing Mexico: Economists from Nationalism to Neoliberalism* (Princeton, N.J.: Princeton University Press, 2001); and Yves Dezalay and Bryan G. Garth, *The Internationalization of Palace Wars: Lawyers, Economists, and the Contest to Transform Latin American States* (Chicago: University of Illinois Press, 2002).

31. David Harvey, *A Brief History of Neoliberalism* (New York: Oxford University Press, 2005), citations on 2–3 and 77 respectively.

32. Ibid., 76.

33. Bourdieu, "Rethinking the State," 15–16, and Loïc Wacquant, "Symbolic Power and the Rule of the 'State Nobility'," in *The Mystery of Ministry*, 133–50.

34. Neil Gilbert, *Transformation of the Welfare State: The Silent Surrender of Public Responsibility* (New York: Oxford University Press, 2002); François-Xavier Merrien, Raphaël Parchet, and Antoine Kernen, *L'Etat social. Une perspective internationale* (Paris: Armand Colin, 2004); and Joel Handler, *Social Citizenship and Workfare in the United States and Western Europe: The Paradox of Inclusion* (New York: Cambridge University Press, 2004).

35. Ralf Dahrendorf, *Life Chances: Approaches to Social and Political Theory* (Chicago: University of Chicago Press, 1981).

36. Desmond King, *In the Name of Liberalism: Illiberal Social Policy in the United States and Britain* (New York: Oxford University Press, 1999), 26.

37. These flaws and contradictions are dissected with precision by Peck, *Workfare States*, and Tonry, *Thinking about Crime*.

38. For a specification of republican and liberal conceptions of democracy at stake here, see David Held, *Models of Democracy* (Stanford, Calif.: Stanford University Press, 1996).

39. Louis Chevalier, *Classes laborieuses et classes dangereuses à Paris pendant la première moitié du XIXe siècle* (Paris: Plon, 1958, expanded edition Pluriel, 1978), and John M. Merriman, *The Margins of City Life: Explorations on the French Urban Frontier, 1815–1851* (New York: Oxford University Press, 1991), especially chapters 3 and 8.

40. Gustave de Beaumont and Alexis de Tocqueville, *On the Penitentiary System in the United States and Its Application in France* (Carbondale: University of South Illinois Press, 1964 [Philadelphia, 1833]), 47. A cogent interpretation of the place of the penal system in Tocqueville's political sociology is Roger Boesche, "The Prison: Tocqueville's Model for Despotism," *Western Political Quarterly* 33, no. 4 (December 1980): 550–63.

Index

LOÏC WACQUANT

is Professor of Sociology at the University of California, Berkeley, and Researcher at the Centre de sociologie européenne, Paris.